Water Resources Policies
in South Asia

Water Resources Policies in South Asia

Editors

Anjal Prakash
Sreoshi Singh
Chanda Gurung Goodrich
S. Janakarajan

LONDON NEW YORK NEW DELHI

First published 2013 in India
by Routledge
912 Tolstoy House, 15–17 Tolstoy Marg, Connaught Place, New Delhi 110 001

Simultaneously published in the UK
by Routledge
2 Park Square, Milton Park, Abingdon, OX14 4RN

Routledge is an imprint of the Taylor & Francis Group, an informa business

© 2013 South Asia Consortium for Interdisciplinary Water Resources Studies
(SaciWATERs)

Typeset by
Eleven Arts
Keshav Puram
Delhi 110 035

All rights reserved. No part of this book may be reproduced or utilized in any form
or by any electronic, mechanical or other means, now known or hereafter invented,
including photocopying and recording, or in any information storage and retrieval
system without permission in writing from the publishers.

British Library Cataloguing-in-Publication Data
A catalogue record of this book is available from the British Library

ISBN 978-0-415-81198-9

This book is printed on ECF environment-friendly paper manufactured from
unconventional and other raw materials sourced from sustainable and identified
sources.

Contents

List of Tables	ix
List of Figures	xi
List of Maps	xiii
List of Abbreviations	xv
Foreword	xxi
Acknowledgements	xxiii

Introduction: An Agenda for Pluralistic and Integrated   1
Framework for Water Policies in South Asia
Anjal Prakash, Sreoshi Singh, Chanda Gurung Goodrich
and *S. Janakarajan*

Part I. Conceptual Framework for Water Resources Policy

1. Interface between Water, Poverty and Gender   19
Empowerment: Revisiting Theories, Policies
and Practices
Amita Shah and *Seema Kulkarni*

2. Seeing Women and Questioning Gender in   38
Water Management
Margreet Zwarteveen

3. "Water Policies are Never Implemented, but   66
Negotiated:" Analyzing Integration of Policies
Using a Bayesian Network
Saravanan V. Subramanian and *David Ip*

vi ≈ *Contents*

**Part II. Informing Water Resources Policies:
The South Asian Experience**

4. Institutional Design Perspective, Capacity Constraints   99
and Participatory Irrigation Management in
South Asia
Jayanath Ananda

5. Integrated Water Resources Management: 116
From Policy to Practice through a Comprehensive
National Water Management Plan: A Case Study
of Bangladesh
Sultan Ahmed

6. Watershed Management Policies and Programs   134
in Bhutan: Empowering the Powerless
Thinley Gyamtsho

7. Scale, Diverse Economies, and Ethnographies of   152
the State: Concepts for Theorizing Water Policy
Priya Sangameswaran

8. Credit Conditionality and Strategic Sabotage: 170
The Tale of the First Decade of Pakistan's
Irrigation Reform
Muhammad Mehmood Ul Hasan

**Part III. Water and Climate Change: Newer
Dimensions That Should Shape Water Policies**

9. Hydro-Hazardscapes of South Asia: Redefining   191
Adaptation and Resilience to Global Climate Change
Daanish Mustafa

10. Climate Change and Groundwater: India's   213
Opportunities for Mitigation and Adaptation
Tushaar Shah

Contents ≈ vii

Part IV. International Experiences of Water Reform

11. Chilean Water Markets: History, Politics and   247
    Empirical Outcomes
    Jessica Budds

12. South Africa's Reformed Water Law and Its   267
    Challenging Implementation
    Eiman Karar

13. Innovation in European Water Policy and the   296
    Need for Exchange on Water Policy Reform at
    a Global Scale
    Claudia Pahl-Wostl

About the Editors	313
Notes on Contributors	315
Index	320

List of Tables

1.1	Two scenarios of water–poverty–gender interface in production sphere	29
3.1	Summary of variables influencing the framing of the problem in Uppala Rajana	79
3.1A	Details of variables influencing the framing of the problem in Uppala Rajana	88
4.1	Design feature analysis of PIM institutions	104
5.1	Existing Water Management Organizations and their members	125
5.2	Changes in irrigation area before and after effective people's participation	127
5.1A	Chronological history of policy development in the water sector of Bangladesh	130
10.1	Groundwater management challenges in different areas of India	217
10.2	Climate change and water storage alternatives	222
10.3	Geographic distribution of electric and diesel irrigation pumps in South Asia	227
10.4	Estimates of electricity consumption by pumpsets in major states of India	227
10.5	An alternative procedure for estimating C-emission from India's groundwater economy	228
12.1	Relative water use distribution in two WMAs	279
13.1	Comparison of characteristics of the current management regime in regulated and controlled rivers with those of a future state that has multifunctional and dynamic landscapes	305

List of Figures

3.1	Framework for analyzing policy processes	70
3.2	Variables influencing the framing of the problem in Uppala Rajana	78
3.3	Scenarios for illustration	81
4.1	Basic structure of PIM in Andhra Pradesh	103
5.1	Organogram of Water Management Organization	124
9.1	Schematic diagram of a *karez* or *qanat*	195
10.1	Growth in agricultural groundwater use in selected countries (1940–2010)	215
10.2a	Groundwater development and water level decline without Managed Aquifer Recharge	232
10.2b	Groundwater development and water level behavior with intensive program of Managed Aquifer Recharge	232
10.3	Aquifer recovery and pre-monsoon water level in 145 districts of India	233
10.4	India's groundwater governance pentagram	236
12.1	Sectoral break-up of water requirements	269
12.2	Macro-policy developments: water and related areas in South Africa (1994–2003)	272
12.3	Number of licences issued to HDIs (Historically Disadvantaged Individuals) vs Non-HDIs by region (1998–2008)	286

List of Maps

9.1	Indus basin and its major infrastructure	200
9.2	Rawalpindi/Islamabad conurbation with the Lai basin outline	203
10.1	Distribution of electric and diesel pumpsets in South Asia	225
10.2	Groundwater-stressed areas of India	231
12.1	Annual rainfall and evaporation	269
12.2	Water Management Areas (WMAs)	275

List of Abbreviations

ADB	Asian Development Bank
AIT	Asian Institute of Technology
AWB	Area Water Board
BAU	Business as Usual
BEM	Benefit Evaluation and Monitoring
BHU	Basic Health Unit
BHWDB	Bangladesh Haors and Wetland Development Board
BN	Bayesian Network
BWDB	Bangladesh Water Development Board
BWFMS	Bangladesh Water and Flood Management Strategy
BWP	Bhutan Water Partnership
CBWM	Community-based Watershed Management
CCB	Chaklala Cantonment Board
CCS	Carbon Capture and Storage
CDA	Capital Development Authority
CEDLA	Center for Latin American Research and Documentation
CEGIS	Center for Environmental and Geographic Information Services (Bangladesh)
CEH	Centre for Ecology and Hydrology (UK)
CEP	Coastal Embankment Project
CIS	Common Implementation Strategy
CMA	Catchment Management Agency (South Africa)
CMS	Catchment Management Strategy (South Africa)
CONADI	Chilean Indigenous Development Corporation
DC	Distributary Committee
DFID	Department for International Development (UK)
DGA	National Water Directorate (Chile)
DoF	Department of Forestry
DRDA	District Rural Development Agency
DRR	Disaster Risk Reduction
DSS	Decision Support System
DWAF	Department of Water Affairs and Forestry (South Africa)

xvi *List of Abbreviations*

ECLAC	Economic Commission for the Latin America and the Caribbean
ECs	Executive Committees
EIA	Environmental Impact Assessment
EPA	Environmental Protection Act
EPWAPDA	East Pakistan Water and Power Development Authority
FAO	Food and Agriculture Organization
FAP	Flood Action Plan (Bangladesh)
FCDI	Flood Control Drainage and Irrigation
FCO	Field Canal Organization
FCRP	Field Crops Research Program
FD	Flood Directive
FO	Farmer Organization
FPCO	Flood Plan Coordination Organization (Bangladesh)
FYP	Five Year Plan
GBM	Ganga–Brahmaputra–Meghna
GCM	General Circulation Modeling
GDP	Gross Domestic Product
GEC	Global Environmental Change
GLOF	Glacier Lake Outburst Flood
GMS	Greater Mekong Sub-basin
GNH	Gross National Happiness
GNP	Gross National Product
GoB	Government of Bangladesh
GoHP	Government of Himachal Pradesh
GoI	Government of India
GoP	Government of Pakistan
GPA	Guidelines for Project Assessment
GPP	Guidelines for People's Participation
GPWM	Guidelines for Participatory Water Management
GWP	Global Water Partnership
HDI	Historically Disadvantaged Individual
HRD	Human Resource Development
HYV	High Yielding Variety
IAD	Institutional Analysis Development
IADP	Integrated Area Development Programme
IB	Irrigation Board
ICIMOD	International Centre for Integrated Mountain Development (Nepal)

List of Abbreviations ☙ xvii

IDS	International Development Studies (UK)
IECO	International Engineering Company
IFI	International Financial Institution
IFPRI	International Food Policy Research Institute
IIMI	International Irrigation Management Institute
IHDP	International Human Dimensions Programme
IMT	Irrigation Management Transfer
INMAS	Integrated Management of Irrigation Schemes
INDAP	Institute for Peasant Agricultural Development (Chile)
INR	Indian Rupees
IPCC	Intergovernmental Panel on Climate Change
IRDC	International Research Development Centre
IRSA	Indus River System Authority
IWM	Institute of Water Modeling
IWDP	Integrated Wasteland Development Programme
IWMI	International Water Management Institute
IWRAM	Integrated Water Resources Assessment and Management
IWRM	Integrated Water Resources Management
JRCB	Joint Rivers Commission (Bangladesh)
LCC	Lower Chenab Canal
LGED	Local Government and Engineering Department
LLZT	*Lingmuteychu Lum Zhinchong Tshogpa*
LWMP	Lingmuteychu Watershed Management Project (Bhutan)
MANIS	Management of Irrigation Systems
MLA	Member of Legislative Assembly
MoA	Ministry of Agriculture
MoIWDFC	Ministry of Irrigation, Water Development and Flood Control
MPO	Master Plan Organization
MRC	Mekong River Commission
NAPA	National Adaptation Plan of Action
NDP	National Drainage Program
NEC	National Environment Commission (Bhutan)
NEDA	Netherlands Environmental Development Agency
NGO	Non-Governmental Organization
NIWRMP	National Integrated Water Resources Management Plan (Bhutan)

xviii *List of Abbreviations*

NMIDP	National Minor Irrigation Development Project
NNIP	Narayanganj–Narsingdi Irrigation Project (Bangladesh)
NWFP	North Western Frontier Province
NWMP	National Water Management Plan
NWMU	National Watershed Management Unit (Bhutan)
NWPo	National Water Policy
NWRC	National Water Resources Council (Bangladesh)
NWRS	National Water Resource Strategy (South Africa)
O&M	Operation & Management
PC	Project Committee
PCAD	Provincial Canal and Drainage
PID	Provincial Irrigation Department
PIDA	Provincial Irrigation and Drainage Authority
PIM	Participatory Irrigation Management
PSRA	Punjab Soil Reclamation Act
PTC	Power Trading Corporation
PUs	Public Utilities
PWA	Provincial Water Accord
PWM	Participatory Water Management
RWMP	Radhi Watershed Management Project (Bhutan)
RCB	Rawalpindi Cantonment Board (Pakistan)
RDA	Rawalpindi Development Authority (Pakistan)
RNR RC	Renewable Natural Resources Research Centre (Bhutan)
RRI	River Research Institute
RSPN	Royal Society of Nature Protection
SMEC	Snowy Mountain Engineering Corporation
SNV	SNV Netherlands Development Organization
SOPPECOM	Society for Promoting Participative Ecosystem Management
SRP	Systems Rehabilitation Project
SUTRA	Social Upliftment for Rural Action
SWIM	Statewide Water Information Management
T&D	Transmission and Distribution
TISS	Tata Institute of Social Sciences
Tk	Taka (currency of Bangladesh)
TVA	Tennessee Valley Authority
UNDP	United Nations Development Programme
UNFCCC	UN Framework Convention on Climate Change

List of Abbreviations ≈ xix

USAID	United States Agency for International Development
WAPDA	Water and Power Development Authority
WAR	Water Allocation Reform
WARPO	Water Resource Planning Organization (Bangladesh)
WB	The World Bank
WFD	Water Framework Directive
WMA	Water Management Association
WMG	Water Management Group
WMO	Water Management Organization
WRC	Water Research Commission
WRBMF	Wang River Basin Management Framework (Bhutan)
WsM	Watershed Management
WSP–SA	Water and Sanitation Program–South Asia
WUA	Water User Association
WWMP	Wang Watershed Management Project (Bhutan)
WWN	Women and Water Network

Foreword

South Asia faces a variety of challenges in water resources governance, management and use. Millions of people in the region do not have access to clean drinking water and sanitation. Many countries in the region rely on groundwater exploitation to supplement their scarce surface water resources. Groundwater dependency reaching about 30–35 percent of the total supply in Bangladesh, India and Pakistan put renewable water resources under medium-to-high stress. The problem of insufficient, ill-managed supply is compounded by the poor quality of fresh water supplies in the region, which are threatened by water pollution due to location, characteristics of ecosystem, land-use patterns, and the degree and type of development. Given the range of water-related challenges faced by the region, many countries have reviewed or revised their national policy on water resources development and management to incorporate approaches and perspectives such as that of integrated water resource management. However, these policies are subject to change, reflecting the dynamic reality of economics, demography and ideology, thereby throwing challenges to civil society organizations and critical academics who have been persistently involved in identifying the existing problems and bringing them to the forefront.

Keeping these issues and concerns in mind, South Asia Consortium for Interdisciplinary Water Resources Studies (SaciWATERs) organized the International Conference on Water Resources Policy in South Asia in Colombo, Sri Lanka, December 17–20, 2008. The conference was part of the Crossing Boundaries Project, a joint initiative of SaciWATERs, India, and Wageningen University, The Netherlands, implemented with university partners in Bangladesh, India, Nepal and Sri Lanka and collaborating organizations in Bhutan and Pakistan. The conference brought together regional and international water professionals, academics, policymakers, activists, and others involved and interested in South Asian water resources issues. As part of ongoing global, regional and national water resources policy dialogues, the conference enhanced the xxii ≋ *Foreword*

understanding of water resources governance, management and use in the region by critically assessing reform agendas. Further, it critically investigated the varied dynamics of existing water resources management in South Asia and compared these with water policy dynamics in other regions of the world.

The present book grew out of the conference. It analyzes water resources policies from a perspective of integrated water resources management, while simultaneously reflecting critically on the notion of "integration." Understanding and analyzing the context in which water policies are formulated, presented and contested, this book argues for a pluralistic and integrated framework in formulating and implementing water policies in South Asia.

This book is part of the effort of SaciWATERs to produce innovative and nuanced knowledge on water resources in South Asia, by crossing national boundaries and thinking about water in a more holistic and integrated framework than is dominant in the region. This new knowledge is expected to help and inspire students studying and teachers teaching Integrated Water Resources Management, help water professionals active in water governance, management and use to more effectively address questions of equity, sustainability and democratic governance, and assist the general public and decision makers to support and advocate responsible approaches to water resource management in the various countries of South Asia.

Peter Mollinga
Professor of Development Studies
School of Oriental and African Studies
University of London

Acknowledgments

This book is the outcome of the papers presented at the International Conference on Water Resources Policies in South Asia held in December 2008 in Colombo, Sri Lanka. Select papers from the conference thus form the chapters in this book. The editors gratefully acknowledge the financial grant from the Government of The Netherlands for organizing the conference and arranging for the travel and stay of the contributors. The support extended by the South Asia Consortium for Interdisciplinary Water Resources Studies (SaciWATERs) office staff–particularly Hemalatha Paul, Office Manager, and Sumathi Shivam, Research Associate–merits profound acknowledgment. The editors also thank participants of the conference for their invaluable and insightful comments, suggestions and critique, since the discussions at the conference shaped this book in more than one way. Altogether, the conference helped in shaping the present form of the book.

The editors acknowledge the support from the external reviewers who reviewed the papers meticulously to enrich its content. We earnestly thank Dr Ajit Menon, Madras Institute of Development Studies, Chennai, India; Prof. Suresh Raj Chalise, Government of Nepal, Kathmandu, Nepal; Prof. Nina Laurie, University of Newcastle, UK; Prof. H. S. Shylendra, Institute of Rural Management, Anand, India; Prof. Vishwa Ballabh, Xavier Labour Relations Institute, Jamshedpur, India; Dr Renu Khosla, Centre for Urban and Regional Excellence, New Delhi, India; Dr Debolina Kundu, National Institute of Urban Affairs, New Delhi, India; Dr Priyanie Amerasinghe, International Water Management Institute (IWMI), Hyderabad, India; Mr Ramaswamy R. Iyer, Centre for Policy Research, New Delhi, India; and Dr Sunder Subramanian, formerly with Development Consulting ICRA Management Consulting Services Limited, Gurgaon, India–all of whom reviewed the papers and gave extensive and nuanced comments to further improve the content of this book.

At the end, the editors are indebted to all those who have directly or indirectly facilitated the production of this book.

Introduction

An Agenda for Pluralistic and Integrated Framework for Water Policies in South Asia

Anjal Prakash, Sreoshi Singh, Chanda Gurung Goodrich and *S. Janakarajan*

Water resources policy processes in South Asian literature bridges a critical gap in understanding how they are developed, influenced and implemented. The significance of water policies is derived from the recent advancements in discourses on water resource management, motives behind their formulation and politics of their implementation. Development of water policies is not devoid of gender, class/caste, urban and rural biases and their successful implementation is largely contested as they have a bearing on people living on the margins. This is more so in stratified societies of South Asia. Thus, identifying potential areas of intervention in order to improve both the formulation and implementation of policies is of paramount importance. This book covers a broad range of issues and water policy imperatives specific to countries within the South Asian region. Highlighting the problems of sustenance of techno-centric and blue print approach, growing influence of international donor agencies and absence of adequate concerns for normative issues such as equity, sustainability, gender sensitivity and diversity in managing water resources in these countries, this book seeks to

2 〜 *Anjal Prakash, Sreoshi Singh, Chanda Gurung Goodrich and S. Janakarajan*

analyze some of the common missing links present in the policies across the countries in South Asia. These issues border on gender orientation, property rights regimes, top-down approach for water management, lack of accountability, and regional conflicts that have been neglected while formulating policies.[1] All these call for serious debates and a political constituency for raising these issues on a sustained basis, and the present book provides the platform for such deliberation.

Further, the water policy discourses and state authorities implementing them have always been mistaken for taking a monolithic approach wherein one form such as market dominates over state or civil society initiatives. This book takes an alternative path in arguing that the state is neither monolithic nor always authoritarian when it comes to forming and formulating water policies.[2] In fact, the state, especially in a democratic set-up tends to work in tandem with two other important players, namely, markets and civil society organizations. Water policies have been drawn up at regular intervals in South Asia and have sought to highlight various ways and means to improve the availability of water for various sectors in order to improve the lives of people, especially those of the less privileged category who have to bear the brunt of water scarcity. Water policies attempt to lay down the allocations of water to various sectors on the basis of differential priorities–allocations that the government plans to implement over a specific period of time. Analyzing the contexts in which water policies are formulated, this book argues for a pluralistic and integrated framework in formulating and implementing water policies in South Asia.

The Context of the Book

At this juncture when water-related issues are at the forefront, the biggest concerns and challenges facing the economy, polity and society of South Asian countries is falling or stagnant agricultural growth, increasing migration from rural to urban areas, swift industrialization process, and unplanned and unregulated urbanization. According to Jairath and Ballabh (2008: 5), "The structure and development of water resources in most South Asian countries is a legacy of colonial times. Emphasis is typically placed on the design of civil engineering structures and hydrological parameters." The problems

Introduction ~ 3

of colonial legacy in water resource management, coupled with the present system of management, have direct and indirect bearing on water policies. The direct impact is the escalating demand for water for non-agricultural uses such as industrial and urban uses. As a consequence, millions of gallons of good quality water are transferred from rural to urban areas every day in most of the urban locations across South Asia. Does the problem stop here? The answer is no. Rising urban and industrial needs for water also enormously contribute to pollution: the South Asian "hydrocracy"[3] at best, focuses on freshwater management, but never ever discusses the issues concerning waste water or used water management practices. Indeed, in most of the South Asian countries, waste water or used water management strategies are considered an integral part of the regular water management strategies. As a result of the neglect of such an important issue, water pollution in South Asia has become the most important concern, which is threatening the very fundamentals of ecology and environment. The waste water generated by urban sewage and industrial effluents is very conveniently discharged into seas, freshwater bodies, low-lying lands/fields, rivers and streams. The problems in the years to come are going to be more severe and frightening. Undeniably, therefore, the sustainability of present levels of industrial development and high economic growth very much depends upon how the environmental and ecological concerns about the use and management of water resources are addressed by the South Asian polity and civil society.

More specifically, water concerns in South Asia are quite critical, varied and complex. First of all, per capita water endowment in South Asia vis-à-vis the rest of the world is quite scanty. South Asia being a home for about one-fourth of the world's population possesses only 4.5 percent (1,945 billion m^3) of the world's annual renewable water resources. Except Bhutan and Nepal, all countries in this region share smaller per capita water availability than the world average. For example, per capita water availability in India has decreased to 1,869 m^3 (6,602 ft^3) from 4,000 m^3 in last two decades and farmers increasingly tap into groundwater resources (Babel and Wahid 2008). Further, per capita water availability needs to be viewed in the context of persisting poverty, unemployment, growing food insecurity and lack of basic needs such as food, safe drinking water, sanitation, health care, etc., in South Asia. According to the World

4 ～ *Anjal Prakash, Sreoshi Singh, Chanda Gurung Goodrich and S. Janakarajan*

Water Development Report-3, more than 60 percent of the world's population growth between 2008 and 2100 is expected to be in sub-Saharan Africa (32 percent) and South Asia (30 percent). The report also indicates that across the world, there are 1.4 billion people who are classified as poor and of which 44 percent live in South Asia (UNWWDR3 2009). The water management challenges in South Asia should therefore be seen in this larger context of demographic pressure, growing rural and urban poverty, and deprivation of access to a critical resource like water.

Second, the structural inequities of caste, class and gender in South Asian societies are compounded by the problem of mismanagement of water resources and produce adverse effects on large sections of people. This is especially so for poor women and men without access to water such as lower castes, or those living on the margins of the mainstream society. The poor need water not only for basic needs such as drinking and sanitation, but also for productive purposes, viz., carry out livelihood-generating activities ranging from field agriculture to household production. In most of the cases, even water for basic needs is denied, leave aside water for production. While reporting cases of water management from India and Nepal, Upadhyay (2006) notes that providing reasonable volumes of water to poor women will encourage them to earn their livelihood, an issue largely ignored in present day water polices that advocate supply of minimum water for basic needs. Sultana (2006) documents a case from rural Bangladesh where the social structure is predominantly patriarchal. Scarcity of potable water brings considerable burden on the daily domestic responsibilities of women. Ahmed summarizes the issue succinctly:

> [T]he water crisis is essentially one of governance—how are our water resources managed at different institutional levels and by whom? Focus on gender, poverty and social exclusion is a significant point of departure from the traditional top-down approach for decentralized community water management initiatives (2005: 211).

Needless to say, equity in distribution of water is an important challenge faced by South Asian societies as water is not accessible to all, especially the ones who need it the most.

Third, even the available water resources are managed in such a way that the sustainability has become a big casuality. Along with

Introduction ~ 5

demographic growth, there is growing mismatch between water supply and demand, competing claims of users and uses over water, rapid urbanization and peri-urbanization and mounting urban stress on water resources, periodic recurrence of floods and droughts, displacement of people in the wake of dam building activities, inequity in and lack of access to safe drinking water and sanitation, groundwater overdraft and depletion, escalating water conflicts, water privatization and water pricing, threatening impact of climate change, disintegrated governance structure, myopic water policies, and most important of all, utter lack of motivation and commitment to protect ecology and environment. Thus, the water policies and programs in South Asia have to address three important challenges which have a bearing on the way water has been traditionally managed and distributed in the region.

The first challenge comes in the form of problems associated with unmanaged urbanization that is becoming the single most important impediment to sound water management in South Asia. Cities in South Asia are already experiencing severe water crisis because of exacerbating pressures on limited natural resources such as land and water; this is reflected in mushrooming of slums, rising urban poverty and utter lack of access of urban poor to safe drinking water and sanitation. All these have a serious effect on ecology and environment of peri-urban areas of major cities. As United Nations Environment Programme's (UNEP's) *State of Environment South Asia 2001* states:

> The growing demand for water, along with poor water resource management and mounting pollution levels, contributes to water supply problems in and around cities. Urbanisation is leading to changes in lifestyle and consumption patterns, which, in turn, is leading to increased demand for water. Industrial demand for water is also on the rise. As the number of people in urban areas increases, so does the demand for food and hence for irrigation in agricultural areas which are close to cities. These pressures can quickly result in a consolidated demand for water that surpasses local water supply (2001: 96).

The growth of industries and housing colonies, and the diversion of water from peri-urban villages to cities have severe effects on the livelihoods of peri-urban population. Water security of peri-urban

6 ≋ *Anjal Prakash, Sreoshi Singh, Chanda Gurung Goodrich and S. Janakarajan*

residents thus has been increasingly compromised by the increasing demand for drinking water in the urban settlements. This water requirement is met from the peri-urban locations which are generally richer in water endowment (Narain 2010). On the whole, the perturbing question is: whether the South Asian water governance system has any definite plan of action to bring sustainability to water supply for its vast and increasing urban populations? The answer lies in water conservation and better initiatives in water governance. Freshwater lakes and rivers provide affordable and easily accessible water, but uncontrolled discharge of domestic sewage and industrial effluents into them has left many urban rivers heavily polluted and their water unsafe for use (UNEP 2001). Consequently, in city after city in South Asia, an emerging trend is that of searching for water sources well beyond the urban boundaries.

The second challenge is the increasing dependency on groundwater for drinking, livelihood and agriculture. In many areas in South Asia, groundwater overdraft has not only resulted in the reduction in groundwater level, but also adversely affected crop yields and farm income, aggravated the problem of migration from rural to urban areas and spoilt the drinking water quality. Farmers have started feeling the pressure of maintaining a well due to "competitiveness in deepening", a phenomenon that has led to a continuous fall in water table and increase in the unit cost of pumping water in most of the South Asian region (Shah 2009). The competing demand for water from industries and urban domestic users has posed a new threat to well–owning agriculturists. This has not only aggravated the problem of decline in groundwater table, but also contributed to severe inequity in groundwater use (Prakash 2005). Well-to-do farmers and urban industrial owners install deep bore wells and pump water round the clock. Such unregulated pumping remains unchallenged because of ambiguity over rights to groundwater use: the right to groundwater use is tied to the right to land ownership, and hence lack of the latter implies the lack of the former and this double deprivation intensifies the problem of exclusion of resource-poor well owners who hitherto had access to groundwater (Janakarajan 1992, 1994; Prakash and Ballabh 2005). And for many, wells have become a source of indebtedness. This, in particular, is true of the low-rainfall, hard-rock regions of South India where unregulated groundwater extraction in the long run have caused distress to society as well as to individual farmers (Janakarajan and Moench 2006). However, groundwater

Introduction ～ 7

is also a politically critical resource in societies characterized by inequitable distribution of power and resources such as South Asia. Studies show how groundwater irrigation has helped in transforming social and production relations which have different implications for different classes and actors, thus contributing to policy formulations for irrigation reform (Mollinga 1998; Gorter 1989). This also shows why groundwater regulations have not been able to check the problem of depletion, and therefore efforts have been directed towards conservation of water rather than its regulation.

The third challenge is grappling with the effects of climate change. The phenomenon of global warming characterized by changes in the seasonal distribution, amount and intensity of precipitation, increased evapotranspiration, accelerated melting of glacial ice, increased coastal inundation and wetland loss from sea level rise would be responsible for increased water-induced hazards such as riverine floods and resultant inundation of fields, soil erosion by flash floods, prolonged droughts, and spread of alien pests that cause harmful crop diseases, thereby exerting a heavy toll on human lives, livelihoods and economic well-being, especially in the South Asian region (Dekens and Eriksson 2009). South Asian economies, which rely more on agriculture, fisheries and other natural resources such as forests, are going to confront the increased risks of high-intensity floods, storms, cyclones and droughts in future (IPCC 2007). Further, the South Asian poor, dependent upon subsistence farming, is more vulnerable to erratic monsoon rainfall. Freshwater availability is expected to become more seasonal since roughly 75 percent of the annual water supply is through monsoon rainfall across South Asia. Accelerated melting of glaciers would seriously affect about half-a-billion people in the Hindu Kush Himalayas (Stern 2007). Erratic monsoon rains in India and Nepal has been found to be highly correlated with large-scale climatological phenomena such as El Nino. It is feared that due to fast melting of the Himalayan glaciers, the presently perennial rivers of South Asia such as Indus, Ganges and Brahmaputra are quite likely to become seasonal rivers (IPCC 2007). The other threats posed by climate change that are particularly relevant to South Asia are increasing intensity of cyclones and storms, floods, beach erosion, landslides, bank cutting, persisting droughts, etc. Water policies of South Asian countries thus are being geared to grapple with the challenges and threats posed by climate change.

8 ∽ *Anjal Prakash, Sreoshi Singh, Chanda Gurung Goodrich and S. Janakarajan*

Thus, South Asia is faced with a concoction of problems in the water sector. In many parts of the region, institutional strengthening needs to take precedence over additional public investment in the water sector. There needs to be resource regulation, re-visioning of existing policies and constant evaluation of such policies which has been the main message in this book, with respect to all the facets of water that effect life in this region. The book, therefore argues for a more integrated and pluralistic framework for water policies in South Asia to counter the challenges outlined above.

About the Book

The book is divided in four sections. Section One provides a conceptual overview of what should inform water resource policy and how, and argues that policies are negotiated spaces within a given society. Chapters in this section also take strong positions on the gendered dimension of water management, which is in much need of attention. Section Two discusses the existing water policies in five South Asian countries in terms of their status, evolution and content, as well as suggestions for modifications therein. Section Three focuses on the impact of climate change and the emerging new challenges and dimensions to water policies in the region. Section Four dwells on international experiences in water policy reforms in three regions of the world, viz., South America, South Africa and Europe.

Section One

In all the South Asian countries, water is clearly a male-dominated sector, as manifest at all levels. Although new reforms and policies have taken cognizance of gender concerns at the micro-level, they have not detailed the feasibility of gender-sensitive water management. Despite these policy spaces, mainstreaming of gender concerns into the sector has become a mere lip service and the answers for this have to be sought at different levels (Kulkarni 2009). Thus, the first two chapters in this section focus on understanding the gender concerns in the water sector and how these influence the water policies.

The first chapter by Amita Shah and Seema Kulkarni covers new ground in the discourse on gender, water and poverty issues, which,

Introduction ≈ 9

in turn, contributes to some of the larger debates on economic growth, efficiency and equity in the water sector. The chapter brings forth the concerns for livelihood security, sustainability and equity, as voiced through various processes of participation, negotiations and contestations, which are some of the important links binding the discourses on water, poverty, and gender. It points out that a nuanced understanding of the trajectory of interface between water, poverty and gender may help to inform policy formulations and implementation at the ground level as water is one of the most critical and contested natural resources for enhancing human well-being and alleviating poverty, as well as a means of creating space for women's participation and empowerment. The chapter also addresses some major concerns in this interface.

The second chapter by Margreet Zwarteveen focussing on irrigation explains why gender and women are "invisible" in conventional water thinking. To this effect, the author identifies three sets of inter-related reasons. The first set relates to some more general features of irrigation thinking, such as its lack of a critical interpretative tradition and its cherishing of this lack as a virtue of modern science. The second set of reasons have to do with the way in which irrigation systems are normally defined and their conceptual boundaries drawn, and in the choice of metaphors used for representing irrigation realities. The third set is that power and politics are bracketed off from the normal analyses of irrigation. Using insights drawn from field experience in South Asia and other developing regions, the author argues that the social construction of gender and power, or rather the lack of it, in irrigation knowledge systems, is reflected in irrigation policy and practice, even those claiming to be participatory and thus, by extension, more socially or "people"–inclined.

The third chapter by Saravanan V. Subramanian and David Ip reveals that water policies are never implemented, but integrated through negotiation with other policies and socio-cultural settings in (re)shaping water resources management. This argument is based on a case-analysis of non-linear and complex integration of policies in framing a water management problem in a hamlet in the Indian Himalayas. The chapter highlights the fact that in spite of various actors incrementally and cumulatively governing water, "fire-fighting" approach is adopted on the presumption that "water is infinite." Policy-makers lack information rule that can enable various actors

10 ≈ *Anjal Prakash, Sreoshi Singh, Chanda Gurung Goodrich and S. Janakarajan*

to communicate and take an informed decision. The actors and their policies are diverse, not confined to a "place-based nexus" to manage watershed, as presumed in the contemporary IWRM programs. In this context, the authors call for government agencies to facilitate the provision of information rule through normative intervention, to carry out a comprehensive feasibility assessment of their policies, and enable actors to debate and negotiate the program.

Section Two

Discussing some existing water policies in five South Asian countries (Sri Lanka, Bangladesh, Bhutan, India and Pakistan) in terms of their status, evolution and content, as well as suggestions for modifications therein, this section has five chapters grounded on studies of the various reforms and approaches in the water management policies.

The first chapter by Jayanath Ananda focuses on Participatory Irrigation Management (PIM). Despite progress in water reforms, particularly PIM, many South Asian countries have been grappling with poor performance in water management, deterioration of canal and tank irrigation systems, high extraction levels of groundwater and related economic and environmental problems. The chapter thus assesses the institutional arrangements of PIM in South Asia using a set of generic institutional design principles and examines the reasons for the poor performance of irrigation management transfer (IMT) and states that reconfiguring the institutional design for PIM requires a greater understanding of socio-political relationships, appropriate spatial and administrative scales and process-based long-term learning.

The second chapter by Sultan Ahmad points out how water policies have changed in Bangladesh and how an integrated approach towards solving water management issues has manifested over time. From the time of Independence, various master plans were prepared and slowly taken up for implementation in Bangladesh. However, it was only in 1999 that the first National Water Policy was adopted for the comprehensive management of water resources of the country with the aim of providing direction to all agencies working in the water sector, and institutions that relate to the water sector in one form or another, for achievement of certain specified objectives. The chapter examines how this comprehensive National Water Policy

Introduction ≋ 11

has been translated into concrete actions and whether the policy statements of the government are only rhetoric, or they have been translated into robust and replicable development practices.

The third chapter by Thinley Gyamtsho draws the scenario of water management in Bhutan, which is endowed with rich water resources. Along with socio-economic development of the country, its water resources are being used for many other purposes such as generation of hydroelectricity, industrial production, recreation, etc., apart from the basic and conventional ones such as drinking and sanitation. However, economic development has done little to enhance the capacity of rural farmers to command these rich water resources. In this context, the chapter looks at the missing links in the Bhutan's water policy and the importance of an IWRM approach to manage a precious resource in this mountain country. The chapter further reflects on whether watershed management policies and programs are geared towards enhancing the people's capacity to command water resources.

The fourth chapter by Priya Sangameswaran, by exploring the categories of analyses of ongoing reforms in the water sector, brings out the merits and shortcomings of reforms in water policies. The chapter argues that many recent developments in social science theory offer useful conceptual tools to deal with some of the shortcomings. Focussing on three such developments–the growing importance of the concept of scale, the diverse economies approach, and ethnographies of the state–the chapter shows how these could be used to generate more nuanced analyses of the water reforms currently underway in India.

The last chapter in this section by Muhammad Mehmood Ul Hasan examines the reform design and implementation experience in Pakistan by focussing on the experiences of the Irrigation Management Transfer (IMT). The chapter argues that regardless of how well-intended and well-designed the policies are, outcomes of their implementation are determined by an interplay of multiple interests held by the most influential strategic groups comprising irrigation bureaucracy and influential farmers. The chapter asserts that donors to developmental projects should pay more attention to learning lessons from public policy research and practice in order to better predict the policy outcomes and improve their understanding of policy transfer processes.

Section Three

In the global climate change debate, the issue with the biggest importance to developing countries is reducing the vulnerability of their natural and socio-economic systems to the projected climate change. Over time, there has been a visible shift in the global climate change discussions towards adaptation (Sathaye et al. 2006). Thus, chapters in this section focus on adaptation and mitigation in the region.

The first chapter by Daanish Mustafa emphasizes the need for capacity building of developing nations for adaptation and social sustainability in the face of climate change, drawing examples from Pakistan, and thereby challenges the pattern of development which is currently in vogue in the South Asian region, which has no element of sustainability. The chapter argues that epistemological commitment to reactive mitigation and adaptation to modeling scenarios of "high-end" climate science is likely to have limited efficacy in the South Asian cultural, institutional and developmental context. The need is for a shift from a modernist *monologue* on vulnerability and adaptation to a *dialogue* wherein "high-end" science and policy can learn from and contribute to vulnerable populations' everyday strategies of adapting to and coping with hazards as well as their struggles for diversified and stable livelihoods.

The second chapter by Tushaar Shah explores India's opportunities for mitigation and adaption in the area of groundwater management in the face of climate change. The chapter stresses that for India, groundwater has become at once critical and threatened, and climate change will act as a force-multiplier, enhancing groundwater's criticality for drought-proofing agriculture and simultaneously multiplying the threat to the resource. From a climate change perspective, India's groundwater hotspots are western and peninsular India which are critical for mitigation of as well as adaptation to climate change. The chapter argues that India needs to make a transition from surface storages to "managed aquifer storage" as the focal point of its water strategy with components of proactive demand- and supply-side management.

Section Four

Water policies do not shape up in isolation. Experiences of other countries and regions serve as strong influences, examples and

Introduction ~~ 13

pointers to water policies and policy reforms of any country. Thus, looking at and examining experiences of other countries and regions is of critical importance. This section has three chapters dwelling on some important international experiences with regard to water reform processes from three regions of the world, viz., South America, South Africa and Europe.

The first chapter by Jessica Budds traces Chile's experience in water rights with a brief history and Chilean political economy of water markets which have been largely promoted by international financial institutions and supported initially by the military state (1973) and later by the Chicago Boys (neoliberal technocrats). The chapter outlines the history and creation of Chile's 1981 Water Code, examines the long-standing and polemic debate over the water markets model, and the government's attempts to reform it after Chile's return to democracy. It also discusses the existing empirical work on water markets in the country, drawing on two case studies which focus on social outcomes in northern Chile. The author argues that water markets in Chile have not yielded any social and environmental benefits and have, in fact, left the poor more vulnerable.

The second chapter by Eiman Karar discussing the contested implementation of water reforms in South Africa focuses on the dichotomy between the objectives of the water law reform in South Africa, as defined by the National Water Act of 1998, and its implementation since then. The chapter provides brief background information on the availability of water resources against the demands over them by different users, and then explains the post-1994 water reforms, the reasons for these reforms, and the resulting new water law, along with its mission and objectives. It outlines the local management of water resources, as it has evolved till date, to illustrate the sequence of events and intentions resulting in the decentralization of water management.

The final chapter by Claudia Pahl-Wostl reports on the latest developments in European Water Policy and argues for the need for an exchange on a global scale. The chapter provides a number of illustrative examples from Europe, arguing for the need of a paradigm shift in the approach to risk management from technical and quantitative assessments to robust and flexible adaptive management strategies. The chapter argues that what is needed is a globally co-ordinated learning process to be able to share lessons

14 ≈ *Anjal Prakash, Sreoshi Singh, Chanda Gurung Goodrich and S. Janakarajan*

learned and to jointly build a global knowledge base. This would also support the development of a "diagnostic" approach which develops tools to analyze the problems embedded in the social context and supports the development of context-specific integrated solutions instead of advocating simplistic technical and institutional panaceas.

Notes

1. For example, the Ganga–Bramhaputra–Meghna (GBM) basin covering about 1.75 million sq. km stretches across five countries out of which four are in the South Asia (Bangladesh, Bhutan, India and Nepal). The GBM region is marked by endemic poverty with about 40 percent of the poor people in the developing world residing there. Managing water regionally and efficiently with co-ordination among the basin countries is of paramount importance for alleviating poverty in the region. However, national water management plans of these countries hardly address the issue of regional integration and on the contrary, there is more conflict than co-operation for water management in the region (Ahmed et al. 2001; Salehin et al. 2012)
2. As against the "linear model" of policy-making that is characterised by objective analysis of options and separation of policy from implementation, Sutton (1999) reveals that, policy and policy implementation are best understood as a "chaos of purposes and accidents." Taking key ideas from such disciplines as political science\ sociology, anthropology, international relations and management, she argues that a combination of concepts and tools from different disciplines can be deployed to put some order into the chaos, including policy narratives, discourse analysis, regime theory, change management, and the role of street-level bureaucrats in implementation. She calls for understanding policy-making as a political process as much as an analytical or problem solving one.
3. The term "hydrocracy" has been derived from the Weberian bureaucracy. It connotes bureaucracy dealing with water issues (Weber 1947).

References

Ahmed, Q. K., Asit K. Biswas, R. Rangachari and M. M. Sainju. 2001. *Ganga-Brahmaputra-Meghna Region: A Framework for Sustainable Development*. Dhaka: The University Press Limited.

Ahmed, Sara. 2005. "Flowing Upstream: Towards Gender Just, Equitable and Empowering Water Management," in Sara Ahmed (ed.), *Flowing*

Upstream: Empowering Women through Water Management Initiatives in India, pp. 211–35. Ahmedabad: Center for Environmental Education.

Babel, Mukand S. and Shahriar M. Wahid. 2008. "Freshwater under Threat, South Asia: Vulnerability Assessment of Freshwater Resources to Environmental Change," UNEP and Asian Institute of Technology (AIT), Thailand, http://www.unep.org/pdf/southasia_report.pdf (accessed September 19, 2011).

Dekens, J. and M. Eriksson. 2009. "Adapting to Climate-induced Stresses and Hazards in the Hindu Kush-Himalayas," in "Water Storage: A Strategy for Climate Change Adaptation in the Himalayas," special issue, *Sustainable Mountain Development*, Winter, 56: 34–37.

Gorter, Peiter. 1989. "Canal Irrigation and Agrarian Transformation: A Case of Kesala," *Economic and Political Weekly*, 24 (39): A94–105.

Intergovernmental Panel on Climate Change (IPCC). 2007. *Climate Change 2007: The Physical Science Basis. Contribution of Working Group I to the Fourth Assessment Report of the Intergovernmental Panel on Climate Change.* Cambridge: Cambridge University Press.

Jairath, Jasveen and Vishwa Ballabh. 2008. "The Context and Problématique," in Jasveen Jairth and Vishwa Ballabh (eds), *Draught and Integrated Water Resources Management in South Asia: Issues, Alternatives and Futures*, pp. 3–39. Water in South Asia Series, vol. 2. New Delhi: Sage Publications.

Janakrajan, S. 1992. "Interlinked Transactions and the Market for Water in the Agrarian Economy of a Tamilnadu Village," in S. Subramanian (ed.), *Themes in Development Economics: Essays in Honour of Malcom Adiseshiah*, pp. 151–201. New Delhi: Oxford University Press.

———. 1994. "Trading in Groundwater: A Source of Power and Accumulation," in Marcus Moench (ed.), *Selling Water: Conceptual and Policy Debates over Groundwater Markets in India*, pp. 47–58. Ahmedabad: VIKSAT and Pacific Institute, Natural Heritage Institute, USA.

Janakarajan, S. and Marcus Moench. 2006. "Wells and Illfare: Conditions and Characteristics of Groundwater Irrigation in Tamil Nadu," *Water Nepal*, 12 (1&2): 47–80.

Kulkarni, Seema. 2009. *Situational Analysis of Women Water Professionals in South Asia*. Hyderabad: SaciWATERs.

Mollinga, Peter P. 1998. *On the Waterfront: Water Distribution, Technology and Agrarian Change in a South Indian Canal Irrigation System*. New Delhi: Orient Longman.

Narain, V. 2010. "Periurban Water Security in a Context of Urbanization and Climate Change: A Review of Concepts and Relationships." Peri Urban Water Security Discussion Paper 1, SaciWATERs, Hyderabad.

Prakash, Anjal and Vishwa Ballabh. 2005. "A Win-Some Lose-All Game. Social Differentiation and Politics of Groundwater Markets in North Gujarat," in Dik Roth, Rutgerd Boelens and Margreet Zwarteveen

16 ≋ *Anjal Prakash, Sreoshi Singh, Chanda Gurung Goodrich and S. Janakarajan*

(eds), *Liquid Relations: Contested Water Rights and Legal Complexity.* New Brunswick, NJ: Rutgers University Press.

Prakash, Anjal. 2005. *The Dark Zone: Groundwater Irrigation, Politics and Social Power in North Gujarat, India.* Hyderabad: Orient Longman.

Salehin, Mashfiqus, M. Shah Alam Khan, Anjal Prakash and Chanda Gurung Goodrich. 2012. "Opportunities for Transboundary Water Sharing in The Ganges, The Brahmaputra and The Meghna Basins," in Infrastructure Development Finance Company, *India Infrastructure Report 2011*, pp. 29–43. New Delhi: Oxford University Press.

Sathaye, Jayant, P. R. Shukla and N. H. Ravindranath. 2006. "Climate Change, Sustainable Development and India: Global and National Concerns," *Current Science,* 90(3): 314–25.

Shah, Tushaar. 2009. *Taming the Anarchy: Groundwater Governance in South Asia.* Washington: RFF Press.

Stern, Nicholas. 2007. *The Economics of Climate Change: The Stern Review.* Cambridge: Cambridge University Press.

Sultana, Farhana. 2006. "Gendered Waters, Poisoned Wells: Political Ecology of the Arsenic Crisis in Bangladesh," in Kuntala Lahiri-Dutt (ed.), *Fluid Bonds: Views on Gender and Water,* pp. 362–86. Kolkata: Stree Publishers.

Sutton, Rebecca. 1999. "The Policy Process: An Overview." Working Paper 118, Overseas Development Institute, London.

UNEP. 2001. *State of Environment South Asia 2001.*UNEP, Regional Resource Centre for Asia and the Pacific (UNEP RRC.AP), and Asian Institute of Technology (AIT), Bangkok: Thailand.

United Nations World Water Development Report 3 (UNWWDR-3): Water in a Changing World. 2009. World Water Assessment Programme, UNESCO, France, and Eathscan Publication, UK.

Upadhyay, Bhawna. 2006. "Poverty and Gendered Livelihoods: Making Water Work," in Kuntala Lahiri-Dutt (ed.), *Fluid Bonds: Views on Gender and Water,* pp. 258–71. Kolkata: Stree Publishers.

Weber, Max. 1947. *The Theory of Social and Economic Organization.* Trans. A. M. Henderson and Talcott Parsons. London: Collier Macmillan Publishers.

PART I

Conceptual Framework for Water Resources Policy

1

Interface between Water, Poverty and Gender Empowerment

Revisiting Theories, Policies and Practices

Amita Shah and *Seema Kulkarni*

The interface between water, poverty and gender has been a less understood one. It rests primarily on the premise that water being one of the most critical resources for human existence and hence contested, may create space for women's participation as well as empowerment. The relationship between the three is also much more complex than is understood to be in the current discourses on the interface between water and poverty, and between water and gender.

Strangely, the contemporary water–poverty–gender discourse has largely remained disjointed, or has seen the three in isolation. Those focussing on water and poverty have been overly concerned with income levels, paying little attention to the other aspects such as health, education, quality of life, property rights regime, equality of opportunities, and sustainability of resources. At the same time, the gender discourse has not moved beyond arguing for rights for women on the efficiency and welfare grounds. Although it does recognize the need for a shift from the earlier eco-feminist approaches wherein assumptions were made about relationships between women and water, little effort has been made to empirically understand the

20 ≈ *Amita Shah and Seema Kulkarni*

dynamic nature of this relationship and problematize it, especially in the Indian context.

It is thus imperative to take forward the two discourses on gender and water, and water and poverty in a manner that leads to a more comprehensive understanding of water–poverty–gender issues. This would necessitate a deeper and nuanced understanding of the interface between the three in a specific socio-economic and geographical context, in the light of major strands of conceptual as well as empirical discourses on the theme.

The chapter aims at addressing these concerns by: *a)* revisiting the dominant theories and contextualizing them in the light of recent trends in policy formulation and actual experience gathered from various participatory initiatives in the water sector in the region; *b)* evolving an analytical framework and identifying key research questions; and *c)* exploring appropriate methodologies for empirical investigation.

The analysis is divided into seven sections including the introduction. Sections 2 and 3 present a brief overview of the recent discourses on water–poverty and water–gender interface in the context of developing economies. This is followed by Section 4 which discusses a tentative framework for conducting empirical investigation for understanding the interface between water, poverty and gender in a specific context. Sections 5 and 6 identify major questions and methodologies for empirically examining the research questions. Section 7 presents some concluding remarks.

Water–Poverty Interface: Evidence and Issues

Access to adequate quantity of quality water, a basic need for all forms of life and for production of food, fibre and fuel, has a significant bearing on human well-being. The two most important and inter-related routes to reduction of water-induced poverty are: *a)* improved state of health and nutrition, and thereby improved quality of life; and *b)* increased productivity, especially of primary products, and thereby increased upward mobility (social as well as economic). While the positive impact on health and quality of life is fairly clear and hence less contested, the link between water and income poverty mainly in the production sphere is mediated by a number of complex factors such as agro-climatic, socio-economic and

Interface between Water, Poverty and Gender Empowerment ≈ 21

cultural ones. While the evidence from a large number of developing agrarian economies in South Asia suggest an overall impact of water, especially for irrigation, on poverty reduction at the macro level, the contemporary discourse has often overlooked the issue of equity in water–poverty interface (Giordano and Hussain 2004; Briscoe and Mallik 2006). This has led to differential outcomes for regions, households and members within the households. Essentially, these differential outcomes tend to reproduce, and at times, aggravate the existing inequalities in terms of resource endowment, ownership and power relationships that obtain at each of these three levels. In the light of this, it becomes important to understand the factors that combine to create scenarios of poverty, or facilitate pathways to move out of it.

Emerging Issues

Sustainability of Groundwater

Another important concern in the context of water–poverty interface is the issue of sustainability of water as an exit route from poverty, given the growing demand and depletion of groundwater resources, the main source of irrigation in large parts of countries such as India and other parts of South Asia (Shah et al. 2004; Shah 2009). For instance, about 50 percent of irrigation in India is through ground water which produces, in turn, nearly one-third of food crops in the country (Shah 2009). A somewhat similar situation with respect to groundwater depletion is observed in countries such as Pakistan and Nepal (Bandopadhyay 2007). Management of groundwater thus is critical for shaping the future of agricultural growth in regions where expansion of large-scale surface irrigation schemes has already started slowing down. The emphasis, therefore, is on rainwater harvesting and recharge of groundwater through various initiatives, especially watershed development.

Experience from micro-watershed projects in India testifies to how such initiatives help in mitigating the adverse impact of droughts and depletion of groundwater. There are, however, not many systematic studies capturing the long-term impact of such micro-level initiatives in recharging of aquifers under varying geo-hydrological conditions. This evidence, by and large, suggests that the positive impact are often confined to fairly limited areas and over a short span of time, mainly for the want of cost-effective devices on a scale required to

22 ≈ *Amita Shah and Seema Kulkarni*

address the problem (Cosgrove and Rijsberman 2000). In fact, the need is to go beyond groundwater recharge and address the issue of ecological services of water so as to ensure long-term sustainability of economic growth in the region.

Water-use Efficiency and Economic Viability

Enhancing value of output per unit of water is yet another important mechanism for impacting farm production and thereby poverty reduction. There cannot be any disagreement on the importance of resource-use efficiency in so far as it helps to promote livelihood support to the poor. The problem, however, emanates from adopting monetary measure of efficiency, i.e., market value of output per unit of water, without necessarily improving the technical efficiency in farm production. A likely fallout of an approach such as this is a drive towards high-value crops as against subsistence crops which are essential for meeting the basic requirements of food, fiber and fuel. It is likely that increasing emphasis on market orientation may further marginalize the poor operating under uncertain rainfall conditions (Prakash 2005). Moreover, emphasis on market-led approaches may further divert the attention from the quality aspect of water which, in fact, has significant bearing on health and human well-being, besides cost saving as suggested by Janakirajan and Moench (2006).

Among technological innovations, agricultural bio-technology seems to assume special significance from the point of view of increased yields from new crop varieties which are pest-resistant, high-yielding, etc. The special emphasis is on developing drought-resistant seeds. However, doubts have been cast on the potential of bio-technology to reach out to the poor farmers.

Absence of an Alternative Perspective

The vision underlying the emerging scenario of water and agriculture in the next two decades thus reinforces centrality of irrigation, groundwater recharge and efficiency in market sense. This may amount to continuing with the same trajectory of agricultural growth with certain modifications. In terms of poverty reduction, it may imply continued and, perhaps, increased dependence on percolation mechanism to reach the maximum number of poor people.

As against this, agricultural growth that leans towards livelihood support and sustainable prosperity for all, may call for an alternative vision of property rights regime, land- and water-use planning,

Interface between Water, Poverty and Gender Empowerment ≈ 23

diversified farming systems, compensatory mechanism for conservation, investment priorities and pricing support. This vision essentially would challenge the dominant paradigm of development and would be shared by a diverse group of actors including communities and civil society organizations. While the World Water Vision presented by the World Water Council (2000) discusses some of these aspects besides several others, the discourse on water and poverty reduction is yet to register a paradigm shift in the composition of agricultural growth which upfront addresses the issue of equity.

As an interesting perspective, the water poverty framework presented by Biltonen and Dalton (2008) offers a useful approach for analyzing availability of water and its use for meeting various developmental objectives, especially poverty reduction, and also for examining the implications of alternative scenarios of water allocation across different uses. While this appears to be a promising framework, its operationalization in a real-life scenario may be difficult in the absence of the aforementioned alternative vision of agricultural growth and of a political commitment that essentially is brought about through various social movements and representations by "agents of change" including women's collective agency.

Apparently, the recent discourse on water and gender discussed in the latter section has critiqued major features of the neoliberal policies for water sector reforms and/or Irrigation Management Transfer (IMT), but without adequately engaging with the issue of nature and composition of economic growth (in terms of production) and poverty reduction. There is an implicit assumption that gendered discourse on water would converge with an alternative vision of growth noted above. However, this may or may not happen depending on how macro-economic policies work to address inequity, and how multiple agencies of women play out under different settings, of region, class, and caste/ethnicity (Jackson 1998). In this context, the following observation by Zwarteveen is quite pertinent:

> Whatever may be the reason for the current disregard for social equity concern, it should be realized that an understanding whether and why irrigation programmes affect different people differently is not just important on the basis of equity concerns. In fact, such an understanding is fundamental to improving the effectiveness and efficiency of the water sector reforms and thus, solving the global problem of water scarcity (1998: 309).

Gender–Water Discourse

Conscious of the fact that environmental problems affect women in significant ways, feminists have been engaged with this issue since the early 1970s. They questioned the notion that the productive capacity of nature can be made limitless with the help of science and technology on the ground that the latter has rendered entire landscapes uninhabitable and unfit for survival of the generations to come.

The recognition of limits to development by nature fueled the search for sustainable solutions to the crisis. In the feminists' attempts to conceptualize sustainable development, the recognition of the connections between the domination of nature and of women provided important insights. This stimulated the debate in the South on women, environment and development, and in the North on nature feminism or ecofeminism.

Women as Victims of Crisis and Solution Providers

In the evolution of debates on women, environment and development since the mid-1980s, there has been a shift in political priorities and positions. The emphasis has gradually shifted from the perception of women as victims of environmental crisis to a recognition of their roles as efficient managers of environment. The argument for increased participation of women in environmental management has largely been derived from their privileged knowledge and experiences of working closely with the environment. A different line is pursued by one group of eco-feminists who suggest that an inherently close affinity of women with nature is based on a feminine principle (Shiva 1989). Nevertheless, the net conclusion of both these positions has been that women are seen as privileged environmental managers or source for solutions to environmental crisis (Baraidotti et al. 1994) By the later 1980s the debate on Women, Environment and Development (WED) had become an established one on international environment agendas. The growing recognition of connections between development crisis and degradation of environment, and between growth of poverty and gender inequalities forced recognition of the need to integrate social aspects with sustainable development.

Emerging Alternatives

In the 1990s, the debates were fairly well-established about the limits to theorization around women as saviors of environment and providers of solutions to environmental degradation. It was, therefore, emphasized that although women are differentially positioned vis-à-vis men in the use of environment and in the process of development, the relationship between these two has to be addressed at a different level.

Around the same time, various alternatives to the position of "women as solutions" were also emerging. These positions were more grounded in a materialist perspective and suggested a historical context to gender relations. For example, feminist environmentalism (Agarwal 1992) and feminist political ecology (Rochleau et al. 1996) speak of a more dynamic relationship between women and nature. The point of difference is largely in the way these alternatives problematize the relationship rather than assume it one way or the other. Feminist political ecology locates the relationship in larger socio-political and cultural context wherein symbolic constructions of power become significant. Feminist environmentalism emphasizes on the material relationship that women and some men have with nature as a result of which they share a more intimate relationship with nature.

Gender and Water

Most of the gender–water discourse traverses a similar path. It continues to be dominated by the instrumentalist approach wherein women's participation becomes critical from the point of view of the larger goal of efficiency and effective management of water resources.

Narrow sectoral biases dominate thinking in the water sector in general, and this is reflected in the gender–water discourse as well. The domestic water sector is seen as the women's sector because of its welfare orientation, and the irrigation sector as dominated by men. Therefore, until recently, the gender–water discourse largely focussed on the domestic water sector, pointing to the women's time and labor spent on collection and utilization of water and thereby arguing for their inclusion in project planning and management (Zwarteveen 1998; Kulkarni et al. 2007). There is little critical engagement with how such a perspective, in fact, lends to stereotyping of women in their current roles as nurturers and carers. Although the discourse has moved ahead and tried to challenge stereotyping of gender roles, water policies and programs continue to be dominated by this image of women as it suits the larger policy and programmatic goals of better and efficient management.

A quick review of literature of the past 10 years on gender and water shows us the range of issues the discourse has been grappling with. From the early 1990s when the focus was clearly on domestic water sector, there has been a shift in the focus towards an attempt to understand the sectoral divide and identify gender aspects of irrigation management (Zwarteveen 1998) largely located in the context of IMT of the post-1990 reform era. This literature calls for addressing some of the challenges thrown up by the introduction of new water policies with their emphasis on water as an economic good and on women's participation and gender relations. Some of the early questions raised were also related to pricing of water as having an impact on cropping patterns and preferences and displacing women from their roles as subsistence agriculturalists (Cleaver 1998; Zwarteveen 1998). These were not backed by context-specific empirical evidence and are yet to be investigated carefully. This investigation becomes important as the rhetoric often is likely to re-emphasize gender stereotypes. Water use and management is gendered and although it is recognized that men and women have differing priorities of and perceptions about water management and use, there is little empirical understanding to contextualize this generalization. This has opened up a larger set of questions around gendered preferences in water use and management which need a careful context-specific examination even today. Do men and women in water-rich areas follow different practices? Do different castes and socio-cultural contexts differ in this respect? Do men and women have different cropping preferences? These kinds of questions may help us acquire a contextualized understanding of gender and water (Jackson 1998).

More recently, there have been efforts to understand the space that has been created by the newly-introduced policies around decentralized water management through people's participation. An instance is the ongoing study by the Society for Promoting Participative Ecosystem Management (SOPPECOM), Utthan and the Tata Institute of Social Sciences (TISS) with the support of the

Interface between Water, Poverty and Gender Empowerment ~ 27

International Development Research Centre (IDRC), Canada, in the states of Gujarat and Maharashtra. These are new processes, and therefore, it is too early to understand and explain the experiences of participation and empowerment through decentralized water management institutions.

It is in this context that the question of institutions too gained currency in these debates, but there is little empirical understanding of the role of formal and informal institutions in water management and their impact on women's participation (Cleaver 2003). Very few questions are asked on women's perceptions about the new institutional forms at the local level that claim to hold the potential for improved participation of women leading to their empowerment. However, there has been no work either on how such empowerment is effected, or on the perception(s) that women and men have about the decision-making process at local level and their role within it. Further, in the Indian context there is very little empirical understanding of the approaches and contributions of men and women to these local institutions and the effect they have on the power relations between them. In the absence of such a nuanced understanding, the general prescription has been to try and increase the representation of women in these committees or institutions. The underlying assumption is that women's representation would lead to better representation of their priorities. There is also very little understanding of how women see these institutions and whether they feel that the process of participation, as it currently presents itself, is empowering to them.

An important contribution to the discourse on sectoral divide is that Cecile Jackson (1996, 1998) who argues for a framework that facilitates an integrated analysis of the domestic and productive uses of water by focusing on subjectivities and embodied experiences of men and women in water works. Such an analysis would allow for an integration of labor and production considerations on the one hand and of health and well-being on the other. The core focus of her argument is on understanding the women's agency as shaped by and resisting structural constraints (Jackson 1998). Here, the individual actor, her perceptions and actions, therefore, are central to understanding the dynamics of water sector.

At the same time, she cautions against an overemphasis on separating genders rather than stressing on the interdependencies of gender relations on the one hand, and on understanding resources

28 ～ Amita Shah and Seema Kulkarni

as physical assets rather than their varied meanings as understood by people on the other. In this context, it might be interesting to get a contextualized understanding of how women look at work around water and what has led to formulating the perceptions they hold.

Interface between the Gender, Water and Poverty Discourses: Exploring an Analytical Framework

This section tries to develop a tentative analytical framework for examining the likely trajectories of water-induced changes in economic (income) well-being, especially in the production sphere, gender empowerment as well as women's agency. There are, of course, possibilities of multiple trajectories linking water–poverty–gender wherein augmentation or additional availability of water operates as the major trigger of the processes of change, both in poverty reduction and gender empowerment in an interactive mode. What kind of trajectories would actually emerge, however, would depend on various factors—natural resource endowments, socio-cultural and techno-economic conditions in a micro-setting. Also, the trajectories may not be pre-defined as they tend to evolve and respond to the larger processes of change in the macro-environment.

Given this backdrop, we have tried to explore at least two broad trajectories which though not mutually exclusive can be treated as analytical constructs that may help in identifying critical research questions for empirical investigation. The trajectories have been identified in the light of the two major strands of economic growth, especially in agriculture and natural resources sector, mentioned in the water–poverty and water–gender discourses in the previous two sections. The central thrust of the enquiry is: whether and in what manner increased water availability may impact poverty across different categories of households and change power relationships between the genders in a specific micro-setting. The following Table 1.1 presents a synoptic view of the two broad categories, which we term as mainly "market-driven" and "process-driven."

Interface between Water, Poverty and Gender Empowerment ≋ 29

Table 1.1: Two scenarios of water–poverty–gender interface
in production sphere

Main Features	Trajectory 1: Market-driven	Trajectory 2: Process-driven
Access to additional water for productive use	Irrigation schemes, private investment in groundwater and watershed development	Minor irrigation works and watershed development
Impact on farm productivity and income	Sure, substantial and immediate	Limited, uncertain and slow
Technology and farm practices/labor intensity	Intensive use of inputs including irrigation	Centrality of soil moisture profile, agronomic practices and labor intensity
Sustainability of resources and benefits	Limited owing to groundwater depletion and neglect of less productive land, especially common property resources	Very positive owing to emphasis on resource regeneration
Intra-community and intra-household equity	Benefits may reach disproportionately to non-poor though it may also help a subset of poor landed households	Better equity within community
Impact on women's work burden and new-opportunities including health and educational outcomes	Expected to be positive on most of these aspects depending on the actual increase in income, given the socio-cultural-spatial features	Not very clear
Women's participation and empowerment within and outside family	Enhancement of economic status	Opening of new spaces within and outside family
Implications for collective identity	May weaken gender identity of women	More conducive

Source: Prepared by the authors.

30 ≋ *Amita Shah and Seema Kulkarni*

Trajectory 1: This refers mainly to a scenario wherein increased availability of water, especially for irrigation, along with the use of mainstream (input-intensive) technology, leads to immediate and substantial increase in crop productivity. Such outcome, however, is experienced by a relatively small subset of households, even among the landed categories. Those benefiting from irrigation, by and large, may belong to relatively higher caste/ethnic categories. Further, it may be postulated that among the beneficiaries of additional irrigation, those with relatively better economic/financial position and at times political power tend to earn greater profit as compared to those having relatively weak resource base.

It is likely that this trajectory of water-induced income enhancement/poverty reduction may generate some adverse environmental consequences owing to adoption of water and input-intensive crops as well as technologies. Also, it may intensify commercialization of agriculture rather than ensure households' food security. This may imply crop-centric approach to land use whereby relatively less productive land may get subjected to sub-optimal use.

Nevertheless, households, at least a subset within the community, may obtain substantial increase in income; hence, improvement in economic well-being including food security. This, in turn, may bring some associated positive benefits to the members of households including women. Some of the benefits could reduce the drudgery and the amount of time spent on collection of water, fodder and fuel as these tasks could be passed onto hired labor, or, these resources could be obtained from market. Another benefit reaching household members could be improved access to health end education, besides recreation, mobility and leisure.

It is still quite likely that these benefits may get distributed disproportionately among the members, often in favor of the male members; among the latter, young men get the better deals. Notwithstanding the gender discrimination, each of the above benefits may bring some kind of empowerment to women within a household, often, without exerting any positive impact on gendered power relations within and outside a family.

One may not, however, completely rule out the possibility that increased economic and social development attainment among some of the female members of the households may trigger a route to empowerment and freedom different from what is generally envisaged. More importantly, it may also lead to changing class

Interface between Water, Poverty and Gender Empowerment ～ 31

identities among women of these households having attained higher economic status. This may involve a new kind of networking, upward social mobility, and perhaps opening of new economic opportunities.

What do all these mean to women's self-esteem, empowerment, agency, collective identity and ultimately gendered power relations? These may need probing in the context of women's own aspirations and the socio-economic-cultural context, which shape them.

Trajectory 2: This refers to an alternative scenario, echoing some of the important features of a wide range of developmental initiatives involving participatory processes and institutions within the domain of watershed, irrigation, and domestic water resources management. This may include initiatives prior to the sector reforms and after that.

As depicted in Table 1.1, this trajectory has a somewhat different starting point for augmenting additional water resources in terms of both technology and processes of decision-making as well as institution building. Without getting into finer details, the trajectory can be described as more sensitive to equity issues which, in turn, may lead to different types of technological interventions for augmentation of water resources and creation of institutional mechanisms for the distribution of the augmented water.

Women and their concerns may find greater space in the augmentation and management of water resources right from the initial stage of the intervention. This is expected to create more equitable outcomes with greater emphasis on provisioning of domestic water and limited but more broad-based access to water for irrigation, especially for crop-survival, covering a large number of relatively poor farmers and marginalized communities.

Centrality of equity, including gender equity, may necessitate different types of land use, crop choices and farm practices. The practices in land use may largely be characterized as technologies with low intensity of irrigation and external inputs; higher labor use; diversified land use promoting allied activities such as livestock, inland fisheries, plantation, kitchen garden, etc., wherein women traditionally have larger space; emphasis on food crops; low dependence on markets; and low risks of crop failure. All these features may be more conducive to environmental sustainability with special emphasis on groundwater recharge. Participatory institutions may help uphold this "virtuous" model as they may create

32 ≈ *Amita Shah and Seema Kulkarni*

greater space for the involvement of the landless, poor and socially marginalized.

Overall, this trajectory may offer more equitable, sustainable and gender-sensitive pathways for strengthening water–poverty–gender interface. It is also likely that the trajectory may lead to further strengthening of collective identity among women owing to their involvement in participatory processes and increased space in public domain. All these may help support the cause of women's empowerment in the context of gendered power relations as compared to Trajectory 1.

How far this has been realized in real-life situations? What are the major facilitating and constraining factors for attaining women empowerment through participatory water resources management? How far a woman's aspirations as an individual converge with that of a collective identity?

These are some questions that may need empirical investigation. An important aspect that deserves special attention is that of linking gender issues with poverty. While it is true that a large proportion of women in developing economies like those in South Asia face severe conditions of poverty and deprivation, it is imperative to bear in mind that women's subordination is not caused by poverty alone, as understood by some feminists. Moreover, the issue of collective identity of women assumes special importance in the context of poverty–gender interface since roles, identities and behavior of non-poor women may exert positive as well as negative influence on poor women (Jackson 1996: 501). The next section dwells on the larger as well as specific questions emerging from the above discussion. Before getting to the empirical questions, it may once again be reiterated that the two trajectories presented above are neither exclusive nor complete in terms of detailed understanding. Also, these are not the only possible trajectories. It is, however, expected that in so far as these trajectories capture the major strands of the contemporary debate, the synoptic view may help to set the stage for identification of relevant questions and the implications thereof, for the theoretical discourse on water–poverty–gender, and in that case, fairly exploratory.

Key Areas of Exploration

Our central enquiry is in the area of exploring the interface between water, gender and poverty. We hope to contribute in a small way

Interface between Water, Poverty and Gender Empowerment ≈ 33

towards understanding the processes that are unfolding in the wake of the current neoliberal economic paradigm in the water sector.

Our substantive concern is to understand the impact of poverty alleviation agenda in the water sector on women across different social groups and on gender relations in general. The water poverty, specifically the income poverty agenda, has missed out on linking the caste and gender concerns while the gender–water discourse, as we have seen earlier, has largely focused on structures of patriarchy as a reason for women's exclusion from water management. Would economic prosperity address gender, caste and other forms of social discrimination both at the intra-household level as well as within the community? Or would participation of women lead to improving the effectiveness of water management programs?

Some of the difficult questions pertaining to broader concern would be on: *a)* the notion of equity across caste, class and gender divide in the context of water resources interventions; *b)* the understanding of empowerment located in water interventions across class, caste, gender and other social groups; *c)* understanding the current access to water (including that created through new interventions) and its meaning across class, caste, tribe, gender, ethnic and religious minorities in the first instance and then at the intra-household level as well to understand the gendered nature of access; *d)* the factors that influence this access across groups such as technology, location, markets; and *e)* the notion of individual access to water in a household and the process of gender discrimination.

The second substantive concern is participation which is informed by discourses on pro-poor agricultural growth, participation and gender relations. Though the current paradigm has created a space for decentralized water management and women's participation, experience is still too fresh to comprehend whether the space has been utilized effectively or not and whether it has contributed to the notions of equity across the different socio-economic groups. Therefore, we may need to look at the possibility of a link between representation and empowerment at different levels and from different dimensions and ways of measuring this. In this context, there is a need to specifically look at economic empowerment and the caste–class differentials for the same. More specifically, the economic benefits to women because of water interventions, in terms of time saved or alternative opportunities of saving time, and the emergence of new forms of gender discrimination need assessment.

The third substantive area is the issue of collective gender identity. Can there be a collective gender identity around water? Since water is a critical input in production, its optimum availability according to the crop type, would lead to increased income which may lead to building of a stronger class identity and perhaps weakening of collective gender identity which may have existed due to other interventions such as SHGs, etc. In this context, the attempt should be to understand the circumstances under which the notion of a collective gender identity evolves or weakens in the context of water interventions. More specifically, we need to understand: a) what was the nature of gendered identities prior to water sector interventions: whether they were Self Help Groups (SHGs), women's rights collectives, or Village Water and Sanitation Committees (VWSC); b) what were the key discourses they engaged in, or the issues they raised; what was their nature and gendered composition (i.e., the kind of women/men affiliated to them); and whether their objective of establishing a collective gendered identity was achieved; and c) whether this identity has been altered since the intervention and to what extent can it be attributed to the water intervention programme meant to alleviate poverty.

The fourth substantive area is a much-contested one, i.e., gender differentials in preferences about water use and management. Though income enhancement and institutional space may hold potential for addressing the issue of equity in general and gender empowerment in particular, the underlying assumptions may need to be examined. Hence, the key question that needs to be asked is: what are the gender differentials in: a) the preferences in land and water use, and b) in the choice of crops/species/technologies?

In this context, we may also further need to probe women's and men's perceptions about the division of labor in water use and management by creating different scenarios of such division and understanding how and why men or women would choose particular scenarios over others. This may lead us to understand the different visions of water sector reforms in the minds of men and women and the underlying differences in their worldview.

The fifth substantive area is the understanding of the interplay between the areas of contestations and stability that define familial relationships and kinship ties.

Here, we need to understand the processes of negotiation, conflict and compromise in some of the key areas of choices such as

Interface between Water, Poverty and Gender Empowerment ≈ 35

health, sexuality and economy. Thus, we may need to understand, for instance, patterns of expenditure in a household (including that on births, deaths and marriages); and decisions about child bearing and sexuality, health and illnesses, education of a girl child, and augmentation or liquidation of women's assets.

Feminist Methodologies

Understanding the interface through a gendered perspective is indeed a methodological challenge, as is evident from the nature of the substantive concerns and some of the specific questions that have been raised in the earlier section. It is a challenge also because it invokes methods from both the disciplines of economics and feminist studies. An interactive and iterative process would be critical in understanding the dynamics between water, gender and poverty. A combination of tools or methods would be needed to understand such a complex set of questions, but the distinctive component of this approach is the research practice and the broader framework of feminist understanding. The analysis of research, then proceeds from the framework employed to understand some of the questions posed earlier. The challenge is in interpreting women's and men's voices and perceptions and whether they can be treated as knowledge especially when we are considering a marriage between two different disciplines.

Concluding Remarks

The chapter tries to link the two largely disjointed discourses on water and poverty on the one hand, and water and gender on the other. Intuitively, some of the important links binding the two discourses seem to be the concern for sustainable livelihood and women's empowerment through various processes of participation, negotiations, and contestations. Equity, including gender equity, is at the center of all these concerns. Ours is thus an effort to cover a new ground in integrating the two discourses, with a hope to contribute to some of the larger debates on economic growth, efficiency and equity in the water sector. While the water–poverty discourse overstates the economic efficiency argument, the gender–water discourse and empirical evidence too has not moved much beyond the welfare and instrumentality approaches. The idea is thus

36　≋　*Amita Shah and Seema Kulkarni*

to go beyond the instrumentalist approach and essentiality of linking gender empowerment with poverty reduction by exploring a new vision of agricultural growth which inter alia, may help to strengthen women's collective agency. Whether and how far is this possible? What are the different pathways? And what role would water-induced processes of change play in attaining these pathways? These are some of the important riders that need empirical investigation in context-specific situations. The chapter has made a modest beginning in this direction by revisiting the major strands of the two discourses, outlining an analytical framework and identifying critical research questions for an empirical enquiry. It is exploratory in nature and seeks to generate substantive engagement among professionals and practitioners in the related fields.

References

Agarwal, B. 1992. "The Gender and Environment Debate: Lessons from India," *Feminist Studies*, 18(1): 119–58.

Bandopadhyay, J. 2007. "Water Systems Management in South Asia: Need for a Research Framework," *Economic and Political Weekly*, 39(12): 863–73.

Biltonen, C. and J. Dalton. 2003. "A Water Poverty Accounting Framework: Analysing the Water Poverty Link," *Water International*, 28(4): 467–77.

Braidotti, R., E. Charkiewicz, S. Hausler and S. Wiering. 1994. *Women, the Environment and Sustainable Development*. London: Zed Books and INSTRAW.

Briscoe, J. and R. P. S. Mallik. 2006. *India's Water Resource Economy for a Turbulent Future*. New Delhi: Oxford University Press.

Cleaver, F. 1998. "Incentives and Informal Institutions: Gender and the Management of Water," *Agriculture and Human Values*, 15(4): 347–60.

―――. 2003. "Bearers, Buyers and Bureaucrats: The Missing Social World in Gender and Water." Paper presented at the seminar "Gender Myths and Feminist Fables: Repositioning Gender in Development Policy and Practice," July 2–4, 2003, Institute of Development Studies, University of Sussex, Brighton.

Cosgrove, W. J. and F. R. Rijsberman. 2000. *World Water Vision: Making Water Everybody's Business*. London: Earthscan Publications Ltd.

Dervis, K. 2006. "Foreword," in United Nations Development Programme (UNDP), *Human Development Report 2006: Beyond Scarcity: Power, Poverty and Global Water Crisis*, pp. v–vi. New York: UNDP and Palgrave Macmillan Ltd.

Girdano, M. and I. Hussain. 2004. "Water and Poverty Linkages: Summary and Lessons," in M. Girdano and I. Hussain (eds), *Water and Poverty Linkages: Case Studies from Nepal, Pakistan and SriLanka*, pp. 105–08. Colombo: International Water Management Institute (IWMI).

Harding, Sandra. 1987. "Introduction: Is There a Feminist Method?," in Sandra Harding (ed.), *Feminism and Methodology*. Indiana: Indiana University Press.

Jackson, C. 1996. "Rescuing Gender from the Poverty Trap," *World Development*, 24(3): 489–504.

———. 1998. "Gender, Irrigation, and Environment: Arguing for Agency," *Agriculture and Human Values*, 15(4): 313–24.

Janakrajan, S. and M. Moench. 2006. "Are Wells Potential Threat to Farmer's Well Being?," *Economic and Political Weekly*, 38(24): 2350–52.

Kulkarni, Seema, Sara Ahmed, Swarnalata Arya, K. J. Joy and Suhas Paranjape. 2007. *Women, Water and Livelihoods: A Review of Policy, Towards Evolving a Gender-just Vision of Water*. Pune: WWN and SOPPECOM.

Prakash, A. 2005. *Dark Zone: The Groundwater, Irrigation, and Social Power in North Gujarat, Wageningen University Water Series*. Hyderabad: Orient Longman.

Rocheleau, Dianne, Barbara Thomas-Slayter and Esther Wangari. 1996. *Feminist Political Ecology: Global Issues and Local Experiences*. London and New York: Routledge.

Shah, T. 2009. *Taming the Anarchy: Groundwater Governance in South Asia, Resources for the Future*. Washington: RFF Press.

Shah, T., C. Scott, A. Kishore and A. Sharma. 2004. *Energy–Irrigation Nexus in South Asia: Improving Ground Water Conservation and Power Sector Viability*. Research Report 70. Colombo: IWMI.

Shiva, V. 1989. *Staying Alive: Women, Ecology and Development*. London: Zed Press; New Delhi: Kali for Women.

World Water Council. 2000. "World Water Vision: Commission Report. A Water Secure World: Vision for Water, Life and the Environment", http://www.worldwatercouncil.org/fileadmin/wwc/Library/Publications_and_reports/Visions/CommissionReport.pdf (accessed November 14, 2012).

Zwarteveen, M. 1998. "Identifying Gender Aspects of New Irrigation Management Policies," *Agriculture and Human Values*, 15: 301–12.

2

Seeing Women and Questioning Gender in Water Management*

Margreet Zwarteveen

Many concerned with gender injustices in the water sector have noted that there is a huge gap between their "paper" recognition on the one hand, and *a*) real grassroots efforts to effectively address them, and *b*) their meaningful integration in mainstream water analyses, on the other (see, for instance, BE et al. 2006). Gender is not as yet seen as belonging to the core of what water management is about. In this chapter I look at one possible reason for the resistance of water professionals to accommodating gender insights: incompatibilities between water experts and gender experts in terms of how they conceptualize and make abstractions about realities of water management.

Focusing on irrigation engineering, I argue that the difficulty of individual water analysts to see the role of women and gender relations in water management does not stem from their unwillingness or persistent biases, but is rather linked to a particular epistemic tradition in water management that is deeply inhospitable to the analysis of social relations and gender. A conclusion that flows from this argument

---

*I have based this chapter on the research I did for my PhD thesis (Zwarteveen 2006), and in particular have used Chapter 3 of the thesis to write it. An earlier and different version of it also appears as Chapter 4 in Boelens et al. 2010 (Zwarteveen 2010).

Seeing Women and Questioning Gender in Water Management ～ 39

is that "thinking" (and acting on) gender in water management additionally and importantly requires active efforts to change the "normal" ways of "knowing" in water management. In this chapter, I critically discuss the terms of discursive existence for water actors in mainstream water thinking from a gender perspective.[1] Important to this exercise is the assumption that scientific water knowledge, like most bodies of knowledge that are systematically produced, possesses regularities and exhibits systems of rules. These rules are, however, seldom formulated by the participants in the knowledge-generating practices, but remain largely unconscious. They make it possible to make claims that count as important, relevant or true within the boundaries of a scientific or epistemic community.[2]

The language, discursive practices and textual resources that form the heart of scientific water knowledge simultaneously form part of a wider range of cultural resources through which water professionals represent and identify themselves, and this contributes to legitimizing professional activities and choices. In this way, the knowledge about realities of water management is as much a reflection of the prevailing professional water cultures and identities (with their own configurations of power, status, authority and funds) as a reflection of realities "in the field." This way of looking at knowledge casts serious doubts on claims of objectivity and neutrality, inviting critical reflection on how knowledge is constructed and by whom, and how the identity and social situated-ness of knowledge producers impact on their claims to truth.

"Seeing" Women in Irrigation

That seeing women in irrigation is difficult is most often attributed to the symbolic, discursive and ideological construction of farmers, irrigators and engineers as masculine and to the fact that being recognized as (relevant) actors in the realm of irrigation requires rights, abilities and personality traits that (are) more often (seen to) belong to men than to women. In this chapter I propose to move beyond these relatively easily identifiable barriers to seeing women in order to suggest that there are a number of less easily recognized but perhaps equally fundamental problems in irrigation thinking that lead to mis-representing women, that prevent the questioning and challenging of gender relations and that mis-represent irrigation realities as gender-less or gender neutral. I believe that identifying

40　♒　*Margreet Zwarteveen*

these problems may help explain why "gender mainstreaming" in water sector remains a difficult and slow process, and may contribute to finding new entry-points for making the water sector a more gender-equitable and just place.

Before going on to further describe these problems, I need to explain how my conceptualization of gender frames the direction and nature of my search for ways to "think" gender in water management. I see gender as a social construction whose meaning is contested and negotiated. Gender, therefore, cannot be treated as something that simply exists and can be known and mapped in a positivist sense. What it means to be a man or a woman is not a given and cannot be determined in any a-historical or transcendental way. As a shifting, dynamic and contextual phenomenon, gender does not denote a substantive trait of character or personality, but is a relative point of convergence among culturally and historically specific sets of relations. Gender roles, identities and relations are matters of continuous (re-)interpretation both in terms of practices and ideas, sometimes leading to controversy and debate.

Such a contextualized and constructivist understanding of gender is hard to reconcile with the feminist desire to establish women as a clearly demarcated political category. It is also incompatible with the habit of mainstream irrigation and water management thinkers to strip away the context and meaning of gender to uncover universal human essence in their efforts to draw generic lessons about the performance of water systems. Indeed, and as I hope to show in this chapter, the difficulty to match feminist representations of the realities of water management with those of engineers or economists largely stems from these ontological and epistemological differences.

Analyzing gender and analyzing water do not just seem to require different ways of ordering and making abstractions about reality; the levels and units of such analyses may also be difficult to reconcile. Manifestations of gendered inequities and injustices in water sector occur, or are most clearly visible at the level of the end-users. If the unit of analysis is a large surface irrigation system, a river basin or even climate change at the global level, the group of end-users is so large that it becomes conceptually difficult to do justice to all diversities and differences, including those based on gender, between stakeholders and actors. In addition, water interests and needs are not usually clearly gendered: although women may have specific interests in water, they are usually not a homogeneous group

Seeing Women and Questioning Gender in Water Management ~ 41

in terms of those interests, rendering it analytically and politically difficult to use gender as a marker of identities based on water use. Understanding gender, therefore, poses some important challenges to the more conventional ways of looking at water issues. I have categorized these challenges into three sets, which are interrelated. The first relates to some of the more general features of irrigation thinking, in particular its lack of a tradition of critical interpretation. These features are related to the positivist epistemological beliefs on which much of the scientific water knowledge is based. The second has to do with the way irrigation systems and realities are ontologically defined and the way conceptual boundaries are drawn between "what matters" for the purpose of knowing irrigation and what can be ignored. And the third relates to how human beings and human behavior are conceptualized, and to the overall bracketing off power and politics from the analysis. I further discuss these conceptual barriers, focusing on their effects on representation of women and thinking about gender.

Power, Perspective and Knowledge

Although different in focus and scope, and drawing on different disciplinary theories, the mainstream strands of professional water thinking share a number of characteristics. First, and importantly, their traditional subject matter is "non-social." Scientific water knowledge is, or used to be primarily concerned with "the resource" water. The physical, biological and chemical characteristics of water, together with the engineering knowledge needed to convey water, constitute the heart of much of the scientific water knowledge. Although efforts are increasingly made to include social questions as well in the analysis of water problems, the preferred scientific languages and methods continue to be derived from the natural and engineering sciences.

Second, much of the scientific water knowledge is visibly rooted in a modernization project, a project that associates positivist science (mathematics in particular) and modern technology with progress and civilization. Although most contemporary irrigation and water professionals no longer share with their (colonial) ancestors a strong faith in technology as a motor of progress, many continue to believe in the superiority—and universal applicability—of scientifically developed irrigation technologies or institutional and economic

42 ~ *Margreet Zwarteveen*

models (also see Boelens 2008). In this positivist tradition, the "god-trick" is pervasive: the assumption that one can see everything from nowhere and that disembodied reason can produce accurate and "objective" accounts of the world.[3] It is marked by a faith in the neutrality of reasoned judgment, in scientific objectivity, in the progressive logic of reason in general and science in particular. Through the omnipotence of reason, transcendence is possible, allowing the knower to escape the limits of body, time and space.

Third, conventional water thinking is pervaded with a belief that given proper technologies, institutions or incentive structures, human beings will display the same behavior in using and managing water everywhere. This belief is rooted in an epistemological claim of human universality and homogeneity, a claim that has it that in essence all human beings are equal and share a common capacity to reason. Differences between people are, therefore, fundamentally epiphenomenal, making it possible to make generic statements about human nature, truth and other universalities.[4] In this humanist or liberal understanding of human beings, gender can only be thought of as an attribute of a person who is characterized essentially as a pre-gendered substance or "core" (called the person). Such a conceptualization does not support a critical feminist inquiry of the meaning of gender, which would require a relational conceptualization of gender, one that acknowledges that what the person "is", and indeed what gender "is" is always relative to the constructed relations in which it is determined (Butler 1999; Scott 1986). In addition, and as feminist political theorists have pointed out, the referent for conceptualizing humanity and the human "core" in much of the social and political theories has been primarily masculine. Indeed, the term "man" as used in liberal thought—even by those who are willing to concede that he/him means "all"—is not simply a linguistic device or a generic label, but a symbol reflecting both masculine virtues and patriarchalist practices (Dietz 1992).

A fourth and related characteristic of much mainstream irrigation thought is its denial of the importance of power to knowledge and of the linkages between the construction of subjectivity and power. This denial is directly linked to the fact that much mainstream irrigation knowledge is produced from the perspective of those who (are deemed to be) in control: planners, administrators and managers.[5] The produced knowledge is aimed at helping *them* realize *their* objectives, and enables them to speak more authoritatively through

Seeing Women and Questioning Gender in Water Management ≈ 43

the disembodied, transcendent voice of reason. Hence, in much of the early engineering thinking the locus of control was situated in the head engineer, at the head-gates. He was the "sovereign," and the irrigators were his "subjects." Although there was debate about the most effective control strategy, the very possibility of effectively controlling and manipulating the behavior of people and flows of water and money was seldom questioned. It is telling in this regard that theoretical models about the determinants of irrigation system performance, such as those embodied in technical designs, or as proposed by neo-institutionalism, are hardly ever empirically tested other than through the deductive method. Measured output is compared to the benchmarks set by the formal models without validating the operational and behavioral assumptions of these models.[6] It is also telling that designers and designs are hardly ever confronted with the operational realities at field level.[7] In this way, the established belief in the model and in the effectiveness of planners' control mechanisms remains unchallenged, and the legitimacy of the water professional and his knowledge remain untouched.[8] Indeed, the persistence of certain basic assumptions in irrigation thinking can be explained as much by their success in generating funds and power (and in bolstering the egos of irrigation practitioners) as by their success in generating valid theses about the determinants of irrigation system performance.

Much scientific water knowledge conceives of knowledge producers, and by extension of head-engineers or managers, as transcendent rational subjects who exist outside time, space and context. Through irrigation knowledge, those (deemed) in control of water are provided with agency and subjectivity, a discursive construction that is conditional upon the simultaneous denial or severe limitation of agency to users, irrigators or farmers. The latter group has a restricted capacity to act and speak; they are the ones who need to be controlled and whose behavior needs to be adjusted to what is deemed "appropriate" by those who "know." The concept of human agency that is often used to explain farmers' and water users' behavior is that of the utility optimizer and rational decision maker who weighs the costs and benefits of alternative choices. This does not leave much conceptual scope for considering the actions and choices of the various players in irrigation from their own perspectives and in their own frames of reference. Nor are culture, tradition and less seemingly rational explanations for behavior allowed for.

44 ≈ *Margreet Zwarteveen*

This is not to deny that contemporary scientific water knowledge takes farmers and other actors more seriously than in earlier days. Calls for more participation of farmers in design and management processes, and the associated appreciation of the value of farmers' knowledge, have led to changes in the production of scientific water knowledge. Yet, and as Shah (2003: 22) convincingly argues, "While inclusion of farmers' knowledge and farmers' choices in the process of "design" is envisaged by the dominant model, the validity of conventional disciplinary–scientific and engineering–knowledge and the context in which this knowledge is generated, is not very frequently questioned." Issues of power and identity, of location and time, continue to be shielded off from scrutiny through appeals to "the technical", "the rational" and "the scientific."

Literary critic and theorist Spivak (1988: 253) once asked, "Can men theorise feminism, can whites theorise racism, can the bourgeois theorise revolution . . .?" She maintains that when the former groups theorize, it is crucial that the members of these groups are kept vigilant about their assigned subject positions. Her question stresses the importance of critically reflecting on how the identities and situatedness of knowers impact on the knowledge they produce. It reaffirms that the production of knowledge about and designs of water systems are deeply social processes in which different stakeholders interact. The nature of these processes and the different perceptions, interests and powers of the stakeholders involved shape the knowledge produced, just as the design choices and the technical characteristics of the ultimate designs (cf. Shah 2003).

This is why challenging norms of objectivity that have long guided science is a central agenda of feminist project in water. In the strong formulation of Catharine MacKinnon (MacKinnon 1987: 50 cited in Langton 2000: 135), "Objectivity is the epistemological stance of which objectification is the social process, of which male dominance is the politics, the acted out social practice." For Haraway (1991: 191), "seeing well" is not just a matter of having good eyesight: it is a located activity, cognizant of its particularity and of the accountability requirements that are specific to its location. "Seeing well" implies the refusal of any subject/object split in the production of knowledge, insisting on "the critical and interpretative core of all knowledge." In situated knowledge-making projects, embodied knowers engage with active objects of knowledge whose agency and unpredictability unsettle any hopes for perfect knowledge and control. Indeed, there

Seeing Women and Questioning Gender in Water Management ≋ 45

are connections and linkages between subjects and objects, and the two can be said to stand in a "dialogic" relationship to each other (cf. Sayer 1992: 22–42). Finding or revealing "truth" in the strictly positivist tradition then becomes impossible. Instead, any effort to represent the sphere of irrigation in one consistent, all-encompassing narrative or discourse is politically dangerous (because of its totalizing and exclusionary effects) and academically suspect (because it hides the knower and her identity and power in cloaks of objectivity). In the words of Nicholson (1995: 5): "Any discursive move which attempts to place itself beyond question automatically invokes suspicion." Indeed, only from the falsely universalizing perspective of those who are, or think they are, in control and command can "reality" have "a" structure. (cf. Flax 1986 cited in Harding 1986: 193).

Gendered Metaphors and Dichotomies

Mainstream irrigation thinking uses a spatial conceptual imagery with strong gender connotations. For one, irrigation systems and what goes on within them are often seen as "the work place", a domain that is spatially and socially distinct from "the home." It separates the place where production for market occurs (and where incomes are earned), from the place where consumption and production for one's own use occur. This place is also the "public" domain which contrasts with the "private" domain of home and family and is associated with men. It rests on the ideological and normative ideas that men should be breadwinners, whereas women should be care-givers, cleaners and mothers. These ideas are reinforced by the masculine connotation of the word "farmer" (and in analogy with it, the words "irrigator" and "engineer"). Although most irrigation thinkers today would no longer explicitly adhere to such gender ideologies, conceptual languages and methodological tools continue to be pervaded by the dichotomies of work–home, production–consumption and public–private. In analogy with this gendered imagery, irrigation is associated with reason and logic, in implicit contrast to the sentiments of emotion and affection that characterize the "non-irrigation" world. What matters to, and characterizes, irrigation professionalism is the "male" side of the dichotomy.

Through the use of concepts based on these dichotomized metaphors, irrigators are seen either as factory workers or as private

46 ≈ *Margreet Zwarteveen*

entrepreneurs. Irrigating and irrigated farming are, as a consequence, seen as the business of one individual whose irrigation practices are primarily informed by irrigation system-related imperatives. Other family members do sometimes assist this individual, but he is the one to be in charge and to make all decisions. This view is problematic since smallholder irrigated farming often is not the sole affair of one individual but a family undertaking. It is also problematic because it is implicitly based on a, by now much-criticized, nuclear family household model and it excludes everything that is associated with private–home–domestic from the analysis. Since these are associated with women, further thinking about women and gender also becomes unnecessary[9], reinforcing the continuous approval of everything "masculine" (to the neglect of all that is "feminine") and limiting the attribution of powers and status to men.

The dichotomous metaphors "infect" irrigation thinking also in more diffuse ways, through associating masculinity with all that matters to irrigation in implicit opposition to femininity with all that is less relevant.[10] Hence, water for productive uses tends to be considered more important than water for domestic uses, crops grown for the market are more important than subsistence crops, and public decisions are more important than private decisions. Also, economic and productionist motivations for behavior are considered more real than (and normatively superior to) those based on emotions, solidarity and affection. Work such as cooking and provision of meals for agricultural laborers is not normally considered part of irrigation work. And the irrigation conflicts and struggles that are most easily observed and named tend to be of the spectacular and violent type, involving stealing, fighting and bribery. The more hidden everyday forms of resistance (cf. Scott 1985), the silences and strategic invisibilities (cf. Jackson 1998) tend to receive less attention. Hence, while often not directly gendered, the conceptual delimitation of what counts and matters in irrigation, of what belongs to the irrigation domain, and the definitions of what is "good" irrigation behavior are deeply colored by gendered images and connotations. Using such delimitations and definitions may have the effect of reinforcing and further legitimizing such gendered divides rather than questioning them.

From the perspective of irrigators and farmers, home and work are often closely inter-connected not only because the first objective of work often is family survival, but also because family circumstances

Seeing Women and Questioning Gender in Water Management ≈ 47

and considerations significantly influence work decisions and behavior. Indeed, the boundaries between public and private, as well as those between production and subsistence, blur on closer examination. And work and genders cannot be easily categorized into two distinct domains, nor are these domains necessarily in harmony (or in conflict, as some feminist scholars have it). Most smallholder farm households display a high degree of interdependence between production and subsistence activities, and between the household's farm functions and its family functions. Domestic (or reproductive) labor is characteristic of all household members' activities, related to agricultural as well as subsistence production, and is not restricted to women's work. Irrigating and farming are not just about production, and not just associated with the activities of men.[11] Maybe more fundamentally, irrigation needs, interests and activities are seldom directly gendered or just a function of a person's gender. Instead, the ways in which gender mediates irrigation realities depends on time and location and is mediated by class, ethnicity and other cultural and socio-economic structures and identities. Rethinking the meaning of "private" and "public" and conceptually reconstructing the relationship between the two because they are in part defined by each other, is therefore central to the feminist project in irrigation.

Some feminisms, and some streams of ecofeminism plea for a revaluation of the feminine through a reversal of the dichotomous hierarchy on which much Western scientific thought is based. Others, instead, have argued in favor of strategies that would facilitate and encourage women's entry into the "masculine" worlds of production, politics and reason. Although I share the belief in the importance of more positively judging all that is associated with the feminine, and although I also see the merits of the integrationist strategy, my argument here is that a more productive form of feminism consists in critically questioning the ways in which the poles are defined. The boundaries that separate nature from culture, private from public, work from home and so on, are not fixed and a-historical, but contingent and socially constructed. Showing that this is so is an important way to start questioning the taken-for-granted gender hierarchies and dichotomies.

In sum, understanding gender relations in irrigation systems is crucially dependent on a thorough rethinking of the metaphorical and spatial (and sometimes ideological and normative) images used. It is crucial to overcome, or at least critically question, the dualistic

48 ～ *Margreet Zwarteveen*

conceptual framework founded upon an opposition between the economic and rational world of irrigation-based production and politics on the one hand, and the affectionate and emotional world of the home and the family on the other. This can, for instance, be done by recognizing the subsistence and livelihood functions of farms. This can also be done by recognizing that men are not just irrigators and farmers, but also husbands and fathers, or by acknowledging the fact that women's identities are not confined to those of mother and (house-)wife, but also often include those of farmers and decision makers. This further includes allowing for the possibility that important irrigation negotiations occur in the domestic domain. And this requires a critical revisiting of what is recognized and defined as irrigation behavior, and of who are recognized as irrigators, for what is included in these definitions may well in itself be gendered. Rather than a priori assuming the meaning and boundaries of irrigation systems, households and farmers, and the criteria for inclusion in the sphere of irrigation, these should be made the object of inquiry. Are these terms negotiable, and are definitions and conceptual categories themselves a way of defining and reconfirming ideas about gender, and of distinguishing masculinity from femininity?

Technical and Management Systems and Boundaries

In much of today's irrigation thinking, the colonial view of farmers as backward and in need of civilization is no longer very popular. Yet, much thinking is still pervaded with an implicit normativity regarding what is "good" and what is "bad" irrigation behavior. In fact, much of the irrigation knowledge seems to show more concern about creating the conditions for people to function as desired by experts, than about understanding what is actually going on. Maybe as a result of this, people tend to "matter" (and discursively exist) in irrigation thinking only in so far as they functionally relate to the irrigation system as conceived in technical designs and management models. Small and Svendsen (1992: 4) in their conceptualization of irrigation performance explicitly posit that "farmers are considered in their roles as irrigators, but their parallel roles in other aspects of crop husbandry are excluded." This distinction, as the authors explain, "is necessary to establish a clear analytic separation between the irrigation system and the broader agricultural system

Seeing Women and Questioning Gender in Water Management 〰 49

of which irrigation is a part" (Small and Svendsen 1992:4). Such a conceptualization rests on the Weberian assumption that individuals can and do consciously separate their irrigation roles and behavior from their other roles. Or at least it suggests that for understanding irrigation realities, a restricted focus on the behavior of users that directly relates to the output and impact of the irrigation system is sufficient. Who farmers are thus only matters as far as their irrigation identities are concerned, the identities they have "achieved" because of their rational involvement in the system. Therefore, and unless irrigation roles are directly gendered (that is, if being a woman or a man in itself is seen as an irrigation role), gender also ceases to matter.

This conceptual insulation of the irrigation system from its environment mirrors the attempts of many irrigation engineers to immunize the irrigation system from outside interferences. It can, in fact, be seen as an attempt to achieve what Latour (1987) calls a process of "closure." Closure is achieved when the possible meaning and use of a technology is no longer contested, and its origins are ascribed to the laws of nature. One of its effects is that the authority to make truth claims about irrigation comes to lie with experts. It is also another illustration of how the irrigation system is metaphorically compared to a factory or work place. The very concept of "role", as used by Small and Svendsen following Coward's 1980 framework, portrays irrigation realities as factory-like settings with strongly pronounced normative definitions of expected modes of conduct. What these roles are is taken as a given, and derived from an ideal-typical model of how the irrigation system should function. Again, who play these irrigation roles and in what social context does not matter. What people do in the "irrigation factory" is conceptualized as a function of the factory, and unrelated to who they are or to their status, position or power outside of the factory. Their gender, as a result, is also inconsequential for understanding the functioning of the irrigation system and therefore does not require further questioning or explanation.

There are an increasing number of studies showing that in day-to-day irrigation realities, the boundaries between the system and its environment are not so easily drawn. People cannot just set aside their non-irrigation related identities and interests for the sake of good performance of the irrigation system. Also, people's decisions on irrigation do not just stem from considerations that are internal to

50 ☙ *Margreet Zwarteveen*

the system. More often, irrigating farmers know each other and relate to each other in many more ways than just through sharing a joint irrigation facility. Irrigation decisions are thus tied to and influenced by wider choices related to farming, livelihoods and social networks.[12] An illustration of this is the case of a widow in Nepal whose access to irrigation water in the absence of formal rights became directly dependent upon the benevolence of her family-in-law. For various reasons (one of which was that she only had daughters), her in-laws were not very accommodating and made it physically impossible for her to irrigate her land by not maintaining part of the canal leading to her field (Schaaf, van der 2000: 174–7).

Not only the physical infrastructural system, but also water users' associations (WUAs) tend to be conceptually defined as relatively insulated from the social context. Instead, in most writings on participatory irrigation management, the group of farmers or irrigators is referred to as a group that is already existing and easily identifiable: those people that are served by a common irrigation facility. Participation is about participation of this group in the project or system of another group, the engineers or irrigation managers who are part of the state irrigation bureaucracy. Implicit in the theory that informs creation of WUAs, sharing the irrigation facility is what binds users together and motivates them to collaborate and meet. Also in theory, for water users' associations to effectively and successfully undertake the tasks they have been assigned, users are expected to "set aside" their non-irrigating roles and identities. The ideal model of a water users' association thus presupposes the absence of social inequalities other than those ordained by the physical lay-out or division of the irrigation system, or by the division of irrigation-related functions.

The ideal water users' association (WUA) is to be an arena in which participants set aside such characteristics as differences in birth, wealth and gender and speak to another as if they are socially and economically equal.[13] Indeed, to many analysts the problem to be solved to make WUAs successful is the problem of "insulating" decision-making processes in irrigation management from what are considered (in liberal terms) non-political or pre-political processes, characteristic, for instance, of the economy (or the market), or the family (or the household) (cf. Fraser 1997). The social context in which community organizations function is not entirely ignored, but seen in view of this problem. The ultimate concern is to unravel

Seeing Women and Questioning Gender in Water Management ≈ 51

the determinants of "well-performing irrigation management institutions", while what good performance means is already decided—based on universal laws of human behavior and nature—and mostly expressed in rather narrow technical, productionist and economic terms. The actually existing situations are thus described and judged on the basis of whether or to what extent they follow, or can be made to follow the ideal model. The existing social relations of power and the existing culture and norms are loosely treated as the raw material from which institutions can be "crafted", "the institutional resource bank from which arrangements can be drawn which reduce the social overhead costs of co-operation in resource management" (Cleaver 2000: 365).

In contrast to such conceptualizations that suppose a clear boundary between the irrigation reality and the rest of the world, "seeing" the social and gender in water management requires acknowledging that water management is embedded (McCay and Jentoft 1998), or that the boundaries between water management and its social and political environment are often permeable in both directions. Oorthuizen (2003), for instance, shows how intimate intra- and inter-familial relationships between farmers, irrigation officials and politicians (either based on kinship or on institutionalized friendship ties) significantly shape (and in their turn are shaped by) water management activities and decisions. Van der Schaaf (2000: 183), in the study referred to earlier, tells the story of a widow whose irrigation water was repeatedly stolen. This widow was hesitant about bringing this up at the meeting of water users since she suspected the thief to be the son of her husband's second wife. Her desire to keep peace in the family prevailed over her anxiety about her crop.

That the insulation of the formal water management domain from its environment reflects experts' ideals rather than ground realities also shows up in women's experiences as participants in users' associations. Women do not stop being (seen as) women (to become gender-less rational deliberators) once they enter the formal public domain. An example comes from an irrigation system in Peru where about half of the members of the WUA were women, and where both women and men attended meetings. It was observed during these meetings that although male members on average talked for about 28 minutes, female members only talked for 3.5 minutes. Although "speaking time" cannot be used as a straightforward measure of influence (see Cleaver 1999), women did explain that

52 ≈ *Margreet Zwarteveen*

they felt diffident about articulating their concerns in meetings and afraid of making mistakes and being ridiculed (Krol 1994). Another example is that of the Buttala irrigation system in Sri Lanka. Here, although 32 percent of the legal cultivators (who were entitled to membership in WUAs and participation in meetings) were women, only 21 percent of the actual members were female. Some of the women who were formally entitled to membership chose not to make use of this right. They preferred, instead, to have their husbands or sons register as members (Kome 1997). Reflecting on the reluctance of women to participate in meetings in an irrigation system in Nepal, van der Schaaf (2000: 186) observed that if a woman would go to the meeting, this would signify the weakness and incompetence of her husband, and (to add insult to disgrace) it would imply admitting that she was smarter and cleverer than he was.

There are many more examples that suggest that gender colors deliberation and decision-making, even in the absence of formal entrance barriers. Public interaction and styles of deliberation are, almost everywhere, gendered in that there are distinct social norms and rules that define what sorts of interaction are permissible for women (and men), in what contexts, and by using which modes of conduct. Fraser (1997) even goes further to suggest that discursive interactions within the public domain are governed by protocols and styles of decorum that are themselves correlates and markers of gender inequality. In the above cited examples, to be outspoken and opinionated are positive characteristics for (some) men, markers of masculine "distinction" in Pierre Bourdieu's sense; a way of defining and reconfirming masculinity and male superiority. Fraser's analysis suggests that (performance in) organizations such as water users' associations may itself be a way of defining and reconfirming the existing gendered norms and practices, and of distinguishing a separate male "public" domain from a female "domestic" or "private" domain.

Just as "the social" does not stop at the boundary of the WUA, water management is often not confined to formal water management institutions. One of the more telling illustrations of this is the story many Andean irrigation professionals often tell when reflecting on gender: the fact that men participating in water management meetings always require a second meeting (the following day or week) to be able to make a decision. As the story goes, they want and need to first consult with their wives at home. There are

Seeing Women and Questioning Gender in Water Management ≋ 53

some more, often rather anecdotal, examples of women playing important but non-formalized (and therefore non-recognized) roles in organizations, or in carrying out collective action. Pradhan (1989), for instance, describes how in the Bhanjayang Tar Ko Kulo in the hills of Nepal, women who were not formal members of the water users' association played key roles in solving a canal maintenance conflict between head- and tail-enders. During the progress of Sreeramsagar project in India, women in one village organized themselves to remove obstructions in the canal and guard the water flow. As an old male farmer said, "We have seen that nobody is bold enough to obstruct women and it made things easy for us" (Rao et al. 1991). While women may not be the formal or official irrigators, canal operators or office bearers of WUAs, there exist quite a few anecdotal examples of women helping their husbands with the work these jobs require, and sometimes even replacing them.

Indeed, water management can be seen to happen in a number of co-existing and partly overlapping "domains of interaction" (Villareal 1994), which are not limited to the ones recognized and designated for water management by policymakers and managers.[14] The very fact that formal water decision-making is, or has come to be seen and defined as something belonging to the sphere of men, may in itself prompt the emergence of alternative ways and networks for managing and dealing with questions of water management. Brunt (1992), for instance, describes how, in an irrigation system in México, male farmers invited canal operators to bars and brothels as a strategy to strengthen and consolidate their access to water. Female farmers, for whom such behavior would be socially unacceptable, instead tried to invest in relations with male water leaders by giving them small presents, or by making them the god-fathers of their children.

Studies such as those by Villareal and Brunt suggest that technical and organizational water systems are embedded in wider social and political relations and hierarchies that are not (all) based on or derived from water. Irrigators belong to wider social, cultural and normative systems, and are informed by locally specific ecological conditions. The recognition of embeddedness opens the conceptual door for the recognition of gender because all social and political environments are gendered, and gender shapes and colors all irrigation interactions and irrigation decisions.[15] The works of Giddens (1984) and Long (1992) can assist in recognizing the social positioning of irrigation actors in the social relations of power, including gender relations.

54 ≈ *Margreet Zwarteveen*

Rather than seeing actors solely in relation to the resource or activity of interest to the knower, Long (1992) suggests perceiving them as complex individuals, partly enrolled in the projects of others and partly involved in their own. Giddens (1984: xxiv) argues for the recognition that a person is positioned in multiple ways, with social relations conferred by specific social identities.

At a deeper level, the implication of embeddedness is that what the system is and how its boundaries are drawn is significantly constituted by the social, political and ecological context in which it is functioning. This realization leads to a different ontological definition of irrigation or water systems than the one used in mainstream thought, one that allows the physical/technical and the social to be analyzed simultaneously, as different but internally related dimensions of a single object (Mollinga 1998). Notions such as "sociotechnical systems" (Mollinga 1998), "waterscapes" (Swyngedouw 1997) and "naturecultures" or "cyborgs" (Haraway 1991) provide important ingredients for an ontology of irrigation systems that allows connecting the water system to its social, cultural and ecological environment. These notions envision human activity and nature as being in negotiation and interaction, shaping landscapes which are dynamic and continuously contested in a process that is constituted by and simultaneously constitutes the political economy of access and control over resources (Haraway 1991; Swyngedouw 1997). Significantly, the boundaries of the system are not static, but change over time and are the subject of negotiation and struggle. In the words of Mollinga (1998: 23), "Time, space, and the properties of water are strategically used, contested and adapted by people when they conduct the activity of irrigation." As Bolding (2004: 135) notes, in their lifetimes, irrigation systems tend to change and be transformed much more, and much more radically (through appropriation by users and frontline management staff and through changing intervention models and policy discourses) than many other technologies. This is why describing and understanding an irrigation system requires what Haraway (2003) refers to as an "ontological choreography". It requires explicit inclusion of how different actors define and manipulate the boundaries and constituent elements of the system.

"Seeing" gender in water management, thus, not just requires allowing women to enter into the already defined and ideal-typical domains of irrigation decision-making. It also and crucially

Seeing Women and Questioning Gender in Water Management ≈ 55

requires rethinking the boundaries of and functioning within these domains. And it includes a critical inquiry of how the drawing of boundaries between the identified domains serves to maintain or erode the existing constellations of gendered power and the existing gendered identities.

Conclusions

In this chapter I have provided an account of how normal professionalism conceptualizes water realities, and tried to show what such conceptualizations imply for "seeing" women or for understanding gender. Water science is a very particular form of science. Many works on irrigation have been funded with the monetary aid under bilateral/multilateral co-operation programs (between/among nations or nations and international bodies) in developmental projects, and a large number of studies have been commissioned to inform specific irrigation programs. A major objective of such research is to help make irrigation systems perform better–though performance is often narrowly defined in technical terms–and this has an important effect on the operating standards of research.

For one, familiarity with the international discourse on irrigation often is of far greater importance than knowledge of a particular country in order for one to become an international expert. Many studies are produced for international consumption by the agencies or universities that sponsored them in the first place, and are circulated only within a privileged circle of policy-makers or academics. Secondly, most studies are predominantly descriptive, providing evidence to substantiate a selection of key themes. Their thrust in general is to provide better irrigation designs or management models rather than produce sharper analysis. Diverse irrigation realities across the world are reduced to "key performance indicators" (see Perry 1996; Molden et al. 1998) which can serve as the basis of comparison to compound "a screening process for selecting systems that perform relatively well, and those that do not" (Molden et al. 1998: 19). Such systematic exclusion of the context or of the specifics of cultural, social and political environment allows sustaining the façade of a universal and generic "water expertise" which can be applied the world over with only minor adjustments. It is an expertise that is intrinsically resilient to seeing gender, even

56 ～ *Margreet Zwarteveen*

when it is accepted that gender is always necessarily about context. It is also an expertise that may not be hospitable to critical reflexivity, more in general, and by more constructivist approaches to knowing– since these risk unveiling and threatening the fundaments of unequal economic and political relations on which it is founded and that it helps sustain.

"Normal" water knowledge often continues to be typically positivist, and much of it continues to be prescriptive: it is concerned with how water realities should be, and possibly with why actual realities are different. It is less concerned with trying to understand the logic and determinants of how such realities actually are. Through prescriptive ways of "ordering" realities (water systems, organizations, institutions, economies), people are also "ordered" and "normalized": they exist in these conceptualizations and narratives almost as little robots that act on the basis of a clearly identifiable and known (to planners, managers, knowers) sets of incentives that can be manipulated or at least to some extent controlled by those (assumed to be) in power. Gender, just like other social differences and social relations of power, are "blackboxed" precisely because these do not belong to what can be generalized about. This "blackboxing" is done either by labeling gender and power as despicable remnants of backward cultures or traditions, or by relegating them to the "non-water" world of the family and the private that do not matter for (understanding) what goes on in the realm of water management and therefore do not need to be studied or explained.

For making women visible, and providing them with a legitimate discursive existence in mainstream water conceptualizations, there are two distinct rhetoric strategies which are, however, not mutually exclusive. The first is to show that there are women among irrigators, water users and managers, or the inhabitants of the world of reason and work. This strategy has it that women are similar to all other irrigators, and its political effectiveness in gaining recognition for and attention to gender significantly rests on convincingly showing that women too are endowed with the gifts of reason and rationality, that they too can irrigate and farm, etc. – in other words, they are humans, too. It rests, in short, on proving that women are like men and thus on questioning the ideological and symbolic association of productive work and public domain with masculinity and domestic work and private domain with femininity. This is a potentially effective strategy to claim rights to water and land for women. Yet, it

Seeing Women and Questioning Gender in Water Management ∼ 57

is not very effective in questioning gender inequities related to water use and management since this mainstreaming of gender issues results in the (discursive) transformation of women into irrigators and water managers, a process during which they (because of the way irrigation and water systems are normally conceptualized) leave aside their non-irrigation identities and thus cease to exist as women. Thus, mainstreaming gender automatically implies its disappearance as a theme that can be discussed or talked about. Women, just like men, are treated as "universal" subjects (who are implicitly modeled on men), and "the gender question" is reduced to one of exclusion or lack of integration.

The second strategy to show that women "matter" is to discursively create them as a distinct functional group in relation to the water system. This is the argument that they are different. This difference can, for instance, be proved by showing that women's water needs are distinct from those of men, or by showing that female farmers systematically have different assessments of the irrigation system's output, impact and internal operations as compared to male farmers. This strategy thus entails, in other words, the establishment of another important category of individuals next to the already existing category of water users and farmers, and claiming some degree of acceptance and "normalcy" for this group as well. It may also entail a change in the ideas about what the irrigation system "produces" or should produce, for instance by including water for domestic uses. And it may further entail shifting the system's boundaries, for instance by including women's homestead gardens in the area that is to be served by the irrigation system. It implies, in other words, the expansion of the water reality with a distinct "women's domain."

This second strategy of making women visible clearly does put them on the water map, and allows thinking about their specific water needs and demands. Yet, it is not without problems. Women are made visible *as women*, as individuals whose identities and needs are derived from the fact that they belong to the female gender. Their link to the water system, and thus their existence in water discourses, therefore, also comes to depend on their gender. Hence, while women's presence in the water system is linked to their gender, that of men is simply a given and unrelated to their social identity. This strategy thus adopts masculinity as the norm while defining femininity as the difference. The definition of the female subject is limited to gender identity, completely bypassing other identities. In

58 ≈ *Margreet Zwarteveen*

this way, a study of the West Gandak irrigation system in Nepal describes different types of members at the lowest organizational level. Next to, for instance, a chairman and a vice-chairman, a woman is mentioned as one type of member (van Koppen et al. 2001). This reductionism discursively constructs women in implicit opposition to other irrigators who are (assumed to be) men. Women's professional identities as farmers and irrigators become difficult to see and understand, while men's identities as irrigators are over-emphasized to the neglect of their other identities. The two categories are thus defined as mutually exclusionary, and dichotomous.

The dichotomous conceptualization of gender as two separate social categories of human beings on which this second strategy is based is analytically problematic. It leads to the universalization and essentialization of gender differences, and thus risks "freezing" rather than questioning and challenging them. It assumes an already existing female identity and sees women as an already constituted, coherent group with identical interests in and aspirations about irrigation, regardless of class, ethnic or racial location, or other contradictions. This group of women exists prior to the process of analysis, and prior to their entry into the arena of social relations or the irrigation system (cf. Mohanty 1991).

Both strategies do not allow a questioning of gender, or of what it means to be a woman or a man at a particular time and place. Such questioning would require a social relations-oriented approach in which men and women are seen as parties to sets of social relations (involving rights, resources, responsibilities and meanings) with other men and women, through which what it means to be a woman (and a man), in that time and social place, is defined, experienced and negotiated. Gender operates within social categories rather than through pre-existing bounded groups of men and women. A critical feminist analysis of water asks for a deconstruction of the categories of men and women, allowing differences within gender divisions, recognizing male gender interests and identities, and separating actually existing women and men from (hegemonic) femininity and masculinity (Connell 1995).

I would like to conclude the chapter by reiterating that a feminist water project is not just concerned with water realities "out there", but also and importantly, with how such water realities are interpreted and understood at different levels of governance and by different actors. Gender is not just a part of water realities in

Seeing Women and Questioning Gender in Water Management ≋ 59

the field, but also fundamentally colors and structures the ways of thinking and making sense of those realities. Struggles over meanings and discourses, and struggles over how claims to "truth" are made in water, are and should therefore assume a central place in the attempts to mainstream gender in water management.

Notes

1. By calling a particular way of "knowing" water management "mainstream," I do not imply that it is uniform and static, nor that it is an uncontested body of knowledge and thinking. Mainstream irrigation wisdoms have always been contested, and continue to be challenged and disputed by various civil society groups as well as water scholars. There thus exists a growing body of critical irrigation texts which radically challenge some of the taken-for-granted assumptions of mainstream thought. I use the word "mainstream" to denote its widespread acceptance and status of "normalcy." Indeed, most produced knowledge about water management needs to refer to it—whether in agreement or in disagreement—in order to be counted as "knowledge," or to have an influence in debates and policies.

2. Diemer (1990: 4–13), in his study about irrigation in Africa, also describes "mainstream" irrigation thinking. He considers irrigation knowledge and thinking a "paradigm" in a Kuhnian sense, and approaches what Foucault calls "the positive unconsciousness of knowledge" with the help of Bourdieu's theory of practice, referring to roughly the same phenomenon as "docte ignorance" or learned ignorance. Chambers also talks about "normal professionalism" of irrigation engineers and defines it as the thinking, values and behavior dominant in a profession (Chambers 1988: 68).

3. The term "god-trick" was coined by Donna Haraway (1991).

4. Mary Dietz, in an essay on feminism and theories of citizenship, elaborates on this liberal notion of humans as "atomistic, rational agents whose existence and interests are ontologically prior to society" (Dietz 1992: 80). As a telling illustration of this notion, she cites Hobbes, who in *De Cive* wrote, "let us . . . consider men as if but even now sprung out of the earth, and suddenly, like mushrooms come to full maturity, without all kinds of engagement to each other" (ibid.: 81).

5. In other words, irrigation knowledge is written "from the center." Chambers refers to this as the "center-outward, core-periphery" perspective (Chambers 1988). Hartsock elaborates on the linkages between power and knowledge, and on the fundamental difference between theorizing from "the center" and theorizing from "the margins" (Hartsock 1998: 205–26).

60 ≈ *Margreet Zwarteveen*

6. Horst notes the "tenacious adherence to design standards (USBR standards in the Philippines) or principles (pursuance of 'technical irrigation' in Indonesia)", resulting in continuous repetition of the same type of design containing the same shortcomings' (1998: 79).
7. This is a frequently mentioned reason to explain why irrigation systems continue to perform poorly. Plusquellec et al. (1994: 1), for instance, state that many irrigation systems are characterized by "dual personalities": "the first is the nominal system that is assumed to conform to the design and norms of operation, and the second is the reality of its operation. The nominal system is rarely adjusted to the changing economic, social and technical reality.
8. Empirical studies of irrigation realities "in the field" provide a much less optimistic account of the controlling powers of head engineers and managers (see, for instance, Halsema 2002; Mollinga 1998; Oorthuizen 2003).
9. Early work on the roots of sexual oppression in anthropology found its basis in the domestic/public divide (cf. Rosaldo and Lamphere 1974). The corresponding political agenda located women's emancipation in the breaking down of barriers between domestic and public domains.
10. Hélène Cixous invokes the following polarities to illustrate that the hierarchical dualisms embedded in Western culture are related to the couple man/woman: "Activity/Passivity, Sun/Moon, Culture/ Nature, Day/Night, Father/Mother, Intelligible/Sensitive, Logos/ Pathos" (Cixous and Clément, 1986: 63). From her viewpoint, the very structures of reason are imbued with gender hierarchies, since reason inheres in a system that subordinates women and all that has traditionally been linked to women: passivity, nature, emotion, and bodily processes.
11. Placing the irrigation system in the productive and public sphere, and conceptually separating it from the domestic and subsistence sphere is not just analytically problematic. It has important political and distributional consequences in guiding plot and water allocation, and through designating specific users and uses of water as legitimate, and qualifying others as less important or even illegal. A question that is now receiving much policy attention is, for instance, the artificiality of the divide between water for productive use and water for domestic use when both are taken from the same irrigation system (cf. Bakker et al. 1999).
12. Some clear examples of embeddedness are provided by Roth (2003) and Oorthuizen (2003).
13. This model of water users' associations can be characterized as politically *liberal* in that it is founded on the autonomy of the political in a strong form. It is premised on the notion of abstract individualism and assumes that all people are equal in the public sphere which is

Seeing Women and Questioning Gender in Water Management ~ 61

characterized by modern values of rationality and impartiality (Fraser 1997; Held 1995; Luckham et al. 2000; Dietz 1992).

14. Villareal (1994: 59) defines domains of interaction as areas of social life wherein practices are routinely organized within specific locales and where certain authorities, values and identities are recognized, reproduced and transformed.

15. Most accounts of embedded realities of water management hardly mention gender perhaps because many of these studies describe and understand irrigation situations in the terms used by irrigation actors themselves, and uncritically accept their gender connotations. Most studies also uncritically adopt either the locally prevalent or conventional methods of identifying relevant actors. Hence, where farmers, irrigators and water leaders in the local perception are men, researchers accept rather than question this. A focus on visible and audible conflicts, and a tacit limitation of observations to the "public" realm of irrigation (fields, and canals, meeting rooms and offices) may further hide gender (and women) from the view of irrigation researchers, at least in situations wherein women's struggles occur in less open and visible ways and wherein women are not routinely among those present in recognized public irrigation spaces.

References

Bakker, M., R. Barker, R. Meinzen-Dick and F. Konradsen (eds). 1999. *Multiple Uses of Water in Irrigated Areas: A Case Study from Sri Lanka.* Statewide Water Information Management (SWIM) Report 8. Colombo: International Water Management Institute (IWMI).

Boelens, R., D. Getches and A. Guevara-Gil. 2010. *Out of the Mainstream; Water Rights, Politics and Identity.* London and Washington: Earthscan Publications Ltd.

Boelens, R. A. 2008. "The Rules of the Game and the Game of the Rules: Normalization and Resistance in Andean Water Control." PhD Thesis, Wageningen University, Wageningen, The Netherlands.

Bolding, A. 2004. "In Hot Water: A Study on Sociotechnical Intervention Models and Practices of Water Use in Smallholder Agriculture, Nyanyadzi Catchment, Zimbabwe." PhD Thesis, Wageningen University, Wageningen, The Netherlands.

Both Ends (BE), Comprehensive Assessment of Water Management in Agriculture (CA) and Gender and Water Alliance (GWA). 2006. "Effective Gender Mainstreaming in Water Management for Sustainable Livelihoods: From Guidelines to Practice." Both Ends Working Paper Series, Amsterdam, The Netherlands.

Brunt, D. 1992. *Mastering the Struggle. Gender Actors and Agrarian Change in a*

62 ~ *Margreet Zwarteveen*

Mexican Ejido. Latin America Studies 64. Amsterdam: Center for Latin American Research and Documentation (CEDLA).

Butler, J. 1999. *Gender Trouble.* 2nd rev. edn. New York and London: Routledge.

Chambers, R. 1988. *Managing Canal Irrigation: Practical Analysis from South Asia.* Delhi: Oxford and IBH Publishing.

Cixous, H. and C. Clément. 1986. *The Newly Born Woman.* Minneapolis: University of Minnesota Press.

Cleaver, F. 1999. "Paradoxes of Participation: Questioning Participatory Approaches to Development," *Journal of International Development,* 11(4): 597–612.

———. 2000. "Moral Ecological Rationality, Institutions and the Management of Common Property Resources," *Development and Change,* 31(2): 361–83.

Connell, R. W. 1995. *Masculinities.* Berkeley: University of California Press.

Coward, E. W. Jr. (ed.). 1980. *Irrigation and Agricultural Development in Asia: Perspectives from the Social Sciences.* Ithaca: Cornell University Press.

Davidson, A. I. 1986. "Archaeology, Genealogy, Ethics," in David Couzens Hoy (ed.), *Foucault: A Critical Reader,* pp. 221–33. Oxford and Cambridge: Blackwell.

Diemer, G. 1990. *Irrigatie in Afrika: Boeren en ingenieurs, techniek en kultuur.* Amsterdam: Thesis Publishers.

Dietz, M. 1992. "Context is All: Feminism and Theories of Citizenship," in Chantal Mouffe (ed.), *Dimensions of Radical Democracy. Pluralism, Citizenship and Community,* pp. 63–85. London and New York: Verso.

Fraser, N. 1997. *Justice Interruptus: Critical Reflections on the "Postsocialist" Condition.* New York and London: Routledge.

Giddens, A. 1984. *The Constitution of Society: Outline of a Theory of Structuration.* Cambridge: Polity Press.

Halsema, G. E. van. 2002. "Trial and Re-trial. The Evolution of Irrigation Modernisation in NWFP, Pakistan." PhD Thesis, Wageningen University, Wageningen, The Netherlands.

Haraway, D. J. 1991. *Simians, Cyborgs and Women: The Reinvention of Nature.* London: Free Association Books.

———. 2003. *The Companion Species Manifesto: Dogs, People and Significant Otherness.* Chicago: Prickly Paradigm Press.

Harding, S. 1986. *The Science Question in Feminism.* Ithaca and London: Cornell University Press.

Hartsock, N. C. M. 1998. *The Feminist Standpoint Revisited and Other Essays.* Boulder: Westview Press.

Held, D. 1995. *Democracy and the Global Order: From the Modern State to Cosmopolitan Governance.* Cambridge: Polity Press.

Horst, L. 1998. *The Dilemma's of Water Division. Consideration and Criteria for Irrigation System Design.* Colombo: IWMI, Sri Lanka, and Wageningen Agricultural University, The Netherlands.

Seeing Women and Questioning Gender in Water Management ～ 63

Jackson, C. 1998. Social Exclusion and Gender: Does One Size Fit All? Mimeo. Norwich, UK: School of Development Studies, University of East-Anglia.

Kome, A. 1997. "Gender and Irrigation Management Transfer in Sri Lanka." MSc Thesis, Department of Gender Studies in Agriculture and Department of Irrigation, Wageningen Agricultural University, Wageningen, The Netherlands; Irrigation Research Management Unit, International Irrigation Management Institute, Colombo.

Koppen, B. van, J. van Etten, P. Bajracharya and A. Tuladhar. 2001. "Women Irrigators and Leaders in the West-Gandak Scheme in Nepal." IWMI Working Paper 15, IWMI, Colombo.

Krol, M. 1994. "Irrigatie is mannenwerk: Genderverhoudingen in een kleinschalig irrigatieprojekt in de Ecuadoriaanse Andes." MSc Thesis, Wageningen Agricultural University, Wageningen, The Netherlands.

Langton, R. 2000. "Feminism in Epistemology. Exclusion and Objectification," in M. Fricker and J. Hornsby (eds), *The Cambridge Companion to Feminism in Philosophy*, pp. 127–45. Cambridge: Cambridge University Press.

Latour, B. 1987. *Science in Action. How to Follow Scientists and Engineers Through Society*. Cambridge: Harvard University Press.

Long, N. 1992. "From Paradigm Lost to Paradigm Regained? The Case for an Actor-oriented Sociology of Development," in Norman Long and Anne Long (eds), *Battlefields of Knowledge. The Interlocking of Theory and Practice in Social Research and Development*, pp. 16–45. London and New York: Routledge.

Luckham, R., A. Goetz and M. Kaldor, with A. Ayers, S. Bastian, E. Gyimah-Boadi, S. Hassim and Z. Puhovski. 2000. "Democratic Institutions and Politics in Contexts of Inequality, Poverty and Conflict. A Conceptual Framework. International Development Institute (IDS)." Working Paper 104, IDS, Brighton, UK.

McCay B. J. and S. Jentoft. 1998. "Market or Community Failure? Critical Perspectives on Common Property Research," *Human Organization*, 57(1): 21–29.

Mohanty, C. T. 1991. "Under Western Eyes: Feminist Scholarship and Colonial Discourses," in Chandra Talpade Mohanty, Ann Russo and Lourdes Torres (eds), *Third World Women and the Politics of Feminism*, pp. 51–78. Bloomington and Indianapolis: Indiana University Press.

Molden, D., R. Sakthivadivel, C. J. Perry, C. de Fraiture and W. H. Kloezen. 1998. "Indicators for Comparing Performance of Irrigated Agricultural Systems." Research Report 20, IWMI, Colombo.

Mollinga, P. P. 1998. "On the Waterfront. Water Distribution, Technology and Agrarian Change in a South Indian Canal Irrigation System." PhD Thesis, Wageningen Agricultural University, Wageningen, The Netherlands.

Nicholson, L. 1995. "Introduction," in Sheila Benhabib, Judith Butler,

64 ≈ *Margreet Zwarteveen*

Drucilla Cornell and Nancy Fraser (eds), *Feminist Contentions. A Philosophical Exchange.* New York and London: Routledge.

Oorthuizen, J. 2003. *Water, Works and Wages: The Everyday Politics of Irrigation Management Reform in the Philippines.* Wageningen University Water Resources Series. New Delhi: Orient Longman.

Perry, C. J. 1996. Quantification and Measurement of a Minimum Set of Indicators of the Performance of Irrigation Systems. Mimeo. Colombo: IWMI.

Plusquellec, H., C. Burt and H. W. Wolter. 1994. "Modern Water Control in Irrigation: Concepts, Issues and Applications." World Bank Technical Paper 246, The World Bank, Washington.

Pradhan, Naresh C. 1989. "Gender Participation in Irrigation System Activities in the Hills of Nepal," in *Proceedings of the Second Annual Workshop on Women in Farming Systems,* September 1989. Rampur and Kathmandu: Institute of Agriculture and Animal Science and USAID.

Rao, S. C., T. Hassan and C. V. Shyamala. 1991. "Role of Women in Water Management: Experiences in Sreeramsagar Project, Andhra Pradesh." Paper presented at a seminar "Men and Women Water Users in Water Management," October 28–29, Indo–Dutch Training Production Management Unit, Hyderabad.

Rosaldo, M. Z. and L. Lamphere (eds). 1974. *Woman, Culture and Society: A Theoretical Overview.* Stanford: Stanford University Press.

Roth, D. 2003. "Ambition, Regulation and Reality: Complex Use of Land and Water Resources in Luwu, South Sulawesi, Indonesia." PhD Thesis, Wageningen University, Wageningen, The Netherlands.

Sayer, A. 1992. *Method in Social Science: A Realist Approach.* London and New York: Routledge.

Schaaf, C. van der. 2000. "Land, Water and Gender in Rupakot Village, Nepal," in Rajendra Pradhan, Franz von Benda-Beckmann and Keebet von Benda-Beckmann (eds), *Water, Land and Law. Changing Rights to Land and Water in Nepal,* pp. 169–94. Kathmandu: FREEDEAL; Wageningen: Wageningen University; Rotterdam: Erasmus University.

Scott, J. 1985. *Weapons of the Weak. Everyday Forms of Peasant Resistance.* Yale: Yale University Press.

———. 1986. "Gender: A Useful Category of Historical Analysis," *American Historical Review,* 91(5): 1053–75.

Shah, E. 2003. *Social Designs. Tank Irrigation Technology and Agrarian Transformation in Karnataka, South India.* Wageningen University Water Resources Series. New Delhi: Orient Longman.

Small, L. E. and M. Svendsen. 1992. "A Framework for Assessing Irrigation Performance." Working Paper 1 on Irrigation Performance, IFPRI (International Food Policy Research Institute), Washington.

Spivak, G. C. 1988. *In Other Worlds: Essays in Cultural Politics.* New York and London: Routledge.

Seeing Women and Questioning Gender in Water Management ≋ 65

Swyngedouw E. 1997. "Neither Global Nor Local: 'Glocalization' and the Politics of Scale," in K. R. Cox (ed.), *Spaces of Globalization: Reasserting the Power of the Local,* pp 137–66. New York: Guilford Press.

Villareal, M. 1994. "Wielding and Yielding. Power, Subordination and Gender Identity in the Context of a Mexican Development Project." PhD Thesis, Wageningen Agricultural University, Wageningen, The Netherlands.

Zwarteveen, M. Z. 2006. "Wedlock or Deadlock? Feminists'Attempts to Meet Engineers." PhD Thesis, Wageningen Agricultural University, Wageningen, The Netherlands.

———. 2010. "A Masculine Water World: The Politics of Gender and Identity in Irrigation Expert Thinking," in R. Boelens, D. Getches and A. Guevara-Gil (eds), *Out of the Mainstream; Water Rights, Politics and Identity* pp. 75–96. London and Washington: Earthscan Publications Ltd.

3

"Water Policies are Never Implemented, but Negotiated"

Analyzing Integration of Policies Using a Bayesian Network*

Saravanan V. Subramanian and *David Ip*

The formulation and implementation of policy packages (consisting of an enabling environment, co-ordinated institutional roles, a participatory watershed approach and treating water as an economic good) with linear implementation strategies are the hallmark of "good policies" in integrated water resources management (IWRM). There is growing realization that the implementation of such policy packages, complex and non-linear, offers opportunities for actors to exploit such policies for claiming competency and legitimacy (e.g., Allan 2003; Cardwell et al. 2006; Mollinga et al. 2007; Mostert 2006; see *Water Alternatives*, Vol. 1, No. 1 2008). The chapter

---

*The chapter is a tribute to Prof. G. T. McDonald and Dr Basil von Horen. We would like to acknowledge Prof. Maria, R. Saleth, Dr John Bromley, Dr David Barton, two anonymous reviewers from the *Journal of Natural Resources Policy Research* and ZEF Research Group on Governance and Institutions, for their comments on a previous draft of this chapter. The support from University of Queensland International Postgraduate Research Scholarship (UQIPRS) and International Water Management Institute (IWMI) Doctoral Fellowship is gratefully acknowledged. The usual disclaimers apply.

"Water Policies are Never Implemented, but Negotiated" ≈ 67

analyzes the integration of policies[1] in framing a water management problem in a hamlet in the Indian Himalayas. Examining this problem from an institutional perspective helps to identify the actors and the rules to strengthen the developmental role of the state (Fritz and Menocal 2007). For this purpose, the water management problem perceived by the households in the case study is analyzed to understand the integration of policies. In particular, the role of diverse actors, contextual factors and the rules are identified and integrated to frame the water management problem.

Policies provide strategic directions for actors to adopt a particular course of action. These policies range from paradigms, public sentiments, programs and frames (Campbell 1998). These policies may be in the form of written policy statements of public and private organizations, national and international organizations, water users groups, religious groups, and other groups of individuals. Similarly, they may be in unwritten form, arising out of community groups, castes, religious groups, or values and sentiments of individuals. These policies are supported with legislation, guidelines, programs, strategies, incentives and other instruments that come together as a policy package. These packages from a diverse set of actors represent a complex process of policy integration in shaping and reshaping water resources management. There is a growing body of literature highlighting the importance of policy integration[2] for sustainable development (e.g., Lafferty and Hovden 2003; Lenschow 2002; Jänicke and Jacob 2005). While most studies focus on integration of strategies, structures and processes within governmental institutions, the attempt to examine the integration of policies across statutory and socially embedded actors and ecological context in influencing water resources management is less common. The chapter applies a Bayesian network (BN) approach to analyze the integration of policies. The second section highlights the significance of applying a BN approach as an analytical tool. The third section outlines a systems approach for analyzing the integration of policies as a process. The fourth section describes the empirical application of this framework using a combination of research methods and usefulness of the BN as an analytical tool. The fifth section reveals the incremental and cumulative interplay of multiple actors with diverse governance arrangements in framing water management problems in a case study. The sixth section draws implications of IWRM and policy. The final section highlights the importance of integrative,

68 ᷿ *Saravanan V. Subramanian* and *David Ip*

adaptive and dynamic policy-making in multifaceted governance arrangements, and the strength of BN as an analytical tool.

Bayesian Network as an Analytical Tool

BN is a modeling tool that quantifies the relationship among variables, even if the relationships involve uncertainty, unpredictability or imprecision. It is based on probability calculus following Bayes'[3] rules. A BN comprises three elements: firstly, a set of variables that represent the factors relevant to a particular environmental system or problem; secondly, the links among these variables; and finally, the conditional probability values that are used to calculate the state of the variables (Bromley 2005). Application of BNs has gained prominence as a Decision Support System (DSS) for IWRM (Batchelor and Cain 1999; Cain 2001; Bromley 2005). Studies[4] that apply BN for IWRM highlight the importance of the model as a DSS. Varis and Kuikka (1999) illustrate the application of BN in a number of water and fisheries management cases. They note that the empirical application of the model is too long, and requires acceptance from established scientific communities. Robertson and Wang (2004) demonstrate the potential impact of water allocation decisions using BN on farmers. Batchelor and Cain (1999) highlight the benefits of BN in using a simple, integrated methodology for modeling complex systems. Molina et al. (2005) apply BN to predict and manage floods through spatio-temporal hydrological modeling. Borsuk et al. (2001) use BN to integrate a combination of process-based models such as multivariate regression and expert opinion of river eutrophication, to predict probability distributions of policy-relevant ecosystem attributes. Varis and Lahtela (2002) analyze basin-wide policy impacts on different user groups in the Senegal river. Ames et al. (2005) use BN to model watershed management decisions on phosphorus management in a small catchment in Utah, the US. These studies have demonstrated that the BN is a powerful tool for understanding the inter-linkages among variables that connect physical, economic and social factors (Batchelor and Cain 1999) in managing water resources.

In brief, the significance of BN includes (Batchelor and Cain 1999; Uusitalo 2007; Barton et al. 2008) the following: *a*) graphical nature of its presentation that demonstrates the interaction among social, cultural, institutional and ecological factors, thereby encouraging interdisciplinary discussions; *b*) suitability for small and

"Water Policies are Never Implemented, but Negotiated" ≈ 69

incomplete data sets when sampling size varies; *c)* ability to specify the relationships among variables; *d)* flexibility to incorporate and combine quantitative and qualitative information; and *e)* explicit treatment of uncertainty in environmental systems. However, its limitations (Barton et al. 2008: 93) include: *a)* inability to capture the cyclic feedback effects in process dynamics; *b)* tendency to make the network too complex given the scale of the management problem; *c)* sensitivity to discretization of probability distributions as there is loss in each node due to discretization assumptions; *d)* diverse techniques to validate the model; and *e)* implicit assumptions of geographical and temporal scale of variables as the consistency across the variables with different sampling regime is difficult to meet.

The past studies have applied BN as a DSS to inform *how to integrate* water resources management. The problem with this approach is the existence of a preconceived logic (among research communities) on what (variables) to integrate, logic, in turn, driven by a theoretical argument in data collection. In the process the researchers attempt to marshal[5] those theoretically relevant variables (and its potential linkages) for understanding the management problem. Second, these studies exclusively rely on BN as a tool for taking policy and management decisions, placing definite boundaries for spatial and temporal variables (Barton et al. 2008). Further, the authors of these studies believe that once the model is built it can remain stable—and possibly updated—and can be useful for future decision-making. Many studies have excluded the dynamic and complex nature of social–political and ecological processes involved in water management. Third, BN is often considered an all-encompassing model to illustrate the interaction process for management decisions, ignoring the conventional quantitative and qualitative approaches to interpreting information. This chapter attempts to overcome some of these challenges by applying BN as an analytical tool to understand the socio-political process of framing water management problems in the watershed.

Understanding Policy Processes— A Conceptual Approach

This chapter applies the institutional integration framework (Sara-vanan 2008) to understand the policy processes. This framework builds on the Institutional Analysis Development (IAD) framework

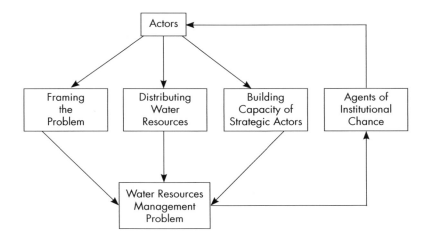

Figure 3.1: Framework for analyzing policy processes
Source: Prepared by the authors.

(Ostrom et al. 1994), but makes amendments by drawing on Dorcey (1986), and Gunderson and Holling (2002). The policy process involves multiple actors to negotiate diverse policies to frame water management problems, distribute water resources, and build capacity of strategic actors (Figure 3.1). These actors collectively structure a water management problem in a region. Given a problem, the agents are active in evolving adaptive strategies for an institutional change (or agency) to overcome inadequacies in the existing institutional arrangements and ecological system. The policy framework is shaped and reshaped by three situational variables: prevailing rules, characteristics of stakeholders and existing bio-physical resources.

Rules are patterned behaviors of a social group, evolved over a period (Mitchell 1975; Ostrom 1998), which interact along with the contextual factors (such as climate, demography, historic evolutions and so on) to govern human activity. They are structures of power relations that actors/agents draw in the socio-political process of water management. They are classified as statutory and socially embedded rules. While there are many rules, Ostrom et al. (1994) broadly classify them as boundary rules (specifying who the actors are), position rules (setting the position for actors to take), scope

"Water Policies are Never Implemented, but Negotiated" ≈ 71

rules (setting the outcome from their decisions), aggregation rules (specifying the outcome), information rules (providing channels for communication), authority rules (setting the actions assigned for actors), and pay-off rules (prescribing the benefits and costs). Rules (along with resources) are drawn by actors and/or agents to interact in diverse arenas through networks. Actors are defined as stakeholders, having legitimate interests in managing water resources. They are organizations and/or groups having an incumbent role and possess a unique social identity. Agents are human individuals possessing a transformative capacity and are members among the actors. These agents draw on the activities of the actors and their rules, along with the bio-physical resources to bring about changes in the existing institutional arrangements and bio-physical resources in a number of decision-making arenas.

Arenas are social settings accessed, activated and created in a strategic context for agents to contest, negotiate, dominate, exchange goods and services, and solve problems (Dorcey 1986), similar to Ostrom's (1998: 68–69) and Long's (2001) arenas. There is no single arena, but multiple ones, existing at various levels in the social sphere (Dorcey 1986) and representing "panarchy" (Gunderson and Holling 2002); this "panarchy" interacts (following Ostrom et al. 1994) with situational variables (bio-physical resources, characteristics of human entities and prevailing rules) in linear, cyclic and non-linear forms of networks. Such a network highlights the power relations and their ability to emphasize the contribution of micro-scale actions to large-scale outcomes (Klijn and Koppenjan 2000).The decision-making process is punctuated at various stages by contextual variables such as geological factors, climate, physiography, demography and other forces punctuating the framework. These characteristics make the policy process adaptive and dynamic. For the purpose of analysis, the framework represents a cyclical process. However, real-life interaction among variables is a complex messy process of shaping and reshaping policies.

This chapter examines how diverse policies integrate in the form of a network influence to frame water management problems in the larger part of policy processes. The application of a network approach to policy analysis in the past has failed to fully explain the driving forces or functions behind the network (Dowding 1995; Klijn 1996). The chapter helps to overcome this limitation by analyzing

72 〰 *Saravanan V. Subramanian* and *David Ip*

the integration of policies from an institutional perspective to identify the activities of the actors and their rules that facilitate the perception of the households to frame the problem.

Methodology

A water management problem exists when there is a discrepancy between: *a*) technically achievable and desired social goals; and *b*) actual outcomes (circumstances) that arise from current institutional arrangements (Livingston 1987: 287). The problem is dialectic, i.e., it is framed differently by different actors depending on how they make sense of their world. For the purpose of this chapter, the framing of a water management problem by households is examined to understand the integration of policies. In such a problem-context there is "a definite ordering and models of complexities" (Crothers 1999: 221) that can be established for analysis. Herein, ethno-methodology is applied in a pragmatic and contextual manner. This approach enables one to capture the assumptions and practices through which the most commonplace activities and experiences are framed by local communities (Pollner 1987: ix). Furthermore, an issue of concern in this chapter is "how society puts together; how it is getting done; how to do it; the social structures of everyday activities," (Garfinkel 1974) in managing water. The ethno-methodological in this chapter combines diverse research methods used in a year-long field research program in 2004: semi-structured interviews, structured interviews, focus group discussions, participatory resource mapping, participant observation, maintaining field notes and information derived from secondary documents (archives and published government records). Structured interviews were conducted with 43 households (40 percent of the total households)[6] semi-structured interviews with 25 officials (with government, non-government, politicians and experts), focus group discussions, participatory mapping exercises (resource mapping, transects and wealth ranking), and participant observation. The combination of methods helped us to contextualize information and also to obtain both quantitative and qualitative information for a comprehensive understanding of the water management problem.

The data collected were analyzed statistically through qualitative interviews and from the researchers' one-year experience in the region to draw on selected variables that influence the framing of

"Water Policies are Never Implemented, but Negotiated" ≈ 73

the water management problem. These selected variables were then applied in a BN. Together with the narratives offered by the respondents, it helped us to understand the integration of policies in a socio-ecological context that facilitate framing the problem. This approach allows one to gain a better understanding of the interaction among the components of the larger policy-making process. The BN approach further helps to integrate both qualitative and quantitative information, and to quantify the probability of relationships amongst the variables. In this network, the variable indicates the actors or the contextual factors. The linkages among these variables indicate the rule (or contextual causal linkages) that governs their relationship and which is derived either through chi-square (significance p value), qualitative statements obtained from field research, the logical reasoning of the researcher, or a combination of all of these. On the basis of a rule in the network, these variables are classified as "boundary," "position," "aggregation," "information," "authority," "scope" and "outcome" variables. The variables and their linkages are applied to a probability model of a BN using Norsys Software Corporation Canada (NETICA) software. A panel of advisors for the research (households, village leaders, bureaucrats, intellectual experts, non-government officials and politicians) validated the findings in the BN to ensure that the model accurately reflects the reality of the situation it is used to understand. In case of conflicting views of the panelists, the authors' critical judgment based on their experiences in this and other regions, the confidence shared by the authors and panelists and the type of information obtained took precedence.

Rajana Watershed—Competing Terrain for Resource Management

The Rajana watershed falls under the jurisdiction of Rajana village (the lowest revenue division in the hierarchy of Indian administrative divisions) in the Sirmaur district of Himachal Pradesh, India. The watershed and the village boundary do not coincide, but a large part of the village falls within the hydrological boundary; the watershed is officially named after the village for carrying out a community-based watershed development program. The watershed represents a diverse fragile ecological region which is rapidly being transformed by market forces and externally aided projects. These contemporary developmental initiatives are embedded within

74 ~~ *Saravanan V. Subramanian* and *David Ip*

socio-cultural, historical and institutional settings to create a water management problem in the watershed.

The Rajana watershed is located in the mid-hill sub-humid zone of the Indian Himalayas. It has limited arable land and is characterized by steep sloping terrain with salty-loamy to clayey soil that is prone to landslides. The watershed has a population of about 1,070 (from 2002 data, compared to 1068 in 2001)[7] spread over six hamlets; the area is politically and economically dominated by the Rajput community which constitutes 36 percent of the population, though numerically the Kohli community (the Scheduled Castes),[8] which constitutes 60 percent of the total population, dominates, with just a few families from other communities. Of the six hamlets in the watershed, more than 95 percent are concentrated in two hamlets, the Uppala (meaning, up in the mountain) Rajana and Nichala (meaning, down the mountain) Rajana. The Uppala Rajana was selected as a case study, as the hamlet had survived without irrigation system for several centuries, but in recent years is demanding for one.

One of the problems facing the hamlet Uppala Rajana is the lack of irrigation system which seems to have deprived the households of livelihood opportunities. The households believe that implementing an irrigation system in the hamlet will give assured returns from cash crops cultivated during the dry months and will increase their income as other livelihood opportunities are limited. Literacy in the hamlet is quite high (about 52 percent of the sampled households are literate), but equally so is unemployment rate, with 60 percent of the literate adult households unemployed. As one of the householders (interviewed on July 15, 2004) remarked:

> It takes about two to three hours to reach Dadahu, the nearest urban centre for any employment. Government jobs (such as those of water operators for pumps to supply drinking water to the villages) within or near the hamlet are limited. The only option is to depend on our agriculture.

For an average household in the hamlet, agriculture contributes 60 percent of the annual income (the average household income of the sampled households in 2004 was INR 68,737). It is supplemented by income from other sources such as wage labor, employment in government organizations and sale of milk products. Rainfed agriculture is practiced higher up the mountain in Uppala Rajana where staple food crops (maize, ragi/finger millet and wheat) are grown for subsistence from October to March, and vegetables

"Water Policies are Never Implemented, but Negotiated" ≈ 75

(tomato, okra, chilli, turmeric and ginger) from March to July. Further, vegetables are organically grown in rainfed conditions, in addition to the staple food grains. The hamlet has loamy soil, producing good yield. As the President of the Rajana Village Development Committee claimed:

> Our village is a remote, poverty-stricken (in terms of the percentage of the resident Scheduled Caste community, one of the criteria set by government for classifying regions as poverty-stricken), but has fertile soil with assured water supply for agriculture so that households get good returns from cash crops and their cultivation generates employment for the poor as well.[9]

Given this situation, the village leaders are actively pursuing the government to get additional sources of irrigation for their hamlet. The settlement in Uppala Rajana dates back to the 14th century, when the Rajput community (hereafter, Rajputs) migrated from the Delhi province in the wake of the invasion of Moghuls from Turkmenistan into India. The incoming Rajput forces occupied and owned (as landlords) most of the resources in Uppala Rajana such as land, water and forests. To meet the labor requirements (for agricultural activity, maintenance of irrigation system, distribution of irrigation water, and sundry menial jobs for the Rajput families), they brought in the Kohli community (hereafter, Kohlis) as tenant cultivators. After India's Independence in 1947, the Land Reforms Act[10] in the 1960s attempted to obscure the distinction between landlord and tenants through land redistribution in order to increase agricultural production and alleviate poverty. The Act redistributed excess lands of the Rajputs among the tenant Kohlis. In the process, the Rajputs gave away less fertile, rocky lands and the ones far away from the main settlements (often near forests) to the Kohlis. Though this gave the Kohlis ownership of land and subsequently met the objective of the Act, most of the land was less productive than that of the Rajputs. The conferment of statehood on Himachal Pradesh in 1971 led to planned development in the state. One of the early developmental initiatives under the first two Five-Year-Plans[11] in the state prioritized agricultural and infrastructural development. The hamlet witnessed the advent of electricity in 1967–68; the construction of roads to nearby townships in the 1970s; and the introduction of bus services, the establishment of educational institutes, health services and access to telephones in the 1990s. Centralized neoliberal programs have been implemented since

76 ~ *Saravanan V. Subramanian* and *David Ip*

2000, including the integrated wasteland development program under the Ministry of Rural Development which implements Community-Based Watershed Management (CBWM) through the respective District Rural Development Agencies (DRDAs) within the state (GoHP 2004). The other program is the Technology Mission for Integrated Development of Horticulture (hereafter, the Horticulture Mission) for making the state the "Fruit Bowl of India" (*Tribune* 2000). This initiative aimed to commercialize agriculture in the state by exploiting the wide-ranging agro-climatic conditions for cultivation of fruits and vegetables. The program offered incentives to expand cultivable areas under horticulture and provided other technical inputs. In addition, the watershed also witnessed externally aided projects promoting community-based resource management programs. These projects include World Bank (WB)-funded HP Mid-Himalayan Watershed Development Project[12] and Department for International Development (DFID)–assisted Himachal Pradesh Forest Sector Reform Project[13] which carries out an integrated area development program (IADP) in the watershed (GoHP 2004). What is interesting about these projects is that each of them (national and international) has its own jurisdiction or sector (such as water, education, forest and infrastructure) for management. Over the decades, these agencies have competed[14] with each other, claiming superior performance in implementation of the physical infrastructural development and social welfare programs and their impact. Though these have opened up the subsistence economy to market forces, these developments have significantly influenced the households to become more vocal about the problem as "lack of irrigation as depriving them of their livelihoods from agriculture." The other problems that the households framed were "inadequate employment opportunities within and outside the region," and "lack of better access to market and urban centers." For the purpose of this chapter, the problem of lack of irrigation was examined to understand how diverse policies integrate to influence the perception of households about framing their water management problem.

Agricultural Prosperity Leading to Demand for Water in Uppala Rajana

In Uppala Rajana small-scale subsistence-level cultivation of vegetables that often depended on virtual water resources (available

"Water Policies are Never Implemented, but Negotiated" ≈ 77

in the form of moisture on land and in the atmosphere) is being transformed into large-scale cultivation. This has placed enormous pressure on the existing virtual water resources, causing, as a consequence, the households to manually irrigate their crops[15], a situation that makes them perceive water as a scarce resource in the village. This, in turn, has led community leaders to demand lift irrigation scheme (through letters to the District Collector and the Member of the Legislative Assembly of this constituency) from the government to remedy water scarcity in the hamlet. Though there is a large number of variables (such as education, social network, knowledge, demographic and other factors), not all have had a significant influence in framing the problem. Only a handful of factors were found to be statistically significant through Chi-square testing, or were highlighted by households and local officials during interviews, or logically inferred by the researcher. In the process, the network combines both qualitative and quantitative information to understand the linkages and probability of their relationship.

Of a handful of variables, the boundary variables set the context of and policies on how the households should frame the problem (Figure 3.2, Table 3.1). These variables were related to contextual factors (climatic conditions for vegetables, nature of product and size of landholdings), socially embedded actors (caste of the household), statutory public actors (GoHP), and statutory private actors (competition from markets, national and international organizations campaigning for CBWM). These boundary variables offer various positions to households. The socially embedded actors influence the choice between the "caste of the middleman" and "location of landholdings;" the statutory public actors take positions based on "opportunities for the "fruit-bowl" economy, while statutory private actors take positions by defining the "nature of market" and the "perception on CBWM." The decision of the households to cultivate the "area under cash crops" depends on their ability to aggregate the position variable (location of land and benefits from incentives) and the boundary variable (size of landholdings). The scope variable, i.e., "access to market" for selling cash crops, is determined by socially embedded actors (the caste of the households). In the market, "income from cash crops" depends on the market forces (position variable: the nature of market, and boundary variable: competition from Mumbai), which authorizes a particular outcome. Similarly, the lower the income, the higher is the demand for irrigation.

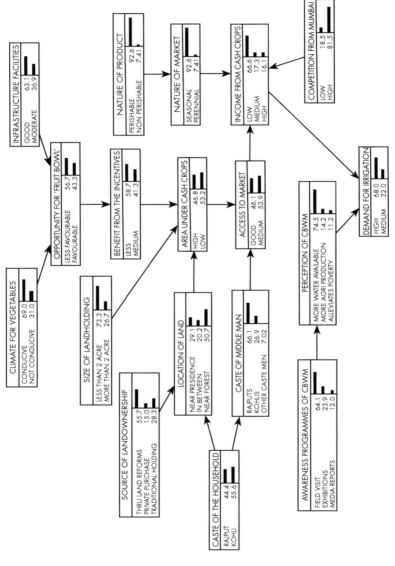

Figure 3.2: Variables influencing the framing of the problem in Uppala Rajana

Source: Prepared by the authors.

"Water Policies are Never Implemented, but Negotiated" ≈ 79

Table 3.1: Summary of variables influencing the framing of the problem in Uppala Rajana

Variables	Contextual Factors	Statutory Actors	Socially Embedded Actors
Boundary			
Climate for Vegetables[a]	Climate	–	
Infrastructural Facilities[a]	–	GoHP	
Size of Landholding	History	–	
Source of Land ownership	History	GoI/GoHP	
Caste of the Household	History	–	Caste
Awareness on CBWM	–	GoI/GoHP/ DfID/WB	
Nature of Product[a]	Natural factor	–	
Competition from Mumbai[a]	–	Market	
Position			
Opportunity for "Fruit-Bowl"[a]	–	GoI/GoHP	
Location of Land	–	–	Caste
Caste of Middleman	–	–	Caste
Nature of Market[a]	–	Market	
Perception of CBWM	–	–	Households
Scope			
Benefit from Incentives	–	–	Households
Access to Market	–	Market	Caste
Aggregation			
Area under Cash Crops	–	–	Caste/ Households
Authority			
Income from Cash Crops	–	Market	Caste
Outcome			
Demand for Irrigation	–	–	Households

Source: Prepared by the authors.
Note: [a]These variables are nominal and ordinal quantified from the responses received through qualitative interviews. The rest of the variables are derived from household interviews. For details on the rules and linkages, please refer to Appendix 3.1A.

80 ~ *Saravanan V. Subramanian* and *David Ip*

Furthermore, this demand is not based on the informed assessment of the household, but on the "perception of CBWM" that is influenced by the boundary variable, viz.,"campaign for CBWM."

The boundary variables, viz., "caste of the household" and "source of landownership" offer positions for the households through "location of land." In this hamlet, there is a 55 percent probability that a household will belong to the Kohli community, rather than the Rajput community. The BN shows that if all households were Rajputs, there would be a 61 percent probability of lands being near the residence (Figure 3.3a), thanks to the Land Reform Act which allowed the Rajput households to retain their lands near their residence—lands that are of better quality and easy to protect from wild animals. In contrast, the probability of Kohli households owning lands near their place of residence was just 3 percent, as against more than 82 percent probability of their owning lands near the forest (often rocky, steep slopes and crops prone to attacks from wild animals) (Figure 3.3b). Caste also influences the households' choice of middleman to gain access to the market and get adequate returns from the sale of cash crops.

A household's decision to cultivate cash crops depends on variables such as the "location of land," the "size of landholding" and the "benefits from incentives." These variables help households to aggregate the "area under cash crops." In Uppala Rajana, there is a 47 percent probability of a household having high "area under cash crops" (more than 0.6 acres in 2004). The probability of Rajputs cultivating high "area under cash crops" is about 78 percent (See Figure 3.3a). The variable "location of land" significantly (p value = 0.02) influences the households in cultivating cash crops. Land near the residence has a higher probability for cultivating cash crops, compared to land near the forest. Cash crops require more man-months especially for weeding and watering during the dry months. In addition, these crops require protection from wild animals (namely monkeys and wild boars). Lands near the residence offers incentives for meeting labor requirements and are easier to protect from wild animals. The importance of the "location of land" renders the "size of landholding" insignificant (p value = 0.049) in terms of influencing the "area under cash crops."

The third variable influencing the "area under cash crops" is the "benefits offered through incentives" under the Horticulture Mission. The Horticulture Mission by Himachal Pradesh attempts to exploit

a. Domination of Rajputs

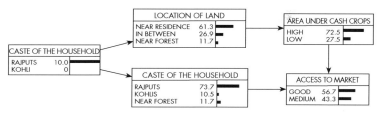

b. Suppression of Kohlis

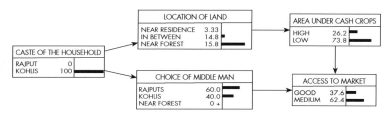

c. Role of Market in Influencing the Demand for Irrigation

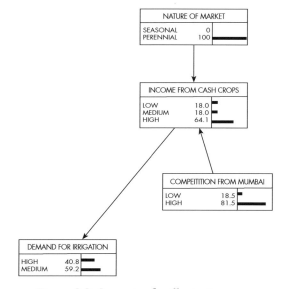

Figure 3.3: Scenarios for illustration

Source: Prepared by the authors from field survey.

82 ~ *Saravanan V. Subramanian* and *David Ip*

the climatic conditions and the existing infrastructural facilities in the state for being a "fruit bowl" of India; the Mission offers assistance in the cultivation of cash crops.[16] An official in charge of horticulture promotion (the Junior Agriculture Officer, Sangrah) in the region claimed that such an initiative would increase the production of cash crops in the region and thereby alleviate poverty (personal communication with the authors). This program has led the government and the market players to offer various incentives for the cultivation of cash crops in the region. However, interviews with officials (government and non-government), influential villagers and experts reveal that there is only a 43 percent probability of villagers supporting this program. Though these incentives have offered opportunities for opening up the village economy, as Subhash Mendhapurkar, Director of an NGO called Social Upliftment Through Rural Action (SUTRA) claimed, these have been "formulated keeping in mind the exploitation of precious land and water resources, and not taking poor people's interest into consideration or the characteristics of landholding in the mountainous region."[17] This opinion was reinforced by a household in the watershed, "The government incentives are only for cultivating the crops, but the market is left to the middleman and brokers who exploit us." For a household, the probability of getting fewer benefits from incentives is higher (59 percent) than that of getting medium benefits such as assistance for area expansion and on-farm water management, and supplies of seedlings. The fewer the incentives received, the less the area under cash crops. The decision of the households to cultivate the required "area under cash crops" depends on their ability to aggregate the "location of land," "size of landholding" and the "benefits from incentives" offered under the Horticulture Mission.

Merely the "area under cash crops" does not enable the household to have "access to market," as such access is socially determined by the position variable ("caste of the middleman"). The probability of a household getting good "access to market" is about 64 percent. As is a common practice in many Indian villages, the middlemen buy the agriculture produce from the households and sell it at higher prices in the *mandi*s (wholesale markets in urban centers).[18] Of the seven middlemen buying the produce in 2004 from this watershed, four were Rajputs, one a Kohli and two from other communities, aligned with Kohlis. The Rajput middlemen offered better prices

"Water Policies are Never Implemented, but Negotiated" ≈ 83

for cash crops—between INR 5 and 8 per kg of tomatoes in 2004, and between INR 12 and 14 per kg of ginger—than others did. Their prices were categorized as good, while those offered by middlemen from other castes as medium. As Rajput middlemen had kinship ties with Rajput households—who had large landholdings located near their residence and more area under cash crop cultivation—many of the latter sold their produce to Rajput middlemen. Often, Kohlis had no option other than sell their produce to the Rajput middlemen because they produced less quantity and chose to gain from the higher prices offered though some were also pressured to do so by the Rajputs. A few Kohli households did engage with two middlemen who were not Rajputs, but offered prices, lower than those offered by their Rajput counterparts. Most of the Rajput middlemen offered good "access to market" as they were involved in marketing at all times (even during off-season for marketing other forest produce) while middlemen from Kohli and other castes operated only during the peak agricultural season. Therefore, in order for a household in Uppala Rajana to get good "access to market," they have to be Rajputs, sell their produce to Rajput middlemen, and cultivate more than 0.6 acres of land. Unfortunately, Kohlis have limited scope (with 37 percent probability of their having good "access to market;" see Figure 3.3b) of cultivating the required "area under cash crops" and hence only limited "access to market."

The scope variable "access to market," along with market forces, influences the authority variable for the households, viz., "income from cash crops." Apart from ginger, all other vegetables are perishable (93 percent probability) and therefore have a seasonal market (93 percent probability). Gaining adequate returns from crops is further problematized by competition from produce coming from Indian plains, locally known as the Mumbai market (as it mainly comes from Maharashtra). Crop markets in India depend on the climate of the producing region. The Himalayan region has a comparative advantage over the rest of the country in the cultivation of cash crops. When many parts of the country are dry (March–August), the Himalayan region is cool, receiving showers that facilitate cultivation of vegetables. This means that households in the Himalayan region are able to exploit the advantage by selling and producing their cash crops before August every year, after which the prices fall as produce from the Indian plains arrives. But in 2004, the late onset

84 ⚉ *Saravanan V. Subramanian* and *David Ip*

of monsoons resulting in late rainfall, along with other conditions led to a delay in the marketing of vegetables. This subsequently affected the prices of the produce with a 59 percent probability of low returns[19] from cash crops.

The authority variable, viz., "income from cash crops" is the deciding factor for households in experiencing the need for an irrigation system. While a diverse set of policies, along with contextual factors, influences the income from cash crops, households attribute their low earnings only to the "lack of irrigation facilities." This perception of the households was legitimized by media, government, NGOs and international agencies portraying a gloomy world where water will be scare and "catching water where it falls" a potential solution. The boundary variable "campaign for CBWM" by national and international agencies–through field visits (organized by project implementing agencies), promotional materials (posters and documents), and sharing of success stories from experiments elsewhere in the world–played an influential role in framing the problem. About 68 percent of the households expressed "high" interest in the demand for irrigation. However, the 32 percent of the households that reported "medium" claimed that improving infrastructure to access market could significantly increase their income from cash crops.

The President of the Rajana Watershed Committee, a leader among the Rajputs and also a lead farmer in the hamlet, has made various pleas to the government for introducing lift irrigation in the watershed. He has interacted with the officials and tapped into his social network with the middlemen outside the watershed in his efforts to obtain adequate returns from cash crops for his fellow villagers. His choice is strategic and spontaneous, as he capitalizes on the market, and the national and international agencies to establish his superior socio-economic status in the village. Though his network reveals the influential role of caste in voicing the demand for irrigation, a scenario analysis reveals that a regulated market could play a prominent role in overcoming the water problem in the hamlet and reducing the influential role of socially embedded actors. If the "nature of market" is controlled, the demand for lift irrigation will be considerably lessened (Figure 3.3c). A farmer, who had served in the Indian Army rightly pointed out, "If we have any technologies to store this produce for a long time, then we can sell it at a time when it fetches a good price." This view was also supported by the District Planning Officer of Nahan (personal communication), who emphasized the need for cold storage facilities for vegetables and fruits in order to promote agro-based industries in the region and thereby ensure good returns from cash crops.

Implication for IWRM

Multiple actors exploit the contextual factors to influence the perception of households about the state of water resources in order to frame the water management problem in the hamlet. The boundary rules are set by contextual factors (e.g., climate and landholding size, etc.), by socially embedded actors (e.g., caste) and by the policies of the national and international agencies promoting CBWM. Statutory public actors (GHP), socially embedded actors (caste of the household) and the statutory private actors (market forces) use these rules to take positions. Interestingly, households exploit these rules as well as socially embedded rules to aggregate their decision to cultivate the required "area under cash crops" and have "access to market." However, the authority to frame the problem is influenced by the statutory private actors (market brokers and middlemen), whose intervention determines the income from the cash crops. This authority, along with the position rules taken by the national and international agencies in portraying the finite nature of water availability and the emphasis on "catching water where it falls," enables households to frame their problem as "lack of irrigation depriving their livelihood." What is important in this integration of policies is the absence of information rules that has constrained the actors to adopt a "fire-fighting approach" towards managing water resources in this hamlet.

The "fire-fighting" approach is adopted depending on the actors' own assessment of the situation and by exploiting the contextual characteristics of the region. In the process, the actors facilitate the perception of the households about framing the water management problem. The Land Reform Acts in the 1960s and 70s attempted to redistribute land, but inherently sanctioned the traditional hierarchical nature of land ownership in terms of the degrees of access to quality land. Subsequent policies of agricultural development such as the Horticultural Mission and other agriculture

86 ≈ *Saravanan V. Subramanian* and *David Ip*

and irrigation development programs exploited the climatic conditions and focused mainly on the expansion of cultivable area under horticultural crops. In the process, they reinforced the existing inequality in landownership promoted by the caste system and ignored other options such as market regulation. Similar is the case of community-based management promoted by The World Bank and DFID in the hamlet. Often, these packages are projected as "blueprints" for the implementation of IWRM. In a recent update of the policy packages to promote watershed development in India, the Honorary Adviser to the Technical Committee on Watershed Programmes (widely known as the Parthasarathy Committee) (GoI 2006) claimed the Committee's report to be "a detailed blueprint of a new course of watershed implementation in rainfed India" (Shah 2006: 2982). The report further claimed that such government reforms held "the key to banishing poverty" (ibid.: 2984). This report was followed by *Common Guidelines for Watershed Development Projects* (GoI 2008). Often, these official statements are based on sporadic successes of NGOs, which are deceptive in their presentation and remain a "black-box"[20] in the Indian democracy.

This is further constrained by inadequate scope rules that do not offer enough incentives to households for cultivating cash crops, and by caste-based access to market. Incentives to households for cash crop cultivation are in turn constrained by the steep and rugged terrain in this region. This terrain determines the marginal and disaggregated nature of landholding, which deters cash crop cultivation. The access to market is caste-based, i.e., largely controlled by Rajput middlemen and brokers who have kinship relations with the better-off Rajput agricultural households in the hamlet. This problem of access is further compounded by poor infrastructure for storage of crops and unregulated market conditions. Therefore, making information available and strengthening the scope rules constitute an important component of comprehensive policy-making.

Chaotic negotiation among different actors and their policies has in part resulted in the current problematic framing of the problem. Also, another contributor to the problem is poor infrastructural development (roads, education and healthcare), rural unemployment and ineffective poverty alleviation programs. These factors have significantly widened the differences between Rajputs and Kohlis in the hamlet in the remotely located and culturally secluded watersheds

"Water Policies are Never Implemented, but Negotiated" ≈ 87

in the Indian Himalayas like Rajana. As one Kohli household women claimed, "It will take one more generation for us to buy a good piece of land in this region." The market for cash crops is open and driven by competition among bidders who are more interested in the quality of the crop than in the process of cultivating it; rarely does the government step in to regulate the functioning of markets. The national and international agencies implementing community-based programs (such as DFID's Himachal Pradesh Forest Sector Reform Project and Ministry of Rural Development's IWDP) unfortunately promote an inaccurate image of water availability and laud the water management practices.

Conclusion

The chapter reveals that the water management problem in the hamlet of Uppala Rajana is the result of interaction of diverse policies (including water policies) over a period of time. Further, water policies are never implemented, but integrated through negotiation with other policies and diverse socio-cultural settings in (re)shaping water resources management. Water is managed by different forms of governance arrangements (state-centric, market-or community-oriented). In this multifaceted water governance system, these institutional arrangements are not superior to each other; rather they incrementally and cumulatively superimpose each other to (re) shape water resources management. In this decision-making process, integration represents a complex blend of statutory and socially embedded actors that bring along diverse rules of negotiation as well as contextual factors. Analyzing the integration from an institutional perspective reveals the absence of information rules and inadequate scope rules which has resulted in the adoption of a "fire-fighting" approach by various actors, without adequate assessment of the context. The statutory public actors can facilitate comprehensive understanding of the context by laying out broad principles in the policy statements. This will allow multiple actors to integrate, adapt and remain dynamic in the policy-making processes by debating and sharing the available information for comprehensive assessment. To facilitate this comprehensive assessment for taking informed water management decisions that are sustainable, the statutory public actors will need to build the capacity of households, regulate water

88 ≈ *Saravanan V. Subramanian* and *David Ip*

distribution, and offer diverse forums for actors to debate and share the available information.

The chapter also highlights the usefulness of BNs to describe policy integration across space and time in framing the water management problem. BN as an analytical tool helps overcome some of the problems raised in the existing Bayesian literature. For example, by focusing on the problem-context, one can examine only those variables that actually influence the framing of the water management problem, thereby rendering the complexity manageable. Similarly, BNs applied with an institutional logic help in identifying the diverse actors (and contextual factors) and rules as well as their interactions involved in framing water management problems. Such an institutional logic also helps to identify the different roles of actors and rules in framing the problem for institutional intervention. Furthermore, by applying BNs from an analytical perspective one can incorporate diverse socio-political processes in interpreting the network. This helps to overcome the slicing of the dynamic policy processes into different sequences for analysis and interpretation. Finally, BNs provide a cross-sectional view of a complex and dynamic resource management process. They do not attempt to include the implicit assumptions of geographical and temporal scale of variables in contemporary studies. The aforementioned advantages, in addition to others recognized by the Bayesian literature (such as graphical presentation, integration of qualitative and quantitative information, suitability of small and incomplete data sets and explicit treatment of uncertainty) can further its application for understanding integration of water resources management practices.

Appendix 3.1A: Details of variables influencing the framing of the problem in Uppala Rajana

Variables	Contextual Factors	Actors	Rules or Causal Linkages
Boundary			
Climate for Vegetables[1]	Climate	–	Conducive climate is opportunity for "Fruit-bowl" economy.
Infrastructural Facilities[1]	–	GoHP	Good facilities are favorable opportunities for "Fruit-bowl" economy.

(contd.)

Appendix 3.1A (contd.)

Variables	Contextual Factors	Actors	Rules or Causal Linkages
Size of Landholding	History	–	Higher the landholding, the more is the area under cash crops (X^2=8.95; df=4, p=0.04, where X^2 is chi-square; Df, degree of frequency; and p, test of signifi cance).
Source of Land Ownership	History	GoI/ GoHP	Land obtained through land reforms were located near forest (X^2=9.61; df=4, p=0.04).
Caste of the Household	History	Caste	If the household belongs to the Rajput caste, higher is the probability of land being located near residence (X^2=12.95; df=2, p=0.001) and higher is the probability of choosing Rajputs as the middlemen (X^2=11.99; df=4, p=0.01).
Awareness of CBWM	–	GoI/ GoHP/ DFID	The greater the number of visits to CBWM field experiments, the more is water availability for development (X^2=.5.85; df=2, p=0.04).
Nature of Product[1]	Natural Characteristics	–	The more perishable the produce, the more seasonal is the market.
Competition from Mumbai[1]	–	Market	Higher the competition from produce from Mumbai, the lower is the price.
Position			
Opportunity for "Fruit-Bowl"[1]	–	GoI/ GoHP	Favorable climate and infra structure, offer incentives to increase area under cash crops.
Location of Land	–	Caste	Lands near residence have higher probability of greater yield of cash crops (X^2=10.79; df=4, p=0.02).

(contd.)

90 ≋ *Saravanan V. Subramanian* and *David Ip*

Appendix 3.1A (contd.)

Variables	Contextual Factors	Actors	Rules or Causal Linkages
Caste of Middlemen	–	Caste	If Rajputs are middlemen, the higher is the probability of getting good access to market (X^2=15.16; df=6, p=0.02).
Nature of Market[a]	–	Market	The more seasonal the market, the lower is the returns from cash crops.
Perception of CBWM	–	Households	The perception that more the water can be harvested, the higher is the demand for irrigation (X^2=13.07; df=2, p=0.00)
Scope			
Benefits from Incentives	–	Households	The lower the benefits from incentives, the lower is the area under cash crops (X^2=11.21; df=33; p=0.01)
Access to Market	–	Caste/ Market	The better the access to market, the higher is the income from cash crops (X^2=13.85; df=3, p=0.00).
Aggregation			
Area under Cash Crops	–	Households	Higher the area under cash crops, the better is the access to market (X^2=7.79 df=3, p=0.04).
Authority			
Income from Cash Crops	–	Caste/ Market	The lower the return, the higher is the demand for irrigation (X^2=12.89; df=3, p=0.01)
Outcome			
Demand for Irrigation	–	Households	The higher the demand for irrigation, the greater the pressure is on agents for seeking government intervention.

Source: Prepared by the authors.
Note: [a]These variables are nominal and ordinal quantified from the responses received through qualitative interviews. The rest of the variables are derived from household interviews.

Notes

1. Integration of policies refers to amalgamation of diverse policies in influencing water management in a context.
2. A similar emphasis is placed in the literature on policy processes (e.g., Sabatier 1999; Keeley and Scoones 1999; Sutton 1999; IDS 2006).
3. Thomas Bayes was an 18th century English clergyman who is known for formulating Bayesian Probability theory.
4. Also refer to the Special Issue on Bayesian belief network in the *Canadian Journal of Forest Research* vol. 36, issue 12, 2006.
5. Though participatory approaches are applied, they provide broad and consensual information and are therefore rarely able to capture the less explicit information.
6. The study was carried out in the hamlet Uppala Rajana in the Rajana watershed in the Indian state of Himachal Pradesh (district Sirmaur). The hamlet has a population of 107 Households as on 2004.
7. Interview with Rajana Village Administrative Officer, May 26, 2004.
8. The caste system is a hereditary social stratification of communities. Scheduled Castes and Scheduled Tribes are groupings of the Indian population explicitly recognized by the Constitution of India as socio-economically deprived.
9. Interview with the President of the Rajana Village Development Committee, May 22, 2004.
10. The Government of India's Land Reforms Act, 1958, was implemented in the State of Himachal as The Himachal Pradesh Transfer of Land (Regulation) Act, 1968, and The Himachal Pradesh Tenancy and Land Reforms Act, 1972, by the Department of Land Revenue in the state.
11. India carries out planned development through Five-Year Plans.
12. This project began after the completion of our research in 2004.
13. The DFID program is targeted at forest management through an integrated development program, while the government of Japan aims to manage floods.
14. The District Project Officer in the DRDA of Nahan (Sirmaur district) claimed that they were the first to enter the watershed and create a good data base, adopt a community-based approach and involve the Panchayat institutions in project implementation. On the other hand, the Divisional Forest Officer, Renuka, claims that their DFID programs allocate more money per hectare and consider an integrated approach within the watershed by linking water management with livelihood activities.
15. Often farmers carry water from springs or from government-supplied sources in order to irrigate vegetable crops during April/May. The terrain being a very steep sloping one, they carry water on their back climbing as high as 500 metres.

92 ≈ *Saravanan V. Subramanian* and *David Ip*

16. The government offers incentives for expanding the area under cash crops, construction of water resources structures, on-farm management, technology, bio-fertilizers and other technical incentives
17. The distribution of non-irrigated landholding in the hamlet revealed that 43 percent of the households owned marginal landholdings (less than 1 acre); 37 percent, small landholdings (between 1 and 2 acres); only 18 percent, large landholdings; and 2 percent, no landholding. On an average, a household had 0.85 acres of land scattered in at least eight plots, given the steep sloping and rugged terrain.
18. At these *mandis*, the products are auctioned to retailers at the market price. The market price depends on the competition for the same produce from other *mandis*, quality of the produce and the timing of its arrival in the market.
19. Income is considered low if annual earnings from cash crop sales are less than INR 20,000, medium if earnings are between INR 20,000 to 60,000 and high if they exceed INR 60,000.
20. The "black box" contains information on how NGOs negotiated watershed and administrative boundaries, how they ensured public participation, how they brought together diverse interest groups to promote environmental management and alleviate poverty, what happened after they formally withdrew from the water sector, and more importantly how much money they actually spent out of the funds they received for meeting the needs of the poor. Unfortunately, this "black box" is unlikely to be opened as these agencies seek legal immunity from disclosure of information.

References

Allan, T. 2003. "IWRM/IWRAM: A New Sanctioned Discourse." SOAS Water Issues Study Group Occasional Paper 50, School of Oriental and African Studies/King's College, University of London, London.

Ames, D. P., B. T. Nielson, D. K. Stevens and U. Lall. 2005. "Using Bayesian Networks to Model Watershed Management Decisions: An East Canyon Creek Case Study," *Journal of Hydroinformatics*, 7(4): 267–82.

Barton, D. N., T. Saloranta, S. J. Moe, H. O. Eggestad and S. Kuikka. 2008. "Bayesian Belief Networks as a Meta-modelling Tool in Integrated River Basin Management: Pros and Cons in Evaluating Nutrient Abatement Decisions under Uncertainty in a Norwegian River Basin," *Ecological Economics*, 66(1): 91–104.

Batchelor, C. and D. J. Cain. 1999. "Application of Belief Networks to Water Management Studies," *Agricultural Water Management*, 40(1): 51–57.

Borsuk, M., R. Clemen, L. Magure and K. Reckhow. 2001. "Stakeholder

"Water Policies are Never Implemented, but Negotiated" ≈ 93

Values and Scientific Modelling in the Neuse River Watershed," *Group Decision and Negotiation*, 10(4): 355–73.

Bromley, J. 2005. *Guidelines for the Use of Bayesian Networks as a Participatory Tool for Water Resource Management*. Wallingford: Center for Ecology and Hydrology (CEH).

Cain, D. J. 2001. *Planning Improvements in Natural Resources Management. Guidelines for Using Bayesian Networks to Support the Planning and Management of Development Programmes in the Water Sector and Beyond*. Wallingford: CEH.

Callon, M. 1991. "Techno-economic Networks and Irreversibility," in J. Law (ed.), *A Sociology of Monsters: Essays on Power, Technology and Domination*, pp. 132–64. London and New York: Routledge.

Campbell, L. J. 1998. "Institutional Analysis and the Role of Ideas in Political Economy," *Theory and Society*, 27(3): 377–409.

Cardwell, H. E., R. A. Cole, L. A. Cartwright and L. A. Martin. 2006. "Integrated Water Resources Management: Definitions and Conceptual Musings," *Journal of Contemporary Water Research and Education*, 135(1): 8–18.

Crothers, C. 1999. "Let's Get Real: Developing Realist Approaches within the Philosophy of Social Science," *South African Journal of Philosophy*, 18(2): 211–22.

Dorcey, A. H. J. 1986. *Bargaining in the Governance of Pacific Coastal Resources: Research and Reform*. Vancouver, British Columbia: Westminster Research Center, Faculty of Graduate Studies, University of British Columbia Press; and Northburn Printers and Stationers Ltd.

Dowding, K. 1995. "Model or Metaphor? A Critical Review of the Policy Network Approach," *Political Studies*, 43(1), 136–58.

Fritz, V. and A. R. Menocal. 2007. "Developmental States in the New Millennium: Concepts and Challenges for a New Aid Agenda," *Development Policy Review*, 25(5): 531–52.

Garfinkel, H. 1974. *Studies in Ethnomethodology*. Cambridge: Polity Press.

Government of Himachal Pradesh (GoHP). 2004. *Draft Annual Plan (2003–2004)*. Shimla: Planning Department, GoHP.

Government of India (GoI). 2006. *From Hariyali to Neeranchal: Report of the Technical Committee on Watershed Programmes in India*. New Delhi: Department of Land Resources, Ministry of Rural Development, GoI.

———. 2008. *Common Guidelines for Watershed Development Projects*. New Delhi: National Rainfed Area Authority, Planning Commission, GoI.

Gunderson, L. H. and C. S. Holling. 2002. "Resilience and Adaptive Cycles," in L. H. Gunderson and C. S. Holling (eds), *Panarchy: Understanding Transformations in Human and Natural Systems*, pp. 25–62. Washington: Island Press.

Institute of Development Studies (IDS). 2006. *Understanding Policy Processes:*

94 ≋ *Saravanan V. Subramanian* and *David Ip*

A Review of IDS Research on the Environment. Sussex: Knowledge, Technology and Society Team, IDS, University of Sussex, Brighton.

Jänicke, M. and K. Jacob (eds). 2005. *Environmental Governance in a Global Perspective: New Approaches to Ecological and Political Modernisation*. Berlin: Free University of Berlin.

Keeley, J. and I. Scoones. 1999. "Understanding Environmental Policy Processes: A Review." IDS Working Paper 89, IDS, University of Sussex, Brighton.

Klijn, E. H. 1996. "Analyzing and Managing Policy Processes in Complex Networks: A Theoretical Examination of the Concept Policy Network and Its Problems," *Administration & Society*, 28(1): 90–119.

Klijn, E. H. and J. F. M. Koppenjan. 2000. "Public Management and Policy Networks: Foundations of a Network Approach to Governance," *Public Management*, 2(2): 135–58.

Lafferty, W. and E. Hovden. 2003. "Environmental Policy Integration: Towards an Analytical Framework," *Environmental Politics*, 12(3): 1–22.

Lenschow, A. (ed.). 2002. *Environmental Policy Integration: Greening Sectoral Policies in Europe*. London: Earthscan Publications Ltd.

Livingston, M. L. 1987. "Evaluating the Performance of Environmental Policy: Contributions of Neoclassical, Public Choice, and Institutional Models," *Journal of Economic Issues*, 21(1): 281–94.

Long, N. 2001. *Development Sociology: Actor Perspectives*. London and New York: Routledge.

Mitchell, B. (ed.). 1975. *Institutional Arrangements for Water Management: Canadian Experiences*. Ontario: Department of Geography, Faculty of Environmental Studies, University of Waterloo, Waterloo, Ontario.

Molina, M., R. Fuentetaja and L. Garrote. 2005. "Hydrologic Models for Emergency Decision Support Using Bayesian Networks'," *ECSQARU*, 3571/2005 (468): 88–99.

Mollinga, P., R. S. Meinzen-Dick and J. D. Merrey. 2007. "Politics, Plurality and Problemsheds: A Strategic Approach for Reform of Agricultural Water Resources Management," *Development Policy Review*, 25(6): 699–719.

Mostert, E. 2006. "Integrated Water Resources Management in The Netherlands: How Concepts Function?," *Journal of Contemporary Water Research and Education*, 135(1): 19–27.

Ostrom, E. 1998. "The Institutional Analysis and Development Approach," in E. T. Loehman and D. M. Kilgour (eds), *Designing Institutions for Environmental and Resource Management*, pp. 68–90. New Horizons in Environmental Economics Series. Massachusetts: Edward Elgar Publishing Limited.

Ostrom, E., R. Gardner and J. Walker. 1994. *Rules, Games & Common-Pool Resources*. Ann Arbor: The University of Michigan Press.

"Water Policies are Never Implemented, but Negotiated" ≈ 95

Pollner, M. 1987. *Mundane Reason: Reality in Everyday and Sociological Discourse.* Cambridge: Cambridge University Press.

Pressman, J. L. and A. Wildavsky. 1984. *Implementation.* 3rd ed. Berkeley: University of California Press.

Robertson, D. and Q. J. Wang. 2004. "Bayesian Networks for Decision Analysis: An Application to Irrigation System Selection," *Australian Journal of Experimental Agriculture,* 44(2): 145–50.

Sabatier, P. A. 1999. "Fostering the Development of Policy Theory," in P. A. Sabatier (ed.), *Theories of the Policy Process,* pp. 261–75. Colorado and Oxford: Westview Press.

Saravanan, V. S. 2008. "A Systems Approach to Unravel Complex Water Management Institutions," *Ecological Complexity,* 5(3): 202–15.

Shah, M. 2006. "Towards reforms," *Economic and Political Weekly,* 41(27–28): 2981–84.

Sutton, R. 1999. "The Policy Process: An Overview." Overseas Development Institute Working Paper 118, Overseas Development Institute, London.

The Tribune. 2000. "HP to be Made Fruit Bowl of India: CM," 29 April.

Uusitalo, L. 2007. "Advantages and Challenges of Bayesian Networks in Environmental Modelling," *Ecological Modelling,* 203(3–4): 312–18.

Varis, O. and S. Kuikka. 1999. "Learning Bayesian Decision Analysis by Doing: Lessons from Environmental and Natural Resources Management," *Ecological Modelling,* 119:177–95).

Varis, O. and V. Lahtela. 2002. "Integrated Water Resources Management along the Senegal River: Introducing an Analytical Framework," *Water Resources Development,* 18(4): 501–21.

PART II

Informing Water Resources Policies

The South Asian Experience

4

Institutional Design Perspective, Capacity Constraints and Participatory Irrigation Management in South Asia

Jayanath Ananda

Notwithstanding the progress in water reforms, particularly Participatory Irrigation Management (henceforth PIM), many South Asian countries still have been grappling with poor performance in the water sector and deterioration of canal and tank irrigation systems, high extraction of groundwater and related economic and environmental problems. Managing water resources in South Asia has never been as critical as it is today with the increasing population levels combined with climatic changes related to global warming, putting global water resources under tremendous pressure. Undoubtedly, institutional arrangements in the water sector largely influence the welfare outcomes for rural masses in South Asia. Designing (and re-designing) of appropriate institutional mechanisms to manage scarce water resources and dwindling river flows is an enormous challenge due to the complex legal, constitutional and social issues involved.

New institutional economics offers a useful framework for analyzing the issues related to PIM.[1] North (1995: 3) defines in-

100 ☰ Jayanath Ananda

stitutions as "the rules of the game in a society or, more formally, the humanly devised constraints that shape human interaction." Institutions can be broadly classified into two groups: formal and informal (ibid.). Bromley (1989: 42) defines the formal institutions from a behavioral perspective as "structured set of expectations about behaviour, and of actual behaviour, driven by shared and dominant preferences for the ultimate outcome as opposed to the means by which that outcome is achieved." Informal institutions, in general, can be regarded as customary rules and traditions of a community. Institutions, though relatively stable, are not eternally immutable (Goodin 1996). They can emerge spontaneously through evolutionary processes or can be intentionally created through political processes (institutional design theory) or through a combination of the above two processes (Kingston and Caballero 2009).

There is little agreement about the appropriate institutional arrangements and criteria for successful institutional design. Various scholars have identified successful design principles to manage common pool resources. They include Olson (1965), Hardin (1968), Uphoff (1986), Wade (1987), Ostrom (1990, 1992, 1993), Ostrom et al. (1994) and Goodin (1996), whose seminal works have been highly influential in debates on the governance of water institutions. Hanna et al. (1995), and Balland and Platteau (1996) also offer alternative sets of design principles (Hussain and Bhattacharya 2004). These propositions have been primarily based on theories such as those of rational choice and collective action. The design perspective of institutional change essentially focuses on which institutional conditions and design principles are the most conducive to creating and sustaining efficient institutions. The quality of the institutional design has a great impact on performance (Merrey 1996).[2] Several researchers have proposed institutional design principles for efficient water management (Merry 1996; Ostrom 1992; Goodin 1996). For instance, Ostrom (1992) developed design principles of long-standing, self-organized irrigation systems. They include clearly defined boundaries, proportional equivalence between benefits and costs, collective choice arrangements, monitoring, graduated sanctions, conflict resolution mechanisms, external recognition of rights to organizes, and nested or federated organizations.

This chapter uses a set of generic institutional design criteria proposed by Pagan (2003) for better institutional outcomes. In particular, the chapter assesses the institutional arrangements of

PIM in South Asia using Pagan's institutional design principles and examines the reasons for the poor performance of irrigation management. The design criteria include clear objectives, interconnection with other formal and informal institutions, adaptiveness and appropriateness of scale and compliance capacity. These criteria are comparable with Ostrom's (1992) institutional principles and consistent with low transaction and transformation costs. The main distinction between the two sets of criteria is that the Ostrom's work specifically focuses on long-enduring and self-managed irrigation systems. However, in most PIM initiatives, farmers do not operate autonomously, but within an overall context of continuing state involvement. Pagan's institutional design criteria are generic in nature and therefore can be applied to a broader set of contexts, i.e., self-organized and externally created institutions as well as partially and fully devolved systems.

The next section briefly outlines the salient features of PIM in South Asia. Section three assesses the performance of PIM using the abovementioned generic design principles. Some concluding remarks are provided in the final section.

PIM in South Asia

As a means of arresting the massive erosion of irrigation capital, many South Asian governments adopted a policy of PIM or Irrigation Management Transfer (IMT) about two decades ago. The policy involved part or full transfer of management of the irrigation systems to Water User Associations (WUAs). The main goals of the policy were to improve the productivity of irrigated agriculture, and to reduce government expenditure on the operation and maintenance of irrigation systems. Many South Asian countries have gathered rich experience with user participation, both in traditional irrigation systems as well as large-scale irrigation projects.

In Sri Lanka, PIM was implemented in a number of major and medium irrigation schemes under three government-sponsored programs: the Integrated Management of Irrigation Schemes (INMAS), the Management of Irrigation Systems (MANIS) program and the systems under the Mahaweli Development Project (Samad 2005). It is estimated that there are about 3,000 Distributary Canal Organizations (or WUAs) and about 15,000 Field Canal Organizations (FCOs) given the responsibility of Operation & Management (O&M) of

102 ≋ *Jayanath Ananda*

irrigation canals in Sri Lanka (ibid.). Despite genuine efforts to make the policy sustainable, a myriad of factors have hindered its effective implementation in Sri Lanka.

In India, many states including Andhra Pradesh, Madhya Pradesh and Maharashtra initially passed legislations to promote PIM (see Gulati et al. 2005 for a recent review of PIM in India). The Andhra Pradesh Farmers Management of Irrigation Systems Act enacted by the government in 1996 and approved by the State Legislative Assembly in 1997 is the first legislation in India, which broadly represents PIM arrangements. The key rationale of the Act was to negate the existing irrigation inefficiency and inequity, low cropping intensities and yields by re-orienting the Irrigation Department as the competent authority to provide technical support to WUAs who would manage the system (Vermillion 1997). WUAs, formed under the Act, are responsible for the operation and maintenance of irrigation networks. Irrigation departments are responsible for making available reliable water supply, rehabilitation of the distributary system, and facilitation and determination of water charges from the users. WUAs in turn receive a portion of water charges to carry out their designated tasks.[3]

The basic structure of PIM in Andhra Pradesh, as stipulated by the Act, is presented in Figure 4.1. WUAs provide the basic platform for all water users. WUAs regulate and distribute water within their respective command areas. Landholders, title holders and tenants as members of the WUA have voting rights. The other water users who do not have voting rights are referred to as co-opted members. The Distributary Committee (DC) is comprised of a group of WUAs under a distributary channel. The DC is responsible for issues related to a distributary. All the WUA presidents are members of the DC. They elect the Managing Committee and the DC President. All the DC presidents will be members of the Project Committees (PCs) which are in charge of the entire project command area. The Apex Committee is headed by the Minister for Major and Medium projects and formulates broad policy guidelines to resolve conflicts (Reddy and Reddy 2002).

WUAs can be classified according to their nature of origin: government-induced, farmer-initiated and NGO-facilitated WUAs. Under PIM initiatives, numerous government-induced WUAs were formed. In some instances, WUAs were promoted to jointly manage

Institutional Design Perspective, Capacity Constraints and PIM

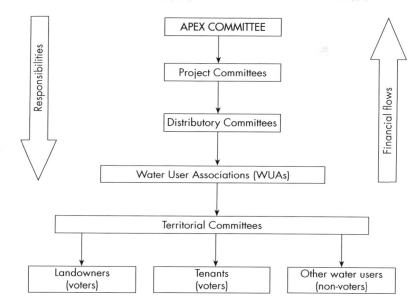

Figure 4.1: Basic structure of PIM in Andhra Pradesh

Source: Modified from Reddy and Reddy (2002: 523).

(partial autonomy) either main or branch canals of the irrigation systems with the irrigation agency. In such cases, a chosen group of farmers or a committee collaborates with the Irrigation Department. In other instances, the whole system has been turned over to farmers (full autonomy).

From an institutional design perspective, it is worth noting that farmer-developed and farmer-managed irrigation institutions have been in existence for up to two thousand years in several South Asian countries including India and Sri Lanka. They have shown a high resilience to various adverse conditions and managed to survive for centuries. These institutions usually operate by adhering to the principles, basic to providing sustainable, fair and affordable services (on a non-cash basis) to beneficiaries. However, despite their historic record, community-managed systems cover less than 1 percent of the total irrigated area in India and have failed to make any inroads into large-scale irrigation systems (Government of India, 1992, quoted in Reddy 1998: 452).

104 ~ *Jayanath Ananda*

Assessment of PIM Institutions

If success is measured by the number of WUAs created, the PIM reforms may be considered a success. However, if irrigation system performance, improvements in service delivery to users and sustainable financing are taken as the criteria for success, then the achievements can be regarded as much more modest, at best (Renault et al. 2007). This section offers a broad comparative assessment of selected Indian PIM institutions using the generic institutional design criteria described in Section 1. Water institutions differ greatly in their physical attributes, geographical location, property rights structure, institutional attributes, socio-political and cultural contexts. However, we contend that it is plausible and desirable to make a comparative assessment based on key design criteria. The assessment made here is predominantly based on secondary literature. However, in some instances case studies conducted in several states of India and personal communication have been used as well. A summarized evaluation is presented in Table 4.1 followed by a detailed evaluation of WUA using each design feature.

Table 4.1: Design feature analysis of PIM institutions

Design Criteria	Government-induced WUA	Farmer-induced WUA4
Clarity of objectives	Low, Moderate[a]	High
Interconnectedness with other institutions	Moderate	High
Adaptiveness	Low[b]	Very high
Appropriateness of scale	Low	Low
Compliance capacity	Poor[c]	Moderate[d]

Source: Prepared by the author.
Notes:
[a]In the case of partial autonomy in IMT (DFID 2001).
[b]Mostly due to poor assessment of resource needs prior to turnover (DFID 2001).
[c]Priority water rights honored by farmers, beneficiaries meet all O&M costs, violators of rules are promptly penalized (DFID 2001).
[d]Based on the Centre for Civil Society (2003).

Clarity of Objectives

A range of objectives are attributed to WUAs in general. They include securing adequate and reliable water supply for irrigation,

Institutional Design Perspective, Capacity Constraints and PIM ≈ 105

water distribution, conflict resolution, equitable access to irrigation water, undertaking O&M activities and the like. In India, the PIM Acts empower WUAs to prepare and implement rotational water distribution for each season (in line with operational plans approved by the DC or PC), and assist in the collection of water charges, maintaining accounts and conducting general body meetings as required. One reason cited for poor cost recovery in ADB-funded PIM projects in Sri Lanka was the perception that the O&M is government's responsibility (Kurian 2001). The objective that is chosen as the principle aim of any institution will ultimately affect the welfare of those people influenced by the institution. The straightforward aspect of good institutional design is often violated simply because there are multiple institutional objectives. Hence, there exists a potentially perverse relationship between the desirability of having clear objectives and a desirable feature, viz., adaptiveness.

The degree of institutional clarity among government-induced WUAs varies from moderate to low. According to a study of 22 WUAs in Madhya Pradesh, the members of WUAs evidently have a clear knowledge of the provisions of the PIM Act: the process of electing and recalling members, water distribution and other collective choice rules (Marothia 2002). Moreover, the study reported that there was total transparency in the functioning of WUAs and existence of a well-specified work plan for maintenance and repair of canal infrastructure (Marothia 2002).

Upscaling Problems

In Sri Lanka, attempts to upscale the unique success of PIM have failed spectacularly. The village irrigation schemes (also known as minor irrigation schemes) have a long tradition of user management (Herath et al. 1989). The forcible formation of Farmer Organizations (FOs, equivalent of WUAs) in Sri Lanka provides a classic example of the failure of "supply-driven" populist approach in institutional building. After the initial success in establishing FOs in Gal Oya[4] in the early 1980s with a combination of roles, rules, norms and values that supported mutually beneficial collective action (see Uphoff and Wijayaratna 2000 for details), the government hastily accelerated the process of establishing FOs. In 1997, there were about 13,000 registered FOs in Sri Lanka. One pilot study has found that only 5 percent of the FOs existing at that time can be considered alive and successful (Razaak and Ananda 1997).

Inter-connectedness with Other Institutions

It is widely believed that bringing about a change in the way social system operates requires changes in the formal and informal institutions of society (e.g., Williamson 1985; Ostrom 1993; Dovers 2001). Inadequacy and erratic water supply have often been cited as reasons for PIM not establishing strong links within the broader institutional setting at the village level. Poor institutional linkages or completely ignoring linkages can become a scale problem to the extent that the issue is scale-dependent and has cross-interactions with other issues. For instance, in India, devolving management responsibilities to Panchayat and Gram Sabhas has created institutional competition among entities within the decision of decision-making organizations. For example, the Amendment to the Indian Constitution for provision of Panchayati Raj charged the local governing bodies with a wide range of tasks including health, education and welfare functions in addition to water management. Hence there is a considerable overlap between the functions of local Panchayats and WUAs, and thereby potential for competition between them. In fact, in some cases, WUAs are referred to as "pani (water) Panchayats" (Gulati et al. 2005). In some tribal areas of central India, there is an apparent conflict between pani Panchayats and tribal Panchayats (Parthasarthy 2004).

Both surface water and groundwater management display cross-level institutional interplay. The horizontal interactions between WUAs and Panchayats are equally important as the vertical interplay between WUAs and their superordinate district-level structure (see Figure 1). The horizontal institutional interplay is further complicated by the tendency of state departments and donor-funded projects to create their own associations and committees. Marothia (2002) reports moderate performance of organizational linkages between WUAs and other related institutions. Some studies report that the leadership often resides with higher caste members (Nikku 2002), indicating the tendency to follow the deeply rooted social norms.

Adaptiveness

Given the universally applied institutional design under the PIM Act, adaptiveness and flexibility of WUAs are restricted. For most WUAs, there is a well-specified work plan for O&M, and each

WUA has to submit its work plan for approval and release of funds, of which WUAs receive compensation according to the irrigation revenue sharing formula. In these situations, the flexibility of the organization and its ability to change plans quickly may be limited. The performance of WUAs and farmer participation in irrigation management is mixed (Meinzen-Dick et al. 2000). They have worked in some areas but not in others. Hence, it is often argued that it requires a complete paradigm shift to ensure effective functioning of WUAs. Sustaining PIM requires a substantial political and bureaucratic will to share power with farmers. Numerous observers have noted that PIM has not delivered to the extent it was envisaged to (Marothia 2003). Performance appears to depend in large part, on whether the WUAs are strong enough to assume management. There have been numerous instances wherein additional direct and indirect costs, including intangible transactions costs, are involved but not balanced by benefits, causing farmer non-participation (Meinzen-Dick et al. 2000).

One of the most common problems with the farmer-managed irrigation schemes is the flawed water delivery systems wherein the tail-enders do not receive water at all (Word Bank 1994 cited in Kurian 2001). Given this problem, the sustainability of WUAs heavily depends on their capacity to ensure adequate water delivery. Although spelt out as an objective of PIM, the equity and reliable supply of irrigation water managed by WUAs is lacking, pointing to the absence of transparency and of an adjustment process. Although WUAs have succeeded in increasing the irrigated area under wet crops such as rice, they have failed to ensure an equitable water distribution among head-enders and tail-enders. Another point of criticism is the degree of equity that prevails with the increased availability of water in the system (IIMI 1997). Problems with the recovery of irrigation service fees is another issue that emerged from an evaluation of 208 World Bank projects, which showed that 68 percent of the projects failed to recover costs satisfactorily (Word Bank 1994 cited in Kurian 2001).

Appropriateness of Scale

An important issue in assigning governance tasks across a hierarchy of decision-making entities in the PIM system is determining the optimal scale for each task. In water management, this issue is further

108 ≈ *Jayanath Ananda*

complicated by water resource regimes (surface water as well as groundwater) which tend to have their own scales and boundaries. Both forms of WUAs were affected by scale mismatches. Inter-state river water disputes in India are typical of the mismatch between human and natural scales. In such cases, the authority or jurisdiction of the management does not coincide with the scale required by the resource either in space or time. Sharing of river water in irrigation and river valley projects, dams and command area development projects often has inter-jurisdictional implications. In fact, these factors provided an impetus for establishing more decentralized systems, particularly empowering Panchayats and WUAs.

At an administrative level, PIM is often structured as a nested system. Different kinds of information are required to carry out specific governance functions in a nested decision hierarchy. Ostrom (1990) lists generic governance functions for nested enterprises. They include appropriation, provision, monitoring, enforcement and conflict resolution. At the operational level, individuals make choices within the constraints of operational rules. For instance, an irrigator in a canal system has to decide on the extent of irrigation and the cropping pattern. This decision entails information on water availability, labor availability, producer prices and marketing arrangements. At the field level, individual irrigators may have to negotiate with each another in clearing the canal system in order to access irrigation water. However, the timing of irrigation for a cropping season may be decided collectively at a higher level of the decision hierarchy say, at the level of WUA. In this case, the scale of the governance problem is limited, and homogeneity and social capital within the WUA may further reduce transaction costs and foster collective action. WUAs take decisions within the constraints of collective choice rules such as the assigning of O&M responsibilities, dispute resolution, rules to implement a *warabandi*[5] schedule, etc.

Current groundwater management in India also epitomizes the mismatch between scales of knowledge and scales of actions. As the state legislation on groundwater extraction is still being developed, various changes to the Environment (Protection) Act, 1986, have been proposed. One such proposal advocates state-level monitoring of groundwater levels through scientific methods under the advisory guidance of Central Ground Water Board (Ministry of Water Resources Planning Commission 2007). The enforcement of the regulation is made at a much lower level through the involvement of Panchayats. In order to be effective, state-level groundwater

Institutional Design Perspective, Capacity Constraints and PIM 〰 109

monitoring should transfer information to lower levels of decision hierarchy in an efficient manner. This information transfer may be rendered inefficient by various transaction costs which, in turn, are caused by poor linkages between state and local levels as well as political economy constraints. In case of surface irrigation too, there is a mismatch between hydrologic units and administrative units of village and district, which form the basis for Panchayats (Gulati et al. 2005). The clear implication is that if Panchayats are given the responsibility to manage irrigation, water users from other villages in the command area can be excluded from the decision-making process.

Compliance Capacity

Most government-sponsored WUAs suffer from erratic water distribution, theft, tail-ender problems (Kurian 2001). There is poor compliance with the regulations since the elected representative would not want to impose them in the view of re-election. Water theft and tampering with irrigation structures are common. One of the key criteria that can test compliance by the members is the irrigation service fee payments. A World Bank evaluation of PIM projects revealed that cost recovery was unsatisfactory in 68 percent of projects (World Bank 1994 cited in Kurian 2001). This implies low compliance with the rules on irrigation service fee payments. Much of this low compliance can be attributed to the fact that most members are not aware of how the money collected is being spent, and mistrust each other. For example, a canal irrigation study carried out in Madhya Pradesh reports that 91 percent of the WUAs studied had low awareness of their financial status and performed poorly in financial management (Marothia 2002). Another key criterion to test the degree of compliance is the level of water supply since the adequacy of water supply is positively related to the degree of conformance with the rules (ibid.). This is also evident in Sri Lanka PIM schemes wherein frequent non-conformance with rules leads to a highly unreliable service provision (Kurian 2001). The adequacy of water supply is arguably the most critical aspect of water governance. However, Marothia (2002) notes that only 5 percent of WUAs had adequate water supply whilst 41 percent and 55 percent had moderate and scarce water supply, respectively.[6] The same study reports that voluntary labor and efforts for saving water, social audit and fund generation were poor (ibid.).

110 ≈ *Jayanath Ananda*

Due to very low collection of water charges, there are instances of the government and WUAs coming together to collect them from the farmers. Traditionally, the Revenue Department collects water charges using its administrative machinery. In this joint collection process, the Irrigation Department, the Revenue Department and WUAs jointly inspect the area irrigated, note the type of crops grown and accordingly collect a water cess will from the farmers. As an incentive for WUAs to participate in this cess collection process, a share of the cess collected is given to them (Nikku 2002). In Sri Lanka, cost recovery process is virtually stalled due to legal and political problems, and the government continues to finance the O&M of canal networks (Samad 2005).

Capacity Constraints

The term "capacity" encompasses several dimensions including financial, physical, human and social capacities (the last two include leadership). Hence, executing a task satisfactorily at a given level of a nested governance structure partly depends on sufficient access at that level to all dimensions of capacity. For instance, even with a high level of social capital, WUAs may not be able to overcome the physical constraints in an ailing irrigation infrastructure. Moreover, although problematic, representations from all relevant actors who have an interest in the task also generally contribute to the successful execution of a given task (Marshall 2008). Panchayat members do not necessarily seek to achieve social goals and may misuse resources. For example, Gram Pradhans who are mostly (70–90 percent) elected from the main village tend to ignore the water needs of surrounding hamlets (Parthasarthy 2004). Even if they desire to carry out their tasks justly, they may not have the requisite skill or capacity to plan and implement. Weak linkages across the governance hierarchy (Figure 1) in terms of administrative and financial control may exacerbate the problem of capacity constraint.

Many states have set up irrigation training institutions in order to train large numbers of farmers and officials on various aspects of PIM (Gulati et al. 2005). To this end, employing community organizers or institutional organizers to mobilize farmers is a popular ploy not only in India but also throughout South Asia. For instance, the Gal Oya Project in Sri Lanka exemplifies the successful deployment of a "change agent" or catalyst in motivating rural masses to organize

Institutional Design Perspective, Capacity Constraints and PIM ∷ 111

themselves and reap maximum benefits from a PIM scheme. The deployment of Institutional Organizers (IOs) as change agents in mobilizing farmers to actively take part in participatory management of irrigation infrastructure is considered a great success. The Gal Oya model employed a learning process approach while examining the behavior at both collective and individual levels and drawing on human potential (Uphoff 1996). In Rajasthan, leadership and social capital (indicated by influential people, number of temples, college graduates, etc.) played a major role in the success of irrigation management (Meinzen-Dick and Raju 2002).

Conclusion

There is evidence that the traditional "farmer-managed" irrigation systems have a significantly different set of institutional features compared to large-scale irrigation institutions established under PIM. These farmer-managed systems are generally highly adaptive to environmental changes, high in compliance and inter-connect well with informal institutions such as social norms and customs. One of the core barriers to the implementation of PIM in South Asia has been constraints on the capacity (including technical and information) of the existing WUAs. The up-scaling of PIM initiatives has also been problematic due to ill-conceived institutional design and poor institutional linkages.

Notwithstanding the initial impact, particularly on improving the water delivery, PIM initiatives are currently at crossroads in many countries. In India, it still receives a great deal of policy attention, but the response from the grassroots levels has not gathered any significant momentum. The core problems facing PIM strategy can be traced back to the problems of institutional design as well as other contextual factors. Many WUAs are falling apart because of poor farmer participation in WUA activities and rundown irrigation infrastructure that continues to disintegrate owing to the inadequate financial autonomy of WUAs. These problems are compounded by the informational and capacity constraints inherent in nested institutional hierarchies as portrayed by water sector decision-making. Moreover, better inter-connections are warranted to resolve the institutional competition between WUAs and Panchayats, while greater attention needs to be paid to socio-political dimensions when reshaping water institutions. It is clear that without genuine

112 ≈ *Jayanath Ananda*

devolution of rights and equitable distribution of responsibilities that match the net benefits, farmers' willingness to take part in PIM will be greatly hindered.

Notes

1. Alternative propositions such as the cultural theory and the contextual theory have also been used to describe institutional arrangements and their performance. Cultural theory (McCay and Acheson 1987) involves the neo-institutional styles that define people's, groups', and organizations' behavior and strategic choices (Mollinga 2001) while the contextual theory (McCay 2002) argues that the context in which a choice has to be made determines its rationality.
2. There is a strong positive correlation between institutional design and performance with four broad categories of performance indicators identified in the literature: technical impact, productivity impact, financial impact and environmental impact (Meinzen-Dick et al. 1994).
3. Water charges are collected by the Revenue Department.
4. The Gal Oya Irrigation and Settlement Project, one of the first irrigation and settlement projects implemented in Sri Lanka, commenced in early 1960s. Later, a USAID-funded water management project was commissioned to increase water use efficiency and promote PIM in this challenging dry zone area. The USAID hired a team comprising members from the Rural Development Committee of the Cornell University and Agrarian Research and Training Institute to undertake this task by establishing necessary "the social infrastructure" or the FOs in the project area. Their work can be considered a pioneering participatory exercise in irrigated agriculture in Sri Lanka.
5. *Warabandi* is a rotational system for distribution of available water within an irrigation system. It specifies the day, time and duration of supply to each irrigator in proportion to the size of his landholding (Bandaragoda and Rehman 1995).
6. It should be noted, however, degree of water availability varied considerably among the WUAs surveyed in this study (scarce for 55percent of them, moderate for 40 percent and adequate for 5 percent) due to a number of factors including the size of the command area, the total number of farmers covered, etc.

References

Balland, J. M. and J. P. Platteau. 1996. *Halting Degradation of Natural Resources: Is there a Role for Rural Communities?* Oxford: Food and Agriculture Organization (FAO) and Oxford University Press.

Bandaragoda, D. J. and Saeed Rehman. 1995. "Warabandi in Pakistan's

Institutional Design Perspective, Capacity Constraints and PIM ෩ 113

Canal Irrigation Systems: Widening Gap between Theory and Practice." International Irrigation Management Institute (IIMI) Country Paper 7, IIMI, Colombo.

Bromley, D. W. 1989. *Economic Interests and Institutions: The Conceptual Foundations of Public Policy.* New York: Basil Blackwell.

Centre for Civil Society (CCS). 2003. "Managing Water Resources: Communities & Markets." CCS Briefing Paper, CCS, New Delhi.

Department for International Development (DFID). 2001. *Sustainable Irrigation Turnover: Report on System Infrastructure.* Knowledge and Research (KAR) Project R7389, Oxon.

Dovers, S. 2001. "Institutions for Sustainability", *TELA: Environment, Economy and Society,* no. 7, April.

Goodin, R. E. 1996. "Institutions and Their Design," in R. E. Goodin (ed.), *The Theory of Institutional Design,* pp. 1–53. Cambridge: Cambridge University Press.

Gulati, A., R. Meizen-Dick and K.V. Raju. 2005. *Institutional Reforms in Indian Irrigation.* New Delhi: Sage Publications for IFPRI.

Hanna, S., C. Folke and K. G. Maler. 1995. "Property Rights and Environmental Resources," in S. Hanna and M. Munasinghe (eds), *Property Rights and the Environment: Social and Ecological Issues,* pp. 15–29. Washington: Beijer International Institute of Ecological Economics and The World Bank.

Hardin, G. 1968. "The Tragedy of the Commons," *Science* (New Series), 162(3859): 1243–48.

Herath, G., S. Sivayoganathan, S. Pinnaduwage and C. Bogahawatta. 1989. *Socio-economic Evaluation of the Village Irrigation Rehabilitation Project.* Report 2. Peradeniya: Department of Agricultural Economics, University of Peradeniya.

Hussain, Z. and R. N. Bhattacharya. 2004. "Common Pool Resources and Contextual Factors: Evolution of a Fishermen's Cooperative in Calcutta," *Ecological Economics,* 50(3): 201–17.

IIMI. 1997. *Impacts of Irrigation Management Transfer: A Review of the Evidence.* Research Report 11. Colombo: IIMI.

Kingston, C. and G. Caballero. 2009. "Comparing Theories of Institutional Change," *Journal of Institutional Economics,* 5(2): 151–80.

Kurian, M. 2001. "Farmer-managed Irrigation and Governance of Irrigation Service Delivery: Analysis of Experience and Best Practice." Working Paper 351, Institute of Social Studies, Hague.

Marothia, D. K. 2002. "Institutional Arrangements for Participatory Irrigation Management: Initial Feedback from Central India," in D. Brennan (ed.), *Water Policy Reform: Lessons from Asia and Australia, Proceedings from an International Workshop held in Bangkok, Thailand, 8–9 June 2001,* ACIAR Proceedings No. 106, Canberra, Australian Centre for International Agricultural Research (ACIAR), pp. 75–105.

Marothia, D. K. 2003. "Enhancing Sustainable Management of Water

114 ≈ *Jayanath Ananda*

Resources in Agriculture Sector: The Role of Institutions," *Indian Journal of Agricultural Economics,* 58(3): 406–27.

Marshall, G. R. 2008 "Nesting, Subsidiarity and Community-based Environmental Governance beyond the Local Level," *International Journal of the Commons,* 2(1): 75–97.

McCay, B. J. 2002. "Emergence of Institutions for the Commons: Contexts, Situations and Events', in National Research Council," in E. Ostrom T. Dietz, N. Dolsak, P. C. Stern, S. Stovich and E.U. Weber (eds), *The Drama of the Commons,* pp. 361–402. Washington: National Academy Press.

McCay, B. J. and J. M. Acheson. 1987. "Human Ecology of the Commons," in B. J. McCay and J. M. Acheson (eds), *The Question of the Commons: The Culture and Ecology of Communal Resources,* pp. 1–36. Tucson: University of Arizona Press.

Meinszen-Dick, R., K. V. Raju and A. Gulati. 2002. "What Affects Organizations and Collective Action for Managing Resources? Evidence from Canal Irrigation Systems in India," *World Development,* 30(4): 649–66.

Meinzen-Dick, R. and B. R. Bruns. 2000. "Negotiating Water Rights: Introduction," in B. R. Bruns and R. S. Meinzen-Dick (eds), *Negotiating Water Rights,* pp. 23–55. London: Vistaar and Intermediate Technology Group Publications.

Merrey, D. J. 1996. *Institutional Design Principles for Accountability in Large Irrigation Systems.* Research Report 8. Colombo: IIMI.

Ministry of Water Resources Planning Commission. 2007. *Report of the Expert Group on Ground Water Management and Ownership.* Delhi: Planning Commission, Government of India (GoI).

Mollinga, P. 2001. "Water and Politics: Levels, Rational Choice and South Indian Canal Irrigation," *Futures,* 33(8–9): 733–52.

Nikku, B. R. 2002. "Water User Associations in Irrigation Management: Case of Andhra Pradesh, South India: Opportunities and Challenges for Collective Action." Paper presented at the 9th Biennial Conference of the International Association for the Study of Common Property, 12–17 June, Victoria Falls, Zimbabwe.

North, D. C. 1995. "The New Institutional Economics and Third World Development," in J. Harris, J. Hunter and C. M. Lewis (eds), *The New Institutional Economics and Third World Development,* pp. 17–26. London: Routledge.

Olson, M. 1965. *The Logic of Collective Action.* Cambridge: Harvard University Press.

Ostrom, E. 1990. *Governing the Commons.* Cambridge: Cambridge University Press.

————. 1992. *Crafting Institutions for Self-governing Irrigation Systems.* San Franscisco: ICS Press.

————. 1993. "Design Principles in Long-enduring Irrigation Institutions," *Water Resources Research,* 29(7): 1907–12.

Institutional Design Perspective, Capacity Constraints and PIM ≋ 115

Ostrom, E. Gardiner and R. Walker 1994. *Rules, Games and Common-Pool Resources.* Ann Arbor: University of Michigan Press.

Pagan, P. G. 2003. "Laws, Customs and Rules: Identifying the Characteristics of Successful Water Management Institutions." Paper presented at the Workshop on "Institutional Issues in Water Resource Allocation: Lessons from Australia and Implications for India," July 17–18, Beechworth, Victoria, Australia.

Parthasarthy, R. 2004. "Decentralisation Trajectories with Multiple Institutions: The Case of PIM Programme in India." Working Paper 147, Gujarat Institute of Development Research, Gota, Ahmedabad.

Razaak, M. G. M. and J. Ananda. 1997. "Farmer Organizations for Agriculture Development: A Case Study in Ambanpola Area," in *Proceedings of the 53ʳᵈ Annual Sessions of the Sri Lanka Association for the Advancement of Science, 8–12 December.* Colombo, Sri Lanka: The Sri Lanka Association for the Advancement of Science (SLAAS).

Reddy, V. R. and P. P. Reddy. 2002. "Water Institutions: Is Formalisation the Answer? (A Study of Water User Associations in Andhra Pradesh)," *Indian Journal of Agricultural Economics,* 57(3): 519–34.

Reddy, V. R. 1998. "Institutional Imperatives and Co-Production Strategies for Large Irrigation Systems in India," *Indian Journal of Agricultural Economics,* 53(3): 440–45.

Renault, D., T. Facon and R. Wahaj. 2007. "Achievements and Remaining Challenges in Participative Management of Large Irrigation Systems in Asia: Insights from the FAO Rapid Appraisal Procedure," in I. Hussain, Z. A. Gill, N. Zeeshan and S. Salman (eds), *Institutional and Technological Interventions for Better Irrigation Management in the New Millennium: Proceedings of the INPIM's 9ᵗʰ International Seminar, December 4–8, 2006,* pp. 40–47. Lahore, Pakistan: International Network on Participatory Irrigation Management (INPIM).

Samad, M. 2005. "Water Institutional Reforms in Sri Lanka," *Water Policy,* 7: 125–40.

Uphoff, N. and C. M. Wijayaratna. 2000. "Demonstrated Benefits from Social Capital: The Productivity of Farmer Organizations in Gal Oya, Sri Lanka," *World Development,* 28(11): 1875–90.

Uphoff, N. 1986. *Local Institutional Development.* West Hartford: Kumarian Press.

————. 1996. *Learning from Gal Oya: Possibilities for Participatory Development and Post-Newtonian Social Science.* London: Intermediate Technology Publications.

Vermillion, D. L. 1997. *Impacts of Irrigation Management Transfer: A Review of the Evidence.* Research Report 11. Colombo: IIMI.

Wade, R. 1987. "The Management of Common Property Resources: Collective Action as an Alternative Privatisation or State Regulation," *Cambridge Journal of Economics,* 11: 95–106.

Williamson, O. E. 1985. *The Economic Institutions of Capitalism.* New York: The Free Press.

5

Integrated Water Resources Management: From Policy to Practice through a Comprehensive National Water Management Plan

A Case Study of Bangladesh

Sultan Ahmed

Water is central to the way of life in Bangladesh and the single most important resource for the well-being of its people. It sustains an extremely fragile natural environment and provides livelihood to millions of people (GoB 1999). Bangladesh is the terminal floodplain delta of three large rivers, the Ganges, the Brahmaputra and the Meghna, with over 90 percent of their catchment areas situated outside the country. These rivers join in Bangladesh to form the world's third largest river, the Lower Meghna, before entering the Bay of Bengal. Fifty-seven rivers flow into Bangladesh from outside. A combination of high monsoon rainfall and full-flowing rivers results in extensive inundation of floodplains, a problem compounded by slow, impeded drainage due to flat topography and often coinciding with high tides of the sea.

Integrated Water Resources Management in Bangladesh ≈ 117

About 20–30 percent of the total area of Bangladesh is inundated every year, flooding over six million hectares to depths ranging from 30 cm to 2 m. Every 10 years, up to 37 percent of the area is inundated due to floods. This situation creates both opportunities and hazards: opportunity for highly productive farming and fishing, but considerable risks from deep flooding, loss of agriculture and aquatic resources, damage to livelihoods, erosion and drainage problems. On the other hand, during the dry season the availability of surface water is considerably reduced, and erratic pre-monsoon rainfall can cause serious deficits in soil moisture.

Bangladesh has a total population of over 150 million and an area of 147,570 sq. km covered by intensive river networks. Poverty is endemic, and the country is prone to natural disasters like floods, erosion, cyclones and tidal surges which result in human casualties and huge economic losses. The poor cannot afford disaster-proof housing and many of them take shelter on high-risk peripheral land, something which makes them more vulnerable to the vagaries of nature. Floods and cyclones aggravate poverty by destroying food stocks and scarce resources of poor households. Further, in the poor households, women, children, elderly and the disabled are more vulnerable than the others. It has been estimated that approximately 50 percent of the total population lives below the poverty line and nine out of every 10 persons reside in the rural areas.

Water management in Bangladesh is further complicated by high population density and expanding economic activities which severely adversely affect its rich and vulnerable ecosystems. Since water is essential for human survival, socio-economic development of the country and preservation of its natural environment, the policy of the Government of Bangladesh (GoB) includes all necessary means and measures to manage national water resources in a comprehensive, integrated and equitable manner. To achieve the national goals of economic development, poverty alleviation, food security, and public health and safety, the GoB has adopted an effective policy, the National Water Policy (NWPo), in 1999 in order to operationalize the policy directives. To set up a planning and institutional framework for the comprehensive management of national water resources, the government adopted the National Water Management Plan (NWMP) in 2004 and the Guidelines for Participatory Water Management (GPWM) in 2000. National experts were involved from the initial stage of conceptualisation to

118　≈≈　*Sultan Ahmed*

that of drafting of the policy, plan and guidelines and development of integrated water resource management (IWRM). Policy, plan, guidelines and regulatory regimes of water sector are conducive to the development and management of water resources following the concept of IWRM.

Genesis of Water Sector Planning and Development

Before examining how a national policy has been interpreted into substantial actions, the water sector planning and development in Bangladesh needs to be investigated. Public sector investment in water resources development dates back to the pre-British period. During that period in Bengal (before partition), there existed a sort of public works program for the construction of local infrastructural facilities such as small reservoirs to reduce the adverse impact of floods and to ensure water for irrigation during dry seasons. Following the devastating floods in 1954 and 1955, a UN mission popularly known as the Krug Mission investigated the possibilities for water resources development in the then East Pakistan (now Bangladesh) (MoWR 2007). On the UN mission's recommendations, the East Pakistan Water and Power Development Authority (EPWAPDA) was created in 1959. The Authority was responsible for planning, design, operation and management of all water development schemes of the land (Chadwick and Datta 2001).

The real beginning of water sector planning in Bangladesh was marked by the completion in 1964 of a 20-year Water Master Plan, prepared by EPWAPDA with the assistance of the United States Agency for International Development (USAID). It envisaged a strategy of massive flood control and drainage to be followed by irrigation in a later phase. However, in actual implementation of the plan, much emphasis was put on the construction of embankments and polders in much of the country, and the construction began in earnest. The activities carried out under the Master Plan brought about immediate results. However, later evaluations noted the rapid rate of decline in performance, especially in terms of operation and maintenance, of much of this infrastructure. The increases in agricultural production in particular failed to materialize as predicted.

The orientation of all water sector development schemes to this time has been almost exclusively aimed at achieving the goal of

Integrated Water Resources Management in Bangladesh ≈ 119

increased agricultural production in order to achieve national food security. This bias towards agriculture meant that solutions tended to be in the form of flood control drainage and irrigation (FCDI) projects (Chadwick and Datta 2001). In reality, emphasis was mainly placed on flood control, and improvement of drainage and irrigation. Development was strictly sectoral with very little inter-sectoral communication. The EPWAPDA, transformed into Bangladesh Water Development Board in 1972, was inclined to seek structural engineering solutions at the expense of all other alternatives. In the absence of other organizations to act as advocates for non-structural development of the nation's water resources, especially where structural ones were inappropriate or costly, water resources in Bangladesh became synonymous with flood control, drainage and irrigation (Chadwick and Datta 2001).

In 1983 the National Water Resources Council (NWRC) was established as an inter-ministerial body. Later, in the same year, the Master Plan Organization (MPO) was created and entrusted with the task of drafting the first National Water Plan (NWP). Development of the Plan was a lengthy process requiring the collection of large quantities of baseline information. As a result, the first NWP (Phase I) was not completed until as late as 1986. An assessment was made in the Plan document of the availability of water from various sources, as well as a projection of the future demand for water by different sectors. The NWP was extended (Phase II) in 1986 and completed in 1991 (MoWR 1998).

A substantial volume of information was generated during Phase II and included the development of a number of planning models and analytical tools for defining and evaluating strategies. The country was divided (initially) into 173 catchments. These were grouped into 60 planning areas, and further aggregated into five regions namely northeast, northwest, southeast, southwest and south central. An important outcome of this process was a baseline assessment of water resources in Bangladesh (Chadwick and Datta 2001).

Bangladesh experienced two severe floods in 1987 and 1988; the latter was the worst in living memory. The flood at its peak inundated approximately 65 percent of the country. They caused massive infrastructural damage, crop loss and human casualties. The event foregrounded the issue of flood control and flood management in international forums and led to renewed and greatly increased levels of assistance. Then came the recommendation for implementing an

120 ☙ *Sultan Ahmed*

integrated approach towards flood mitigation based on the concept of "controlled flooding" over the next 20–30 years.

As a result, 26 components of the Flood Action Plan (FAP) were implemented. The FAP was seen as a five-year rolling plan, which would be reviewed every two years. Various plans of action were shown as outputs of the FAP studies ranging from improved flood forecasting and warning systems to high-cost embankment schemes aimed at changing the entire hydrological regime of Bangladesh.

In 1995 the FAP final report, the Bangladesh Water and Flood Management Strategy (BWFMS), was approved by the government, and the implementation strategy laid out in the BWFMS report was also endorsed by the associated development partners in 1995. Following the recommendations of the BWFMS, the institutional arrangements for the planning of water resources were reviewed leading to transformation of the Flood Plan Co-ordination Organization (FPCO) into an expanded Water Resource Planning Organization (WARPO) in 1996. A chronological history of water sector development in Bangladesh has been presented in Annex 1.

National Water Policy (NWPo) 1999

The NWRC led the process of formulation of a water management policy, and the first NWPo was published in 1999. The NWPo aims to provide direction to all line agencies working in the water sector and institutions related to it in one way or the other, for achieving specified objectives.

These objectives are broadly:

a. To address issues related to the harnessing and development of all forms of surface water and groundwater and management of these resources in an efficient and equitable manner.
b. To ensure the availability of water to all sections of society including the poor and underprivileged, and to take into account the particular needs of women and children.
c. To accelerate the development of sustainable public and private water delivery systems with appropriate legal and financial measures and incentives, including delineation of water rights and water pricing.

Integrated Water Resources Management in Bangladesh ≈ 121

d. To bring about institutional changes that will help decentralize the management of water resources and enhance the role of women therein.
e. To develop a legal and regulatory environment that will help the process of decentralization and sound environmental management, and improve the investment climate for the private sector in water development and management.
f. To develop a state of knowledge and capability that will enable the country to design future water resources management plans by itself with economic efficiency, gender equity, social justice and environmental awareness to facilitate achievement of water management objectives through broad public participation.

Water Institutions

Over 40 different agencies and organizations are involved in the water sector, of which 35 are related to central government and have their institutional set-up up to the district and sub-district level. At least 13 different ministries are involved directly or indirectly with these organizations. The NWRC is responsible for co-ordinating all aspects of water management and issues directives through its Executive Committee (EC). Under the NWPo, WARPO has been made the Secretariat to the NWRC and is responsible for preparing the NWMP and subsequent updates, and monitoring their implementation. Agencies are responsible for preparing their own sub-regional plans within the framework established by the NWMP. Ministry of Water Resources (MoWR) is the apex body of the government responsible for comprehensive development and management of water resources of the country. Bangladesh Water Development Board (BWDB), Water Resources Planning Organization (WARPO), River Research Institute (RRI), Joint Rivers Commission-Bangladesh (JRCB), Bangladesh Haor and Wetland Development Board (BHWDB), Institute of Water Modeling (IWM), and the Center for Environmental and Geographic Information Services (CEGIS) have been working under the aegis of the Ministry. BWDB implements, operates and maintains development and FCDI projects; WARPO is responsible for macro-planning of water resources; JRCB for sharing

122 ≈ *Sultan Ahmed*

of waters of trans-boundary rivers; and RRI, BHWDB, IWM, and CEGIS are the research and knowledge management institutions.

National Water Management Plan (NWMP)

The government prepared the NWMP, with the intention of operationalizing the directives laid down in the NWPo. In so far as it reflects the objective of rationalizing and decentralizing the management of water sector, the Plan is a framework plan within which line agencies and other organizations are expected to plan and implement their own activities in a co-ordinated manner. The Plan is presented in three phases: in the short-term (2000–05) it is considered a firm plan of ongoing and new activities; in the medium-term (2006–10) it is an indicative plan; and in the long-term (2011–25) it is a perspective plan. Implementation of the Plan is to be monitored regularly and it is to be updated every five years.

The NWMP is intended to identify the needs and priorities for water resources management, the institutional structure through which these resources should be managed, and the process through which both institutional reform and priority interventions can be realized. It is hoped that the NWMP would represent a radical break with the past and provide a framework for more effective management of these resources in the future. The NWMP has been prepared to respond to these challenges and paradigms, with three central objectives consistent with the Policy aims and national goals.

These objectives are:

a. Rational management and wise use of Bangladesh's water resources.
b. Improvement of people's quality of life through equitable, safe and reliable access to water for production, health and hygiene
c. Availability of clean water in sufficient quantities at the right time, for multi-purpose use, and preservation of aquatic and water-dependent eco-systems.

The Plan is structured in such a manner that the objectives of 84 different programs planned for the next 25 years contribute individually and collectively to the attainment of both the overall objectives as well as the intermediate sub-sectoral goals. The programs

Integrated Water Resources Management in Bangladesh ∼ 123

are grouped into eight sub-sectoral clusters and spatially distributed across eight planning regions of the country. The three main categories of programs are Cross-Cutting Programs, National-level Programs and Regional Programs.

From Policy to Practice

The NWPo was adopted in 1999 with the intention of guiding both public and private actions in the future for ensuring optimal development and management of water that benefits both individuals and the society at large and for achieving certain specified objectives. One of them is IWRM. Though the Policy did not coin the term IWRM explicitly, it holistically advocates social equity, conservation of natural environment and efficiency of water management–the basic components of IWRM. The Policy aims "to ensure progress towards fulfilling national goals of economic development, poverty alleviation, food security, public health and safety, a decent standard of living for the people and protection of the natural environment" (GoB 1999: 2).

The policies set forth are considered essential for addressing the objectives of improved water resources management and protection of the environment. Every public agency, every community, village and each individual has an important role to play in ensuring that the water and associated natural resources of Bangladesh are used judiciously and sustainably.

The NWMP and the GPWM are also adopted by the government and are in practice. The country is now having comprehensive policy, plan and guidelines for her water resources development and management in an integrated manner. A Water Act has been drafted but is yet to be passed by the Parliament. After the enactment of the Water Act, the water sector will be fully equipped with all the systemic instruments necessary for the sound management of the national water resources. The NWPo through its various provisions emphasizes the issues of participatory water management (PWM) and highlights the importance of stakeholder participation.

People's Participation

People's participation in water management projects implemented by BWDB and the Local Government Engineering Department

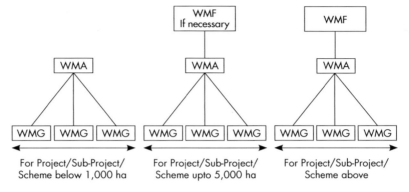

Composition of WMF
- WMF will be formed for apex level of the Project/sub-project/scheme.
- Representative from the general members of the WMA will be the general members of the WMF.
- Representatives from the concerned LGIs (Upazila Parishad/Zila Parished) will be the advisors of WMF.

Composition of WMA
- WMA will be formed for either the apex level of project/sub-project/scheme or the mid-level for each sub-system of the project/sub-project/scheme.
- Women and men belonging to the households of farmers, fisherman, small traders, craftsmen, boatmen, aquaculturist, landless people, destitute women, PAP etc. will be the general members of WMA or representatives from the general members of the WMG will be the general members of WMA. Representatives from the concerned LGIs (Union Parishad/Upazila a Parishad) will be the advisors of WMA.

Composition of WMG
- WMG will be formed for each smallest hydrological unit or social unit (Para/Village) of the project/sub-project/scheme.
- Women and men belonging to the households of armers, fishermen, small traders, craftsmen boatmen, aquaculturist, landless people, destitute women, PAP etc. will be the general members.
- Representatives from the concerned LGI (Union Parishad) will be the advisors of WMG.

Figure 5.1: Organogram of Water Management Organization

Source: GoB (2000: 22).

(LGED) has been made compulsory and has been in practice since the adoption of the NWPo and the GPWM. The GPWM provides a broad outline for the people's/stakeholders' participation in water management projects. The agencies responsible for implementation will develop their own procedures, manuals, formats, etc., as required.

Until 2006, more than 2,82,000 men and women became members of the Water Management Groups (WMGs) under 104 projects of BWDB. The Board plans to constitute more than 50,000

Integrated Water Resources Management in Bangladesh 〰 125

Water Management Organizations (WMOs) in the near future. The people's participation in the BWDB projects is numerically expressed in Table 5.1.

Table 5.1: Existing Water Management Organizations and their members

Water Management Organization	Number of Organizations	Number of Members
Water Management Groups	7898	282554
Water Management Association	166	13995
Water Management Federation	8	675

Source: MoWR (2006: 18).

It is apparent that the WMO retains its central position within the overall project framework. Among other things, the success of a project in attaining its objectives depends on its ability to create a viable WMO and strengthen the operation and maintenance activities by institutionalizing beneficiaries' participation.

To attain the objective of increasing public participation, a medium-scale FCDI project of BWDB has been chosen for pilot testing following guidelines of the GPWM. In effect, the performance of different indicators are closely examined in order to assess the pros and cons of the guidelines and thereby come-up with recommendations for future water management practices in Bangladesh.

A Case Study of Successful People's Participation

A pre-eminent example of the implementation of policy guidelines is Narayanganj–Narsingdi Irrigation Project, which is a success story of people's participation in water sector projects of Bangladesh and a model example of transformation from policy to practice.

Narayanganj–Narsingdi Irrigation Project (NNIP)

It is a medium-scale project of BWDB with gross area of 3,000 ha. This project started its operation since 1991, but the desired benefit from the project was not achieved mainly due to inefficiency in water distribution and increasing urbanization. Local people and BWDB ranked this project as a sick project due to its inability to deliver as desired. Then, in 2004–05, a pilot research study was initiated by BUET and DUT, under the BUET–DUT Linkage Project-III

126 ≈ *Sultan Ahmed*

(2001–06) to evolve a suitable water management solution for this project. A PWM approach as laid down in the policy plan and guidelines was applied at NNIP. The principle focus of the experiment was to check the adaptability of PWM approach and enumerate its impact in terms of benefits achieved and sustainability. After the application of PWM, the big farmers were benefited because of increased production and monetary return. A financial analysis on *boro* cultivation shows that post PWM, the average per hectare per household monetary return from *boro*, a dry-season high-yielding variety (HYV) paddy cultivated through irrigation, substantially increased in comparison to that in the pre-PWM period. Thus, PWM ensured the involvement of all stakeholders in water management as regular partners in managing the project.

Immediately after implementation of NNIP in 1993, farmers were provided with irrigation satisfactorily for about two or three seasons only. However, the performance of the project fell below expectations largely due to inadequate operation and maintenance, lack of supervision by the nodal agency, and co-ordination between it and the beneficiaries. Supply of water for irrigation by BWDB was not on time, and rather mostly uncertain and inadequate at the tail-end of the canals; this seriously affected paddy production and significantly reduced the yield. A pilot research was thus undertaken to evolve a suitable management practice in line with the GPWM. Application of PWM at NNIP was again embarked in 2002–03 to observe its performance in the subsequent seasons. This experiment with PWM was meant to examine the nature of its O&M in order to ascertain the project's long-term self-sustainability. A two-tier WMO was set up to take over the control of the day-to-day project management from BWDB. The membership of WMO was also made open to all project-affected people.

The application of PWM approach showed an outstanding improvement in agricultural production and subsequent socio-economic development. The production of *boro*, in particular, doubled due to timely and adequate supply of irrigation water. In the second year, the cultivated area was doubled due to assured availability of irrigation water (see Table 5.2). As a consequence, the standardized gross value of production increased by more than 110 percent from the pre-PWM period. Each farm household received an additional return up to Tk. 12,000/acre only from *boro* cultivation, which was about 80 percent of the total available return during the pre-PWM

Integrated Water Resources Management in Bangladesh 〰 127

Table 5.2: Changes in irrigation area before and after
effective people's participation

Before People's Participation (March 2003)		After People's Participation (April 2005)		
Boro paddy	Target	Pre-PWM	Post-PWM	
		2002–03	2003–04	2004–05
Cultivated Area (ha)	1194	750	1165	1231
Yield (ton/ha)	6.10	4.25	5.70	5.50

Source: BUET (2006: 49).

period. Thereby, poverty was also significantly reduced. The ratio of return between small and large farmers was significantly reduced in terms of incremental return per unit of family labor available. The contribution of the incurred investment, about Tk. 5.5 million over two years, to the national economy was also immense. The net present value and benefit–cost ratio of the investment derived from the discounted cash flow analysis for an estimated project life of 25 years were found to be Tk. 71 million and 2.14:1 respectively (BUET 2006).

The cornerstone behind the success was nothing but the effective participation of stakeholders, commonly termed as people's participation. A two-tier water management institution was established following the GPWM-prescribed framework for medium-scale schemes, as shown in Figure 5.1, in the pilot area that consists of 40 WMGs headed by a WMA. A sample survey carried out under NNIP showed that 98 percent of the local farmers were aware of the water management institution and 57 percent directly involved in the institution formation process. Around 70 percent of the water users identified WMGs as key water managers, a phenomenon which reflected a clear transfer of the responsibility for water management from traditional government-employed water managers to local stakeholders. More than 50 percent of the water users acclaimed the success of WMGs in water management and O&M activities. Around 95 percent of the water users agreed to pay the irrigation service charge for fairer water distribution, which also reflected their stake to ensure sustainability.

After one year of successful trial operation of their activities, the beneficiaries decided on the number of levels/tiers of WMOs to be formed for the project following the rules and regulations

128 ≈ *Sultan Ahmed*

regarding composition and formation, function, legal framework and monitoring to make WMOs sustainable. At this stage, interface with the implementing agency and other agencies and local institutes and administration would give WMOs the necessary leverage to negotiate matters related to their benefits. Beneficiaries were informed beforehand about the responsibilities they would have to take up at their own risk. At the same time they were apprised of their benefits and financial involvement for running the project on their own. Any mistake at this stage would tend to ruin the future sustainability of the project.

Thus, direct benefits in terms of micro- and macro-economic returns were quite evident, but the institutional process for ensuring full-scale devolution of responsibilities demanded some nurturing. Till the completion of the research project, WMGs were facing some risk of intrusion from local elites, who had no direct connection with agriculture or water management process, into the ECs. Historically, in other development projects of Bangladesh, this group usually tried to take financial advantage by participating in the ECs and disrupting the entire institutional formation process in violation of the norms of participatory management (BUET 2006). Further, while the water users mostly opined that the water supply was regular and adequate, EC members were not pro-active in O&M as they were not enjoying any financial benefit. Furthermore, WMG executive members were in general focused on service charge collection, thereby ignoring other important activities of the institution. Another problem was that officials of the implementing agency as well as other policy-makers and donors translated the PWM approach through two indicators, cost recovery and sustainability, by collecting service charge, rather than providing water management service and support. This approach should have been avoided as it often caused annoyance to the beneficiaries.

Application of PWM was embarked during 2002–03 to observe its performance in the subsequent seasons. In order to ascertain the project's long-term self-sustainability, evaluation and monitoring of the O&M activities was necessary. While experimenting with the PWM approach under this project, it was recognized that there were quite a few experiences related to the application of PWM by the LGED to small-scale water sector projects and other large-scale flood control, drainage and irrigation projects of BWDB. The benefit evaluation and monitoring (BEM) of the small-scale water

Integrated Water Resources Management in Bangladesh ☙ 129

resources development and management projects of the LGED are being carried out to examine the improvement in the socio-economic condition of the primary stakeholders of these projects. The case of NNIP is a success story of people's participation in the water sector development projects of Bangladesh, and it should be replicated in other publicly managed projects to ensure the sustainability in terms of food security and combined economic growth.

Conclusion and Recommendations

Systemic instruments such as policies, plans, guidelines and laws are crucial for the development and management of a service sector such as water in Bangladesh which is fully devoted to the production of public goods. This also helps the adoption of a sector-wide approach with aid alignment and harmonization. Such a sector needs adoption of a comprehensive policy, which should be translated into time-based–short-term (firm plan), medium-term and long-term comprehensive plan, an approach which Bangladesh has already adopted.

People's participation in public goods production activities such as in water management for crop production and drinking water is very crucial. Comprehensive guidelines for all stakeholders in participatory water management are a pre-requisite. Thus, compliance with GPWM in all such water management projects is inevitable. Sustainable effectiveness of WMGs in managing the community's water resources mostly depends on the process through which the groups are formed. Unbiased, objective and careful judgment in selecting genuine members is very crucial. The time and place of the WMG meetings are also very important and should be convenient to the community. Several meetings over a period of at least one year are required to find genuine, self-motivated and sincere members. Quick selection will hardly work and a group selected in a hurry may be a burden for the project and the community. Re-selection of members in such a case becomes inevitable and creates divisions in the community which is very detrimental to the project.

The tasks of operation and maintenance of new small-scale water management projects after proper rehabilitation of the old ones should be transferred to the community for building a sense of ownership and ensuring better management. Bangladesh has adopted a national water policy, plan and guidelines. The Water Act

130 ∾ *Sultan Ahmed*

of Bangladesh has also been drafted and needs to be passed without any further delay. Then the entire system will flow from policy to law and will be in place, something very essential for IWRM. Without a parliamentary act, the implementation of government policies can be impeded at every step because water sector management throws up many cross-sectoral issues involving multiple institutions and stakeholders.

Appendix 5.1A: Chronological history of policy development in the water sector of Bangladesh

Year	Major Events
1952	Embankment and Drainage Act comes into force.
1956–1957	Krug Mission fielded by the United Nations submits its report.
1958	Coastal Embankment Project (CEP) and polder construction is started by East Pakistan Irrigation Department.
1959	East Pakistan Water and Power Development Authority (EPWAPDA) is created.
1964	Master Plan formulated by the International Engineering Company (IECO) of the USA recommends 58 large-scale Flood Control Drainage and Irrigation (FCDI) projects.
1965	CEP and polder development takes place rapidly and continues till 1980s. A total of 140 polders are constructed.
1972	EPWAPDA is restructured as Bangladesh Water Development Board (BWDB) by the Presidential Order.
1975	Farakka Barrage is put on trial run and continues to be built.
1977	Indo-Bangladesh agreement on the Ganges water sharing is signed.
1979	A joint review of BWDB by the Government of Bangladesh (GoB) and the World Bank recommends restructuring of BWDB and formulation of a new National Water Plan.
1982	The Ganges agreement expires, and a memorandum of understanding (MoU) is signed.
1983	Master Plan Organization (MPO) is established by the Ministry of Irrigation, Water Development and Flood Control (MoIWDFC) and tasked with the preparation of a long-term water resources development plan. Phase I of National Water Plan starts.
1985	New MOU on the Ganges water sharing is signed.

(Contd.)

Integrated Water Resources Management in Bangladesh ≈ 131

Appendix 5.1A (contd.)

Year	Major Events
1986	National Water Plan (Phase I) completes its first report. The availability of water from various sources and the projected future demand for water by different sectors are assessed.
1987 & 1988	Major flood studies are undertaken by the GoB, UNDP, USAID, Government of Japan and France.
1989	National Water Plan (Phase II) continues Flood Action Plan (FAP) approved in the Donors' meeting in London held in December.
	FAP consists of 11 main components and 15 supporting studies.
	For co-ordination of FAP activities, Flood Plan Co-ordination Organization (FPCO) is created under the MoIWDFC.
1990	MPO is restructured as Water Resources Planning Organization (WARPO) under the MoIWDFC.
1992	Systems Rehabilitation Project (SRP) under the BWDB is launched with support from the World Bank, Netherlands Environmental Development Agency (NEDA), the EU and the World Food Program (WFP). National Minor Irrigation Development Project (NMIDP) is launched to investigate and develop groundwater resources with the EU funding under the Ministry of Agriculture.
1993	MoIWDFC is re-named as the Ministry of Water Resources (MoWR), a name that reflects a holistic and wider vision on water.
	Under FPCO several guidelines–Guidelines for People's Participation (GPP), Guidelines for Project Assessment (GPA), and Guidelines for Environmental Impact Assessment (EIA)–are drafted and approved.
1994	MoWR approves GPP and circulates it for its application in the new projects of BWDB.
1995	FAP's final report is produced; GoB approves Bangladesh Water and Flood Management Strategy (BWFMS).
1996	FPCO is merged with WARPO.
	WARPO gets an extended mandate.
	Initiative to prepare the National Water Management Plan (NWMP) addressing all resource management issues is undertaken under supervision of the WARPO.
	The GoB and India sign the Ganges Water Sharing Treaty.

(Contd.)

132 ≈ *Sultan Ahmed*

Appendix 5.1A (contd.)

Year	Major Events
1998	Major floods both in terms of area coverage and duration occur.
1999	National Water Policy is adopted by the government. BWDB is mandated to implement all major surface water development projects and other FCDI projects with command area above 1,000 ha. LGED is mandated to implement FCDI projects having a command area of 1000 hectares or less after identification and appraisal through an "interagency project appraisal committee."
2004	National Water Management Plan is formulated.
2005	National Coastal Zone Policy is formulated.
2007	Water Management Improvement Project is initiated.

Source: Adapted from Datta (1999: 1) and updated by the authors.

References

Adnan, S. and A. M. Sufiyan. 1993. *State of the FAP: Contradictions between Policy Objectives and Plan Implementation*. Dhaka: Research and Advisory Service (RAS).

Bangladesh University of Engineering and Technology (BUET). 2006. *Final Technical Report: BUET–DUT Linkage Project Phase-III (Research Project No. 4)*. Dhaka: BUET.

Chadwick, M. and A. Datta. 2001. *Livelihood–Policy Relationship in South Asia in Bangladesh*. Dhaka: DIFD.

Datta, A. (ed.). 1999. *Planning and Management of Water Resources: Lessons from Two Decades of Early Implementation Projects in Bangladesh*. Dhaka: University Press Limited.

Government of Bangladesh (GoB). 1999. *National Water Policy*. Dhaka: Ministry of Water Resources, GoB.

———. 2000. *Guidelines for Participatory Water Management*. Dhaka: Ministry of Local Government, Rural Development and Cooperatives, GoB.

Halcrow. 2000a. *National Water Management Plan Project, Draft Development Strategy, Volume No 3, Annex A: Policies*. Dhaka: Water Resource Planning Organization, Ministry of Water Resources, GoB.

———. 2000b. *National Water Management Plan Project, Draft Development Strategy, Volume No 2, Main Report*. Dhaka: Water Resource Planning Organization, Ministry of Water Resources, GoB.

Integrated Water Resources Management in Bangladesh 〰 133

Ministry of Water Resources (MoWR). 1998a. *Overview of Water Resources Management and Development in Bangladesh.* Dhaka: Ministry of Water Resources, GoB.

_____. 1998b. *National Water Policy.* Dhaka: Ministry of Water Resources, GoB.

_____. 2006. *Annual Report 2004–2005.* Dhaka: Ministry of Water Resources, GoB.

_____. 2007. *Annual Report 2005–2006.* Dhaka: Ministry of Water Resources, GoB.

MoWR and Ministry of Local Government, Rural Development and Cooperatives (MoLGRD&C). 2000. *Guidelines for Participatory Water Management.* Dhaka: Ministries of Water Resources and Local Government, Rural Development and Cooperatives, GoB.

6

Watershed Management Policies and Programs in Bhutan

Empowering the Powerless

Thinley Gyamtsho

Bhutan is a small country located in the Eastern Himalayas with an area of 38,394 sq. km. It rises sharply from the Indo-Gangetic plains in the south at an altitude of about 200 m to more than 7,500 m into the Himalayas forming a natural border with China in the north. Due to extreme variation in altitudes, climatic conditions vary from hot and humid tropical and subtropical conditions in the southern foothills to cold and dry tundra conditions in the north.

Bhutan has a total population of 672,425 with 69 percent living in the rural area and 31 percent in the urban (OCC 2005). The sources of livelihood of the rural population are subsistence agriculture, livestock rearing, and forest products. However, only 8 percent of land is used for agriculture. Bhutan has a high proportion of forest cover at 64.4 percent (Rai 2005) and protected areas at 43 percent (DoF 2008), followed by rugged mountains, open pastures and glaciers.

The modern development process in Bhutan was initiated with the launching of the First Five-Year-Plan (FYP) in 1961. Bhutan is currently into the third year of the 10th FYP. Prior to 1961, service facilities like modern education, health services, transport and

Watershed Management Policies and Programs in Bhutan ≈ 135

communication services and agriculture services did not exist. However, through planned development, service facilities were built and made accessible to majority of the population. Some of the statistical indicators of these achievements at present include:

- a. 476 modern educational institutions,
- b. 29 hospitals and 176 Basic Health Units (BHUs) with 145 doctors serving 90 percent of the population,
- c. 4,393 km of road network and 231 bridges to improve accessibility to the remote areas,
- d. 33,709 fixed telephone connections and new mobile services,
- e. Electricity generation capacity of 2,520.2 million units mainly from hydropower benefiting 46 towns and 1,210 villages (NSB 2007a)
- f. Constitutional democracy in place with Gross National Happiness (GNH) as its development philosophy.

These achievements have brought about significant improvement in the socio-economic conditions of the people. Unfortunately, not all sections of the society enjoy the benefits equally as 23.2 percent of the population has been living below poverty line since 2006. Of this, 98.1 percent resides in the rural areas (NSB 2007b). Although the proportion of people living below poverty line has declined from 31.7 percent in 2004 to 23.2 percent in 2007, the subsistence poverty[1] figure increased from 3.8 to 5.9 percent during the same period.

Objective

The overall objective of this chapter is to provoke discussion and debate on identifying the best possible ways to manage water resources in Bhutan by placing the farming communities at the centre of water resources development. Some of the specific objectives are: *a*) to justify the requirement of concerted efforts to manage water resources as they play an important role for socio-economic development of the country; *b*) to review the current policies and programs related to water resources management; *c*) to make critical assessment of whether currently conceived policies will deliver the GNH development goals; and *d*) to provide suggestions for the re-formulation of watershed policies and programs in line with the GNH concepts.

136 ≈ *Thinley Gyamtsho*

Framework for Analysis

This chapter employs the concepts of GNH as the overall framework to assess the possible outcome of standing water resources policies and programs. The concepts of equity, sustainability, participation, decentralization and empowerment are employed within the backdrop of GNH principles. The overall aim of the chapter is to provoke more debate on the formulation of water resource governance policies so that the outcome is relevant to the Bhutanese people. Specifically, the intent is to identify ways to empower the poorest sections of the society and ensure that they benefit from these policies and programs as suggested by the title of this chapter.

The basic principle of GNH is that development should serve the well-being of the people and that economic growth is only a means to, not the end of development (CBS 2007). Now, let me take the liberty to provide a personal interpretation of GNH concept in the context of natural resources management in Bhutan using the analogy of a pie. Here, a pie represents natural resources which support the livelihood of rural farmers. Management (water resources policy/program) is analogous to how the pie is shared among the people (citizens). From the individual perspective, GNH in this case would mean: "I want the smallest possible fraction of the pie so that many others would benefit from the remaining fraction." The national perspective is: "how can we make the pie small to minimize the use of resources so that adequate resources are spared for future generations and shared equally among the citizens?"

Individual perspective on GNH represents intra-generational equity to access, limiting wants, avoiding conflicts, making personal sacrifices for the welfare of others, letting others benefit more than me, and so on. Limiting our wants helps to sustain our resources, thus ensuring inter-generational equity. A personal sacrifice for the welfare of others represents self-disempowerment so that the disempowered sections of the society are empowered to enhance their social well-being. Power sharing is premised on self-disempowerment because of the inverse relationship between empowerment and disempowerment. Unless people in power give up some of their power, empowerment of disempowered would never happen because disempowered people would never be able to demand their rights. Hence, the starting point of resource-sharing is self-

Watershed Management Policies and Programs in Bhutan 〰 137

disempowerment which is essential to the concept of GNH; the spiritual component of GNH is the realization of the impermanence of materialistic comforts of life.

At the national level, minimizing the size of a pie without undermining the basic livelihood requirement of the citizens represents sustainability of resource systems. This perspective ensures that utilization of resources is within the limits of their natural regenerative capacity, and it focuses on enhancing the efficiency of resource utilization rather than increasing the capacity to use more resources. We see that there are four possible combinations of making and sharing a pie:

a. making a big pie but with people in power taking the major chunk;
b. making it big and sharing equally;
c. making it small, but with people in power taking the major chunk; and
d. making it small but sharing equally.

Among the four combinations the last one represents the GNH approach. Ideally, a GNH-seeking nation should pursue for making a reasonably small pie but distributing its shares equally among the citizens.

Water Resources Management Issues

Rich Endowment of Water Resources: What It Means to Poor Farmers?

Bhutan is rich in water resources with per capita availability of 75,000 m^3 per year which is one of the highest in the region (BWP 2003). However, people's capacity to utilize this resource is very limited. Evidence from Lingmuteychu Watershed indicates that a typical farmer who cultivates rice has a capacity to use only 650 m^3 of water annually from the total per capita availability of 15,000 m^3 at the watershed level. This utilization fraction represents only 4.3 percent of the available water resources. When this utilization capacity is considered at the national level, it represents less than 1 percent of the total available water. For a dry land farmer this figure would be even smaller.

138 ≋ *Thinley Gyamtsho*

The main reason for farmers having limited capacity to use water resources is the lack of infrastructural facilities like irrigation channels to bring water from where it is available to where it is required and water storage mechanism which can help store water when it is available and use it when it is required. At the moment apart from the existence of a few irrigation channels which irrigate 12.5 percent of the total arable land (BWP 2003), there are no water management systems in place for managing water for food production from 87.5 percent of the arable land. Therefore, whatever water is being utilized by the majority of farmers is rainwater.

Apart from the national water availability figure, Bhutan does not have a figure for national-level individual water utilization capacity. My guesstimate is that the figure would be far less than that for the Lingmuteychu Watershed (650 m^3 per person per year), given the fact that this watershed has 84 percent of arable land under irrigation (Gyamtsho 2003) as against only 12.5 percent of the arable land under irrigation at the national level.

The issue here is not getting precise statistics, but appreciating what this figure means in relation to high per capita water resource availability of 75,000m^3 per year. According to the Falkenmark indicator or water stress index, a threshold value of 1,700 m^3 of renewable water resources per capita per year is proposed, based on the water requirement in household, agriculture, industry, energy sector, and environmental needs (as cited in Rijsberman 2006). Therefore, any country is said to be water-stressed if the renewable water supply falls below this threshold. Likewise, when the supply falls below 1,000 m^3, a country experiences water scarcity, and when it falls below 500 m^3, absolute scarcity. Bhutan faces absolute water scarcity, going by these threshold values. This is confirmed by the incidence of: *a*) delayed rice transplantation due to limited water supply; *b*) wet lands (irrigated paddy fields) left fallow due to unavailability of water; *c*) wetland converted to dry land due to lack of water; and *d*) an increasing incidence of inter- and intra-community conflicts stemming from water scarcity. It is really unfortunate that symptoms of water scarcity loom large in a country said to be very rich in water resources.

The Uncomfortable Paradox

An uncomfortable paradox has risen in Bhutan: a situation of water scarcity (less than 500m^3/person/year) amidst the highest

Watershed Management Policies and Programs in Bhutan ཞ 139

endowment of water resources (75,000 m³/person/year) in the region if not in the world. To explain this paradox, the International Water Management Institute (IWMI) has made an assessment of future (2025) adaptive capacity by taking into account the share of renewable water resources available for human needs and the primary water supply. Accordingly, countries are classified into two groups, namely, "physically water scarce" (those countries that will not be able to meet the estimated water demand even after accounting for future adaptive capacity), and "economically water scarce" (those countries that have sufficient renewable resources, but would have to make a very significant investment in water infrastructure to make these resources available to people) (Rijsberman 2006). Going by this model, Bhutan falls in the economically water scarce category. This explains the paradox that Bhutan has adequate water resources at the national level, but people have limited capacity to use them because the physical infrastructure for water management is very limited. The next question one might ask is what good is it if the rich water resources are not beneficial to the society?

Is Hydropower Development Aligned along GNH Concepts?

Although Bhutan is making huge investments in the development of hydropower through various bilateral collaborations that have an immense potential to increase the value of water resources at the national level, these developments will not directly benefit the common people. Notwithstanding the fact that hydropower's contribution to GDP increased from 10 percent in 2001 to 12.4 percent in 2004 (NSB 2007a), there is no concerted effort to share these benefits (water value) with the common people who are ideally the custodians of water resources.

The counter-argument to the above is that if the value generated from hydropower goes to the government then it automatically benefits farmers through implementation of development programs. Through such a distribution mechanism, every stakeholder—whether a farmer, a shareholder or an employee of a hydropower company— is benefited equally, irrespective of his/her role in managing water resources.

However, some questions that automatically follow from this argument are:

140 ≈ *Thinley Gyamtsho*

a. Why should a farmer do more and get little?
b. Why should farmers reduce the number of cattle to reduce the pressure on grazing lands in the forest?
c. Why should farmers stop practicing shifting cultivation when it is their primary source of livelihood?
d. Why should farmers stop burning forests for a better management of pests and crop diseases?
e. Why should farmers sacrifice their basic livelihood entitlements for the sake of maintaining forest cover?
f. By a simple logic, if farmers do not have the right to get a share of the value generated from water resources, then no other stakeholders have the right to benefit from it.

The existing consumption pattern suggests that farmers evidently have not benefited directly from state investments in hydropower development. It shows that on an average 20 percent of national population consumes 6.7 times more than the poorest 20 percent of the population (NSB 2007b). The argument here is that while the country embarks upon the task of developing infrastructure to enhance the value of renewable water resources, it is equally crucial to develop a mechanism to sustain these benefits through watershed development approaches with appropriate direct incentive mechanisms which will be discussed later.

Though some investment in the construction of some irrigation channels has improved the access to water resources to some extent, the major investment made in the development of hydropower has not enhanced the access to water resources. In absence of any formal mechanisms to plough back the value generated from water resources, hydropower development will widen the gap between the poor and the rich. Since Bhutan is already pursuing the goal of attaining GNH as the development philosophy and poverty reduction as part of the 10th FYP through a democratic process, there should be no room for excuses for not achieving the socio-economic welfare of the citizens of Bhutan. Since water resources constitute the key to socio-economic development of the country, it is vital to manage it through policies and programs that serve the interest of all the citizens. In particular, one way of managing water resources is through watershed approach which is the central theme of this chapter. Therefore, the following section try to highlight some of the issues and concerns that help shape the policies and programs of watershed development in Bhutan.

Review of Watershed Policies and Programs

Bhutan has started well in terms of formulating policies and programs related to water resources management during the last couple of years. Owing to the lack of strong knowledge base for water resources management, the principle and concepts on which these policies and programs are founded are rather weak. This section intends to provide some background in this context.

Policy Environment for Water Resource Management

At the highest level, policy environment is the most conducive to the sustainable management of natural resources in Bhutan. The fourth king of Bhutan, Jigme Singey Wangchuk, has always emphasized that enhancing GNH is more important than increasing Gross National Product (GNP) (DoA 1990). The Government of Bhutan decided to take proactive measures at present rather than react later and pay a heavy price extracted from the land and people if development is left unregulated. This intervention is based on the premise that socio-economic development, and environmental and cultural integrity are not mutually exclusive, but interdependent and equally critical for the long-term viability of Bhutan (NEC 1998: 18).

Bhutan Vision 2020 recognizes hydropower resources as one of the four pillars of development in the country. It envisages that the country should embark on watershed management (WsM) to sustain the benefits from water resources. Development and implementation of major river basin management plans by 9th FYP was set as a milestone to ensure this sustainability. But, unfortunately nothing has been done to achieve this vision in the 9th FYP.

Water Management Research Program

The first water management research project was started at the Renewable Natural Resources Research Centre (RNR RC), Bajo, in 1997 with the primary objective of increasing agricultural productivity through better management of on-farm irrigation water. The Netherlands Development Organization (SNV) provided a modest fund support along with an expatriate consultant which started from 1997. Most of the project activities were implemented

142 ≈ *Thinley Gyamtsho*

in Lingmuteychu Watershed, as presented in the watershed section below. While the SNV support came to an end in 2000, the project itself was institutionalized as part of the Field Crops Research Program (FCRP) with a sub-program status. This status means a limited priority and focus placed by the government on the project. Despite these limitations, water management research program continues to be implemented on a small scale. This essay represents one of the outcomes of this program.

Bhutan Water Partnership: Drafting of Water Policies/Acts/Visions

Bhutan Water Partnership (BWP) was established in August 2001 to co-ordinate all programs related to water resources management. The mandates of BWP are:

a. to co-ordinate and formulate a broad National Water Policy along with necessary legislation;
b. to co-ordinate and prepare the Bhutan Water Vision for the next 25years;
c. to co-ordinate and prepare water action plans for integrated water resources management;
d. to co-ordinate and prepare an institutional linkage mechanism within and beyond the water resources sector;
e. to review and co-ordinate the preparation of a comprehensive Human Resource Development (HRD) plan in the water resources sector; and
f. to act as the national counterpart to consultants involved in policy formulation and management of water resources.

The formation of this inter-ministerial partnership was initially driven by the insights gained from the water management experience in Lingmuteychu Watershed. The researcher involved in the water management research in RNR RC provided the initial thrust in shaping this partnership. The BWP drafted the Bhutan Water Policy, Water Act and Vision.

Water Resources Co-ordination Division

In the process of formulating the draft Water Act, National Environment Commission (NEC) was identified as the apex body for the overall co-ordination of water resources management in the country. Accordingly, Water Resources Division was instituted within NEC with a mandate to prepare the National Integrated Water Resources Management Plan (NIWRMP), co-ordinate the formulation of water policies and acts, foster institutional linkages, and develop water quality monitoring and management strategies.

WATERSHED MANAGEMENT DIVISION

National Watershed Management Unit (NWMU) was established under the Social Forestry Division of the Department of Forestry (DoF) in 2003 (Wangchuk 2008). The DoF was mostly involved in reforestation and afforestation, contributing to the maintenance of a healthy watershed. Since reforestation and afforestation were not planned from a WsM point of view (ibid.), it deterred the actual emergence of a clear WsM program and policy direction. So far, the unit has conducted several workshops to draw a road map for developing WsM programs and policies. Its latest output is the Wang River Basin Management Framework (WRBMF). The overall goal of the framework is to promote economic and ecological sustainability while its specific objectives (DoF 2009) are:

a. to manage the basin effectively for ensuring reliable supply of quality water and sustainable livelihoods of the stakeholders;
b. to formulate socio-economic welfare strategies and programs that would enhance income and well-being of stakeholders while promoting ecological sustenance; and
c. to identify and instate institutional mechanisms and policy measures that create an ambient environment for implementing water management projects.

Over time, the scope and mandate of the unit has increased and by 2010 the unit was upgraded as Watershed Management Division under the DoF.

WATERSHED MANAGEMENT RESEARCH

In 2004, RNR RC Wengkhar was mandated to carry out WsM research following a disaster caused by heavy rainfall in 2003. Incessant rainfall in the east caused landslips and devastating floods which destroyed farmlands, livestock, houses and social infrastructures. Degraded watersheds were perceived to have aggravated the problem. As such RNR RC Wengkhar conducted

144 ⁓ *Thinley Gyamtsho*

consultation meeting to set up an institute for WsM at various levels in mid-2008, which resulted in the publication of Gamri Watershed Management Plan. This watershed is situated in Trashigang district encompassing an area of 745 sq. km at an altitude of 600–4,465 m above sea level. The objective of this plan is to: *a)* increase the productivity of land; *b)* conserve and utilize natural resources in the watershed region in a sustainable manner; and *c)* improve the quality of water (RNR RC Wengkhar 2006).

OTHER INSTITUTIONAL PROGRAMS

The Irrigation Division under the Ministry of Agriculture responsible for irrigation water supply was initially focused on delivering water from the sources to the fields through construction of channels. Over the years the focus has shifted to the development of sustainable irrigation systems through formation of water users groups (WUGs). The Rural Water Supply Scheme under the Ministry of Health mandated for providing drinking water in rural areas, now focuses on the protection of water sources apart from infrastructural development.

Watershed Projects in Bhutan: An Evaluation

The following sections detail the current status of watershed projects in Bhutan that have not been able to fully apply the concepts of watershed principles as yet.

Lingmuteychu Watershed Management Project

Lingmuteychu Watershed Management Project (LWMP), the first of its kind in Bhutan, was initiated by RNR RC Bajo in 1997 in a small watershed with an area of only 34 sq. km located at the junction of three districts. Its initial objective was to conduct on-farm research (crop verity trials) as the project site had broad agro-climatic conditions ideal for the systematic testing of technologies. The concepts of farming systems research gained popularity in late 1990s in Bhutan, allowing the tag name of watershed management to be attached to what was originally intended to be an on-farm research.

A multidisciplinary diagnostic study conducted towards the end of 1997 identified several issues and concerns at the watershed level which included shortage of irrigation water during rice transplanting.

Subsequently, a confirmatory study was conducted to understand and characterize the nature of the problem. It revealed the causative factors, ranging from bio-physical to socio-cultural. It not only helped understand the impact of these factors, but also underscored the need for sound water management policies in the country.

While the watershed research project generated a rich knowledge base for the researchers, it could do very little to improve the problem of water shortage in reality. By 2003, the research focused on addressing the watershed issue through the development of local capacity. In late 2005, a watershed management group (WsMG) known as *Lingmuteychu Lum Zhinchong Tshogpa* (LLZT), the first of its kind in Bhutan, was formed with the primary objective to enhance water productivity for food production based on the watershed approach. Since then, LLZT has managed to draw support from three donor agencies to implement several priority projects and now has WsM plans geared towards prioritizing the development activities in future.

Radhi Watershed Management Project

Radhi Watershed Management Project (RWMP) was started in 2003 by RNR RC Khangma, Trashigang district, and has now been shifted to Wengkhar, Mongar district. Its main objective was to address the issues of environmental degradation caused by overgrazing in the upper catchment and mismanagement of irrigation water (Wangchuk 2008). The need for a multi-sectoral approach, for cost-effective management, for nestling of local institutions and for local institutional capacity building, together with the role of local beliefs and practices–all shaped the need for a water management group. Therefore, the Radhi WMG was formed in 2006, with a WsM plan to prioritize and implement watershed development activities.

Wang Watershed Management Project

Wang Watershed Management Project (WWMP), a project much bigger in scale than others, was started in 2000 by MoA in four districts of Thimphu, Paro, Ha and Chukha. Despite its huge scale, it was not implemented as a WsM project in its true sense and was not different from other development projects (Wangchuk 2008). However, some of the crucial aspects identified were: the need for a

146 ～ *Thinley Gyamtsho*

holistic approach for improving farming systems, better co-ordination among the agencies under MoA and need for efficient management of water schemes by WUGs. Although land degradation is not a major issue in this basin, farmers are not willing to undertake soil conservation measures as they are labor-intensive. The project came to an end in 2006, but NWMU within DoF is in the process of developing a management plan.

Discussion

It is seen that Bhutan has always favored policies that support the social welfare of citizens. This is indicated by the government's strong emphasis on enhancing GNH rather than GDP. Utilization of Bhutan's rich water resources is identified as one of the four pillars of development. As per the draft Bhutan Water Policy, water will continue to be in abundance to enable the pursuit of socio-economic development in Bhutan. Present and future generations of Bhutanese people will have assured access to adequate, safe and affordable water to maintain and improve their quality of life (BWP 2003).

There are a number of agencies involved in programs and projects on water resources management. Although drinking and irrigation water schemes are the oldest water-related programs, of late hydroelectric and industrial uses of water have emerged as the new stakeholders in the water sector. But unfortunately, there is no institution to oversee and coordinate these projects and programs at the national level.

The draft Bhutan Water Policy document recognizes that the existing water user institutions have weak functional linkages at policy, planning and programming levels. The different sub-sectors have been discharging their respective responsibilities independent of each other. This has resulted in fragmentation of data, duplication of efforts and poor resource management, at the cost of synergy of integration. For instance, drinking water program, currently in operation, is being looked after by two ministries: urban water supply by the Ministry of Communications, and rural water supply by the Ministry of Health and Education. While the Ministry of Agriculture handles irrigation and land use, hydropower and hydro-meteorological data collection comes under the purview of the Ministry of Economic Affairs. Above all, a national perspective

Watershed Management Policies and Programs in Bhutan ~ 147

on water resources sector is missing, leading to potential conflicts among the sub-sectors (BWP 2003).

The formation of technical advisory BWP in 2003 provided some hope for the integration of water resources management programs at the national level. Despite the initial success, subsequent progress completely stagnated due to the endemic politics amongst the concerned agencies over where the secretariat of the technical advisory BWP would be housed. The observation is that agencies like to sit on a huge pile of national mandates but deliver very little. While there is a lack of nationally co-ordinated efforts for water resources management, some progress had been made through the efforts of individual agencies. The general observation of three WsM projects shows that the term "watershed" was used more as a tag in the initial stages. This was inevitable because the implementation did not follow a purely conceptual understanding of the principles of watershed development when the project started. However with time, the project got realigned along those principles. The key lesson learnt is that it is important to conceptually understand watershed development correctly in the first place, rather than apply them from the very beginning or ensure that the implementers are equipped with the requisite skills. It is encouraging to note that RNR RC Wengkhar was mandated with WsM research and that NWMU is making some effort to find directions for the WsM program. The WsM consultation meeting has started the process of drafting WsM framework, though a lot needs to be done in terms of debating and deepening concepts, approaches, focuses and setting the right context. Watershed development visions, goals, objectives and approaches need to be re-aligned with the GNH goals, and specifically for poverty reduction themes of 10th FYP. General observation so far is that the approach seems to have not considered the perspectives of rural farmers who are the main stakeholders of WsM.

a. The process at the moment is completely driven by the government agenda, i.e., WsM for sustaining hydropower production. This is obvious from the fact that the proposed institutional body, WsM Committee, is housed within the government institutions. The argument here is that it is necessary to qualify the roles of the committee. In case this committee represents a decision-making body, then it is not

148 ≋ *Thinley Gyamtsho*

aligned to the decentralization policy. Then, how should we implement genuine decentralization?

b. Besides recognizing the need for a WsM program, there is also a need to identify how to pursue it rightly. Firstly, there is a need to understand the context: what should be the purpose of WsM (drinking, food production/agriculture, ecological functioning, energy generation, industrial production, or recreation); who are the stakeholders (farmers, government servant, corporations [BPC], government, or NGOs) and what are their roles and responsibilities; and who (i.e., stakeholders) pays the cost and who benefits?

c. The primary purpose of WsM is to increase water productivity which will help increase food production, or may stabilize the supply by ensuring that water is available when it is required through storage/harvesting system, and where it is required through development of relevant infrastructure.

d. While undertaking management, one needs to prioritize the following sectors: *i*) drinking; *ii*) food production and ecosystem functioning; *iii*) energy production; *iv*) industrial use, and *v*) recreational purpose (BWP 2003).

e. WsM should primarily focus on enhancing the social welfare of farmers and not the ones who are providing services. Hence, farmers should be made the main stakeholders in WsM projects. This implies that food production is the primary concern. Other stakeholders like civil servants, NGOs, and corporations are providers of services to farmers.

f. WsM should have management groups/committees/organizations/associations. All members of such bodies should be representatives of rural communities/villages with complete decision-making powers.

g. The local watershed groups should be supported by a technical committee comprising representatives of support providers/outsiders including government agencies, NGOs, corporations, etc. The role of this committee should be to provide technical support and advice to watershed organizations.

h. The smallest watershed organization would comprise a village or a cluster of a maximum of 10 to 15 villages depending on the physical orientation of watersheds. But watershed boundaries and resource dynamics should be the first criterion to determine the size of the watersheds.

Watershed Management Policies and Programs in Bhutan 〰 149

i. Watershed institutions should be nestled at the basin level through the formation of river basin management groups by watershed associations. The chairman of the smaller watersheds should become a member representative at the basin level. Again, this basin-level organization should have decision-making powers. A similar hierarchy of associations should be formed within the technical support providers.

j. All the costs and benefits of WsM should be worked out in detail both at the basin and the watershed level. Accordingly a mechanism should be developed to distribute the costs and benefits among the stakeholders during and after the project execution phase.

k. While developing the cost- and benefit-sharing mechanism, it is crucial to ensure that the principles of GNH, poverty reduction theme of the 10th FYP, equity, sustainability, participation, decentralization and empowerment are not only respected but actually applied.

Conclusions

Since Bhutan has 64.4 percent of geographical area under forest cover, in addition to the rich endowment of water resources (75,000 m³/person/year), the need for WsM policies and programs may seem out of context. But it really depends on the perspective one views them from. If one views them from the perspective of watershed conservation, with the exception of a few, most watersheds in Bhutan are in good condition. But if one views them from the farmers' point of view that is guided by their need for water for food production, there exists water scarcity in a water-rich country. Despite the high per capita availability of water resources at the national level, it is insufficient in reality. To judge utility of water at the individual level, it is necessary to consider the spatial scale (is water available when it is needed?) and temporal (is water available when it is needed?) aspects of water distribution.

Since Bhutan is a mountainous country, most of the farmlands are located at the upper reaches of the slope where supply of water is limited, and big rivers are situated at the bottom of the valleys where there are limited farmlands. In addition, the distribution of rainfall has a unimodal pattern, i.e., more than 90 percent of rainfall occurs within three months. Further, the demand peaks a month

150 ≈ *Thinley Gyamtsho*

(i.e., during rice transplantation season) before the peak rainfall. All these factors create the problem of water scarcity for food production in Bhutan, and poses tremendous challenge to the management of water resources. Hence, WsM with the objective of enhancing food production per unit quantity of water is very crucial for the farming communities.

Currently, the farming community represents 69 percent of the national population and earns its livelihood from arable lands which constitute 7.8 percent of the country's total geographical area. The implementation of WsM policies and programs can offer a huge scope for the farming communities to benefit from the value generated from the remaining 92.2 percent of the country's area. Thus, it is important to start believing that the government's primary role is to enhance the social well-being of citizens especially the farmers.

Note

1. Subsistence poverty is defined as the level of consumption which is less than food poverty line of Nu.688.96 per person per month (NSB 2007b).

References

Bhutan Water Partnership (BWP). 2003. *Bhutan Water Policy* (Draft). Thimpu: BWP, Royal Government of Bhutan.

Centre for Bhutan Studies (CBS). 2007. *Gross National Happiness and Material Welfare in Bhutan and Japan.* Prepared by Tashi Choden, CBS, and Takayoshi Kusago, Kokoro Shirai, Osaka University, Japan.

Department of Agriculture (DoA). 1990. *Main Document of Irrigation Policy Exercise.* Thimpu: Irrigation Division, DoA, Ministry of Agriculture, Royal Government of Bhutan.

Department of Forest (DoF). 2009. *Wang River Basin Management Framework to Promote Economic and Ecological Sustainability of the Wang River Basin.* Thimpu: Social Forestry Division, DoF, Ministry of Agriculture, Royal Government of Bhutan.

Gyamtsho, Thinley. 2003. "Irrigation Water Conflicts in Lingmuteychu Watershed." Paper presented at Banff Mountain Summit "Mountains as Water Towers," November 23–26, Celgary, Canada.

Mcdonald, Bernadette and Douglas Jehl. 2003. *Whose Water is it? The Unquenchable Thirst of a Water-hungry World.* Washington: National Geographic.

Watershed Management Policies and Programs in Bhutan ≈ 151

National Environment Commission (NEC). 1998. *The Middle Path: National Environment Strategy for Bhutan.* NEC, Royal Government of Bhutan. Thailand: Keen Publishing Co. Ltd.

Nature Conservation Division (NCD). 2004. *Bhutan Biological Conservation Complex: A Landscape Conservation Plan: A Way Forward and Living in Harmony with the Nature.* Thimphu: NCD, Department of Forestry Services, Ministry of Agriculture with support from WWF Bhutan Program.

NSB (National Statistical Bureau). 2004. *Poverty Analysis Report of Bhutan 2004.* Thimphu: NSB, Royal Government of Bhutan.

NSB. 2007a. *Statistical Yearbook of Bhutan 2007.* Thimpu: NSB, Royal Government of Bhutan.

————. 2007b. *Poverty Analysis Report of Bhutan 2007.* Thimphu: NSB, Royal Government of Bhutan.

Office of the Census (OCC). 2005. *Population and Housing Census of Bhutan 2005.* Thimpu: OCC Commissioner, Royal Government of Bhutan.

Rai, B. 2005. "Bhutan's Forest: The Real Picture." *Kuenselonline News,* 8 October, 2005, @ 01:48:47 EDT. http://www.kuenselonline.com/modules.php?name=News&file=article&sid=6120 (accessed September 21, 2012).

Renewable Natural Resources Research Centre (RNR RC) Bajo. 2006. *Facilitating the Change: Research-led Watershed Experiences from Lingmuteychu Watershed.* Wangdue: RNR RC Bajo.

Rijsberman, Frank R. 2006. "Water Scarcity: Fact or Friction?," *Agriculture Water Management,* 80(2006): 5–22.

RNR RC Wengkhar. 2006. *Integrated Approach to Watershed Management in Radhi: The Experiences, Lessons and Way Forward.* Mongar: RNR RC Wengkhar.

RNR RC Wengkhar. 2008. "Proposal to Set Up Institute for Watershed Management at Various Levels," in *Proceedings of Watershed Management Workshop and Proposal conducted in Wengkhar from 12 to 13 February 2008.* Mongar: RNR RC Wengkhar:

RNR RC Wengkhar. 2009. *Gamri Watershed Management Plan.* Mongar: RNR RC Wengkhar.

Wangchuk. 2008. *The Status of Watershed Management in Bhutan: Situational Analysis Report.* Mongar: RNR RC Wengkhar, CoRRB, MoA.

7

Scale, Diverse Economies, and Ethnographies of the State

Concepts for Theorizing Water Policy*

Priya Sangameswaran

—

The domain of water has seen a wide variety of changes in the last decade. Often euphemistically labeled as "water sector reforms," changes in water policies include elements such as participatory irrigation management, cost-sharing by users, greater power to local bodies, establishment of regulatory bodies, greater involvement of corporate bodies, and growing importance of the economic dimension of water provision. These changes have been the subject of much debate, with protagonists taking one of two normative positions. On the one hand, the water sector reforms are believed to lead to greater efficiency, equity, and sustainability. For instance, the new demand-oriented rural drinking water schemes are viewed as providing more choices to local communities with respect to the kind of projects and the personnel they hire for different functions, and as resulting in better management of water systems (GoM, n.d.). On the other

---

* This chapter draws on a larger research project on neoliberalism and water reforms and many of the arguments made here draw on material presented in a book titled *Re-Forming Development through Water Reforms* currently under review at Orient Blackswan.

Scale, Diverse Economies, and Ethnographies of the State ⚕ 153

hand, the reforms have also been interpreted as part of a discourse of neoliberalism and as attempts to extend capitalist exploitation to newer arenas such as water, a move that is considered inevitable as other sources of profit dry up. Thus, Harvey (2003) and Swyngedouw (2005) argue that reforms such as the privatization of water are instances of "accumulation by dispossession" and feed into a process of global accumulation. Apart from these two normative positions, there is also a more applied strand which is action-oriented and concerned with making immediate interventions (such as how best to improve the design and implementation of a given project). Such studies too have a particular normative position implicit in them; however, some wish to downplay it for pragmatic reasons, while others wish to steer clear of ideological debates and hence claim to be "apolitical."

This chapter is sympathetic to the second normative position albeit with a number of qualifications. The argument that the ongoing water sector reforms are a specific manifestation of the process of neoliberalization at work in many parts of the world since the 1980s has been made not only in the context of changes in the water sector, but also with respect to changes in a variety of realms ranging from other natural resources such as forests to health, education, banking, etc. Limitations of this argument have also been pointed out particularly in critical geography, wherein the relationship between neoliberalism and environment has received a lot of attention, and in critical development studies, wherein the question of how to understand social change in a globalized world has preoccupied many theorists. A major critique of both fields has been about the use of metanarratives and how these often present an oversimplified teleological story, thereby losing sight of the complex and often messy trajectories of many of the reforms. This chapter aims to discuss three concepts/approaches that have been put forward in critical geography and critical development studies that would help complicate the kind of questions that we ask about water sector reforms and thereby result in more nuanced theoretical analyses. This, in turn, would draw attention to some of the spaces that the reforms open up for progressive change, even if inadvertently.

The next section would critically discuss the normative literature on water sector reforms in India. Then in the subsequent section, the three aforementioned concepts–scale, diverse economies, and ethnographies of the state–will be introduced, along with some illustrations about the kind of questions that they would help raise and the processes that

154   ≋   *Priya Sangameswaran*

they would make visible in the context of water sector reforms. The chapter finally concludes with some general comments.

Analyses of Water Reforms

Broadly speaking, studies in water sector reforms in India have adopted one of the two normative positions outlined in the introduction. One set of studies cites the failure of the welfare state and of top-down technocratic approaches put in place by it as a justification for major restructuring of the water sector. Such studies are usually celebratory of the current reforms, and if anything, bemoan their slow uptake (see, for instance, Briscoe and Malik 2006). While there are differences among the studies adopting this broad position on a number of issues such as the relative importance to be given to markets vis-à-vis civil society organizations, the specific pricing principles to be adopted, and the kind of governance structures required, the basic trends underlying the reforms—decentralization, privatization, commodification and regulation—are not themselves subject to critical scrutiny. Many of these studies, although not all, stem from an environmental economics/institutional economics perspective and the methodology of these approaches influences the kind of questions asked, e.g., what kind of factors would facilitate collective action. The second normative position also accepts the failure of the welfare state, although it concedes that the welfare state had at least some achievements to its credit; however, it is much more sceptical about the current nature of reforms (see, for instance, Dwivedi and Dharmadhikary 2006). Those who hold this position include academics and activists from a variety of backgrounds, but who can be broadly characterized as having an interest in questions of power (both in terms of representation of the reforms as well as actual practice) and in a critical appraisal of production processes, technology and ecological conditions.

This chapter will focus on the second position. In general, while this position draws attention to the wide variety of ongoing changes and sometimes effectively mobilizes opposition against the factors that are believed to be problematic (e.g., the movement against the proposed privatization of the Delhi Jal Board), it often tends to lay all blame at the door of a singular, seemingly omnipotent neoliberalization/globalization agenda and ends up obscuring some significant issues. For instance, Aiyer (2007) points out that struggles

Scale, Diverse Economies, and Ethnographies of the State ≈ 155

around water which have typically been posited as struggles by a community against the practices of a transnational corporation (e.g., against Coca-Cola in Plachimada in southern India) also need to be treated as part of an unfolding agrarian crisis, which although related to globalization and neoliberalization, involves local, regional, and national dynamics. While there are important and exceptional studies that offer more nuanced analyses and draw attention to the historically and geographically contingent nature of the reform process (e.g., Coelho 2006; Shah 2008), they are often studies of particular cases in the sense that they deal with a very specific aspect of the reform process and/or are rooted in a particular locale. This has given rise to concerns about the theoretical and philosophical implications of carrying out case studies and calls for greater analytical precision in the use of concepts/categories, particularly in critical geography (see, for instance, Castree 2005). It is hoped that the three concepts discussed in the chapter would be useful in this regard.

Another field which has seen debates that would be useful for a better understanding of water sector reforms is developmental studies. From the post-World War II period until about the 1980s, there were two broad metanarratives that dominated development studies: theories of modernization and dependency. The post-development turn of the 1990s seemed to ring the death knell of all metanarratives, and in fact often of the concept of development itself, leading to fears of a development impasse. Yet a variety of new studies emerged, particularly from anthropology and sociology, which used a wide range of theoretical approaches to engage with questions of development in more creative ways.[1] These studies also raised concerns about the relationship between agency, structure and explanation; the reconstitution of political economy on a non-essentialist and non-teleological basis; and the relevance of theory for practical intervention (see, for instance, Booth 1993)–concerns that have acquired even greater importance as developmental policy has been re-invented in a neoliberalized and globalized form. Many of these issues are very relevant to analyses of water policy, as we shall see in the following section.

Concepts for Theorizing Water Policy

In this section, I discuss three concepts which have been the subject of considerable discussion in recent times in social science

156   ≋   *Priya Sangameswaran*

scholarship, and which are potentially useful in theorizing the ongoing changes in water policy. The concepts themselves are not new, but have either acquired different or more nuanced meanings, or have been deployed more fruitfully in discussions on globalization and neoliberalism. Further, although the insights offered by these concepts are already implicitly present in at least some of the work on water policy reforms, an explicit engagement with these concepts can further improve our understanding of the reforms.

First, I introduce each of the concepts, and then point out the kind of questions that it will help to raise in the context of water policy reforms and/or the potential insights it can provide, using illustrations from the Indian context, and more specifically from a recent study of water policy reforms in the state of Maharashtra in western India.

Scale

Discussions about scale have always had an important place in development studies and the broader social science literature. In developmental economics, for instance, the question of whether production (of goods and services) should take place on a small scale or on a large scale has been the subject of much debate.[2] Debates about structure and agency, which are linked to (although not restricted to) the question of the scale of decision-making, too have had a long history in sociological tradition.[3] Further, the related debate about the "local" versus the "global" implicitly draws on the notion of scale. Moreover, discussions of developmental policy often make references to the particular scales at which policies are framed and implemented.

In recent times, there has been a revival of interest in the concept of scale (along with attempts to re-conceptualize it) in at least the two aforementioned disciplines of critical geography and development studies. In development studies, there is concern with the ideal scale at which to analyse any phenomenon as well as the meaning of terms such as "micro", "local" and "macro." For instance, Gupta (1998) and Sivaramakrishnan and Agrawal (2003) make a distinction between location, space and scale, and emphasize that the terms "local" and "macro" (or "macrological") refer not so much to specific sites or locations but to relative scales. Thus, a macro-level factor or a macrological discourse is not defined by location (in other words,

Scale, Diverse Economies, and Ethnographies of the State ☷ 157

that it arises in sites "outside" or "beyond" the village), but by the fact that it is relevant to the supra-local and/or involves reference to linkages between different sites, and is therefore best explained at larger scales. Similarly, critical geography has paid attention to the relation between scale and power. For instance, Herod and Wright (2002) focus on questions such as how our world is scaled, how we think about such scaling, and how this allows people to exercise power or deny it to others. What is important in this conceptualization is not the choice between different scales, but rather the articulation or relation between the different scales at which various events, actions, and institutions occur (Gupta 2003), as also how the shift from one scale to another occurs and what is at stake in such shifts (Herod and Wright 2002). Such an exercise becomes even more critical in the context of globalized societies where scalar boundaries have become more obfuscated than ever before.

To get a sense of the difference that a focus on scale would make, it is useful to consider Gibson-Graham's (2002) discussion of the global–local dualism. Gibson-Graham point out that in most analyses of globalization, the global is associated with strength, domination and action, and the local with its antithesis. That is, size and extensiveness are taken to be coincident with power. This dualism, in turn, feeds into the hegemony of a discourse of globalization because the global is accepted as the scale at which capital is seen to hold political and economic sway over the local. The association between capital, power and the global in taken to imply that local struggles (against globalization) need to be upscaled if they are to be successful. In contrast to this, Gibson-Graham argue that conventional analyses overlook the constitutive power of small and local processes. In general, then, the privileging of processes at a particular scale can have adverse consequences.

The global–local dualism has also evoked another kind of response. Sivaramakrishnan and Agrawal (2003) propose the term "regional"[4] in order to go beyond the local and global scales and deal with either the nation-state or other sub-national and supra-national units of analyses. The term "regional" (in their framework) has a spatial connotation, but is not to be identified with a specific scale or geographical size; instead, it is a relative concept that would depend on the kind of subject/questions under consideration. At each given scale, the concept would focus on the networks, struggles and differentiated place-making that people engage in in everyday

158 ☙ *Priya Sangameswaran*

contexts. Sivaramakrishnan and Agrawal also make a case for one particular variant of the regional, viz., the national. They argue that the nation-state continues to be important in a time increasingly defined by globalization; in contrast, the recent writings on development emphasize either its local performances, or its global/international discourses and agents. To give an example from the realm of water, this would mean, for instance, that the manner in which water sector reforms work in the Indian context would be influenced by the constitutionally mandated decentralization process (by way of the 73rd and 74th Constitutional Amendments); the latter has often resulted in state governments being bypassed as well as, ironically, the central government acquiring greater powers (especially by way of central government schemes such as the Jawaharlal Nehru National Urban Renewal Mission).

Questioning of the local–global dualism and all that it implies is just one instance of the difference that a focus on scale can make. I provide three more illustrations of the potential of the concept. First, Swyngedouw and Heynen (2003) argue that the continuous re-organization of spatial scales is an integral part of social strategies to combat and defend control over limited resources and/or a struggle for empowerment. For instance, conflicts over the appropriate scale for organizing water systems (local, river basin, national or trans-national) evoke different power geometries and may lead to radically different socio-ecological conditions. In the case of the state of Maharashtra, as in many other parts of the country, the post-reform period (i.e., since the beginning of the 21st century) has seen a shift in the scale of organization of water systems (from Regional Rural Schemes to individual village-based schemes) and in the scale of decision-making (from centralized to decentralized forms). A variety of processes are at play in each shift; in turn, each scalar shift also gives rise to its own trajectory of changes, a point that has been discussed in greater detail in Sangameswaran (2008). Hence, the shifts in the scale of organization of water systems and in the scale of decision-making can be read neither as a straightforward move from state control to local/community control or as privatization and commodification of a service which was once public.

Second, the scale of organization of water systems can also refer to how widespread any particular form of organization, individual or regional, is. At one level, this is dependent on the availability of resources (such as capital investment)[5] as well as the perceived

Scale, Diverse Economies, and Ethnographies of the State ≈ 159

success of any initial pilot projects that may have been undertaken. But in water sector interventions, as in other developmental interventions, there does not seem to be much critical interrogation of the implementation process and outcomes of pilot projects. Thus, the pilot projects undertaken by the Government of India as part of its Sector Reforms Program—which were later upscaled to *Swajaldhara* and which have provided the base for all the rural demand-driven drinking water projects in the country—had a number of problems. For instance, NGOs in the state found the shift to a demand-driven approach difficult to deal with; further, there were not even enough NGOs to extend the project beyond the districts where the pilot projects were carried out, let alone NGOs with the requisite expertise.[6] Yet the approach was upscaled, and understanding the factors feeding into this in different parts of the country would be an interesting exercise.

Third, the question of scale also comes into play in the decision of whether water is provided to one household or multiple households (i.e., private or communal sources of water). In *Jalswarajya*, a World-Bank sponsored demand-driven drinking water project in rural Maharashtra, private connections were usually encouraged (with some exceptions such as in regions with dispersed houses).[7] The emphasis on individual household connections is, in turn, related at least partly to the current emphasis on cost-recovery. But while the idea of recovering costs may make sense in the context of deteriorating state finances, a totally different picture emerges when one considers the repayment stipulations of the World Bank loan or the inability to pay off many individuals/groups at the village level. Thus, what might seem benign or beneficial at one scale where one set of evaluative criteria are used might seem problematic when judged using different criteria at other scales.

Diverse Economies

Apart from questioning the local/global dualism (as discussed in the previous sub-section), Gibson-Graham (2002) also question the capitalist/non-capitalist dualism by using the concept of "diverse economies." The concept draws on the work done in a number of areas (such as feminist theory, post-structuralist Marxism, and studies of the informal sector) and questions the idea that the capitalist form of production is *the* dominant form of production today. Two

160 ≈ *Priya Sangameswaran*

points are made to show this. First, Gibson-Graham emphasize that not all markets are for capitalist commodities. Further, apart from alternative forms of markets, there are also non-market transactions. Second, these non-capitalist spaces (whether market-based or non–market-based) are important *in their own right*, and not just in terms of the contribution they make to the capitalist sector. To shake off the spectre of global capital, Gibson-Graham argue that it is necessary to make these non-capitalist activities visible and show that they can be viable *in the economic terrain* (as against only representing different cultural practices). In other words, recognizing the non-capitalist spaces within contemporary capitalism would provide a fulcrum from which to imagine and develop real alternatives.

Following from the preceding discussion, two points in particular are worth emphasizing in the context of water sector reforms. First, in much of the literature on reforms, the terms "markets" and "commodities" are used with predominantly negative connotations. The critique of the concept of "commodity" usually arises from its definition as a good or service whose price is determined by the market. The argument is then made that not all social, cultural and environmental values can be captured by a market price; further, the market price may not be affordable to large sections of society, thereby resulting in inequitable access. But irrespective of the validity of these concerns, one can also have a different understanding of commodities and markets (Gibson-Graham 2002). For instance, one can think of commodities as goods and services produced for the market, and of markets as not being naturally expansive or dominant. Further, as Li (2001) points out in her discussion of the boundaries (or lack thereof) between communities, markets and states, markets have been in existence for a long time within communities. Hence, it is necessary to understand the ways in which current markets differ from older ones, to distinguish between different kinds of existing markets, as also varied social, political and economic conditions under which production for the market could potentially be equitable and markets play a more progressive role.

Consider, for instance, the case of rural groundwater markets for irrigation. Water-sharing arrangements or exchange of goods and services for water have existed for a long time in rural areas. But the specific sense in which water markets have received attention since the 1990s are "localized, village level institutional set-up[s] through which owners of *modern water extraction methods* supply

Scale, Diverse Economies, and Ethnographies of the State ☙ 161

water to other members of the community at a price" (Shah 1993: 44; emphasis added). Although there are claims that groundwater markets are both efficient and equitable (e.g., Shah 1993), there are also counter-claims to this argument (e.g., Bhatia 1992). But instead of making generalized claims about the equity and efficiency of these markets, it might make more sense to consider the actual micro-level functioning of markets at different locations (Dubash 2002). Thus, Dubash describes how problems of incentives and information shape contracts for purchase and sale of groundwater and how norms and rules help solve these problems.

The diverse potentialities of markets have also been brought out by experiments that aimed to give water rights to the landless such as the NGO Proshika's efforts in Bangladesh and the Andhi Khola Irrigation Scheme in Nepal. Proshika helped landless groups in Bangladesh obtain water rights by giving them financial and other support to acquire minor irrigation technologies and develop collective sources of groundwater (Wood et al. 1990). By selling water to landowners, the landless not only began to enjoy improved material conditions, but also better social and political status, as well as increased leverage and bargaining power in other areas such as informal credit, grazing rights, and wages (ibid.). In the case of the Andhi Khola Irrigation Scheme, a land redistribution scheme was designed and implemented along with a water allocation system in which everyone could earn tradable water rights through participation in construction work (Etten et al. 2002). But equal water rights did not benefit the poor partly because of the lack of a market for water (i.e., a mechanism for exchange with others who needed water and were willing to compensate for it) (ibid.).[8] In the Indian context, the only way in which the landless (usually the ones who lease in land for farming) have been involved in groundwater markets seems to be as *buyers* of groundwater (Dubash 2002). But the legal changes being made in the context of the ongoing water reforms can be used as a space to provide water to the landless and other groups traditionally denied access to it.

The second point that follows from the concept of "diverse economies" is that commodities can be produced by non-capitalist firms as well as by capitalist firms and involve alternative forms of labor and market relations (such as in the case of co-operatives). The idea of alternative economic models or alternative forms of organization is not a new one. But Gibson-Graham emphasizes that

162 ≈ *Priya Sangameswaran*

the project of developing non-capitalist sites is not an easy one. First, a language of economic difference (wherein there is space for non-capitalist enterprises and for economic dynamics other than the quest for profitability) needs to be created and people need to be actively subject to it. Second, even when such a language exists, it is likely to be voiced in terms of community-building and environmental sustainability, i.e., as non-economic and therefore marginal to the mainstream economy.

I would like to conclude this sub-section with a cautionary note. The concept of "diverse economies" put forward by Gibson-Graham forces us to rethink many received binaries. However, it can also slip into a conservative agenda, especially if inadequate attention is paid to the reconstitution of the meanings of commonly used terms such as "markets" and "commodities" in the popular as well as official imaginations.

Ethnographies of the State

For social theorists engaged in understanding the process of change as well as activists seeking to bring about change, engagement with "the state"—whether seen as an abstract entity (usually discrete and autonomous), or whether taking on the concrete forms of a national government, provincial government, specific departments, or particular bureaucratic officials—is inevitable. This is even more so in the context of debates about neoliberalism and globalization wherein the changing role of the state and the implications thereof have received a lot of attention (see, for instance, Sharma and Gupta 2006). One approach that is useful in this regard is the anthropology of the state that pays "careful attention to the cultural constitution of the state—that is, how people perceive the state, how their understandings are shaped by their particular locations and intimate and embodied encounters with state processes and officials, and how the state manifests itself in their lives" (ibid.: 11). In the realm of water, this approach would lead to several questions. What are the concrete manifestations of the withdrawal of the state? What views do villagers themselves hold about the relative importance of district-level government units vis-à-vis sub-district and village-level units as well as NGOs, and how do these differ across different classes/genders of villagers? What does the failure of the state mean in an era when appointments to many state and parastatal bodies

Scale, Diverse Economies, and Ethnographies of the State ≋ 163

are increasingly on a contractual basis? What kind of nexus exists between knowledge and power, a question that has been discussed in the Indian context, for instance, by Dharmadhikary (2008)?

The focus of this sub-section will be on ethnographies of the state that use Gramscian and Foucauldian approaches to understand the operation of hegemony and the constitution of power. A detailed discussion of Gramsci and Foucault is beyond the scope of this chapter. Instead, I selectively mention some of their key ideas followed by examples from the realm of water. In doing so, I draw on the discussion in Simon (1982), and Ekers and Loftus (2008).[9]

Gramsci's concept of hegemony refers to the maintenance of one social group's dominance over subordinate groups by creating a "common sense" about how the world is, what can be changed and what cannot. The state is crucial to Gramsci's understanding of hegemony; more specifically, it is both centralized and diffused. Power is consolidated in many ways, including via institutions normally considered outside the state. Further, the Gramscian concept of hegemony is not just a relation of domination by force, but also of consent by means of political and ideological leadership. It is also important to note that ideology in Gramsci has a material existence in the social practices of individuals. That is, ideology is not just a system of ideas, but something that shapes individuals' beliefs and actions.

Foucault was not explicitly concerned with the problematic of hegemony; rather he attempted to radically redefine government as the regulation of conduct and pointed out that governmental relations are dispersed throughout society. Governmentality à la Foucault refers to the emergence of a distinctive, modern form of power which seeks to govern or regulate the conditions under which people live their lives. That is to say, conditions are set so that people will be inclined to behave as they should, but without any attempt to dictate terms to or coerce them.

What do these ideas imply in terms of water? First, water is an important domain for constituting the hegemony of particular ways of thinking and acting (such as cost-recovery). In fact, given the critical nature of water in satisfying both basic needs (e.g., drinking) and economic purposes (e.g., producing goods and services), water is perhaps best regarded as not just one more domain for hegemonic struggles, but rather as a domain where such struggles are inevitable. Ekers and Loftus (2008) point out, for instance, how alliances between

164 ≈ *Priya Sangameswaran*

and within specific groups are forged through the provision of water to certain areas. Similarly, getting/giving a water connection is a means of establishing/granting the "legality" of migrant populations in urban locales.

Second, in order to understand the operation of hegemony, one needs to appreciate the subtle ways in which power works through everyday hydraulic and other practices. As Larner (2003) puts it, one needs to get at the apparently mundane practices (best practices, audits, contracts, benchmarks) through which neoliberal spaces, subjects and states are constituted in particular forms. For this, a Foucauldian understanding of governmentality is useful because it points out how the new forms of governance encourage both institutions and individuals to conform to the norms of the market (Larner 2000). Consider, for instance, the practice of double-entry accounting that is now insisted upon as part of the restructuring of urban and rural local bodies in general, and also specifically with regard to water functions. On the one hand, this seems like a move to bring in greater transparency and accountability. On the other hand, it can also serve as a means to control the earlier practice of cross-subsidizing less remunerative water supply options such as public standposts with more remunerative options. Similarly, the separation of water budgets from other budgets in both rural and urban local bodies has implications for the extent to which water provision has to be "self-sufficient," as well as the extent to which the idea of fiscal decentralization has moved away from the official agenda even though the rhetoric of the 73rd and 74th Constitutional Amendments continues to be employed. A third example is how 24×7 supply of water 24 hours a day, seven days a week–is posited as not only possible but necessary especially in urban areas (WSP–SA 2003).

Third, applying Gramscian/Foucauldian insights to water would mean moving away from a conceptualization of power as something that is held by some to a conceptualization of power as productive, in the sense of materializing a reiterated norm (Ekers and Loftus 2008). For example, private property relations, considered to be critical for the functioning of markets, require individuals to not only act in new ways, but also become new kinds of subjects; thus owners of property are made to be efficient, profit-seeking, rational individuals (Mansfield 2007). Another example is the idea of villagers having greater choice and empowerment in the new

Scale, Diverse Economies, and Ethnographies of the State ≋ 165

demand-oriented drinking water projects, and how this leads to the labeling of those who do not attend village-level meetings as "undeserving" and not worthy of getting water by other villagers and the NGO/officials involved; this is even when there are good reasons for their non-participation such as the fact that they might often go out of the village to work, or may have suffered at the hands of village elites in the past.[10]

Further, unlike purely Foucauldian approaches which might overemphasize the power of government action to fix the meanings of words and regulate the behavior of people, a Gramscian understanding of hegemony would emphasize the partial, unstable and contested nature of even dominant strategies. Consider, for instance, the emphasis on piped water schemes in the new demand-driven rural drinking water projects. One important reason for such an emphasis is that billing and recovery of water charges is believed to be easier in case of private provision of water to houses (which is only possible via piped water). But another important reason, and one that is often used in the official discourse of the project, is the idea of a new development vision which involves the urbanization of the rural, perhaps best exemplified in the promise of one district-level bureaucrat that the new piped water schemes would enable village women to throw away once and for all the pots that they typically use to carry water.[11] This served as an important motivational/inspirational point for many villagers and NGOs particularly in the initial stages. But what this vision left out was the fact that the project itself would finance only the installation of the main pipelines; the cost of the connections to the individual houses would have to be borne by the concerned households. Further, in certain regions, ecological/topographical factors would render inconceivable any consideration of supplying piped water. Hence, in the later stages of the project, there was a lot of disillusionment with the idea of piped water for all.[12]

Conclusion

Given the multifaceted nature of water, it is but natural that diverse disciplines have engaged with it. The discussion in this chapter has drawn on concepts from two such disciplines to show how one might make better sense of the ongoing changes in water policy, and especially of the relation between water reforms and neoliberalism.

166 ∻ *Priya Sangameswaran*

The illustrations used show that any engagement with neoliberalism is necessarily a difficult and challenging process because neoliberalism is about much more than just markets or privatization. But this very fact can also open up spaces for intervention. That is, critiquing water reforms and positing alternatives would be most effective if this is done across different scalar levels, along with the creation of new discourses about markets and economies, a focus on the power relations implicit in waterscapes and other practices in the water sector, as well as attention to both how beliefs and subjectivities are constituted and the concrete material effects resulting from them.

Notes

1. For a brief discussion of some of the new approaches in development studies, see, for instance, Gardner and Lewis (1996).
2. This debate was perhaps most heated in the 1970s; see, for instance, Schumacher (1973).
3. For a brief discussion of the concept of structure, see Sewell (1992). For a discussion of the concept of agency, particularly in the context of agrarian development, see Long and van der Ploeg (1994).
4. More specifically, Sivaramakrishnan and Agrawal (2003) propose the term "regional modernity." Although their aim is to discern patterns in the various local productions of modernity, one can also extend the concept to theorize the effects of globalization and neoliberalism.
5. Note that sometimes the logic also works in the opposite direction. That is, the scale becomes the justification for a particular level of capital investment, and therefore for borrowing from international institutions such as the World Bank, along with acceptance of the conditionalities that go with such borrowing.
6. Interview with a former member of Maharashtra Jeevan Pradhikaran, a parastatal agency for the provision of water in Maharashtra, July 15, 2007.
7. Interview with a member of the Reforms Support and Project Management Unit (the agency in charge of externally funded rural drinking water projects in Maharashtra), March 23, 2007.
8. Some of the other reasons were differences in the ability of the poor to make use of rules stipulating equality and their exclusion from decision-making bodies.
9. While Simon (1982) gives a brief introduction to Gramsci's ideas, Ekers and Loftus (2008) argue how understanding the state through the lens of Gramsci and Foucault would enrich the debates on urban water provision.

Scale, Diverse Economies, and Ethnographies of the State ≈ 167

10. Field work in Thane district of Maharashtra, May–June 2008.
11. This promise, and the fact that it was unrealistic and eventually led to disillusionment (due to reasons outlined below), came up in a discussion with a member of an NGO working in the *Jalswarjya* project in Maharashtra. This discussion took place during a visit to a village in the western part of the state where a similar promise had been made and not fulfilled (Field discussion, May 26, 2008).
12. Field work in Thane district of Maharashtra, May–June 2008.

References

Aiyer, Ananthakrishnan. 2007. "The Allure of the Transnational: Notes on Some Aspects of the Political Economy of Water in India," *Cultural Anthropology*, 22(4): 640–58.

Bhatia, Bela. 1992. "Lush Fields and Parched Throats: Political Economy of Groundwater in Gujarat," *Economic and Political Weekly*, 27 (51/52): A142–70.

Booth, David. 1993. "Development Research: From Impasse to a New Agenda," in Frans J. Schuurman (ed.), *Beyond the Impasse: New Directions in Development Theory*, pp. 49–76. London: Zed Books.

Briscoe, John and R. P. S. Malik. 2006. *India's Water Economy: Bracing for a Turbulent Future*. Washington: The World Bank and Oxford University Press.

Castree, Noel. 2005. "The Epistemology of Particulars: Human Geography, Case Studies and 'Context'," *Geoforum*, 36(5): 541–44.

Coelho, Karen. 2006. "The Slow Road to the Private: A Case Study of Neoliberal Water Reforms in Chennai." Paper presented at the workshop on "Water, Law and the Commons," organized by the International Environmental Law Research Centre at Society for Participatory Research in Asia (PRIA), December 8–10, New Delhi.

Dharmadhikary, Shripad. 2008. *The World Bank as a Knowledge Producer*. Badwani: Manthan Adhyayan Kendra.

Dubash, Navroz K. 2002. *Tubewell Capitalism: Groundwater Development and Agrarian Change in Gujarat*. New Delhi: Oxford University Press.

Dwivedi, Gautam, Rehmat, and Shirpad Dharmadhikary. 2006. *Water: Private, Limited*. Badwani: Manthan Adhyayan Kendra.

Ekers, Michael and Alex Loftus. 2008. "The Power of Water: Developing Dialogues between Foucault and Gramsci," *Environment and Development D: Society and Space*, 26(4): 698–718.

Etten, Jacobijn van, Barbara van Koppen and Shuku Pun. 2002. "Do Equal Land and Water Rights Benefit the Poor? Targeted Irrigation Development: The Case of the Andhi Khola Irrigation Scheme in Nepal." Working Paper 38, International Water Management Institute (IWMI), Colombo, Sri Lanka.

168　〜　*Priya Sangameswaran*

Gardner, Katy and David Lewis. 1996. *Anthropology, Development and the Post-Modern Challenge*. London: Pluto Press.

Gibson-Graham, J. K. 2002. "Beyond Global Versus Local: Economic Politics Outside the Binary Frame," in Andrew Herod and Melissa W. Wright (eds), *Geographies of Power: Placing Scale*, pp. 25–60. Malden: Blackwell.

Government of Maharashtra (GoM). n.d. "Vision for the Rural Water Supply and Sanitation Sector," Water Supply and Sanitation Department, GoM, http://mahawssd.gov.in/scripts/policies.htm (accessed September 26, 2007).

Gupta, Akhil. 1998. *Notes from Postcolonial Developments: Agriculture in the Making of Modern India*. Durham: Duke University Press.

———. 2003. "The Transmission of Development: Problems of Scale and Socialization," in K. Sivaramakrishnan and Arun Agrawal (eds), *Regional Modernities: The Cultural Politics of Development in India*, pp. 65–74. New Delhi: Oxford University Press.

Harvey, David. 2003. *The New Imperialism*. Oxford: Oxford University Press.

Herod, Andrew and Melissa W. Wright (eds). 2002. *Geographies of Power: Placing Scale*. Malden: Blackwell.

Larner, Wendy. 2000. "Neo-Liberalism: Policy, Ideology, Governmentality," *Studies in Political Economy*, 63: 5–25.

———. 2003. "Guest Editorial," *Environment and Planning D: Society and Space*, 21: 501–12.

Li, Tania Murray. 2001. "Boundary Work: Community, Market, and State Reconsidered," in Arun Agrawal and Clark C. Gibson (eds), *Communities and the Environment: Ethnicity, Gender and the State in Community-Based Conservation*, pp. 157–79. New Brunswick: The State University of New Jersey.

Long, Norman and Jan Douwe van der Ploeg. 1994. "Heterogeneity, Actor and Structure: Towards a Reconstitution of the Concept of Structure," in David Booth (ed.), *Rethinking Social Development: Theory, Research and Practice*, pp. 62–89. London: Longman Publishing Group.

Mansfield, Becky. 2007. "Privatization: Property and the Remaking of Nature–Society Relations," *Antipode*, 39(3): 393–405.

Sangameswaran, Priya. 2008. "Scale-Process Interplay in Water Policy in Western India". Paper presented at the workshop on Political Ecology, Department of Sociology, Delhi School of Economics, Delhi University, March 6–7, 2008.

Schumacher, E. F. 1973. *Small is Beautiful: A Study of Economics as if People Mattered*. London: Abacus.

Sewell, William H., Jr. 1992. "A Theory of Structure: Duality, Agency and Transformation," *American Journal of Sociology*, 98(1): 1–29.

Shah, Esha. 2008. "Resources, Rules and Technology: Ethnography of Building a Water Users' Association," in Vishwa Ballabh (ed.), *Governance*

Scale, Diverse Economies, and Ethnographies of the State ≈ 169

of Water: Institutional Alternatives and Political Economy, pp. 137–58. New Delhi: Sage Publications.

Shah, Tushaar. 1993. *Groundwater Markets and Irrigation Development: Political Economy and Practical Policy*. Bombay: Oxford University Press.

Sharma, Aradhana and Akhil Gupta (eds). 2006. *An Anthropology of the State: A Reader*. Oxford: Blackwell Publishing.

Simon, Roger. 1982. *Gramsci's Political Thought: An Introduction*. London: Lawrence and Wishart.

Sivaramakrishnan, K. and Arun Agrawal. 2003. "Regional Modernities in Stories and Practices of Development," in K. Sivaramakrishnan and Arun Agrawal (eds), *Regional Modernities: The Cultural Politics of Development in India*. New Delhi: Oxford University Press.

Swyngedouw, Erik. 2005. "Dispossessing H_2O: The Contested Terrain of Water Privatization," *Capitalism Nature Socialism*, 16(1): 81–98.

Swyngedouw, Erik and Nikolas C Heynen. 2003. "Urban Political Ecology, Justice and the Politics of Scale," *Antipode*, 35(5): 898–918.

Water and Sanitation Program-South Asia (WSP–SA). 2003. "24-hour Water Supply: Is this goal achievable?" in Nagari, Fifteenth Meeting of the Urban Think Tank, September 23–24, 2003, Hyderabad, India. New Delhi: WSP–SA, The World Bank.

Wood, Geoffrey D. and Richard Palmer-Jones, with Q. F. Ahmed, M. A. S. Mandal and S. C. Dutta. 1990. *The Water Sellers: A Cooperative Venture by the Rural Poor*. Connecticut: Kumarian Press.

8

Credit Conditionality and Strategic Sabotage

The Tale of the First Decade of Pakistan's Irrigation Reform

Muhammad Mehmood Ul Hasan

The water resource development in Pakistan has resulted in a number of small and large multipurpose reservoirs and 43 high-capacity main canals. These provide water for irrigation and hydroelectricity, and boost employment in the textile industry. At the same time, however, water resource development has displaced hundreds of thousands of families, caused salinization and water-logging in some areas, and depleted precious groundwater aquifers in others. The water scenario of Pakistan has been, and remains, a contested arena for several actors, including the agents representing various hierarchical levels of federal and provincial governments, farmers and rural communities, Non-Governmental Organizations (NGOs) and researchers, as well as international development agencies.

Most often, the policy and institutional changes in the water sector have been coincidental to the infrastructure development. For example, Pakistan's federal water authority emerged as an outcome of the Indus Basin Replacement Project. Since the macro-economic reforms pushed by the International Financial Institutions (IFIs) through their structural adjustment programs have generally affected the poorest segments more adversely (ActionAid 2006), it has become a natural tendency for the press and media to oppose and resist any advice regarding institutional reform that can be seen as coming from IFIs. The staunch critics of international aid agencies such as Bosshard (2007) tend to even blame the co-operation between the government and IFIs in the field of infrastructural development, for pursuing high-risk strategies that have triggered conflict, reinforced the deadlock in Pakistan's water sector and wasted valuable time and financial resources. In this backdrop, regardless of how good the designed policies are, their implementation usually remains contested. One could argue that policies are rarely fully implemented as designed and intended; rather what is implemented is the outcome of various negotiation processes taking place amongst the strategic groups (Hodgkinson 1997) of influential actors, with diverse and competing interests.

The latest water policy drafted in 2004 (GoP 2004) still awaits its implementation in full. Some elements of the new water policy such as statements on full cost pricing of water, increasing the storage potential, and devolving the management of irrigation systems to farmer's organizations and private sector have the potential to trigger further controversies amongst various strategic interest groups of the society, and become sticking points in policy implementation.

Irrigation sub-sector is the largest water user. The draft water policy confirms the expansion and further deepening of the on-going reform in the irrigation sub-sector. This chapter examines the emergence and implementation of water policy related to Irrigation Management Transfer (IMT), which had been the bone of contention amongst various actors in the water policy arena. The chapter restricts itself in large parts to the IMT experience in the Punjab province, the major part of Pakistan's irrigated area and thus the biggest user of water diverted for agricultural use.

Section 2 of the chapter briefly describes how IMT in Pakistan was conceived; Section 3 presents a few key design features of IMT and comments on its implementation; and Section 4 examines the IMT experience through the prism of key concepts in public policy research and concludes the discussion.

The Conception of IMT in Pakistan

In the 1990s, on the advice of the World Bank, Pakistan's government embarked on major institutional reforms in irrigation management. The original reform proposal by the World Bank (World Bank 1994) was too revolutionary for both the government and the farmers. It proposed to treat water as a tradable commodity rather than a public good, to create private water markets by disconnecting farmer's water rights from land, to divide the four provincial irrigation departments (PIDs) into 43 autonomous public utilities (PUs) one for each canal command area. It also proposed that the PUs should have a business-style management commensurate with the provisions of the Companies Ordinance 1984.

The provincial governments dismissed the World Bank proposal on the ground that it was divorced from reality (Nakashima 2005), and that its ideas did not match the prevalent socio-economic conditions in Pakistan (Haq et al. 1996). The federal government initiated discussions with the World Bank for improving the reform model. The discussions and debates continued until 1997, when finally the World Bank and the federal government agreed on a revised reform model.

The revised model envisaged a three-tier irrigation and drainage management structure (Ul-Hassan and Chaudhry 1998). Farmer Organizations (FOs), established through the representation of water users, were to supply water to irrigators, be responsible for operation and maintenance (O&M) of secondary irrigation canals and to levy and collect water charges. FOs had to pay the canal-level Area Water Boards (AWBs), the cost of supplying bulk water to them. The operating PU was to be the AWB, with an average command area of a million hectares (ha) which would manage and distribute irrigation water through formal volume-based contracts with FOs, and trade water with other utilities. The Provincial Irrigation and Drainage Authorities (PIDAs) would be responsible for such functions as province-wide water delivery, system maintenance and development, and sales of water beyond the amounts contracted with AWBs (Nakashima 2005; Ul-Hassan and Chaudhry 1998).

The Bank decided to influence the reform process through its disbursement mechanisms and made its US$ 800 million loan to the government under its National Drainage Program (NDP) conditional upon the latter's ability to promulgate reform legislation

Credit Conditionality and Strategic Sabotage ≋ 173

as proposed by the Bank. The federal government pushed the provincial governments to accept the reform proposal by making the disbursement of NDP funds conditional upon the progress demonstrated in carrying out the reform in the manner proposed by the Bank. Thus, the issue of reform remained a bone of contention between federal and provincial governments throughout the period of implementation (Dinar et al. 2004).

The Design and Implementation of IMT Policy

Objectives of IMTs

Global experience shows that either a serious breakdown in services, an environmental disaster affecting large numbers of people, a fiscal crisis making the status quo untenable, or a combination of some of these, usually drive IMTs (Vermillion and Sagardoy 1999). The irrigation and drainage sector of Pakistan had gone through profound changes since independence and was found to be trapped in a vicious cycle of "poor funding, poor maintenance, poor infrastructure condition, poor supply, poor productivity, poor recovery" (World Bank 1994). The water management and usage habits resulted in the lack of farmers' trust in the authorities, anarchy, inequity, and lack of transparency. The Bank identified these as the symptoms of deep-rooted problems of poor accountability and lack of transparency (Dinar et. al. 2004).

The surface irrigation and water supply services in Pakistan was managed as a virtual exclusive monopoly of government agencies which did not provide services to many—especially the tail-end farmers many of whom were smallholders (Hussain et al. 2004)—and provided poor quality services to those who already had access (Meinzen-Dick 1997). Merry (1996) attributes the lack of accountability in large irrigation systems in part to the management by bureaucracies. The overall situation in Pakistan was that the state agencies monopolizing the supply of water for public irrigation faced no competition, and the accountability was only upwards in so far as farmers were accountable to authorities for water use, but the authorities were not accountable to farmers for a quality water supply (Dinar et al. 2004). The status quo suited two important groups in the society, namely the irrigation department officials who were extracting rents from farmers by making water

174 ≋ *Muhammad Mehmood Ul Hasan*

artificially scarce and its supply unpredictable, and the influential landowners who would want to have as much water as they could get (Dinar et al. 2004). This situation provided opportunities for partnership between corrupt irrigation officials and big landowners both of whom would benefit from this symbiotic relationship. The big landowners would be ready to bribe irrigation officials and get water at the cost of smaller and relatively powerless farmers, and the corrupt irrigation officials would be ready to use their discretionary powers to provide this water to big landowners against kickbacks or favors like for transfers to financially lucrative government posts.

The essence of real reforms would be to reduce monopoly power of state agencies and introduce transparency in the allocation and distribution of water, thus greatly reducing the scope for exercise of discretionary powers and resultant corruption. The reforms had to be introduced with the explicit objective of redesigning irrigation management institutions in order to transform them from government monopolies to public utilities that would be responsible for sustainability of its assets, provision of quality irrigation and drainage services to its clients, and that would discharge its responsibilities in a business-like fashion with full accountability to its clients.

However, Punjab's reform legislation overlooked the essence of accountability. The preamble of the PIDA Act of 1997 (see Government of Punjab 1997: 1) conceived four key objectives of reform:

a. to implement the strategy of the government for streamlining the irrigation and drainage system;
b. to replace the existing administrative set-up and procedures with more responsive, efficient and transparent arrangements;
c. to achieve economical and effective operation and maintenance of the irrigation, drainage and flood control system in the province(s); and
d. to make the irrigation and drainage network sustainable on a long-term basis and introduce participation of beneficiaries in the operation and management.

Though references to responsiveness, transparency and efficiency are implicitly related to accountability in the PIDA Act, this legislation does not explicitly refer to making the bureaucracies accountable to users, which in part, reflects the lack of will of policy-makers to address the core issues for which the reforms were deemed essential.

Lack of Political Will and Resistance from Stakeholders

The media picked up the proposed reform and various stakeholders engaged themselves in a hot debate, questioning the rationale, modalities, as well as the perceived outcomes of the reform. For example, it was reported in the newspapers that the government was going to sell the irrigation canals to the World Bank (Nakashima 2005), and the farmers had the perception that the water charge for irrigation purposes would rise dramatically, and would be collected in advance (Bandaragoda et. al. 1997). People did not like, above all, the idea of a utility company, which would disconnect a water supply just because water charges were not paid on time (Nakashima 2005). There was strong resistance to the proposed reform program from the key stakeholders: irrigation bureaucracy, irrigation field staff and farmers.

The bureaucracy of the PIDs and their field staff feared the loss of their discretionary authority to distribute water and maintain irrigation systems. The influential farmers feared the loss of water that they had been receiving in excess of what had been authorized. Smaller farmers and tenants feared that water rates would go up and influential farmers would exploit them.

While the federal government agreed to the need for reform by signing the loan agreement, the PIDs did not quite share the same feeling. The federal government also gave mixed signals initially, for example by delaying the acceptance of offer from the Asian Development Bank (ADB) for formulating water sector strategy, as ADB had agreed to support the formulation of comprehensive national and provincial institutional and policy reforms and infrastructure development plans for all water sub-sectors. "The Government's lack of interest was perceived to cause a delay in its execution by almost three years. Only after a drought raised awareness of water issues, the follow-up missions of ADB was able to convince the Government of the need for the technical assistance and then the Government supported the technical assistance" (ADB 2005). The accounts of the reform donors (e.g., see ADB 2005; Dinar et al. 2004; World Bank 2005) and analysts (e.g., see Bandaragoda 1999, Bandaragoda 2006; Nakashima 2005; Shafique et al. 2001; Shah

176 ～ *Muhammad Mehmood Ul Hasan*

et al. 2000; van der Velde and Tirmizi 2001) indicate that the irrigation bureaucracies tried to sabotage the reform from the beginning. The engineers of the PIDs opposed the reform through their formal forums[1] (e.g., see Haq et al. 1996). They feared that reform would entail dissolution of their services and a breakdown of existing rent relationships (Shafique et. al. 2004; van der Velde and Tirmizi 2001). Another disincentive for the PID staff was that of leaving the relative security of service with the government for more novel contractual work with more transparent and accountable institutions (World Bank 2005). The PID staff obstructed the reform initially by considerably delaying the passage of the legislation (Bandaragoda 1999) and used various tactics to delay the handover of management to FOs until 2005, when the first FO was finally allowed to manage its canal in the AWB (Baig et al. 2008). The donors had to threaten to withdraw the loan (van der Velde and Tirmizi 2001) to make the first management transfer happen. Seeing that non-implementation was no more an option, the PID in Punjab strategically chose one of the most challenging irrigation systems to pilot the reform, wherein the farming communities were usually at odds with each other over water issues (e.g., see Malik et al. 1996)[2] and thus the likelihood of successful formation of FOs was too little.

Even those segments of farmers who were benefiting from the status quo had also opposed the reform (Nakashima 2005). The Farmer Association of Pakistan, a forum for the most influential farmers of Pakistan were the most opposed to change, since their members had been gaming with the system for decades (Dinar et al. 2004; van der Velde and Tirmizi 2001). Many accounts of reform in earlier years (e.g., see Nakashima 2005; Shafique et al. 2001; van der Velde and Tirmizi 2001) indicate that the reforms were felt to be failing because of inadequate top-level support, technical support to the farmers and vested interests of bureaucracy and influential farmers.

Legal Pluralism and the Resultant Controversies

A myriad of legislative acts govern irrigation and drainage systems in Pakistan, namely:

a. Provincial Canal and Drainage (PCAD) Acts of 1873
b. Water and Power Development Authority (WAPDA) Act of 1958

Credit Conditionality and Strategic Sabotage ≈ 177

c. Indus River System Authority (IRSA) Act of 1992
d. Environmental Protection Act (EPA) of 1997
e. The Punjab Soil Reclamation Act (PSRA) of 1952
f. Water Users Association (WUA) Ordinance of 1981
g. The Provincial Water Accord (PWA) of 1991
h. Provincial Irrigation and Drainage Authority (PIDA) Act of 1997

Enactment of reform legislation was a major success of the reform program as the provincial acts are legally binding. To demonstrate its commitment and support on paper, the Punjab PID went even further to issue legal rules and regulations for the operation of PIDA, AWBs and FOs, election rules for FOs, and guidelines for system operation and maintenance, etc. From PIDA's own viewpoint, these rules were meant to support and guide reform. However, formalizing everything endangered flexibility, innovativeness and dynamism, especially amongst the newly emerging and relatively inexperienced but enthusiastic FOs which felt constrained by too detailed dictations on how they should be carrying out their business (van der Velde and Tirmizi 2001).

Besides, there were contradicting, overlapping and overriding provisions in the laws mentioned above, which in certain cases caused confusions, misunderstanding and remained susceptible to misinterpretations (GoP 2004). There are clear tensions between the main irrigation and drainage legislations of provinces. For example, the PCAD of 1873, whose "overall tenor is that of a colonial document meant to facilitate control over a population than a legislation meant to facilitate efficient and equitable provision of a public service to the public" (Mustafa 2001), does not allow farmers to interfere in the irrigation system beyond the tertiary level. The PIDA Act of 1997, on the contrary, require farmer organizations to manage secondary canals. The PCAD Act would require farmers to report any interference by other farmers to irrigation departments, whereas the latter would require them to settle it themselves. The PIDA Act is silent on a legal situation of contradiction in clauses of these and earlier laws.

Besides, the PIDA Act specifies that

[a]ll employees of the Irrigation Wing of the Provincial Irrigation and Power Department except such employees as may be specified by the Government in this behalf shall, subject to any other provisions

178 ※ *Muhammad Mehmood Ul Hasan*

contained herein, on coming in force of this Act, become the employees of the Authority [and] the Area Water Boards have to become financially self-sufficient in 7–10 years from the passage of this act (Haq 1998: 122).

As of 2008, the irrigation wing of the PIDs and AWBs operated, as they used to during the past century, in the canal command areas. The pilot AWBs had not achieved financial self-sufficiency until 2007 as recommended by the law. One could argue that the lack of progress in converting the governmental monopolies into efficient PUs was a rather strategic attempt, as the PIDs "kept on debating modalities rather than focusing on instituting arrangements for transition management" (World Bank 2005). This legal plurality prevents IMT from being successful because of contradicting the essence of IMT by the earlier legislation, especially the PCAD Acts.

IMT Implementation

Punjab became the first province to present its PIDA bill in its provincial parliament and got it passed, albeit in a hurry by a single "stroke of pen" (World Bank 2005) and without much debate and understanding amongst the legislators. Other provinces had just waited for Punjab to pioneer, and then followed suit. Even after the passage of the legislation, political support for reform remained mixed, indicated by the frequent changes of the leadership of Punjab PIDA. The first leadership had provided a championing discourse in early years of reform, and the reforms slowed down and changed course after its replacement. The Punjab government replaced the leadership of the PID to speed up the reforms, once the World Bank again threatened to exclude Punjab from future investments.

In 2004, the Punjab PID recruited its own social mobilizers and quickly organized farmers into FOs within a span of one year, but these FOs proved to be rather symbolic and lacked enthusiasm for managing the irrigation and drainage systems. Blaming their unwillingness and incapacity, the PID assigned simpler, but socially negative roles of reporting offenders to FOs and called it "the Punjab Model of Reforms."[3] The FO members perceived this role as that of spying against their neighbors.[4] By 2003, the PIDA had installed an AWB and formed 85 FOs in the Lower Chenab Canal (LCC) East, but did not attempt until 2007 to ensure farmer's representation

Credit Conditionality and Strategic Sabotage ～ 179

in the AWB which played just an advisory role instead of AWB autonomously managing the canal command area.

Upon the donor pressure, PIDs focused only on the establishment of FOs, and to some degree AWBs. The contractual arrangements between FOs and AWBs remained one-sided and top-down, where FOs were accountable to AWBs and PIDAs, but not otherwise. The PIDA and AWB's rights to water remained unchallenged, while their obligations to deliver water to water user associations (WUAs) were not legally binding (World Bank 2005). Some analysts even argue that an alliance between water professionals, politicians and rich landowners existed to make sure that an informal rule system would override the formal law (Bandaragoda and Firdousi 1992). This alliance did not want the reform to transfer discretionary powers from the professional elite to the democratically elected FOs. The alliance made the reform negotiations between the majority of local stakeholders and the policy-makers extremely difficult and expensive (Bandaragoda 2006), so that the reforms were either withdrawn or implemented sub-optimally due to high transaction costs of implementation.

PIDAs still retain a number of discretionary powers, for example to cancel the contract, to declare some canal command areas exempt from water charges, etc. For the emerging AWBs and PIDAs to be accountable and transparent to their respective clients, it would require a clear contract between AWBs and FOs, which would define the rights and responsibilities for water supply and for payments to both parties. The absence of such contracts is one of the major reasons why PIDAs and AWBs still act as monopolies, as they remain unaccountable to users and information sharing remains very poor and opaque.

The later assessments of the Bank showed that "the reform effort failed to address the realities of political economy embedded in the profound changes the reforms sought" and that the overall performance of the effort "remained unsatisfactory" (World Bank 2005: 15), due to the following reasons:

a. The reforms focused too much on organizations and organizational designs, but completely ignored the instruments and incentives.
b. Lack of a detailed strategy for implementing the key elements of the reforms: the PIDA Acts envisaged a "stroke of the pen"

conversion of PIDs into PIDAs but lacked the knowledge of important details for implementing the reform strategy such as job transition for irrigation staff under new arrangements.

c. The donor's underlying assumption that transition plans, severance packages and change management arrangements would be defined and developed during implementation did not materialize due to constant distraction from other implementation issues and battles of turf and jurisdiction among the various participating agencies. Similarly, the naïve expectations that AWBs and PIDAs would introduce transparent volumetric measurements, bulk water sales, and water charges based on volume during implementation also did not materialize as they received far lower priority from the implementers than the easier-to-implement rehabilitation works.

d. From 1999 onwards, the prevailing drought and resulting water shortages dominated the water sector debate in Pakistan and the issues surrounding new storage proposals distracted the Government's attention from drainage and institutional reform issues.

Discussion and Conclusion[5]

There is a growing tendency amongst international financial institutions (IFIs), development donors, and technical co-operation agencies to undertake "lesson drawing"[6] from policy initiatives and practices of various sectors by looking at the potential for innovation by cross-sectoral and cross-national learning, and then carrying out "policy transfers." Policy transfer refers to the process in which knowledge about policies, administrative arrangements, institutions, etc., in one time and/or place is used in the development of policies, institutional arrangements and institutions in another time and/or place (Dolowitz and Marsh 1996). The earlier reform efforts about irrigation sponsored by IFIs in Chile, Mexico, Turkey and Egypt inspired the IMT policy in Pakistan, which provides an interesting case of the application of the above concepts.

The lesson-drawing exercises are useful in that these identify both the symptoms and the root causes of the existing policy failure, as these base themselves on a detailed analysis of the existing contextual setting, as was the case with the World Bank's analysis of the situation in Pakistan (World Bank 1994). While in the Bank's interpretation, the anarchy, chaos, and deterioration were all the symptoms, the core of the problem was identified as the monopolistic nature of irrigation institutions that lacked transparency in their operations and accountability to the clients (World Bank 2005). Therefore, the Bank through its proposal for policy transfer tried to argue for a reform model that not only treated symptoms, but also addressed the core problem of inducing accountability to clients. However, the Banks' own assessments indicated that the reforms had failed to address the fundamental issues (ibid.).

Since the policy transfer was directed towards breaking the monopoly of the most powerful stakeholders, i.e., the PIDs and the influential farmers who were benefiting from the status quo, they resisted and frustrated the reform strategically. The irrigation engineers brought their opposition to the table in course of their deliberations in the Engineering Congress (e.g., see Haq et al. 1996) and were reported to spread rumors that the irrigation and drainage system was being privatized in such a manner that small farmers would be deprived of their water (Ul-Hassan et al. 1998) and that water would become much more expensive that before. PIDs in their turn strategically delayed the reform by protracted discussions on modalities, by choosing pilot areas where reforms had the highest risks of failures due to non-cooperation of farmers, by making the operation of FOs too complicated through the imposition of detailed technical guidelines and complicated rules of business, etc. The rich farmers also obstructed formation of FOs and threatened the social mobilization staff wherever they could (Ul-Hassan et al. 1996). Later, when the rich farmers realized that the government would pilot the reform anyway due to its commitments to the donors, they managed to secure important positions in FOs in many cases (van der Velde and Tirmizi 2001). It is argued that a number of problems that have frustrated the reform effort could have been avoided, if the Bank itself would have learned the "lessons" from public policy research.

First, as is clear from the above analysis, the IMT policy in Pakistan was largely seen as a "policy irritant" (Teubner 1998), at least by the PIDs, one of the key stakeholders. The donor's style of carrying out "lesson drawing" exercises contributed much to creating such perceptions. A team of pertinent international and local consultants are engaged to carry out such exercises, generally comprising disciplinary sectoral experts, socio-economic experts,

182 〰 *Muhammad Mehmood Ul Hasan*

environmental experts and the like. The local consultants are usually highly knowledgeable about the local situation and its evolution, and the current challenges and issues facing the particular sector, whereas the international experts bring in knowledge about similar situations elsewhere. However, the staff of organizations under study sees the consultants as "outsiders." For example in case of carrying out a diagnostic analysis of irrigation service, a local consultant from federal government's WAPDA, a university staff member, or staff from a research institute not affiliated with PIDs would always be considered as an "outsider." Thus, the PID staff would regard his/her contributions to the analysis of a situation as partial, biased, and based on half-truths. Besides, the international experts' role is associated with connotations of "not contributing anything substantially new, rather crunching the old information provided by the organization in a new fashion."[7] Commenting on World Bank's proposal of 1994, a high-level technocrat in Pakistan, for example, characterized the consultant in 1997 as "a person, who borrows your watch, looks at it, tells you the time, and charges a very high fee for his service, and the Bank pays it in the name of service to our country." Therefore, the first reaction from the key PID staff to the critical recommendations and suggestions coming from such a team is likely to be met with some degree of skepticism. While the main stakeholders including the policy-makers would not challenge the main argument of the analysis as it would imply lack of interest in the loan, they would tend to challenge the proposals of the reforms. During the informal discussions in the presence of the researcher, statements like, "it will not work in our conditions," "Pakistan is not Mexico or Turkey," "the recommendations suit more to the Banks wishes rather than our reality," would usually be made by the high- and mid-level officials. While these statements might partly be true, such perceptions reflect the initial skepticism of the key governmental decision-makers from the donee country about the lessons from the "lesson drawing" exercises carried out in usual project identification exercise. One way of avoiding such perceptions would be to ensure that institutionalized arrangements exist for the inclusion of the perspectives of the recipient organizations in the "lesson drawing" exercises.

Second, the adoption of IMT policies in Pakistan represents a case of a "coercive policy transfer" as opposed to a "voluntary policy adoption" (Dolowitz and Marsh 1996) at all levels. State

Credit Conditionality and Strategic Sabotage ~ 183

bureaucracies are a key to the success of the reform in countries with large irrigation and drainage infrastructure like Pakistan (Scheumann 2002). The perceived lack of political will and support by state bureaucracies can be attributed to the coercive nature of the reform. The Bank forced the federal government to adopt IMT policy by attaching conditionality to further loan disbursement, and the federal government pursued the same strategies for ensuring compliance by the PIDs. One can argue that the partial success of IMTs was very much inherent in the coercive approach followed by the Bank who tried to push its design against the willingness of the recipients. Dolowitz (2000) identifies three main reasons for policy failure in policy transfer cases: *a*) uninformed transfer; *b*) incomplete transfer; and *c*) inappropriate transfer. In case of Pakistan, it appears that all the three reasons were quite evident when the debate started. The staff of the federal as well as provincial water administration had little or no knowledge of how to transform governmental monopolies into accountable and corporate-style PUs. They assumed that enactment of legislation would be enough to transform the irrigation bureaucracies into self-accounting PUs. The transition management was significantly delayed and did not start till 2007. The IMT policy simply ignored the crucial elements of PUs such as accountability-based contractual arrangements and detached property rights to water. Since the policy transfer was coerced, PIDs strategically focused more on relatively harmless elements of the policy lessons, i.e., organizational designs and arrangements of FOs and AWBs (World Bank 2005) to demonstrate compliance with loan conditionality, but completely ignored the need to devise and introduce reform instruments that could reduce its monopoly power. The PIDs ignored attending to: *a*) assignment of clear water rights for FOs; *b*) making AWBs accountable to FOs; and *c*) putting in place strategies for capacity-building of FOs, AWBs, and PIDAs to undertake their jobs in a new fashion.

Thirdly, the initial opposition and resistance from the bureaucracy should have been understood as an indicator that the policy-learning by PIDs would be rather overly backward and conservative. PIDs would never transform of their own unless their current path dependencies (Pierson 2000) of being an engineering organization were altered before the reforms.

Finally, and perhaps more importantly, a governmental bureaucracy that has its roots in the colonial system of administration

184　�　*Muhammad Mehmood Ul Hasan*

(Mustafa 2001), would not easily give up its authority and powers to farmers and be accountable to those farmers many of whom were uneducated. A reform design based on drawing lessons from elsewhere and expectation that such a bureaucracy would reform itself proved to be too naive to create the targeted service-oriented PU that would be accountable to its clients, whom it had been considering as beneficiaries. The policy transfer exercise as perceived by donors in this particular case was not as successful as envisaged by the international donors. A successful policy transfer in this case would require a facilitated in-depth joint problem analysis by various groups of providers and users of the service. Such a problem analysis should focus on yielding a collaborative action plan for addressing and eliminating both the symptoms and the deep-rooted causes of underperformance, and then putting in place transparent mechanisms to undertake the proposed reforms. The implementation of such actions should have been jointly monitored and evaluated by all stakeholders; the criteria and indicators should have addressed both the quantity and quality aspects of performance. The failed policy transfer in this case can therefore be explained by inappropriate, inadequate and uninformed policy transfer as shown in this chapter. To make future policy transfers successful, the donors need to look at the process of policy transfer and make context-specific adjustments to their policy transfer exercises.

Notes

1. Engineering Congress is a professional forum for engineers and a large majority of its membership is from the irrigation engineers from various provinces.
2. For example, Malik et al. (1996) in their study of six watercourses in the Junejwala minor canal of the LCC East canal report that the top three most frequent disputes were related to water.
3. Staff member of PIDA monitoring unit, pers. comm., 2005.
4. Ibid.
5. The chapter deliberately does not provide references to the statements made by officials for the sake of respect for anonymity of the sources of information.
6. See Rose (1991) for a detailed account of the concept and James and Lodge (2003) for a critique.
7. Several high- and mid-level water officials in the provincial and federal capitals referred to this perception during their private interactions with the researcher during 1995–99.

References

ActionAid. 2006. Report of the Regional Conference on "Impact of Economic Globalization on Women's Work & Empowerment Issues," November 22–23, Islamabad, http://www.docstoc.com/docs/21488787/Effects-of-Economic-Globalization-on-Womens-Work-and-Empowerment (accessed July 31, 2012).

Asian Development Bank (ADB). 2005. *Technical Assistance Completion Report: 3130-PAK-Water Resources Strategy Study.* Islamabad: ADB.

Baig, I. A., M. Ashfaq, S. Hassan, and K. Mushtaq. 2008. "Impact of Financial Reforms in Irrigation Sector of Punjab, Pakistan," *Journal of Animal and Plant Sciences*, 18(4): 145–50.

Bandaragoda, D. J. 1999. *Institutional Change and Shared Management of Water Resources in Large Canal Systems: Results of an Action Research Program in Pakistan.* Research Report 36. Colombo: International Water Management Institute (IWMI).

———. 2006. "Limits to Donor-driven Water Sector Reforms: Insight and Evidence from Pakistan and Sri Lanka," *Water Policy*, 8(1): 51–67.

Bandaragoda, D. J. and G. R. Firdousi. 1992. "Institutional Factors Affecting Irrigation Performance in Pakistan: Research and Policy Priorities." International Irrigation Management Institute (IIMI) Country Paper–Pakistan 4, IIMI, Colombo.

Bandaragoda, D. J., M. Ul-Hassan, M. A. Cheema, Z. L. Mirza and Waheed-Uz-Zmana. 1997. *Organizing Water Users for Distributary Management: Preliminary Results from a Pilot Study in the Hakra 4-R Distributary of the Eastern Sadiqia Canal System of Pakistan's Punjab Province.* Research Report R-25. Lahore: Pakistan National Program, IIMI.

Bosshard, P. 2007. "The World Bank and Pakistan's Water Sector: A Recipe for Conflict and Deadlock," http://www.wdev.eu/wearchiv/53168697580b82701.php (accessed July 31, 2012).

Deutsch, K. 1963. *The Nerves of Government: Modles of Political Political Communication and Control.* New York: Free Press.

Dinar, A., T. K. Balakrishnan and J. K. Wambia. 2004. "Politics of Institutional Reforms in the Water and Drainage Sector of Pakistan," *Environment and Development Economics*, 9(3): 409–45.

Dolowitz, D. 2000. "Introduction," *Governance*, 13(1): 1–4.

Dolowitz, D. and D. Marsh. 1996. "Who Learns What from Whom: A Review of Policy Policy Transfer Literature," *Political Studies*, 44(2): 343–57.

———. 2000. "Learning from Abroad: The Role of Policy Transfer in Contemporary Policy-Making," *Governance*, 13(1): 5–24.

Government of Pakistan (GoP). 2004. *National Water Policy* (draft), http://cms.waterinfo.net.pk/pdf/NationalWaterPolicy.PDF (accessed July 31, 2012).

Government of Punjab. 1997. "Punjab Irrigation and Drainage Act, 1997," in *Provincial Gazette*. Lahore, Pakistan: Punjab Printing Press.

186 ～ *Muhammad Mehmood Ul Hasan*

Haq, A. U. 1998. *Case Study of the Punjab Irrigation Department: Consultancy Report.* Lahore: Pakistan National Program, IIMI, Lahore.

Haq, A. U., B. A. Shahid and A. Ul-Haq. 1996. "Privatization and Commercialization of Irrigation Management: Are the New Strategies Workable in Pakistan's Setting?," in *Proceedings of the Pakistan National Engineering Congress,* September 22–24, 1996, Pakistan Engineering Council, Lahore.

Hodgkinson, G. P. 1997. "The Cognitive Analysis of Competitive Structures: A Review and Critique," *Human Relations,* 50(6): 625–54.

Hussian, I., M. Mudasser, M. A. Hanjra, U. Amrasinghe and D. Molden. 2004. "Improving Wheat Productivity in Pakistan: Econometric Analysis Using Panel Data from Chaj in the Upper Indus Basin," *Water International,* 29(2): 189–200.

James, O. and M. Lodge. 2003. "The Limitations of 'Policy Transfer' and 'Lesson Drawing' for Public Policy Research," *Political Studies Review,* 1(2):179–93.

Malik, S., W. U. Zaman and M. Kuper. 1996. "Farmer's Organized Behaviour in Irrigated Agriculture of Pakistan's Punjab: A Case Study of Six Watercourse Command Areas in June Jwala Minor, Lower Chenab Canal System." Working Paper 39, IIMI, Colombo.

Meinzen-Dick, R. 1997. "Farmer Participation in Irrigation: 20 Years of Experience and Lessons for the Future," *Irrigation and Drainage Systems,* 11(2): 103–18.

Merry, D. J. 1996. "Institutional Design Principles for Accountability in Large Irrigation Systems." Research Report 8. Colombo: IWMI.

Mosse, D. 2003. *The Rule of Water: Statecraft, Ecology and Collective Action in South India.* London: Oxford University Press.

Mustafa, D. 2001. "Colonial law, Contemporary Water Issues in Pakistan," *Political Geography,* 20: 817–37.

Nakashima, M. 2005. "Pakistan's Institutional Reform of Irrigation Management: Initial Conditions and Issues for the Reform," www.intl. hiroshima-cu.ac.jp/~nakashim/Nakashima/PakHJIS.pdf (accessed July 31, 2012).

Pierson, P. 2000. "Increasing Returns, Path Dependencies, and the Study of Politics," *American Political Science Review,* 94(2): 251–67.

Rose, R. 1991. "What is Lesson Drawing?," *Journal of Public Policy,* 11(1): 3–30.

Scheumann, W. 2002. *Institutional Reform in the Irrigation Sector: The Cases of Turkey and Pakistan.* Bonn: German Development Institute.

Shafique, M. S., W. Clyma and M. A. Gill. 2001. "Institutional Reforms in the Agricultural Sector." Paper 012054, 2001, American Society of Agricultural and Biological Engineers (ASABE), http://asae.frymulti. com/abstract.asp?aid=7311&t=2 (accessed September 25, 2008).

Shah, T., I. Hussain and S. U. Rehman 2000. "Irrigation Management in Pakistan and India: Comparing Notes on Institutions and Policies." Working Paper 4, IWMI, Colombo.

Teubner, G. 1998. "Legal Irritants: Good Faith in British Law or How Unifying Law Ends up in New Divergences," *Modern Law Review*, 61(1): 11–32.

Ul-Hassan, M. and M. G. Chaudhry. 1998. "Assessing Water Charges in the Changing Irrigation Management in Pakistan: A Methodological Framework," *The Pakistan Development Review*, 37(1): 1–17.

Ul-Hassan, M., Z. L. Mirza, and D. J. Bandaragoda. 1996. *Mobilizing Social Organization Volunteers: An Initial Methodological Step towards Establishing Effective Water Users' Organizations.* Research Report R-9. Lahore: Pakistan National Program, IIMI.

Van der Velde, E. and J. Tirmizi. 2001. "Irrigation Policy Reforms in Pakistan: Who's Getting the Process Right?," in P. Mollinga and A. Bolding (eds), *The Politics of Irrigation Reforms: Contested Policy Formulation and Implementation in Asia, Africa and Latin America*, pp. 207–39. Aldershot, England: Ashgate Publications.

Vermillion, D. and J. A. Sagardoy. 1999. "Transfer of Irrigation Management Services: Guidelines." Food and Agriculture Organization (FAO) Irrigation and Drainage Paper 58, FAO, Rome.

World Bank. 1994. *Pakistan Irrigation and Drainage: Issues and Options.* Report 1184-PAK. New York: Agriculture and Rural Development Unit, South Asia Region, International Bank for Reconstruction and Development (IBRD).

―――. 2005. *Pakistan Country Water Resources Assistance Strategy.* Report 34081PK. New York: Agriculture and Rural Development Unit, South Asia Region, IBRD.

PART III

Water and Climate Change

Newer Dimensions That Should Shape Water Policies

9

Hydro-Hazardscapes of South Asia

Redefining Adaptation and Resilience to Global Climate Change

Daanish Mustafa

Epistemological commitment to reactive mitigation of hydro-hazards and adaptation to modeling scenarios of high-end climate science are likely to have limited efficacy in the South Asian cultural, institutional and developmental context. The almost universal hegemony of narrowly defined developmental and technocratic discourses at the policy level, coupled with pervasive poverty, cultural diversity and multiple drivers of vulnerability at the local level in South Asia, is a major challenge to the transference of a Western agenda of adaptation to climate change. The need is for changing the modernist *monologue* on vulnerability and adaptation into a *dialogue* wherein high-end scientific research and policy-making can draw lessons from and contribute to the vulnerable populations' everyday strategies of adapting to and coping with hydro-hazards as well as their struggles for diversified and stable livelihoods. In this chapter I use the idea of "hazardscapes" that I had proposed in my earlier work (2005) as a conceptual lens to apprehend the pattern of vulnerability to hydro-meteorological extremes and water issues

192 ≈ *Daanish Mustafa*

in Pakistan. In this chapter I propose that vulnerability and its alter-ego, resilience, if suitably redefined and recentered between the three communities of practice—climate change policy, water resources and hazards management—can be useful concepts around which integrated pro-poor development, which reduces vulnerability and enhances resilience against climate change, can be conceived and practiced.

In addition to the above, there are other substantial challenges to successful adaptation to climate change in South Asia, not the least of which is the role of South Asian communities of practice as consumers of knowledge generated in the North on climate change, mitigation, and adaptation. The role of South Asian academic and policy communities will continue to be that of passive consumers of knowledge, unless they engage with the largest repository of experiential environmental knowledge and resource management skills in their midst—the rural and urban underclass of farmers, artisans, fishermen, healers and entrepreneurs of South Asia. This is not to romanticise some a-historical miracle-working indigenous wisdom, but rather an invitation to engage in a dialogue between the high-end science and everyday strategies of livelihood and resource management of the people so as to enrich both. Following Wescoat (1991), I propose a different approach towards adaptation to climate change and generation of knowledge on the environment and development problematique that will be more suitable to the South Asian context.

In the following section, by drawing upon appropriate literature, I outline the conceptual framework for analyzing case studies of drought and groundwater management, urban flood plain management and surface irrigation water management in Pakistan. I then proceed to review evidence from the case studies to substantiate my theoretically modest but practically ambitious claims.

Defining the Hydro-Hazardscapes and their Discontents

The case studies draw their intellectual capital from the tradition of research in hazards, water and climate change within the discipline of human geography. This approach within human geography pioneered by the American geographer Gilbert White and his students has spawned multiple intellectual perspectives to engage with hazards. This academic tradition that White was associated with,

Hydro-Hazardscapes of South Asia ≋ 193

posits that beyond engineering approaches to water management or controlling the impact of physical extremes, attention must be paid to the role of perception in influencing individual and collective behavior towards hazards and water management (White 1945; Kates and Burton 1986 a and b; Whyte 1986). Researchers of hazards in the tradition of political ecology have further moved on to focus on socially determined vulnerability as a key variable affecting the distribution and intensity of loss suffered by victims of hazards. They have been concerned with the politico-economic contexts that define differential vulnerability (Watts 1983; Wisner 1993; Blaikie et al. 1994; Mustafa 1998, 2002a; Pelling 2003).

The conceptual approach of these case studies combines the insights of the two hazards research traditions within human geography described above and uses the integrative concept of a "hazardscape" to apprehend the complexities of vulnerability, disaster-response and disaster-recovery. Elsewhere, I have defined the term "hazardscape" as

> simultaneously an analytical way of seeing, which asserts power, and a social space where the gaze of power is contested and struggled against to produce the lived reality of hazardous places. Hazardscapes are therefore constitutive of the ideological filters used to view hazardous spaces and the produced social spaces where those ideologies are contested and struggled over (Mustafa 2005: 570).

The above definition suggests that vulnerability profiles and strategies of hazard mitigation in specific geographic localities are the outcome of the various stakeholders' perceptions regarding the root causes of disasters and their cultural and institutional biases on what to do about them. Different stakeholders within a hazardscape have varying levels of social power and clash of ideas between them spawn the material configuration of the hazardscape. This perspective highlights the importance of perceptions of all stakeholders and how varying social power of stakeholders can create obstacles and opportunities for social actors to pursue policy-level and community-level interventions for reducing risk and vulnerability, or encouraging adaptation to changing nature and incidence of hazards including those effected by climate change.

For managing the Indus basin in the context of global climate change, Wescoat (1991) proposed four conceptual approaches–

194 ≋ *Daanish Mustafa*

climate scenario assessment, critical water management problems, historical antecedents and analogies and Muslim political reconstruction–in the first volume of, what is now a flagship journal, *Global Environmental Change.* Of the four approaches, climate scenario assessment has received the most attention and funding. The glamorous high-end science of atmospheric physics, cutting-edge computing, and General Circulation Modelling (GCMs) are the main tools of studying climate change that we know about and use. While many policy-makers in the poorer countries of the South pay polite attention to these tools, especially when donor money for climate-related programs is involved, there is little attempt at internalization or little realization of the urgency of climate change science and scenarios based on that science. Instead, the focus of the policy-makers and the people in the South are on critical water management problems. Wescoat (1991) argues that maybe engaging with present-day water management issues is a better guarantee for future resilience to climate change.

However, the cultures and populations of South Asia are no strangers to the vagaries of climate. There is a wealth of anecdotal, historical and proto-historical knowledge to be harvested on how communities and societies have coped with such vagaries (Wescoat 1991).

And finally in a cultural mode, I restate what Wescoat (1991) calls "Muslim political reconstruction" as "politico-cultural reconstruction" because it applies to all religious and cultural communities in South Asia. In making a case for this cultural approach, he alludes to the set of ethical and cultural standards of society, violation of which under the conditions of (forced?) developmental modernity is causing the problems that we are witnessing. I agree with his argument that the cultural approach has the utmost potential to modify behavior at the grass roots level in response to climate change.

Productivity Maximization versus Resilience in Groundwater Management in Pakistan

To revisit queries about the need for technological transitions from traditional to modern water management systems is desirable, inevitable, or part of the inexorable process of development. I outline the social, environmental and economic consequences of transition from the ancient *karez* system to the modern electric tube well technology in the Balochistan province of Pakistan. This change has been initiated to engage with the problematic of productivity maximization versus resilience as a core objective of groundwater development in Pakistan.

Karez irrigation is an ancient system of underground water channels where water flows in by gravity from the "mother well" dug into the water table (Figure 9.1). The water channel is underground for a distance of a few hundred meters to a few kilometers before it emerges from the ground at the "day-light point." The underground channel has a series of wells for the purpose of maintenance. Water can be used for irrigation and other purposes only from the daylight point onwards. The slope of the *karez* canals is less than that of the surrounding land and the water table, and one of the main advantages of the system is that it significantly reduces the otherwise heavy water loss due to evaporation. Because the *karez* system depends on passive tapping of groundwater, the water supply from it varies with changes in groundwater levels and does not pose a threat to the natural water balance. However, the system is under threat from modern tubewell pumps in Balochistan (van Steenbergen and Oliemans 2002), just as it is on steady retreat from

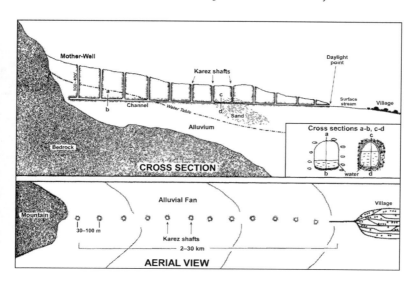

Figure 9.1: Schematic diagram of a *karez* or *qanat*

Source: Prepared by the author.

196 ≋ *Daanish Mustafa*

most of the other places where it is practiced (Lightfoot 1996 a and b; Beaumont et al. 1989). The tube well pumping has excessively lowered the water table in Balochistan, so much so that the mother wells of most *karez*es have gone dry.

Karez system has been the locus of social organization in the semi-arid environment of Balochistan. Very well-established rules of collective management, water distribution and conflict resolution have evolved around *karez* management. A select person, or a group of persons are responsible for the enforcement of rules of *karez* management, as well as for the maintenance and expansion of *karez*, and handling of other water-related issues including enforcement of the *harim* rule (under which an exclusion zone of 1500 feet from the *karez* is demarcated where no additional *karez* wells or tube wells can be constructed). In Balochistan, the person responsible for *karez* management is known as *Mir-e-aab* (water leader) or *Rais*. The *Mir-e-aab* is member of the village elite and occasionally the village head himself. His–the person is invariably male–source of authority and standing in the community is with regard to water management, the basis of rural economic life in the semi-arid Balochistan.

Karez water is perpetually flowing and is distributed among the shareholders on the basis of a fixed time rotation system. A cycle of water distribution typically ranges from 12–22 *shabana*s (24-hour cycles). The *shabana*s are further subdivided into three-hour increments locally known as *pass*. There are active water markets in *karez* water, and sometimes a privately or communally held *shabana* of water when auctioned can fetch as much as PKR 190,000 (US$ 3,200 approx.). This money in case of communally held *shabana*s goes towards *karez* maintenance, as do the annual cash contributions of shareholders, and occasional government grants. The *karez* shares are well established and well known, with the result that conflict over *karez* water share is virtually unknown (Mustafa and Qazi 2007). The substitution of *karez* by tube well irrigation has often led to mostly intra–but also some inter-community conflict. A tube well is expensive to install and has high operation and maintenance costs as electricity is expensive. It is more restrictive in use and cash-dependent. Further, as a result of its use, there has been a decline in the water table, water wastage is high and soil erosion higher (Mustafa and Qazi 2008).

Balochistan province in Pakistan, much like the rest of the country and the global South has been a venue for development praxis.

Hydro-Hazardscapes of South Asia ∷ 197

Development in the sense of modernization, increased economic productivity and social transformation is a dominant feature of the water resources policy discourse and practice (Wescoat et al. 2000; Shah et. al. 2003). As early as the 1970s Western management consultants and Pakistani water engineers identified *karez* system as an overly wasteful water management system and technology because of the apparent wastage of constantly flowing water in the *karez*es without any productive or high-value use expect during the summer growing season (van Steenbergen 2002). However, this assessment did not take into account the other uses of the flowing *karez* water particularly for women in their domestic chores and for farm animals, as documented by Meinzen-Dick and van der Hoek (2001). The greater nationwide emphasis in the realm of groundwater management was on promoting tube well installation through soft loans, and mostly through subsidized electricity. In case of Balochistan, flat electricity charges were levied on tube wells regardless of the duration of use. The Pakistan government's attempts at promoting groundwater exploitation with electric tube wells were successful beyond expectations. The subsidies on tube well installation and electricity were largely withdrawn or cut in the three other provinces of Pakistan in the 1990s, except in Balochistan, where they continue to this day.

The promotion of tube well irrigation in Balochistan is deemed to be part of the larger project of modernizing and thereby developing agriculture in rural Balochistan. Even the local water users are quite cognizant of the modernist and modernizing underpinnings of the diffusion of tube well technology:

> Our elders tell us that in olden times there was so much water in the *karez* that people working far away in the fields would receive their mid-day meals through the *karez*. The women folk would put food in a buoyant sealed container called "Danko," and put it in the *karez* near them. The *karez* would then take the containers to the farmers working downstream. Now those were the days! Nowadays times have changed, *new technology is coming in, with new machines, and new people who like latest machines.* The traditional irrigation is progressively being forgotten.[1]

The consequences of the general adoption of tube wells and the subsidies on electricity have meant that all the water users compete with each other in drawing as much groundwater as possible. The

198 ※ *Daanish Mustafa*

consequently declining water tables have caused considerable alarm among the farmers as well as the policy-makers, but yet have not instigated any concrete action to prevent it. The decline in water tables has also led to rural-to-urban migration and pauperization of small farmers.

Large farmers have become more powerful and prosperous, and there has been a breakdown of social capital, which had been built around *karez* water management. There has been a greater integration of rural Balochistan into the monetary economy of Pakistan. On the other hand, water quality for domestic use has improved and the tubewells have helped in coping with the drought and sustaining some livelihoods. However, majority of the people in Balochistan, however, still maintain that *karez* system was better for them and that the system can be and should be saved from extinction (Mustafa and Qazi 2007).

The *karez* system has sustained community life, economic well-being and ecological balance in Balochistan through various natural climatic variations for millennia. Therein lies the proof of its relevance for a future with human-induced climate change. However, attitudes towards and technologies of resource management in moist regions are being uncritically applied in the arid areas. The society and ecology of drylands will be all the more vulnerable to climate change as a consequence. Studies by Mustafa and Qazi (2007, 2008) reveal that the transition from *karez* to tube well irrigation was neither inevitable nor necessarily more advantageous, but rather the outcome of deliberate policy choices by the government. The diffusion of tube wells is weakening the traditional resilience of the local communities to episodic manifestations of environmental stress, such as droughts. The richer farmers might be able to take advantage of non-local income generation opportunities and supplement income from agriculture involving locally intensive and non-sustainable water use. But the local poor who are doubly dependent upon local resources and accompanying social capital around those resources are at a particular disadvantage (Desakota Study Team 2008). Pro-poor policies of agrarian adaptation to climate change will have to take into account the changing context of resource use.

At the policy level, the differential power of the discourse of modernization, coupled with the social influence of rich farmers, is facilitating rapid diffusion of tube wells in Balochistan. The transition from *karez* to tube well irrigation has negative consequences for social equity and environmental quality. The current problem of declining water tables because of over-pumping of groundwater with tube wells is illustrative of the types of stresses that agro-ecological system in Balochistan is likely to face in the wake of the impact of climate change in the future.

I argue that climate change research agenda at its core is really about adaptation to an increasingly uncertain future. Modern groundwater management techniques, much the same as in other sectors, are predicated upon an understanding of the hazardscape of Balochistan where past environmental averages will prevail in the future. The local farmers on the other hand are aware of and concerned about uncertainty inherent in the dryland hazardscape. Most of the local poor deem socio-cultural continuity that entailed strong bonds of reciprocity, as key to resilience to droughts. Accumulative development strategies based on technocratic hazardscapes with a narrow vision of development and modernization are likely to render the future of fragile drylands like Balochistan much more perilous in any future climate change scenario.

Debating Surface Irrigation in the (Post-) Dog-Days of Engineering in Pakistan

The semi-arid environment of the Indus basin is home to more than a quarter of a billion people with some of the lowest human development indicators in the world (UNDP 2002). Given the stakes involved, in terms of the survival of millions of people inhabiting the area, the Indus basin has been a veritable laboratory for international and national research on various problems of water distribution, development, and management especially as they pertain to issues of water efficiency, equity, hazards and environmental quality (Michel 1967; Mustafa and Wescoat 1997; van Steenbergen and Oliemans 2002; Wescoat et al. 2000).

The massive water development carried out in both India and Pakistan as part of the Indus Basin Water Development Project in the aftermath of the Indo-Pakistan Indus Basin Treaty in 1960, was a temporary boon to agricultural water supplies in the basin. Furthermore, the changing demographics of the basin with the rise in urban population, and the widening of the international water resources agenda from a singular focus on water development to equity in water resources, water management, environmental quality

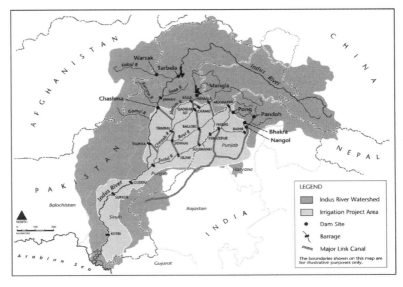

Map 9.1: Indus basin and its major infrastructure

Source: Department of Geography, King's College, London. Used with permission.

and domestic water supply and sanitation meant that the old recipe of responding to growing demands for water and hydro-hazards with more water development projects was no longer as readily practicable (Wescoat et al. 2000). The water bureaucracies in the basin being dominated by engineers with a very strong institutional bias towards mega water development projects continue to operate as if the multipoint agenda of flood prevention, ecosystem health, upstream–downstream conflict resolution and livelihood resilience with regard to water resources, can only be addressed by more engineering interventions (Mustafa 2002b). Much of the adaptation challenges in the Indus basin and the conflicts arising over water can be understood, at least partially with reference to this dissonance between the multidimensional demands on water resources by the public, international donors, and politicians, and unidimensional solutions offered by the basin's water managers.

The Indus hazardscape is characterized by the aforementioned dissonance between the engineers' perception of the river as a source of water to be controlled, and the multidimensional public perception of it as a source of hazard, resource, and conduit for negotiating ethno-national identity. The inter-provincial water conflict between upstream Punjab and downstream Sindh is an exemplar of this hazardscape. The first substantial inter-provincial water allocation treaty between Punjab and downstream riparian Sindh dates back to 1945, which allocated 75 percent of the waters of the main-stem Indus River to Sindh with the remainder going to Punjab. The treaty further allocated 94 percent of the water from the five eastern tributaries of Indus to Punjab, with the residual water going to Sindh (Michel 1967, Talpur 2001). The partition of the Indo–Pak subcontinent in 1947 and the subsequent signing of the Indus Basin Treaty by India and Pakistan in 1960 allocated most of, what was once Punjab's share of the Indus basin waters according to the 1945 Sindh–Punjab Agreement to India, and provided for construction of storage and link canals from the western half of the Indus basin to the eastern half to compensate for the water lost to India. The proposed Kalabagh Dam on Indus in the Punjab province of Pakistan is highly controversial[2] and perceived by the Sindhis as yet another insult to the long series of injuries that Punjab province has inflicted on them by appropriation of Sindh's rightful share of water (Mustafa 2007a).

The official argument in favour of the construction of the Kalabagh Dam on Indus paints the picture of a scarce water resource being wasted by being allowed to flow out to the sea, and spells a doomsday scenario should additional storage not be built on Indus (GoP 2005). The controversy is beginning to polarize the public opinion in Pakistan, particularly in the Sindh province, in the aftermath of the drought in southern Pakistan in the latter half of the 1990s that resulted in severe water scarcity.

The drought, coupled with single-minded focus of the Pakistani water bureaucracy on water development, has made the issue of Kalabagh Dam project and the existing water scarcity in the Sindh province a surrogate for a litany of Sindhi grievances against a Punjabi-dominated political, military and bureaucratic system in Pakistan (e.g., see Eckholm 2003). On the other hand, for the Pakistani water managers, Kalabagh Dam has become a metaphor for the persistent meddling of the "untrained" and "non-expert" politicians in what they perceive or wish to be a purely engineering issue. The dam project at the moment is in cold storage particularly on account of the combined opposition of not just Sindh, but the provinces of Khyber-Pakhtunkhwa (formerly North Western Frontier Province)

202 ≋ *Daanish Mustafa*

and Balochistan as well. Sindh is also reluctant to lend its support to the project because of its suspicions based on the poor record of the Pakistani government in providing for the rehabilitation of those displaced by the earlier large dam construction projects.

In addition to the objections raised by smaller provinces to the construction of additional storage canals on Indus, convincing arguments have also been made by environmental and citizen groups in Pakistan, pointing out that Pakistan's irrigation sector has some of the lowest conveyance efficiencies in the world. Furthermore, others (e.g., Mustafa 2002a, 2002c, 2007a) have argued that the key issue in surface water irrigation in the Indus basin is equity at the local level, which is unlikely to be addressed by dams.

Paying attention to the immediate problems of inequity and inefficiency in the surface water management system of Pakistan, according to Wescoat (1991), will be a more appropriate approach to building resilience to future climate change. A coupling of critical water problems approach and the hazardscape approach which broadens the parameters of the discourse from purely engineering concerns to wider social, cultural, environmental, equity- and justice-related concerns about water resources is more relevant for the Indus basin.

Urban Hazardscapes

The Rawalpindi/Islamabad conurbation is the fifth most populous urban area in Pakistan with a combined population of 2.1 million, including 1.5 million in Rawalpindi and the remaining in Islamabad (GoP 2000). As the capital of Pakistan, Islamabad houses all the administrative structures of the federal government, while Rawalpindi is the headquarters of the Pakistan Army, the most important institution in Pakistan. Flood hazard in the local stream Lai is endemic for the twin cities. Most recently, Lai flooded on July 24, 2001, affecting 400,000 residents of the twin cities, mainly people of the poorest class. The death toll stood at 74, including 64 fatalities in the downstream city of Rawalpindi (The United Nations Relief Web 2001). The official estimate of the damages from the flood stands at PKR 15 billion (approximately US$ 250 million), though unofficial estimates have been as high as INR 53 billion (approximately US $ 930 million) – an enormous sum of money for a country with a total official GDP of US$ 60.5 billion (World Bank 2003;

JICA 2003). In the recent past, Lai also flooded in 1995, 1996, and 1997; 1997 calamity caused 84 fatalities and destroyed 1,000 houses (NEC 2002).

The Lai basin drains a total area of 244 sq. km south of the Margalla hills, with 55 percent of the watershed falling within the Islamabad Capital Territory and the remaining portion within the

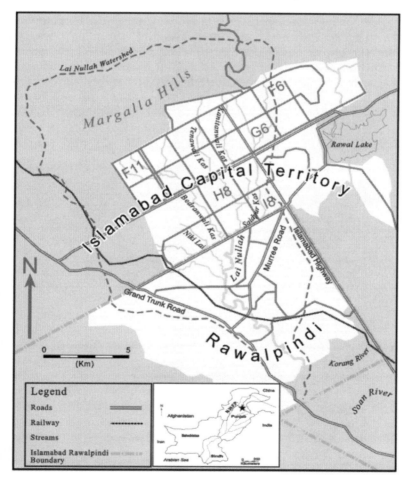

Map 9.2: Rawalpindi/Islamabad conurbation with the Lai basin outline
Source: Prepared by the author.

204 ≈ *Daanish Mustafa*

downstream Rawalpindi Municipal and Cantonment limits (see Map 9.2).[3] The stream has five major tributaries: Saidpur Kas, Kanitanwali Kas, Tenawali Kas, Bedranwali Kas, and Niki Lai, in addition to 20 other minor tributaries. The maximum length of Lai from its source to its final confluence with the Soan River does not exceed 45 km, thereby allowing very little time for any flood warning in its middle reaches within the Rawalpindi municipal limits.

The institutional hazardscape of Lai is characterized by multiple, fragmented jurisdictions. At the macro-scale, the upper basin is under the federally controlled Capital Development Authority (CDA) and its various directorates, e.g., for water supply, sanitation, and environmental management. The middle basin falls under the Rawalpindi Town Municipal Administration (TMA) as well as the provincially-controlled Rawalpindi Development Authority (RDA). The lower basin is again under federally controlled Rawalpindi and Chaklala Cantonment Boards (RCB and CCB) and their various departments. The assorted stakeholder institutions within the Lai basin display all the specialized bureaucratic structures and disciplinary backgrounds, from public administrator to civil engineers, particular to a modernist state apparatus. Where Islamabad's urban geography may be the poster child for the high modernist ideology inherent to "seeing like a state" (Scott 1998), the state institutions operating within the Lai basin also manifest what Dove and Kammen (2001) call disconnect between the fluid and diverse "vernacular models of development" and the "official models of development." Bureaucratic objectives are disconnected and unco-ordinated: the Sanitation Directorate of the CDA is preoccupied with solid and liquid waste disposal, while the Relief Commissioner of Rawalpindi focuses solely on floods. The messy inter-linkages between issues, although widely recognized, do not and supposedly *must* not distract the public servants from their assigned tasks.

Lying upstream, Islamabad is a preplanned modern city designed by a Greek architect, Constantinos A. Doxiadis. Its grid pattern with wide, tree-lined boulevards and relatively low urban density, presents a sharp contrast to the mostly curving, narrow streets of its older neighbor, Rawalpindi. European concepts of distinctions based on social class and civil service rank are written into the Islamabad Master Plan, and manifest themselves poignantly in the geography of the city (Meier 1985).[4]

Idealistic urban planning did not change social and environmental realities, but rather exacerbated them. In the city plan by Constantinos A. Doxiadis, there was a mention of the lowest ranking government servants residing in working-class neighborhoods, while the poorest of the poor–garbage collectors, street sweepers, housemaids, beggars and day laborers–did not figure in the plan. His idealism, played out on sketches, diagrams and scale models, overlooked the impact that local topography had on the social geography of the absolute poor in the city. It is little surprise, then, that wherever the topography dips below the putative plain of human habitation, by the banks of the tributaries of Lai, one finds unplanned shantytowns or *katchi abadi*s (Spaulding 1996). More than 3 percent of the population of Islamabad, i.e., about 3,000 households, lives in these *katchi abadi*s and they are also the only neighborhoods that repeatedly suffer damage from floods. They were, as a result, especially affected by the floods in 2001.

The Lai basin already receives most (90 percent) of its water flows within a period of one-and-a-half month. The current carrying capacity of Lai is about 10,000 cusecs, while the 25-year return period flood carries 35,000 cusecs of water causing inundation in the most densely populated areas of Rawalpindi. Predictions of increased precipitation on approximately the same number of rainy days as a result of climate change–in effect, higher intensity storm events–will exacerbate this situation. Similarly, Islamabad is in an accelerated process of developing new sectors in the upstream watershed, further reducing its absorption capacity. The mix of these factors is expected to significantly increase the flood intensity in Lai.

While the policy-makers are largely focussed on coping with the more dramatic flood hazard in Lai, the residents of the Lai basin perceive a range of hazards within the basin (Mustafa 2005). For instance, solid waste disposal is the main issue of concern to the residents of the Lai flood plain. The problem of mortality and diseases caused by unhygienic living conditions and consumption of contaminated drinking water around Lai may actually be claiming more lives than the floods. In fact, some of the female residents of the Lai flood plain see floods as a benefit. As one Mrs. Ijaz said, "Floods in the Lai annually clean up Rawalpindi and Islamabad, otherwise the trash in the Lai would generate unbearable diseases–clothes would start walking with vermin."[5] Concurring with this, Ms Rabeea

206 ≈≈ *Daanish Mustafa*

opined, "The damage caused by floods is more visible to the people, but the floods also clean up the Lai, something that the government is not capable of doing."[6]

One reason for women's greater attention to the beneficial aspects of floods could be their greater responsibility towards and engagement with the domestic sphere. Since it was the women who had to spend more time coping with the health and sanitary hazards of the pollution in Lai, they were also more concerned about those hazards in addition to the floods. The evidence thus suggests a strong gender dimension to human interaction with the environment, something that can have important ramifications for future adaptation initiatives.

Another dimension of vulnerability to the multiple hazards endemic to the Lai basin is class-based: people feel disempowered vis-à-vis the state and do not think that their lives and health are a priority for the authorities.

The attention, however, does not seem to be promising any sustainable disaster risk reduction measures that may enhance resilience. For instance, though the government wants to pave the Lai channel and build an expressway along its banks, how long will the channel lining last and what consequences it will have for the downstream unlined parts are questions that few are willing to contemplate. Mercifully, with the advent of PPP government to power in 1999 the project is in cold storage. Other proposals include diversion of the channel, early flood warning system, building of a dam in the upper reaches of the stream and straightening and lining of the channel. All the proposals being considered at the policy level are heavily structural with the exception of the warning system. In none of the proposals is the multidimensional hazardscape of the Lai flood plain residents being considered (Mustafa 2005).

The Lai hazardscape is produced by the convergence of multiple material processes and ideologies governing official and public views of the hazardscape. The large rural-to-urban migration driven by rural poverty and urban industrialization creates armies of urban poor living on marginal low-lying areas of Rawalpindi and Islamabad. Official corruption and indifference creates the land-grabbing mafias, who cash in on the desperate housing needs of the poor by creating neighborhoods on marginal lands exposed to multiple hazards. The policy-makers, depending upon their institutional biases, view a single hazard at a time—ranging from waterborne diseases to flooding–instead of multiple, inter-related hazards. Furthermore, the solutions to hazards rarely involve meaningful public participation or consultation, but are rather driven by donor agendas and deeply modernist assumptions about controlling and manipulating physical systems. The production of the Lai hazardscape and its geography of vulnerability is therefore the outcome of the many inter-related factors.

Future adaptation to climate change in such a context of recurrent hydro-hazards will have to take a more holistic view of the hazardscapes, where multiple hazards spawned by the complexity of urban living must be addressed. Participatory and environment-friendly hazard mitigation initiatives are likely to enhance resilience both in the short and long run. The concern as per the above discussion is about issues of long-term environmental health and quality of human life. Factoring these concerns into the policies of hazard mitigation and of climate change adaptation will be the most fruitful way of moving forward towards sound water and hazard management in South Asia, particularly the Indus basin of Pakistan.

Conclusion: Towards a More Democratic Adaptation Praxis

South Asia, like the rest of the world is undergoing unprecedented changes in its environmental and social conditions. The case studies of water-related conflicts and hazards in Pakistan illustrate the kind of changes happening all over the region. From technological transformations in case of Balochistan producing and then re-producing social change and migration patterns, to the dissonance between engineering and public concerns about surface water irrigation, to urban flood hazard, there are complex hydro-hazardscapes requiring sophisticated and unconventional thinking. The sophisticated thinking in these scenarios is not just about more complex algorithms, or stronger, higher water control infrastructure, or stronger policing of landuse, but about dialogue and a spirit of shared learning. The Disaster Risk Reduction (DRR), development and climate change communities of practice need to listen to each other and most importantly to the societies they are concerned with.

In all the three case studies, communities are adapting to an uncertain future through migration and diversification of their livelihoods, as has been documented by a recently concluded

208 ≈ *Daanish Mustafa*

study by the Deskota Team (2008). A deeper study of the existing adaptive strategies to deal with environmental hazards and water scarcity, along with an empathetic engagement with politco-cultural reconstruction of environmental and social ethics and a creative focus on the current water problems, has the greatest potential of creating resilience to the promised uncertainty of a changed global environment. Genuine participatory democracy in water management, not better calibration of a computer model at NCAR in Boulder (Colorado), may yet hold the best prospects for adaptation to climate change in South Asia.

Notes

1. Interview with Khaliqdad, farmer from Kunghar *karez*, July 2004; emphasis added.
2. This is a proposed dam on Indus near the town of Kalabagh in northwestern Punjab. The project has been on the drawing board since the 1960s, but vigorous opposition from the three less populous provinces of Pakistan has kept the project in abeyance.
3. This spelling comes closest to the phonetic pronunciation of the name and is most widely used. Other spellings, e.g., Leh and Lei, are also in use.
4. By the European sense I mean the relatively recognizable division of economic classes in the industrialized societies of Europe, e.g., the working class, the petit bourgeoisie, the bourgeoisie and the ruling classes (also see Gramsci 1971).
5. Interview with Mrs Ijaz, July 2003.
6. Interview with Ms Rabeea, August 2003.

References

Abbasi, A. N. G. and A. M. Kazi. 1998. "Kalabagh Dam: Look before Your Leap," http://www.sanalist.org/kalabagh/a-7.htm (accessed June 13, 2012).

Adger, W. N. 2006. "Vulnerability," *Global Environmental Change*, 16 (3): 268–81.

Agarwal, A. 1995. "Dismantling the Divide between Indigenous and Scientific Knowledge," *Development and Change*, 26(3): 413–39.

Beaumont, P., P. Bonin and K. McLachlan. 1989. *Qanat, Kariz and Khettara*. Wisbech: Menas Press.

Blaikie, P., T. Cannon, I. Davis and B. Wisner. 1994. *At Risk: Natural Hazards, People's Vulnerability, and Disasters*. New York: Routledge.

Desakota Study Team. 2008. *Re-imagining the Rural–Urban Continuum:*

Understanding the Role Ecosystem Services Play in the Livelihoods of the Poor in Desakota regions Undergoing Rapid Change. Kathmandu, Nepal: ISET-Nepal.

Dove, M. R. and D. M. Kammen. 2001. "Vernacular models of development: An analysis of Indonesia under the 'New Order'," *World Development,* 29(4): 619–39.

Eckholm, E. 2003. "A Province is Dying of Thirst and Cries Robbery." *The New York Times,* March 17, http://www.nytimes.com/2003/03/17/international/asia/17STAN.html (accessed June 13, 2012).

Gilmartin, D. 1994. "Scientific Empire and Imperial Science: Colonialism and Irrigation in the Indus Basin," *The Journal of Asian Studies,* 53 (4): 1127–49.

————. 1995. "Models of the Hydraulic Environment: Colonial Irrigation, State Power and Community in the Indus Basin," in D. Arnold and R. Guha (eds), *Nature, Culture and Imperialism: Essays on the Environmental History of South Asia,* pp. 237–59. New Delhi: Oxford University Press.

Government of Pakistan (GoP). 2000. *Statistical Pocketbook of Pakistan 2000.* Islamabad: Federal Bureau of Statistics.

————. 2005. "Report of the Technical Committee on Water Resources." *Dawn,* December 27, http://archives.dawn.com/2005/12/27/nat16.htm (accessed June 13, 2012).

Hewitt, K. (ed.). 1983. *Interpretations of Calamity.* Winchester: Allen & Unwin Inc.

————. 1997. *Regions of Risk: A Geographical Introduction to Disasters.* Harlow: Longman.

Gramsci, A. 1971. *Selections from the Prison Notebooks.* New York: Qunitin Hoare and Geoffrey Nowell Smith & International Publishers.

Ingram, H. with F. L. Brown. 1987. *Water and Poverty in the Southwest.* Tucson: University of Arizona Press.

Japan International Cooperation Agency (JICA). 2003. Comprehensive Flood Mitigation and Environmental Improvement Plan for Lai Nullah Basin, Islamic Republic of Pakistan. Islamabad Pakistan: JICA and Federal Flood Commission (FFC).

Kamal, S. 2001. "Apocalypse Now." *Newsline Magazine,* April.

Kates, R. and I. Burton. 1986a. *Geography Resources and Environment: Selected Works of Gilbert F. White.* Vol. 1. Chicago: University of Chicago Press.

————. 1986b. *Geography Resources and Environment: Themes from the Work of Gilbert F. White.* Vol. 2. Chicago: University of Chicago Press.

Khan, S. R. 2003. "The Kalabagh Controversy," in K. Bengali (ed.), *The Politics of Managing Water,* pp. 174–81. Karachi: Oxford University Press.

Lightfoot, D. R. 1996a. "Moroccan Khettara: Traditional Irrigation and Progressive Desiccation," *Geoforum,* 27(2): 261–73.

————. 1996b. "Syrian *Qanat* Romani: History, Ecology, Abandonment," *Journal of Arid Environments,* 33(3): 321–36.

210 ☡ *Daanish Mustafa*

L'vovich, M. I. and G. F. White. 1995. "Uses and Transformation of Terrestrial Water," in B. L. Turner, W. C. Clark, R. W. Kates, J. F. Richards, J. T. Mathews and W. B. Meyer (eds), *The Earth as Transformed by Human Action: Global and Regional Changes in the Biosphere over the Past 300 Years*, pp. 235–52. Cambridge, UK: Cambridge University Press.

Malik, A. H. 2000. "Integrated Urban Lei River (North Pakistan) Water Resources Management," *Water Resources Development*, 16(1): 97–117.

Meier, R. 1985. "Islamabad is already Twenty-Five," *Ekistics*, 52: 212–16.

Meinzen-Dick, R. S. and W. van der Hoek. 2001. "Multiple Uses of Water in Irrigated Areas," *Irrigation and Drainage Systems*, 15(2): 93–98.

Michel, A. A. 1967. *The Indus Rivers: A Study of the Effects of Partition.* New Haven: Yale University Press.

Mustafa, D. 1998. "Structural Causes of Vulnerability to Flood Hazard in Pakistan," *Economic Geography*, 74(3): 289–305.

———. 2002a. "To Each According to His Power? Participation, Access, and Vulnerability in Irrigation Water and Vulnerability to Flood Hazard in Pakistan," *Environment and Planning D: Society and Space*, 20(6): 737–52.

———. 2002b. "Linking Access and Vulnerability: Perceptions of Irrigation and Flood Management in Pakistan," *Professional Geographer*, 54(1): 94–105.

———. 2002c. "Theory vs. Practice: The Bureaucratic Ethos of Water Resources Management and Administration in Pakistan," *Contemporary South Asia*, 11(1): 39–56.

———. 2005. "The Production of an Urban Hazardscape in Pakistan: Modernity, Vulnerability and the Range of Choice", *The Annals of the Association of American Geographers*, 95(3): 566–86.

———. 2007a. "Social Construction of Hydropolitics: The Geographical Scales of Water and Security in the Indus River Basin," *Geographical Review*, 94(4): 484–502.

———. 2007b. "Transition from Karez to Tubewell Irrigation: Development, Modernization and Social Capital in Balochistan, Pakistan," *World Development*, 35(10): 1796–813.

Mustafa, D. and J. L. Wescoat Jr. 1997. "Development of Flood Hazard Policy in the Indus River Basin of Pakistan, 1947–1995," *Water International*, 22 (4): 238–44.

Mustafa, D. and U. Qazi 2007. "Transition from Karez to Tubewell Irrigation: Development, Modernization and Social Capital in Balochistan, Pakistan," *World Development*, 35(10): 1796–813.

———. 2008. "Karez versus Tubewell Irrigation: Comparative Social Acceptability and Practicality of Sustainable Groundwater Development in Balochistan, Pakistan," *Contemporary South Asia*, 16(2): 171–95.

National Engineering Corporation (NEC). 2002. "Study for Social Environment: Comprehensive Flood Mitigation and Environmental

Improvement Plan of Lai Nullah Basin in the Islamic Republic of Pakistan." Unpublished report submitted to Japan International Cooperation Agency (JICA).

Pelling, M. 2003. "Toward a Political Ecology of Urban Environmental Risk: The Case of Guyana," in K. S. Zimmerer and T. J. Bassett (eds), *Political Ecology: An Integrative Approach to Geography and Environment-Development Studies*, pp. 73–93. New York: Guilford Press.

Schipper, L. and M. Pelling 2006. "Disaster Risk, Climate Change and International Development: Scope for and Challenges to, Integration," *Disasters*, 30(1): 19–38.

Scott, J. C. 1998. *Seeing Like a State*. New Haven: Yale University Press.

Shah, T., A. D. Roy, A. S. Qureshi and J. Wang. 2003. "Sustaining Asia's Groundwater Boom: An Overview of Issues and Evidence," *Natural Resources Forum*, 27 (2): 130–41.

Spaulding, F. 1996. "Architecture and Islamabad." Paper presented at the American Institute of Pakistan Studies Workshop on the State of Pakistan Studies, September 18–22, Washington.

United Nations Development Programme (UNDP). 2002. *Human Development Report 2002: Deepening Democracy in a Fragmented World*. New York: Oxford University Press.

United Nations Relief Web. 2001. "Pakistan Floods Update Report No. 5," http://www.reliefweb.int/w/rwb.nsf/0/bc6dfcbb0fdd8bf3c1256ada0050 5cc8?OpenDocument (accessed October 2, 2008).

van Steenbergen, F. 1995. "The Frontier Problem in Incipient Groundwater Management Regimes in Balochistan (Pakistan)," *Human Ecology*, 23(1): 53–74.

———. 1997. "Understanding the Sociology of Spate Irrigation: Cases from Balochistan," *Journal of Arid Environments*, 35 (2): 349–65.

van Steenbergen, F. and W. Oliemans. 2002. "A Review of Policies in Groundwater Management in Pakistan 1950–2000," *Water Policy*, 4(4): 323–44.

Watts, M. 1983. "On the Poverty of Theory: Natural Hazards Research in Context," in K. Hewitt (ed.), *Interpretations of Calamity*, pp. 231–62. London: Routledge.

Wescoat, J. L. Jr. 1987. "The Practical Range of Choice" in Water Resources Geography,' *Progress in Human Geography*, 11(2): 41–59.

———. 1991. "Managing the Indus River Basin in the Light of Climate Change: Four Conceptual Approaches," *Global Environmental Change: Human and Policy Dimensions*, 1(5): 381–95.

Wescoat, J. L. Jr., S. Halvorson and D. Mustafa. 2000. "Water Management in the Indus Basin of Pakistan: A Half-Century Perspective," *International Journal of Water Resources Development*, 16(3): 391–406.

White, G. F. 1945. "Human Adjustment to Floods." Research Paper 29, Department of Geography, University of Chicago, Chicago.

212 ≋ *Daanish Mustafa*

Whyte, A. 1986. "From Hazards Perception to Human Ecology," in R. Kates and I. Burton (eds), *Themes from the Work of Gilbert F. White*, vol. 2, pp. 240–71. Chicago: University of Chicago Press.

Wisner, B. 1993. "Disaster Vulnerability: Scale, Power, and Daily Life," *Geojournal*, 30(2): 127–40.

World Bank 2003. "Pakistan Data Profile", http://web.worldbank.org/WBSITE/EXTERNAL/COUNTRIES/SOUTHASIAEXT/PAKISTANEXTN/0,,menuPK:293057~pagePK:141159~piPK:141110~theSitePK:293052,00html (accessed October 12, 2012)

10

Climate Change and Groundwater

India's Opportunities for Mitigation and Adaptation

Tushaar Shah

Evolution of Indian Irrigation

Irrigation has always been central to the life and society in the plains of South Asia, i.e., India, Pakistan, southern Nepal, Bangladesh and Sri Lanka. According to Alfred Deakin, a three-time Australian Prime Minister and an irrigation enthusiast of the early 20th century who toured British India in 1890, the region had 12 million ha (ha) of irrigated land compared with 3 million ha in the US, 2 million ha in Egypt, 1.5 million ha in Italy and a few hundred thousand ha each in Ceylon, France, Spain, and Victoria (Australia) (*The Age* 1891). Although Egypt and Sri Lanka are better known as hydraulic civilizations of yore, a century ago British India was the world champion in irrigation. This is not surprising, as in a normal year, India receives 4,000 km^3 of rainfall, a large volume by any standards. But a large part of it falls in eastern India. Moreover, almost all of it is received within 100 hours of torrential downpour, making storage and irrigation critical for the survival of agrarian societies. Considering that parts of India, chiefly the Indo-Gangetic basin, were densely populated and intensively cultivated even before 2000

214 ≈ *Tushaar Shah*

years suggests that water-managed agriculture has been the bedrock of civilization in this part of the world. However, the technology of water-managed agriculture has undergone profound changes over the millennia. Three distinct eras of evolution of irrigation can be identified according to the technology used and the institutions it spawned. They are:

a. *Era of adaptive irrigation:* Since time immemorial until the early 1800's, farming communities have adapted their agrarian lives to the hydrology of river basins. There are records of numerous, often gigantic, irrigation systems constructed by kings and managed by specialized bureaucracies. This induced historians like K. Wittfogel (1957) to famously claim that irrigation drove state-formation in oriental societies like India's, and the administrative requirements of managing large, state-run systems were at the root of despotic authority in these societies during a period when many countries in Europe had well-entrenched republican institutions. However, the sum total of the evidence suggests that farming communities and local landlords, rather than the monolithic state, were key irrigation players in Mughal India and earlier. Diverting and managing monsoon floodwaters to support riverine agriculture was the dominant mode of irrigation in northern India and Pakistan with sandy alluvial aquifers where harvesting and storing rainwater in unlined surface tanks and reservoirs was subject to high seepage losses. In contrast, using monsoon floodwaters to fill up countless small reservoirs was the standard procedure in hard-rock parts of peninsular India where seepage losses from water storages were insignificant (Shah 2009).

b. *Era of canal construction:* Around 1810, the British East India Company began changing this adaptive irrigation regime by undertaking gigantic projects that reconfigured river basins. The Indus canals transformed north-western (British) India from a pastoral region to an intensively cultivated terrain. Large canal projects were also undertaken in southern India. In undertaking these ambitious irrigation projects, the colonial rulers combined the "interests of charity and the interests of commerce" (Whitcombe 2005: 677). The state and centralized irrigation bureaucracies replaced village communities and local landlords as key players in the new regime. Civil engineering began to dominate water resource planning, and construction and management of irrigation infrastructure, and continued to do so even after India became independent. In fact, dominance of civil engineering in water sector persists even today. The colonial era left India and Pakistan with some of the world's largest gravity flow irrigation systems, complete with a highly centralized, bureaucratic irrigation management regime.

c. *Era of atomistic irrigation:* The colonial irrigation strategy, however, created pockets of agrarian prosperity in canal commands (i.e., areas below the reservoir/weir irrigated by gravity canals) which even as recently as in 2000 encompassed no more than 15 percent of India's farmlands. However, India experienced an explosion in agricultural population from 1960; and the land-to-man ratio declined from over 0.4 ha/person in 1900 to less than 0.1 ha/person in 2000. Peasants across the country felt the need to secure their means of

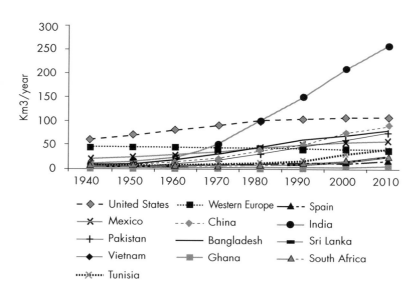

Figure 10.1: Growth in agricultural groundwater use in selected countries (1940–2010)

Source: Shah et al. (2007: 399)

216 ≈ *Tushaar Shah*

irrigation that could permit intensification and diversification of land use. The availability of small mechanical pumps and boring rigs provided a technological breakthrough. Beginning in 1970, this combination of circumstances catalyzed a groundwater revolution all over South Asia. This was a wholly new phenomenon that the water establishment was unfamiliar with. North-western India had seen some well irrigation even during colonial times; however, irrigation of field crops with groundwater was wholly new to humid eastern India and hard-rock peninsular India. In India, the number of irrigation wells equipped with diesel or electric pumps increased from some 150,000 in 1950 to nearly 19 million by 2000. Around 1960, India was a relatively minor user of groundwater in agriculture compared to countries like the US and Spain; by 2000, the country had emerged as the global champion in groundwater irrigation, pumping around 220–230 billion m^3/year, over twice the amount the US did, as the chart in Figure 10.1 shows.

India's water policy-making is yet to fully factor in the epochal transformation in the way its farmers water their crops, and successive governments have kept investing billions of dollars on constructing new surface reservoirs and canal networks even as the existing ones have begun falling into disuse. Evidence from land use survey data released by the Union Ministry of Agriculture, Government of India (GoI) as well as five yearly minor irrigation censuses suggests that since 1990, central and state governments in India have invested over US$ 20 billion on building new and rehabilitating existing surface irrigation systems; however, the net area served by surface structures, small and large, has actually *declined* by over 3 million ha (Shah 2009; Thakkar and Chandra 2007). In contrast, the net area served by groundwater has been steadily rising. Small farmers looking for opportunities to intensify and diversify their agricultural activity need on-demand year-round irrigation with greater frequency. Tanks and canal systems are unable to meet this need, but groundwater wells are. Groundwater wells are also a better insurance against droughts than tanks and canal systems. As a result, since 1990, Indian irrigation has been transformed from a centrally managed surface irrigation regime to an atomistically managed water-scavenging irrigation regime involving tens of millions of pump-owners who divert surface and groundwater at will. Even

Climate Change and Groundwater ≋ 217

Table 10.1: Groundwater management challenges in different areas of India

Hydro-Geological Settings	Socio-economic and Management Challenges			
	Resource Depletion	Optimizing Conjunctive Use	Secondary Salinization	Natural Groundwater Quality Concerns
A. Major Alluvial Plains	••	••	•••	•
A.1. Arid	•	• • •		••
A.2. Humid				
B. Coastal plains	• •	•	• • •	•
C. Inter-Mountain Valleys	•	••	•	•
D. Hard-rock Areas	• • •	•	•	• • •

Source: Prepared by the author.
Note: The number of dots suggests the scale and severity of a challenge (1 dot = minor, 2 dots = significant, 3 dots = severe).

as groundwater irrigation has helped South Asia's small-holders survive, unmanaged overexploitation of groundwater resource has affected the environment in myriad ways. Table 10.1 outlines the key consequences of intensification of groundwater use in agriculture in different parts of the subcontinent.

This transformation, and the socio-ecological threats it posed, necessitated a totally new policy response from governments and water planners. The meteoric rise of the atomistic groundwater economy demanded a bold new thinking and resource allocation strategy to evolve a groundwater management regime with practical supply- and demand-side strategies. However, steeped in colonial irrigation thinking, Indian water planners still keep spending billions of dollars on the canal irrigation technology that farmers throughout India have been roundly rejecting. If canals are ending up as groundwater recharge structures by default, the question is whether it would not be more effective to do so by design.

Even as India's groundwater irrigation economy remains pretty much ungoverned, climate change will present new challenges and uncertainties, and demand new responses from the region's water planners. The rise of a booming groundwater economy and the

218 ≋ *Tushaar Shah*

decline in surface irrigation necessitates a totally new understanding of the operating system of India's water economy and how best it can mitigate as well as adapt to the hydro-climatic change.

India's Hydro-climatic Future

Climate change is expected to significantly alter India's hydro-climatic regime over the 21st century. It is widely agreed that the Indo-Gangetic basin is likely to experience increased water availability from snow-melt up to around 2030, but is also likely to face gradual reductions thereafter. Parts of the Indo-Gangetic basin may also receive less rain in India's hydro-climatic future than in the past, but the rest of India is likely to benefit from greater precipitation. According to IPCC (2001), most Indian landmass below the Ganges plain is likely to experience a 0.5–1°C rise in average temperatures in the period 2020–2029 and 3.5–4.5°C rise in 2090–2099. Many parts of peninsular India, especially Western Ghats are likely to experience a 5–10 percent increase in total precipitation (ibid.)[1]; however, this increase is likely to be accompanied by greater temporal variability. Throughout the subcontinent, it is expected that "very wet days" are likely to contribute more and more to the total precipitation suggesting that more of India's precipitation may be received in fewer than 100 hours of thunderstorms–and half in less than 30 hours–as has been the case in the recent decades. This is likely to mean higher precipitation intensity and larger number of dry days in a year.[2] Increased frequency of extremely wet rainy seasons (Gosain and Rao 2007) is also likely to mean increased runoff. According to Milly et al. (2008), compared to 1900–1970, most of India is likely to experience an increase in the annual runoff by 5–20 percent during 2041–2060. All in all, India should expect to receive more of its water through rain than through snowmelt; get used to a faster and incidence of snowmelt; cope with less soil moisture in summer and higher crop evapotranspiration (ET) demand as a consequence.

For Indian agriculture, hydro-climatic change will mean the following:

a. Kharif (monsoon) season crops will experience heightened risk of floods as well as droughts;
b. Rabi and especially summer crops will experience enhanced ET needing greater and more frequent irrigation;

c. Surface water storages–large and small–will benefit from increased runoff but will also suffer increased evaporation from large open surfaces of reservoirs and open canal networks as a result of higher mean temperature;
d. Irrigating the same area through canals will necessitate larger reservoir storage; more frequent droughts will also mean greater need for multi-year reservoir storage capacity of which India has very little as of now.

As can be inferred from these points of view, managing groundwater storage will acquire greater significance for India than ever before. However, besides affecting groundwater demand, climate change is expected to impact groundwater supply too in direct and myriad ways.

Impact of Climate Change on Groundwater

To the extent that climate change results in spatial and temporal changes in precipitation, it will significantly influence natural groundwater recharge. Moreover, since a good deal of natural recharge occurs in areas with high vegetative cover, such as forests, changing ET rates resulting from rising temperatures may reduce infiltration rates from natural precipitation and thus reduce recharge. Recharge responds strongly to the temporal pattern of precipitation as well as soil cover and soil properties. In the African context, Carter (2007) has argued that replacing natural vegetation by crops can increase natural recharge by up to a factor of 10. If climate change results in changes in natural vegetation in forests or savanna, these too may influence natural recharge; however, the direction of net effect will depend upon the pattern of changes in the vegetative cover. Simulation models developed by Australian scientists have showed that changes in temperatures and rainfall influence growth rates and leaf size of plants that affect groundwater recharge (Kundzewicz and Döll 2009). The direction of change is conditioned by the context: in some areas, the response of vegetation to climate change would cause the average recharge to decrease, but in other areas, groundwater recharge would more than double. Changing river flows in response to changing mean precipitation and its variability, rising sea levels, changing temperatures will all influence natural recharge rates (ibid.).

We know little about how exactly rainfall patterns will change, but increased temporal variability seems guaranteed. This will mean intense and large rainfall events in short monsoons followed by long dry spells. All the hydro-geological evidence we have suggests that groundwater recharge through natural infiltration occurs only beyond a threshold level of precipitation; however, it also suggests not only that run-off increases with precipitation but also that runoff coefficient (i.e., runoff/precipitation) itself increases with increased rainfall intensity (or precipitation per rainfall event) (Carter 2007). Higher variability in precipitation may thus negatively impact natural recharge in general. What will be the net impact of such variability on the state of natural recharge of a given location will depend upon the change in both the total precipitation and the variability of that precipitation.

The Indo-Gangetic aquifer system has been heavy recharged by the Himalayan snowmelt. As snowmelt-based runoff increases during the coming decades, its contribution to potential recharge may increase. However, a great deal of this potential recharge may end up as "rejected recharge" and rather enhance river flows and intensify the flood-proneness of eastern India and Bangladesh. As the snowmelt-based runoff begins to decline, a decline in runoff as well as groundwater recharge in this vast basin[3] can be expected.

A major interplay of climate change and groundwater will be witnessed in coastal areas. Using the records of coastal tide gauges in the northern part of Indian Ocean for more than 40 years, Unnikrishnan and Shankar (2007) have estimated an annual sea level rise between 1.06 mm and 1.75 mm, consistent with the IPCC estimate of 1–2 mm annual global sea level rise. Rising sea levels will threaten coastal aquifers. Many of India's coastal aquifers are already experiencing salinity ingress. This problem is particularly acute in Saurashtra coast of Gujarat and Minjur aquifer of Tamilnadu. In coastal West Bengal, Sundarbans (mangrove forests) are threatened by overland intrusion of saline seawater, which is affecting its aquifers. Thus, the precarious balance between freshwater aquifers and seawater will come under increased stress as sea levels rise and coastal aquifers will likely face serious threats from climate-change–induced sea level rise.

Some scientists (e.g., Kundzewicz and Doll 2007) suggest that climate change may alter the physical characteristics of aquifers themselves.[4] Higher CO_2 concentrations in the atmosphere, they argue, may influence carbonate dissolution and promote the

Climate Change and Groundwater ≋ 221

formation of Karst which, in turn, may negatively affect infiltration properties of top soils. Others (like Tim Green), however, argue the opposite (*Science Daily* 2007). From experimental data, some scientists have claimed that elevated atmospheric CO_2 levels may affect plants, vadose zone and groundwater in ways that may hasten infiltration from precipitation by up to 119 percent in Mediterranean climate and up to 500 percent in subtropical climate (*Science Daily* 2007).

Rethinking Storage

Aquifers respond to droughts and climate fluctuations much more slowly than surface storages. As a result, compared to surface storages, they act as a more resilient buffer during dry spells especially when they have large storage. This is the reason why India has experienced explosive growth in groundwater demand during the recent decades, and this is also the reason why groundwater demand will expand further in the wake of climate change. For millennia, groundwater wells have been the principal weapon Indian farmers have used in order to cope with droughts (Shah 2009). This is evident in the fact that well-digging has tended to peak during droughts. This practice continues even today and will likely increase with heightened hydro-climatic variability. All in all, while we can predict with confidence that climate change will enhance the demand for groundwater in agricultural and other uses, there is no clarity on whether climate change will enhance or reduce natural groundwater recharge in net terms under Business As Usual (BAU) scenario.

For millennia, India has relied on building surface storages and providing gravity flow irrigation to water crops. With the groundwater boom, India's irrigation economy has been fundamentally transformed, bringing into question its age-old emphasis on surface structures. Climate change raises new questions about the continued reliance on surface storage of water and its transport to agricultural fields, and demands that India fundamentally rethink its storage strategy. Table 10.2 compares the four storage alternatives India faces along a dozen criteria using a ten-point scale that assigns up to five "↑" signs for positives (benefits) and up to five "↓" signs for the negatives (costs, disadvantages). The four alternatives are:

a. The first–advocated by environmental and civil society groups–emphasizes numerous small decentralized storages

222 ≈ Tushaar Shah

close to the point of use and with short canals. India's age-old traditional water harvesting structures—such as tanks in southern and eastern India, *ahar-pyne* system[5] of southern Bihar, homestead ponds of West Bengal and north Bihar, *johad*s[6] of Rajasthan—represent this class (see Choppra 2005);

Table 10.2: Climate change and water storage alternatives

		Small Surface Storages	Large Surface Reservoirs	Aquifer Storage (BAU)	Managed Aquifer Storage
1	Makes water available where needed (space utility)	↑↑↑	↑↑	↑↑↑↑	↑↑↑↑↑
2	Makes water available when needed (time utility)	↑	↑↑	↑↑↑↑	↑↑↑↑↑
3	Level of water control offered (form utility)	↑	↑↑	↑↑↑↑	↑↑↑↑↑
4	Non-beneficial evaporation from storage	↓↓↓↓	↓↓	↓	↓
5	Non-beneficial evaporation from transport	↓↓	↓↓↓	↓	↓
6	Protection against mid-monsoonal dry spell (2–8 weeks)	↑↑	↑↑↑	↑↑↑↑↑	↑↑↑↑↑
7	Protection against a single annual drought	↑	↑	↑↑↑	↑↑↑↑↑
8	Protection against two successive annual droughts	↑	↑	↑↑	↑↑↑↑
9	Ease of storage recovery during a good monsoon	↑↑↑↑↑	↑↑↑↑	↑↑	↑↑↑
10	Social capital cost of water storage, transport and retrieval structures	↓↓	↓↓↓↓↓	↓↓	↓↓↓
11	Operation and maintenance of social costs of storage, transport and retrieval structures	↓	↓↓	↓↓↓↓↓	↓↓↓
12	Carbon footprint of agricultural water use	↓	↓↓	↓↓↓↓↓	↓↓↓

Source: Prepared by the author.

Climate Change and Groundwater ≈ 223

b. The second–advocated by bureaucracy–represents the dominant colonial and post-colonial strategy of creating large reservoirs at hydraulically opportune sites and transporting water through a vast network of surface canals;

c. The third represents the groundwater boom India has experienced, as a result of which mostly shallow aquifer storage has been relentlessly exploited through atomistic action by millions of small farmers without any demand-side management or a systematic strategy of enhancing aquifer recharge;

d. The fourth represents an option that is as yet non-existent but can be operationalized with a paradigmatic shift in the country's water management thinking. It recognizes that groundwater demand will increase, but given India's hydrology, aquifer storage can sustain this increase with proactive demand management and a nation-wide program of Managed Aquifer Recharge.

Rows 4, 5, 10, 11, and 12 include costs or disadvantages of different storage structures; the rest are benefits/positives. Of the benefits and costs, some, like operating costs (Row 11), quality of access (Rows 1, 2 and 3) are private in nature and drive the choices of individual farmers. Others are "public" (or social) in nature. For instance, the carbon-footprint of alternative storage systems may not directly influence individual farmer decisions but has to be factored into the national calculus.

Especially since the 1970s, the high scores of groundwater irrigation on space, time and form utility (Rows 1, 2 and 3) have driven India's groundwater boom. Also important has been groundwater's resilience to dry-spells and drought (Rows 6, 7 and 8). Surface storages have fared poorly on these counts. These benefits will become more valuable as climate change heightens the hydrological variability. From the society's viewpoint, aquifer storage has the advantage of minimum non-beneficial evaporation (Rows 4 and 5). For a mostly semi-arid country, where surface reservoirs can lose 3 m or more of their storage every year simply through pan evaporation, this is no mean gain. The major social disadvantages of heavy dependence on groundwater are three: *a)* aquifers are slow to recharge and hard rock aquifers that underlie 65 percent of India have limited storage;

224 ≋ *Tushaar Shah*

b) while gravity flow irrigation from canals needs little or no energy, groundwater irrigation is energy-intensive; and *c*) since the bulk of the energy used in pumping groundwater is drawn from diesel or electricity generated with coal, India's transition from flow irrigation to pump irrigation has created a massive carbon footprint.

Carbon Footprint of India's Groundwater Economy

Transformation of Indian irrigation from gravity flow to lift has made it highly energy-intensive, but the arithmetic of computing the carbon footprint of this economy is fraught with widely divergent estimates. Around 2000, Indian farmers lifted some 150 km^3 of groundwater using electric pumpsets and around 80 km^3, using diesel pumpsets. Lifting 1,000 m^3 of water to a height of 1 m uses up to 2.73 kWh of energy without friction losses and at peak efficiency.[7] Indian electric irrigation pumps probably operate at 40 percent efficiency. Moreover, transmission and distribution losses in delivering power to pumpsets are of the order of 25 percent or higher. This implies that electricity actually used to lift 1,000 m^3/m in India is of the order of 9.1 kWh. If we assume that a representative electric pump lifts water to a dynamic head of 20 m, then lifting 150 km^3 of groundwater requires 27.3 billion kWh of electricity. This estimate is highly sensitive to the assumption about the dynamic head over which a representative electric pumpset lifts water. Taking a figure of 40 m yields an electricity consumption figure of 55 billion kWh. This estimate compares well with the estimate (54.50 billion kWh) made by the more detailed International Food Policy Research Institute (IFPRI), as set out in Table 10.5, but is lower than those made by J. Rao at 87 billion kWh, as shown in Table 10.4.

Using India's 2001 Minor Irrigation Census data on groundwater irrigated area (GoI 2005a) and the energy consumed in agriculture from (Planning Commission of India 2007: Annex. 2.4) combined with some assumptions, J. Rao[8] pegged the total electricity consumption in groundwater irrigation at 87 billion kWh. Another indirect estimate is provided from the numbers circulating in the electricity industry. Total power generation in India is around 560 billion kWh, and many observers suggest that the power used by irrigation pumps may be around 15 percent of the total power generated (ibid.). However, this means that either the transmission

Climate Change and Groundwater ≈ 225

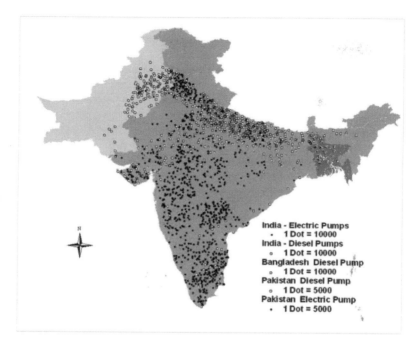

Map 10.1: Distribution of electric and diesel pumpsets in South Asia
Source: Prepared by the author using Minor Irrigation Census.

and distribution (T&D) losses are much higher than 25 percent, as we assumed[9] or that the dynamic head over which a representative electric pumpset in India lifts water is more like 50–60 m rather than 20 m that our estimate of 27.3 billion kWh is based on. The latter appears highly unlikely. The 2001 Minor Irrigation Census (GoI 2005a: Table 6.2) found that just around 8.5 percent of India's villages had static water level deeper than 50 m; in 75 percent of the villages, depth to static water level was less than 15 m. True, pumping depth can be much higher than static water level; yet, such a huge difference is difficult to explain.

Diesel pumps are even less efficient but they lift water to a smaller head. Moreover, diesel does not face the T&D losses that electricity suffers and a liter of diesel provides equivalent of 10 kWh of energy. Some 80 km^3 of groundwater lifted by diesel pumpsets uses around 4–4.5 billion liters of diesel. Nelson et al. (2009) have taken the

226　〰　*Tushaar Shah*

carbon intensity of electricity and diesel at 0.4062 kgC/kWh and 0.732 kgC/liter respectively. This would imply that groundwater pumping in India results in the emission of a total of some 14.38 million mt of Carbon (C): 11.09 million mt from electric pumps and 3.29 million mt from diesel pumpsets. Nelson et al. tentatively estimate the C-emission from groundwater irrigation as higher, i.e., at 16 million mt, roughly 4 percent of India's total C-emissions.

Two interesting aspects of the carbon footprint of India's groundwater economy are that: *a)* lifting a 1000 m³/m using electricity emits 5.5 times more C than lifting the same amount using diesel does, and diesel pumps are concentrated in eastern India with rich alluvial aquifers; *b)* C-emission of groundwater irrigation is highly sensitive to the dynamic head over which groundwater is lifted because for one, higher head leads to higher energy use and C-emission; second, beyond a depth of 10–15 m, diesel pumps become extremely inefficient forcing irrigators to switch to electricity which has a larger C-footprint anyway. Map 10.1 shows that most of India's diesel pumps are concentrated in eastern India and her electric pumps, in western and peninsular India. Table 4 presents this distribution for all of groundwater-irrigating South Asia, i.e, India, Pakistan, Bangladesh and Nepal terai (densely cultivated farming areas, grasslands and forests at the base of the Himalayas in India, Nepal and Bhutan). Indeed, as the calculations made by J. Rao in Table 4 show, 96 percent of India's electricity consumption in groundwater pumping is concentrated in 11 states of western and peninsular India. Even amongst these, the biggest C-culprits are states like Karnataka, Tamilnadu, Andhra Pradesh and Gujarat which have large areas under deep tube well irrigation. Deep tube wells have a huge C-footprint; according to the IFPRI preliminary calculations, India's deep tube wells irrigate only 4.1 million of the 31 million ha under electric pumpset irrigation; but these account for nearly two-third of C-emission from groundwater pumping with electric pumpsets.

An alternative procedure for estimating C-emissions from India's groundwater economy, set out in Table 5, too draws heavily on the data provided by the Minor Irrigation Census. The Census provides numbers of different groundwater and lift irrigation structures, diesel as well as electric pumps, and gross area irrigated by each type of irrigation structure. Several micro-level surveys suggest that deep tube wells in India operate for around 1,600 hours/year, that diesel

Table 10.3: Geographic distribution of electric and diesel irrigation pumps in South Asia

	Number of Irrigation Pumps (million)	Diesel (%)	Electric (%)
Pakistan	0.93	89.6	10.4
Bangladesh	1.18	96.7	3.3
Eastern India: Assam, West Bengal, Bihar, Jharkhand, Orissa, Uttar Pradesh, Uttaranchal, and West Bengal	5.09	84.0	16.0
Western and southern India: Andhra Pradesh, Gujarat, Haryana, Karnataka, Kerala, Madhya Pradesh, Maharashtra, Punjab, Rajasthan, and Tamilnadu	11.69	19.4	80.6

Sources: Pakistan figures are from Government of Pakistan (2004). Bangladesh figures are from Mandal (2006). Figures for Indian states are from the *Report on Third Census of Minor Irrigation Schemes (2000–01)*.

Table 10.4: Estimates of electricity consumption by pumpsets in major states of India

States	Gross area irrigated with electric pumps	Average kWh used per ha of irrigation	Total electricity used by electric pumps (gWh)
Rajasthan	3844	1111.8	4274000
Uttar Pradesh	14010	353.4	4951000
Haryana	2267	2432.1	5514000
Madhya Pradesh	2783	2006.5	5583000
Punjab	5748	1086.2	6243000
Karnataka	1285	6997.0	8993000
Tamilnadu	1666	5630.9	9382000
Maharashtra	3311	3193.0	10572000
Andhra Pradesh	2294	5863.4	13448000
Gujarat	2713	5293.6	14361000
Other states	5060	7436.0	3762500
Total	44,981	1,934.9	87,031,584

Source: J. Rao, pers. comm., 2008[10]

228 ≋ *Tushaar Shah*

pumps, because of high fuel cost, operate for around 600 hours, but electric pumps, subject to flat tariff charge operate for 800–1,000 hours. Without having to estimate the energy needed to lift water from different depths, I have assumed annual hours of operation for different structures based on survey data. Average horse power ratings of different structures are obtained from the data provided by the Census. T&D losses in power between the generating station and

Table 10.5: An alternative procedure for estimating C-emission from India's groundwater economy

		Deep tube wells	Shallow tube wells: electric	Shallow tube wells: diesel	Dug-wells: electric	Dug-wells: diesel	Surface lift: electric	Surface lift: diesel
1	Number of structures (m)	0.53	3.26	4.37	6.15	1.99	0.33	0.21
2	Gross area irrigated (m ha)	4.09	11.61	16.06	9.99	3.23	1.22	0.78
3	Av. Horse power	9.66	6.26	6.26	4.43	4.43	5.1	5.1
4	Energy use/ hour at well-head	7.3 kWh	4.7 kWh	1.25 liter	3.3 kWh	0.9 liter	3.83	1
5	Average hours of operation/ year	1,600	900	600	900	600	600	600
6	Average hours/ha	207.3	252.8	163.5	554.2	369.6	162.2	162.2
7	T&D efficiency[a]	70%	70%		70%		70%	
8	Total Energy Used[b]	8.34 b kWh	19.7 b kWh	3.28 b kWh	26.1 b liters	1.07 b kWh	1.1 b liters	0.13 b liters
9	Total estimated emission (met)[c]	3.39	8.0	2.4	10.6	0.78	0.45	0.1
10	Emission/ha (C-mt)	0.83	0.69	0.15	1.06	0.24	0.37	0.13

Source: Prepared by the author.

Notes: [a]Transmission and distribution efficiency in conveying power between generating station and well-head.

[b]Computed by multiplying rows 5, 4 and 1.

[c]C-emission per kWh of electricity is assumed to be 0.4062 kg and per liter of diesel at 0.732 kg (Nelson and Robertson, pers. comm., 2008).

the well-head are assumed to be 30 percent. This procedure: *a*) yields a total C-emission of 25.64 million mt from India's lift irrigation economy, some 60 percent higher than the IFPRI estimate and around 6.4 percent of India's total emissions; *b*) shows deep tube wells to be more GHG-emitting than the IFPRI procedure makes them out to be; and *c*) shows diesel pumps to have a much lower carbon footprint than electric pumps, as the IFPRI analysis suggests.

Scientific studies on the possible impact of climate change on groundwater resources are at a very early stage in India. However, preliminary studies show massive scope for reducing the C-footprint[11] of India's groundwater economy. Using the data for Haryana and Andhra Pradesh, Shukla et al. (2003) built a quantitative model to estimate the marginal impacts of a host of factors on GHG emissions from pumping. Some of the conclusions of the study are: *a*) decline in pumping water levels by every single meter increases GHG emissions by 4.37 percent in Haryana and 6 percent in Andhra Pradesh; *b*) the elasticity of GHG emissions with reference to the percentage of area under groundwater irrigation (i.e., the percentage increase in GHG induced by a 1 percent increase in groundwater-irrigated area) is 2.2; and through the 1990s, groundwater-irrigated area in these two states increased at a compound annual growth rate (CAGR) of 3 percent/year resulting in an increase in GHG emission by 6.6 percent/year; *c*) every 1 percent increase in the share of diesel pumps to the total number of pumps reduces GHG emissions by 0.3 percent; and *d*) the elasticity of GHG emissions with reference to irrigation efficiency is high at 2.1. The most important determinant of the C-footprint of India's pump irrigation economy is the dynamic head over which farmers lift water to irrigate crops. The larger the head, the higher the energy consumption and more likely that electrified deep tube wells are used for pumping groundwater, multiplying the C-footprint of groundwater pumping.

Groundwater Recharge for Adaptation and Mitigation

From the climate change viewpoint, India's groundwater hotspots are concentrated in arid and semi-arid areas of western and peninsular India especially in the seven states of Punjab, Rajasthan, Maharashtra, Karnataka, Gujarat, Andhra Pradesh, and Tamilnadu, as is evident from the map of areas with overexploitation of groundwater (Map

230 ~ *Tushaar Shah*

10.2). Continued overexploitation of groundwater has severely curtailed the resilience of their aquifers and their ability to stabilize farmers' livelihoods in the face of heightened hydro-climatic variability. Groundwater in these states is pumped from increasing depths mostly using coal-based electricity. Hence, these are also the regions which account for an overwhelmingly large proportion of GHG emissions from groundwater pumping. Accepting the present groundwater-dependence of agriculture as a fait accompli should lead policy-makers to evolve a strategy of proactive management of aquifer storage as the central plank of India's water strategy in the years to come. This strategy needs to incorporate effective means to manage agricultural water demand as well as to enhance natural groundwater recharge through large-scale "Managed Aquifer Recharge" investments. Without demand- and supply-side management of the pump irrigation economies, groundwater levels in most Indian aquifers display a behavior caricatured in Figure 10.1a. In the initial years, water level fluctuations before and after monsoon get amplified. However, as pre-monsoon water levels drop considerably below the vadose zone, natural recharge rates decline and the pumping head increases rapidly. With proactive demand- and supply-side management, the situation desired is caricatured in Figure 10.1b. With groundwater development, fluctuations will amplify; however, as long as post-monsoon water levels bounce back to pre-development levels with Managed Aquifer Recharge, a steady state can be approached, albeit with rising average pumping head. There is considerable evidence to show that nature itself helps aquifer recover during monsoons. India's Minor Irrigation Census compiles data on pre-monsoon and post-monsoon water levels in wells from over 500,000 villages. Map 10.2 plots this data aggregated for 145 districts and arranged in ascending order of pre-monsoon water level. Without significant efforts to enhance natural recharge, this data suggests that monsoonal recovery of water levels tends to increase with pre-monsoon depth to the water level except at very high levels of the latter. Survey data from some 250 villages around the Indian subcontinent in 2002 also suggested a similar positive relationship between pre-monsoon water level and monsoonal rise in water level (Shah et al. 2006). This suggests that in the absence of groundwater development, much floodwaters from surface runoff as rejected recharge; and that to some considerable extent, post-monsoon groundwater extraction helps increase the natural

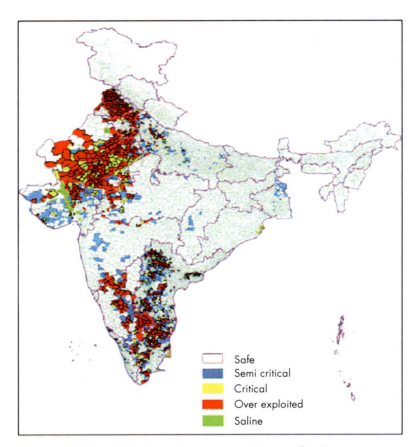

Map 10.2: Groundwater-stressed areas of India

Source: Planning Commission of India (2007: 9).

recharge. An aggressive, nation-wide Managed Aquifer Recharge program can enhance natural recharge rates to bring them closer to groundwater utilization rates on an annual basis.

India has witnessed growing debates on how best to manage the runaway expansion in agricultural demand for groundwater and for the energy needed to pump it. Laws and administrative regulations such as licensing have been extensively discussed and even attempts have been made to draft them. However, the key challenge lies in enforcing these on several tens of millions of widely

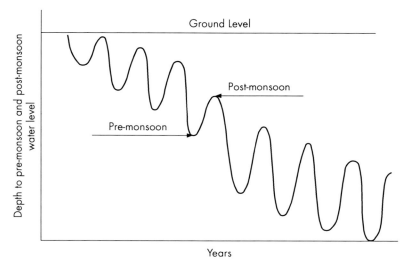

Figure 10.2a: Groundwater development and water level decline without Managed Aquifer Recharge

Source: Prepared by the author.

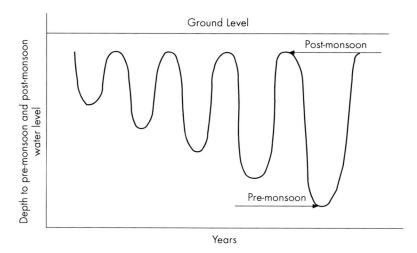

Figure 10.2b: Groundwater development and water level behavior with intensive program of Managed Aquifer Recharge

Source: Prepared by the author.

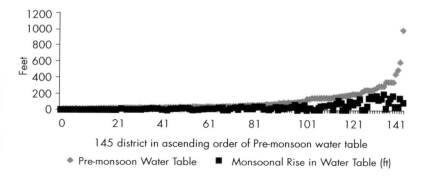

Figure 10.3: Aquifer recovery and pre-monsoon water level in 145 districts of India

Source: Report on Third Census of Minor Irrigation Schemes (2000–01).

dispersed pumpers in the vast countryside (Planning Commission 2007). Many observers have also suggested pricing of groundwater, but the administrative and logistical challenges of doing so are even more formidable. Groundwater irrigation is the mainstay of India's small farmers and the rural poor. Therefore, successive governments and political leaders have been reluctant to adopt a heavy-handed approach to curtail groundwater demand (Shah 2009). The political objective, therefore, is to achieve environmental goals in ways that do not hit the poor. The International Water Management Institute (IWMI), Colombo, has argued for over a decade that in the short run the only effective and practical approach towards groundwater demand management in India is through rationing of agricultural power supply (Shah et al. 2004). In the recent years, Gujarat in western India has experimented with this approach with considerable success. The government of this state invested US$ 250 million in rewiring rural Gujarat's electricity infrastructure under *Jyotirgram* Scheme[12] to separate feeders supplying power to farm-consumers from those supplying power to non-farm rural consumers. This done, the electricity company has been rationing farm power supply, forcing farmers to use power and groundwater more efficiently, and curtailing aggregate groundwater withdrawals significantly (Shah et al. 2008). The states that are weighed under heavy burden of farm power subsidy—such as Gujarat, Rajasthan, Maharashtra, Tamilnadu and Andhra Pradesh—also aggressively promote drip irrigation

234 〰 *Tushaar Shah*

technologies among farmers not so much to save water but to save energy. Numerous field studies show that the use of drip irrigation reduces the quantity of groundwater pumped per hectare by 30–70 percent depending upon the crop and the season. In many other states, farmers use expensive energy to pump groundwater but then lose much of it in evaporation and seepage while conveying it in earthen field channels. Promoting piped conveyance can in this case save a great deal of energy.

On the supply side, the key transition India needs to make is from surface storage to aquifer storage. Intensive groundwater development has created problems, but also opportunities. As mentioned elsewhere, it is unique to India that farmers in command areas of many canal irrigation systems depend on pumping groundwater for irrigation. Punjab is an excellent example. It has India's largest and best canal network. Yet, 75 percent of Punjab's irrigated areas depend upon tubewells for irrigation (Shah 2009). Conjunctive management of surface and groundwater offers large opportunities for improving water productivity as well as saving energy. Conjunctive management can aim at minimizing, throughout the command area, average pumping depth of groundwater by spreading water over the command area. This would involve modifying the protocol for main system management as illustrated for the Mahi command area in Gujarat by Shah (1993).

Outside canal commands, the challenge is bigger. Until the 1960s, when India used to withdraw 10–20 km^3 of groundwater, it experienced very little natural recharge to its pre-development aquifer storage; most of the runoff was rejected recharge. Today, India's Central Groundwater Board estimates that some 10 percent of India's annual precipitation of 4,000 km^3 ends up as natural recharge without any significant human intervention. If a fraction of the resources and energies that India expends on building new surface reservoirs and canal systems is directed to promoting large-scale groundwater recharge in her groundwater hotspot areas of western and peninsular India, the country can not only greatly reduce its GHG emissions from pumping but also restore the resilience of its aquifers to protect agriculture from heightened hydro-climatic variability (Shah 2008).

Groundwater recharge, therefore, needs to become the new mantra for India's water policy. In this respect too, India needs to evolve strategies and technologies that suit its unique conditions.

Climate Change and Groundwater 〰 235

In hard-rock areas of India, farmers have built over 9 million large open wells at their own cost. These can be up to 8 m in diameter and 60–70 m in depth. Many have also invested in several–sometimes dozens–of horizontal and vertical bores inside them to enhance their connectivity with nearby water-bearing fractures. So far, these wells are used only for withdrawing water, but these can as well be used as excellent recharge structures if the sediment load of surplus flood waters during monsoons could be reduced using simple filtering and desilting technologies. True, with dugwell recharge, there are threats of groundwater contamination and these threats need to be contained by intensive campaigns to enhance farmer knowledge about improving the quality of water as an input, as far as practical.[13] However, Indian thinking on groundwater recharge is shaped by the experiences and technologies used in the western US and Australia. As a result, government hydro-geologists tend to prefer large spreading-type recharge structures rather than working with millions of well-owners to modify their wells for recharge. India needs to use the vast technological experience of Australia and the US to design recharge programs but in a manner that incorporates its own unique features. While there is no substitute for large spreading-type recharge structures in recharging large confined aquifers, not using millions of farmer-owned open wells for recharge is a great opportunity lost (Shah 2008).

Conclusion: Need for a Paradigm Change

In 2001, India's Central Ground Water Board produced a Master Plan for Groundwater Recharge (GoI 2005b). While the Plan had many limitations and flaws, its most striking contribution was its objective: of stabilizing static post-monsoon groundwater level throughout India at 3 m below the ground through a national program of groundwater recharge. Pursuing such a bold objective can be India's best feasible response to climate change mitigation as well as adaptation. However, doing this requires that India does a major rethink of its water policy and administration.

Re-orienting India's water strategy to meet the challenge of hydro-climatic change demands a paradigm change in the official thinking about water management. Although the groundwater agencies of the government are the custodians of our groundwater resource, in reality, multiple agencies in public and private sectors are

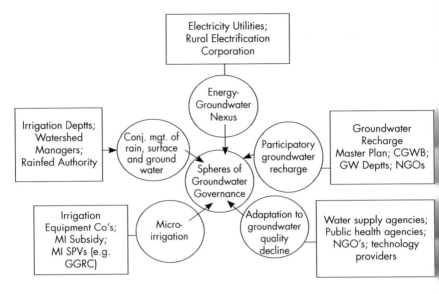

Figure 10.4: India's groundwater governance pentagram

Source: Prepared by the author.

major players in India's groundwater economy. As climate change transforms groundwater into a more critical and yet threatened resource, there is dire need for co-ordinating mechanisms to bring these agencies under an umbrella framework to synergize their roles and actions. Even as governments evolve groundwater regulations and their enforcement mechanisms, more practical strategies for groundwater governance need to be evolved in five spheres as outlined in Figure 10.2 (Shah 2009). Synergizing the working of agencies in these spheres offers the best chance to bring a modicum of order and method to the region's water-scavenging irrigation economy.

As of now, managing the energy-irrigation nexus with sensitivity and intelligence is India's principal tool for groundwater demand management. Gujarat's experiment was already mentioned earlier; but other ideas need to be tried, given that energy-irrigation nexus holds the key to minimizing the C-footprint of Indian irrigation. There has been a debate on the value of aggressively promoting micro-irrigation technologies. Some experts have argued that micro-

Climate Change and Groundwater ≈ 237

irrigation technologies–such as drip irrigation–saves water that would have otherwise returned to the aquifer for later use (Shah and Keller 2002; Narayanamoorthy 2004; Kumar 2003). However, in the climate-change context, micro-irrigation is important for energy savings even more than water savings. Indeed, in the context of climate change, water management structures and strategies need to achieve joint maximization of water productivity as well as energy-efficiency.

In hard-rock India, together with intelligent management of the energy–irrigation nexus, mass-based decentralized groundwater recharge offers a major short-run supply-side opportunity. Public agencies are likely to attract maximum farmer participation in any programs that augment on-demand water availability around farming areas. Experience also shows that engaging in groundwater recharge is often the first step for communities to evolve norms for local, community-based demand management.

In alluvial areas with aquifers, conjunctive management of rain, surface water, and groundwater is the hitherto underexploited big opportunity for supply-side management. Massive investments being planned for rehabilitating, modernizing, and extending gravity flow irrigation from large and small reservoirs need a major rethink in India. In view of the threat of climate change, India needs to rethink its storage technology itself. Over the past 40 years, India's landmass has been turned into a huge underground reservoir, more productive, efficient, and valuable to farmers than surface reservoirs. For millennia, it could capture and store little rainwater because in its pre-development phase it had little unused storage. The pump irrigation revolution has created 230–250 km^3 of new, more efficient storage in the subcontinent. Like surface reservoirs, aquifer storage is good in some places and not so good in others. To the farmer, this reservoir is more valuable than surface reservoirs because he has direct access to it and can obtain water on demand. Therefore, he is far more likely to collaborate in managing this reservoir if it responds to his recharge pull (Shah 2009).

In mainstream irrigation thinking, groundwater recharge is viewed as a byproduct of flow irrigation, but in today's India, this equation needs to be turned on its head. Increasingly, the country's 250 odd km^3 of surface storage makes economic sense only for sustaining on-demand groundwater irrigation in extended command areas. A cubic meter of recharged well water, available on demand, is valued

238 ≈ *Tushaar Shah*

many times more than a cubic meter of water in surface storage. Farmers' new-found interest in local water bodies throughout semi-arid peninsular India reflects the value of groundwater recharge. This is evident in south Indian tank-using farming communities that are converting irrigation tanks into percolation tanks, and in Saurashtra and Kutch, where a new norm intended to maximize groundwater recharge forbids the use of small surface reservoirs for irrigation in order to ensure the maximization of recharge (Shah and Desai 2002).

In the areas of India that experience massive evaporation losses from reservoirs and canals but high rates of infiltration and percolation, the big hope for surface irrigation systems–small and large–may be to reinvent them in order to enhance and stabilize groundwater aquifers that offer water supply close to points of use, permitting frequent and flexible just-in-time irrigation of diverse crops. Already, many canal irrigation systems create value not through flow irrigation but by supporting well irrigation by default through farmers investing in tube wells in command areas. But canal systems need to be redesigned for maximizing recharge over a larger area than the command. While farmers are doing their bit, the management of the system itself tends to be totally antithetical to optimal system-wide conjunctive use (Shah 1993:176–201). Surface system management is clearly in dire need of reinvention.

Surface systems in water-stressed regions of western India need to be remodeled to mimic the on-demand nature of groundwater irrigation. In the areas of Rajasthan receiving water from the Indira Gandhi Canal, the government is subsidizing farmers to make farm ponds, to be filled by canal once a month and then used to supply water on demand. Gujarat is following suit through a new program of supporting farmers in command areas to build on-farm storage from which they can irrigate on demand. Integrating large canal irrigation projects in the groundwater irrigation economy may support the case for rethinking their modernization in ways previously unimagined. Replacing lined canals with buried perforated pipes that connect with irrigation wells or farm and village ponds, creating recharge paths along the way, may be a more efficient way of using surface storage than flow irrigation.

There is a new groundswell of enthusiasm for pipes rather than open channels to transport water. The use of pipes for water transport is also valued for at least two other benefits: first, it saves scarce farmland otherwise used for digging watercourses and field channels,

Climate Change and Groundwater ≋ 239

and second, it offers opportunities for micro-irrigation. In the Sardar Sarovar Project in Gujarat, western India, the major reason for water user associations' refusal to build water distribution systems was land scarcity. In an agrarian economy with already high population pressure on farmland, flexible pipes for water distribution make more sense than surface channels, and buried pipes are even better. Pipes also support micro-irrigation technologies. This is what explains a boom in the use of plastics in many parts of Indian agriculture. And if China's experience is any guide (Shah et al. 2004), this boom will continue to generate water as well as energy savings.

By far the most critical response to hydro-climatic change in India's water sector demands exploring synergies from a variety of players for a nation-wide groundwater recharge program. Evolving a groundwater recharge strategy appropriate to India needs to begin with an appreciation of the variety of actors that can contribute through different kinds of recharge structures as suggested by Shah (2008). Public agencies with strong science and engineering capabilities need to play a major role in constructing and managing large recharge structures. However, in India, an intelligent strategy can also involve millions of farmers and householders–and thousands of their communities–each of whom can contribute small volumes to recharge dynamic groundwater. When we approach the problem thus, new strategic avenues present themselves. India's water policy has so far tended to focus on what governments and government agencies can do. Now, it needs to target networks of players, each with distinct capabilities and limitations. If groundwater recharge is to be a major response to hydro-climatic change, the country needs to evolve and work with an integrated groundwater recharge strategy with role and space for various players to contribute.

Notes

1. In some ways, this trend may reflect a continuation of some past ones. Based on analyses of rainfall data in the 1872–2005 period, Basishtha et al. (2007) identified secular decline in rainfall in north India barring Punjab, Haryana, west Rajasthan, Saurashtra and an increase in rainfall in southern India.
2. Goswami et al. (2006) by analyzing a daily rainfall data set have shown a rising trend in the frequency of heavy rain events and a significant decrease in the frequency of moderate events over central India from 1951 to 2000.

240 ≈≈ *Tushaar Shah*

3. Monitoring data on Himalayan glaciers present a confusing picture. They indicate recession of some glaciers in recent years, but the trend is not consistent across the entire mountain chain (Singh and Arora 2007).
4. Aquifers are also of interest to climate researchers for other reasons. Growing literature on Carbon Capture and Storage (CCS) and Geological Sequestration hints at opportunities that aquifers–especially saline and otherwise unusable–offer as "carbon storehouses." However, this chapter, focusing on climate change–groundwater–agriculture interaction, does not deal with these aspects.
5. *Ahar-pyne* system is a traditional system of irrigation popular in south Bihar. *Ahar* is a rectangular water harvesting structure with raised embankment on three sides. *Pyne* is a diversion channel that may divert water from a river or a stream into the *ahar*. Cuts are made into the embankment to divert stored water to irrigation fields.
6. A *johad* is a large village pond used more for irrigation, livestock and groundwater recharge than for washing and bathing.
7. Gerald C. Nelson and Richard Robertson, IFPRI, pers. comm., 2008.
8. J. Rao, pers. comm., 2008.
9. A study by the Indian Institute of Management (IIM), Ahmedabad, claims that of the "actual calories used by farmers out of 100 calories generated at the power plant is barely 2%" (Shukla et al. 2003: 93). This excludes the fossil energy used in mining and transporting the fuel for the thermal plants.
10. https://login.yahoo.com/config/login_verify2?.intl=us&.src=ygrp&. done=http%3a//groups.yahoo.com%2Fgroup%2FWaterWatch%2Fme ssage%2F6680 (accessed November 14, 2008).
11. C-footprint in the context can be viewed as the volume of Greenhouse Gas (GHG) released per hectare of groundwater-irrigated area.
12. This scheme was the "second-best" answer to the challenge of controlling subsidies on farm power supply. The best solution advocated was to install meters on each tube well and charge farmers tariffs based on their actual power consumption. However, groundwater irrigators in many states have opposed such a move over recent years. The next best option was to ration power supply to farmers for a fixed number of hours every day. But this could not be done effectively when the same feeder lines provided power to farmers as well as other rural users such as households, cottage industries, hospitals, schools, etc. In a clever move, Gujarat invested US$ 250 million in rewiring rural Gujarat. By separating the feeders supplying power to farmers from those supplying power to other rural users, Gujarat is now able to effectively impose a power ration on farmers, forcing them to use their electricity ration more efficiently. For a study of the impacts of this scheme, see Shah et al. (2008).

Climate Change and Groundwater 241

13. Many Western countries permit groundwater recharge only after ensuring that the quality of water is brought up to the level of drinking water quality. In developing countries like India, this may become practical but only in the long run. In any case, the degree of fertilizer and pesticide use in much of India is a small fraction of the degree of their use common in Western countries. As a consequence, chemical contaminant load of monsoon runoff is likely to be much smaller than that in the West. Moreover, in many parts of India, geogenic contaminants–fluoride, arsenic, etc.–are more of a public health hazard, and experience shows that the concentration of these, especially fluoride, declines where vigorous groundwater recharge programs are undertaken.

References

Basishtha, A., N. K. Goel, D. S. Arya and S. K. Gangwar. 2007. "Spatial Patterns of Trends in Indian Sub-divisional Rainfall," *Jalvigyan Sameeksha*, 22(1 & 2): 47–57.

Carter, R. C. 2008. "Climate, Population and Groundwater in Africa." Paper presented at the International Conference on Groundwater and Climate in Africa, June 24–28, Kampala, Uganda.

Choppra, K. 2005. "The Raining Nature," http://www.boloji.com/index.cf m?md=Content&sd=Articles&ArticleID=5468 (accessed November 10, 2008).

Gosain, A. K. and S. Rao. 2007. "Impact Assessment of Climate Change on Water Resources of Two River Systems in India," *Jalvigyan Sameeksha*, 22(1 & 2): 1–20.

Goswami, B. N., V. Venugopal, D. Sengupta, D., M. S. Madhusoodanam and P. K. Xavier. 2006. "Increasing Trend of Extreme Rain Events Over India in a Warming Environment," *Science*, 314(5804): 1442–45.

Government of India (GoI). 2005a. *Report on Third Census of Minor Irrigation Schemes (2000–01)*, Minor Irrigation Division, Ministry of Water Resources, GoI, New Delhi, http://wrmin.nic.in/micensus/mi3census/ reports/integrated/integrated_report.htm (accessed December 15, 2010).

———. 2005b. *Master Plan for Artificial Recharge to Groundwater in India*. New Delhi: Central Groundwater Board, Ministry of Water Resources, GoI.

Government of Pakistan (GoP). 2004. *Pakistan Agricultural Machinery Census*. Lahore: GoP.

Intergovernmental Panel on Climate Change (IPCC). 2001. *Climate Change: Impacts, Adaptation and Vulnerability*. Third Assessment Report of Intergovernmental Panel on Climate Change. Cambridge: Cambridge University Press.

242 ≋ *Tushaar Shah*

Kumar, M. D. 2003. "Food Security and Sustainable Agriculture in India: The Water Management Challenge." Working Paper 60, IWMI, Colombo.

Kundzewicz, Z. W. and P. Döll. 2009. "Will Groundwater Ease Freshwater Stress under Climate Change?," *Hydrological Sciences Journal*, 54(4): 665–75.

Mandal, M. A. S. 2006. "Groundwater Irrigation Issues and Research Experience in Bangladesh." Paper presented at the International Workshop on Groundwater Governance in Asia, November 12–14, Indian Institute of Technology (IIT), Roorkee.

Milly, P. C. D., J. Betancourt, M. Falkenmark, R. M. Hirsch, Z. W. Kundzewicz, D. P. Lettenmaier and R. J. Stouffer. 2008. "Stationarity is Dead: Wither Water Management?," *Science*, 319(5863): 573–74.

Narayanamoorthy, A. 2004. "Drip Irrigation in India: Can it Solve Water Scarcity?," *Water Policy*, 6(2): 117–30.

Nelson, G. C., R. Robertson, S. Msangi, T. Zhu, X. Liao and P. Jawajar. 2009. "Greenhouse Gas Mitigation: Issues for Indian Agriculture." IFPRI Discussion Paper 900, IFPRI, Washington.

Planning Commission of India. 2007. *Report of the Expert Group on Ground Water Management and Ownership*, GoI, New Delhi, http://planningcommission.nic.in/reports/genrep/rep_grndwat.pdf (accessed October 12, 2012).

Science Daily. 2007. "Climate Change Likely To Help With Groundwater Recharge", October 9, http://www.sciencedaily.com/releases/2007/10/071006091012.htm (accessed October 12, 2012).

Shah, T., et al. 2007. "Groundwater: A Global Assessment of Scale and Significance," in D. Molden (ed.), *Water for food, water for life: A Comprehensive Assessment of Water Management in Agriculture*, pp. 395–423. London: Earthscan; Colombo: IWMI.

Shah, T. 1993. *Groundwater Markets and Irrigation Development: Political Economy and Practical Policy*. Bombay: Oxford University Press.

——. 2008. "India's Master Plan for Groundwater Recharge: An Assessment and Some Suggestions for Revision," *Economic and Political Weekly*, 43(51): 41–49.

——. 2009. *Taming the Anarchy? Groundwater Governance in South Asia.* Washington: RFF press.

Shah, T. and J. Keller. 2002. "Micro-irrigation and the Poor: A Marketing Challenge in Smallholder Irrigation Development," in Hilmy Sally and Charles Abernethy (eds), *Private Irrigation in Sub-Saharan Africa*: *Proceedings of a Regional Seminar on Private Sector Participation in Irrigation in Sub-saharan Africa*, pp. 165–83. Colombo: IWMI.

Shah, T. and R. Desai. 2002. "Creative Destruction: Is That How Gujarat is Adapting to Groundwater Depletion? A Synthesis of ITP Studies." Pre-publication Discussion Paper presented at the IWMI-Tata Water

Climate Change and Groundwater ≈ 243

Policy Research Program Annual Partners' Meet, Indian Institute of Rural Management Anand (IRMA), February 19–20, Anand, Gujarat.

Shah, T., C. Scott, A. Kishore and A. Sharma. 2004. *Energy-Irrigation Nexus in South Asia: Improving Groundwater Conservation and Power Sector Viability.* Research Report 70. Colombo: IWMI.

Shah, T., O. P. Singh and A. Mukherji. 2006. "Some Aspects of South Asia's Groundwater Irrigation Economy: Analyses from a Survey in India, Pakistan, Nepal Terai and Bangladesh," *Hydrogeology Journal*, 14(3): 286–309.

Shah, T., S. Bhatt, R. K. Shah and J. Talati. 2008. "Groundwater Governance through Electricity Supply Management: Assessing an Innovative Intervention in Gujarat, Western India," *Agricultural Water Management*, 95(11): 1233–42.

Shukla, P. R., R. Nair, M. Kapshe, A. Garg, S. Balasubramaniam, D. Menon and K. K. Sharma. 2003. "Development and Climate: An Assessment for India." Unpublished report submitted to UCCEE, Denmark, by IIM, Ahmedabad.

Singh, P. and M. A. Arora. 2007. "Water Resources Potential of Himalayas and Possible Impact of Climate," *Jalvigyan Sameeksha*, 22(1 & 2): 109–32.

Thakkar, H. and B. Chandra. 2007. "Rs 100 000 crores Spent, but No Additional Benefits, No Addition to Canal Irrigated Areas for 12 Years," *Dams, Rivers & People*, 5(8–9):1–6.

The Age. 1891. "Deakin on Irrigation," February 7, http://150.theage.com.au/view_bestofarticle.asp?straction=update&inttype=1&intid=437 (accessed November 1, 2006).

Unnikrishnan, A. S. and D. Shankar. 2007. "Are Sea Levels trends along the North Indian Ocean Coasts Consistent with Global Estimates?," *Global and Planetary Change*, 57(1 & 2): 301–307.

Whitcombe, E. 2005. "Irrigation," in D. Kumar and M. Desai (eds), *The Cambridge Economic History of India, c 1757–c 1970*, pp. 677–737. Vol. 2. Hyderabad: Orient Longman.

Wittfogel, K. A. 1957. *Oriental Despotism: A Comparative Study of Total Power.* New Haven: Yale University Press.

PART IV

*International Experiences of
Water Reform*

11

Chilean Water Markets

History, Politics and Empirical Outcomes

Jessica Budds

—

The application of economic and market principles has been a significant policy shift in the international water sector over the last two decades. It has taken two main forms: private sector participation in urban water supply and schemes for tradable water rights. Tradable private water rights have been recommended on the basis that market mechanisms are able to increase the efficient management of *scarce* water resources, by encouraging water allocation to higher value uses (Simpson and Ringskog 1998). Importantly, however, these *economic* gains have been extended to other advantages, including *social* benefits. For example:

> This approach has the potential to increase the productivity of water use, improve operations and maintenance, stimulate private investment and economic growth, reduce water conflicts, rationalize ongoing and future irrigation development, and free up government resources for activities that have a public good content or positive externalities. And *it is likely to especially benefit the poor* and to help conserve natural resources (Thobani 1995: n/p; emphasis added).

The promotion of water rights markets for low-income countries has drawn heavily on the case of Chile, which, since 1981, has operated

248 ≋ *Jessica Budds*

a system of private water rights that can be freely traded with almost no government regulation (Bauer 2004). The World Bank in particular has heralded the Chilean system as successful, and has incorporated it into its water resources management strategy (WB 1992) and recommended its replication to other Latin American countries. However, this vigorous promotion is not based on any empirical evidence. The extent to which water markets have produced social and resource management benefits is greatly contested in Chile itself (Bauer 1998), despite bold yet unsubstantiated assertions of success by Chilean writers (Donoso 2006; Gazmuri 1994; Gazmuri and Rosegrant 1996; Ríos and Quiroz 1995). For example:

> Perhaps the most important achievements of Chilean water policy are social benefits through redistribution of wealth and eradication of poverty (Gazmuri 1994: 76).

> The establishment of tradable water rights and redistribution of a large portion of these water rights to former landless laborers was seen as a substantial improvement in equity (Rosegrant and Gazmuri 1994: 19).

Such assertions have been widely, but uncritically, cited by several World Bank publications, which have dismissed the possible negative social impact of Chilean water rights system (Briscoe 1996; Briscoe et al. 1997; Hearne and Easter 1995, 1997; Simpson and Ringskog 1998; Thobani 1995). For example:

> Evidence from Chile suggests that not only are negative impacts small, but that the agricultural regions have benefited substantially from water trading (Rosegrant and Gazmuri 1994: 30).

> Even though some specific equity problems might be involved with the initial implementation of a private water right market, it seems to be a non issue in the case of Chile given the traditional operation of a water market among farmers (Ríos and Quiroz 1995: 27).

This chapter presents an account of Chilean water markets and their empirical outcomes for low-income water users. Following this introduction, the chapter starts with outlining the history and creation of Chile's 1981 Water Code. The following section examines the long-standing and polemic debate over the water markets model,

Chilean Water Markets ~ 249

and attempts to reform it after the return to democracy. The next section presents existing empirical work on water markets in Chile, and then two studies focusing on their social outcome in Northern Chile. The first case explores the access of peasant smallholders and commercial farmers in La Ligua river basin to new water rights, in particular, to groundwater, while the second one examines the demand for water rights from mining and its consequences for indigenous groups and wetlands in the Atacama. The final section draws some conclusions about the social implications of Chilean water markets.

Chile's Neoliberal Model and the 1981 Water Code

In Chile, water rights, or concessions allowing the exclusive use of water, have existed in various forms since colonial times. During the colonial period water was a public resource that could be allocated to private parties as water grants. The first Water Code of 1951 replaced water grants with fixed-term water use concessions, or water rights. Once granted and in use, water rights became a private property that could be sold or rented, and only canceled with compensation, unless they had not been used for five years (Bauer 1998; Muchnik et al. 1997).

In 1967, the 1951 Water Code was revised in line with agrarian reform to reinstate government control over land and water. The government canceled the existing water rights without paying compensation by amending the 1925 Constitution and declaring water as "national property for public use", meaning that water rights reverted to administrative concessions (Bauer 1998; Muchnik et al. 1997). Water rights for irrigation could no longer be traded or separated from land and were no longer registered in property registers (Bauer 1998).

Following the military coup in 1973, the military government under Augusto Pinochet immediately reversed the statist policies of the previous governments under Eduardo Frei Montalva and Salvador Allende. This reversal included suspension of land reforms and return of the expropriated lands to their former owners. By 1980, the situation with water rights became chaotic, partly because no records of water allocation had been kept since 1967, but mainly because the statist water law was incompatible with the new market-

250 ≈ *Jessica Budds*

oriented politico-economic order whose construction was underway (Bauer 1998).

Chile's military government is often noted for its two key characteristics: political authoritarianism and a neoliberal economic program. This historical-political context—which has always been missing from mainstream policy accounts of Chilean water markets— had profound implications for the formulation of the Water Code in 1981, and the form of water governance and management that it created.

When the military seized power, it recruited civilian advisers from its allies to implement reforms. Instated in secondary positions, these advisors included experts from two related groups: the *Gremialistas* and the "Chicago Boys" (Huneeus 2000). The *Gremialistas* belonged to an ultra-conservative political movement, founded at the Catholic University of Chile to lead student opposition to Allende. The label "Chicago Boys" is widely used to refer to the group of Chilean neoliberal economists who undertook undergraduate studies at the Catholic University and postgraduate training at the University of Chicago, the then leading centre of the so-called neoliberal thought. Although the *Gremialistas* and the Chicago Boys are often portrayed as separate, many were either supporters or members of the *Gremialistas* (Huneeus 2000).

The Chicago Boys were the chief advisers in the designing of the neoliberal economic model, which entailed a drastic reduction in the state's role in the economy and society. The neoliberal reforms were designed to promote private sector participation in the economy, based on exports of natural resources (minerals, timber, agricultural produce) (E. Silva 1993). The political reforms were led by the *Gremialistas* and centred on the complete rewriting of the 1925 Constitution in 1980. The new constitution embodied the legal and institutional framework to create a free market economy and prevent a future return to statism. Much of the literature on the politics of this period in Chile describes the political and economic reforms as *separate*, whereby the *Gremialistas* established a new legal framework of reduced state intervention and more private liberty, while the Chicago Boys established a free market economy, supposedly without other political interests (Huneeus 2000). However, economic and political reforms were mutually reinforcing because the constitution contained measures to acquire and protect private property, which was necessary for market mechanisms to operate. This was designed

Chilean Water Markets ≈ 251

to prevent future legislators from modifying private property rights. Importantly, such radical neoliberal political and economic reforms were possible under the *authoritarian* regime (Huneeus 2000; P. Silva 1993); although they also gained popular support due to Chile's economic boom from 1978 to 1981. The new Water Code was passed at the height of neoliberalism in 1981. Its economic and market features were designed to consider water as a commodity, which entailed its separation from land in order to attribute a real cost to it.[1] The new Water Code had three objectives: to privatize water rights and prevent state intervention in land and water; to increase the efficiency and productive value of water by enabling re-allocation to higher value uses; and to foster private investment in water infrastructure to replace state funding. The economists considered water taxes a crucial element that would put a realistic price on water and thus encourage efficiency through re-allocation. However, taxes were strongly opposed by economic sectors, especially agriculture, as farmers supported private water rights, but opposed paying for water. This opposition forced the economists to withdraw taxes, although they were satisfied that the new water law would limit state power (Bauer 1998).

The 1981 Water Code introduced a number of important changes. Water rights were defined as private property, which:

a. were separate from those in land;
b. could be freely traded or transferred;
c. were guaranteed by the state and could only be expropriated for compensation at market value;
d. were governed by private law; and
e. were under no obligation to be used.

Water rights were applied to all surface water and groundwater resources, measured in liters per second. Existing water rights could be regularized, and rights were allocated to land redistributed under agrarian reform. New rights could be obtained by applying to the National Water Directorate (DGA). Water rights were granted free of charge and, if water were available, could not be refused. Once all available rights had been allocated, future reallocation was to take place through market transfers, as long as rights were registered. Water rights were to be registered at the local property registries, but only those rights that had been regularized, newly granted or

252 ～ *Jessica Budds*

formally traded, meaning that the record would not be complete. By the mid-1990s, however, many historic rights had still not been regularized, and many more had not been formally registered (ibid.).

Political Debate over the Water Code and Its Reform

The transition from the military government to democracy occurred in 1990. Although the incoming centre–left coalition government pledged its commitment to retaining the neoliberal model, it *did* intend to bring about some reforms, including modification of the Water Code (ibid.).

In 1992, the DGA proposed reforms to the Water Code, which focused on softening its most extreme neoliberal features, especially the possibility of water rights being obtained purely for speculative pruposes, and on expanding the role of the DGA from administrative functions to water resources management. In particular, it proposed a statement of planned use for new water rights applications and cancelation of water rights not used for five years without compensation. However, the proposed reforms were strongly opposed by three groups of conservatives: right-wing politicians, large-scale economic sectors, and independent "experts". This opposition forced the government to withdraw the proposals.

In 1996, the proposal was revised and re-submitted to the National Congress. It aimed to address the non-use of water and strengthen environmental regulation by the DGA. Its main difference with the 1992 proposal lay in its proposition to charge water users a fee for non-use of water instead of canceling their water rights and require from them a statement justifying the quantity of water requested for new rights. The revised reforms again encountered staunch opposition from the conservatives, based on practical concerns over the economic effects of a change in the law, and more ideological arguments in favor of neoliberalism.[2]

The proposed non-use fee was very controversial because it was considered to constitute de facto expropriation without compensation. The mining and hydroelectric power sectors were the strongest opponents of the non-use fee because they had the most unused water rights, and argued that the proposed fees were too high and the periods for non-use were too short for large-scale investment projects. The main concern of the agriculture sector

Chilean Water Markets ∽ 253

was that the rules for non-use were unclear and the definition of non-use would depend on the subjective interpretation of a DGA official.

A more ideological argument was that the proposed measures undermined the fundamental elements of the neoliberal model by infringing private economic liberty and weakening the security of private property rights, and thereby reducing the objective role of market in water allocation.

The third controversial aspect was the perception that the reforms signified a return to statism, by giving the DGA too much power. In turn, this perception led to the accusation that the government was reneging on the market mechanisms of the Water Code and the neoliberal model itself.

The strongest argument was that canceling or placing new restrictions on water rights without paying compensation would violate the constitutional guarantee of private property. However, this argument was weakened, but not dismissed, after the Constitutional Court declared that the proposal was not unconstitutional.

More debate centered on the need to reform the Water Code. While some accepted that some problems had risen, strong disagreement persisted about their scale and how to address them. Some thought that the extent of speculation and hoarding was unknown and probably confined to particular sectors, and resented the proposal of modifying the entire legislation. Others supported strengthening the existing institutional framework, and perfecting economic incentives and market mechanisms to address inequitable distribution and environmental concerns, as opposed to increasing state regulation. Still others continued to argue that the Water Code worked well as long as it was applied correctly.

The debate over the modification shows that the Water Code is highly politicized: the arguments marshaled against the reforms are articulated in politico-ideological terms and are strongly linked to political affiliations or vested interests. The debate is consistently framed in terms of the state versus the private sector, and reflects wider disagreements about the merits of the statist approach embodied by Allende compared with the neoliberal program of the military government of Pinochet. For instance:

> [The modification] has produced a war of attrition between the public and private sectors that is very damaging for the country, and it is more about a political vision with no technical justification, because

254 ≈ *Jessica Budds*

the idea is to change everything that was a legacy of the former government under General Pinochet (*El Diario* 2002).

The arguments for strengthening the market and minimizing the role of the state are so forcefully voiced because they constitute more than a debate over optimal water management; they represent a compromise with the interests of the largest and the most powerful economic sectors in Chile which directly benefit from a system of private, liberal and marketized water allocation.

Empirical Outcomes of Water Markets

Existing Research

Despite the importance of the Chilean model in international water policy, only limited empirical research has been done in Chile. The first comprehensive field study was undertaken by Carl Bauer (1998) who examined the practical operation of the Water Code in relation to agriculture and hydroelectricity, and identified a number of problems and limitations. In particular, he observed that water markets were largely inactive, even when users economized water because of barriers related to geography, infrastructure, legal and administrative systems, cultural attitudes and transaction costs. Concluding that market principles operated differently on the ground than at the theoretical level, he writes, "Markets are not automatic or self-regulating but depend on their social, institutional and geographic contexts" (1998:119).

Later empirical research, mostly based on economic analyses in the agriculture sector, confirmed that water markets were inactive (Hearne and Easter 1995, 1997). However, this inactivity was attributed to the "optimal" original allocation of water rights which resulted in low sales (Ríos and Quiroz 1995). An exception is the Limarí basin in northern Chile which has an active market in *leasing* of water rights but not their *sale*, due to three storage reservoirs that enable users to predict the amount of water available for each growing season. However, further research suggested that the sale of water rights that did occur was largely by small to large farmers, especially in times of hardship faced by the former (Romano and Leporati 2002). Although Bauer (1998) did not specifically study the implications of water rights transfers for peasant farmers, his observations in the agriculture sector led him to conclude that

Chilean Water Markets ≈ 255

they were worse off than commercial farmers due to their fewer formalized legal rights, poorly maintained infrastructure, little influence in water users organizations, avoidance of the legal system and state bureaucracy, and inability to undertake private bargaining. However, others argue that rural poverty is more deep-rooted:

> There is nothing very serious, because users have kept on using the water as they did before 1981—nothing has changed . . . The problem is not the Water Code itself, but the social context within which it is implemented.[3]

Peña maintained that there was no evidence of the monopolization of water rights by wealthier users, although he accepts that data were neither complete nor had been analyzed for these purposes. However, he referred to two cases in which he suggested that the transfer of water rights led to efficiency and economic gains: the sale of indigenous water rights to mining companies in the Atacama, and leasing of water rights in the Limarí valley. In both of these cases, peasant smallholders sold their water rights to wealthier users rather than produce low-value crops themselves.

The next two sub-sections will consider these issues by presenting some empirical research on the impact of water rights markets in two case studies in northern Chile (Budds 2009).

Agriculture and Irrigation in La Ligua River Basin[4]

La Ligua is a semi-arid river basin in central-northern Chile. The Ligua River receives its greatest flow in spring (from snowmelt) and has a reduced flow in the summer. The valley also contains a shallow alluvial aquifer. Land in the valley was re-organized under agrarian reform. Under the 1967 Water Code, water rights were assigned to land, but full allocation was an still unresolved issue by 1981. The Water Code contains two clauses to regularize historic water rights. The first recognizes historic rights that have been in continuous use since 1976, and involves an application for recognition of these rights to the civil court, supported by a DGA technical report. The second recognizes water rights pertaining to the land reallocated under the agrarian reform program at a fixed flow rate of one liter per second per hectare, and the application is dealt with by the Agricultural

256 ～ *Jessica Budds*

and Livestock Service (SAG). SAG rules that the second clause only applies to water rights for land originally assigned as *irrigated*, and in use *at the time* of assignation, and believes that most of the wells subject to this eligibility criterion under this clause have already been regularized.[5]

From 1990s, La Ligua underwent a shift and expansion from annual crops (wheat, potatoes, beans, maize) for the domestic consumption to fruit production (avocados, citrus fruits, nuts) for export. Increased avocado production was made possible by two factors. First, much rain-fed land on the slopes of Li Ligua valley owned by peasant communities remained untilled. The temperature on the slopes is slightly higher than that on the valley floor (which is optimal for cultivation of avocados), and the price of land on slopes is much lower than that of irrigated land on the valley floor, because the former does not have access to water. Peasants sold tracts of this land because they were not working it, nor had the resources to do so. Second, the rise in avocado production followed advances in well-drilling and mechanized pumps to extract groundwater, as well as new irrigation technology, in particular drip systems, which came to be mass-produced and hence cost-effective. These systems had the significant advantage of being able to transport water uphill.

Wealthy farmers increasingly brought more land under avocado cultivation. Seeking to invest in production for export, they bought much of the rain-fed land on the slopes of the valley for starting new plantations. Many peasant smallholders also sold their land parcels to such investors, often due to indebtedness. Peasant farmers have been slower to shift to fruit production, but, encouraged by micro-credit and subsidies from the Institute for Peasant Agricultural Development (INDAP), they have increasingly converted some, or in some cases all, of their land to orchards.

The expansion of fruit plantations led to an increase in demand for water, especially groundwater, for two reasons. First, surface water rights were fully allocated, whereas groundwater was plentiful and available. Second, groundwater is cleaner and more reliable during dry periods. Many irrigation wells now exist in the valley and most farmers have at least one. Some wells have been adapted from old drinking-water boreholes, but most have been drilled for irrigation.[6] Farmers on the valley floor tend to use surface water as their main source and groundwater as a backup, while those with new irrigation technology, which includes all those with slope plantations, pump

Chilean Water Markets ☰ 257

groundwater. As the water table is usually quite deep on the slopes, most farmers have purchased a piece of land on the valley floor, in order to drill wells and transport water to the slopes.

The increase in groundwater use led to a rise in applications for new groundwater rights, primarily from large farmers. In 1996, the DGA suspended groundwater allocation pending a hydrological assessment.[7] Applications for new rights formed a waiting list of applicants for any rights that would later be allocated. The suspension did not affect the regularization of historic rights. Regularization then became the principal mechanism for acquiring legal groundwater rights. However, it has been used mostly by large farmers, and widely abused as well.[8] Many applications are either dubious or clearly false in terms of both the length of time and the volume of water used historically.[9] While it is difficult to ascertain the age of wells, applications were submitted for wells on rain-fed land that had never been irrigated. If the DGA's technical report expressed doubt, applicants either abandoned the application or summoned false witnesses to give testimonies.[10]

When water rights are fully allocated, the intended mechanism for transfers is the market. In La Ligua, since many groundwater rights are unregistered, and most farmers want to buy and not sell, the market is limited. When water rights are offered for sale, the price is high.[11] However, even when farmers switched to groundwater, they did not sell their surface water rights. For example, as a peasant said, "You can't sell the water and leave the parcel without water rights, otherwise you wouldn't be able to sell the land. If you don't have water, the land is no good for anything."[12]

Local evidence suggests that the majority of wells are illegal.[13] While this affects all farmers, larger ones have the resources to regularize rights, legitimately or otherwise, and apply for new water rights. Moreover, they attach more importance to legalization, partly to access state irrigation subsidies (which require legal water rights), partly to protect their water against potential infractions (only legal rights can be defended), and partly due to the value of water as private property. Illegal water use has not been controlled because the DGA has no regulatory powers.[14] In La Ligua, some large farmers have also violated peasant smallholders' water rights.

Many farmers fear that the expansion of plantations will exacerbate water scarcity in the valley. The drought in 2007–08 occurred even when the cultivated area was twice that in 1996–97, and it seriously

258 ~ *Jessica Budds*

affected all farmers. However, in particular, the peasants, who had mono-cropped their land with avocados, were the least able to cope with the losses. Even the small and shallow wells legalized by a special mechanism under the 2005 reform ran dry.

The construction of a water storage reservoir in the upper La Ligua valley, with generous state subsidies, is widely held as the solution to the problem of water scarcity, especially by a consortium of large farmers. However, this solution re-positions the problem of overexploitation of groundwater by them as physical water scarcity due to the river's natural regime. The scheme is also justified by peasant smallholders' lack of access to water; yet it is precisely they who contribute the least to groundwater overexploitation, but have become most vulnerable as a result.

In La Ligua, private tradable water rights have brought few benefits for peasant smallholders, but have better positioned large farmers to access water resources at the expense of their irrigation security. In the words of one peasant leader, "The law [Water Code] works for the large farmers, not the small ones."[15]

Mining and Water in the Atacama[16]

The Loa River and the Salar de Atacama basins are located in the Atacama desert in northern Chile, an area marked by barren landscape, hot climate with virtually no precipitation. This part of the Atacama is inhabited by diverse indigenous groups collectively denominated as Atacameños under the 1993 Indigenous Law (Gundermann 2000).

Surface freshwater is scarce, but flows in streams emerging from the Andes, the Loa River and the subsurface springs that sustain the wetlands. Saline surface water is present in salares, the largest being the Salar de Atacama. Groundwater is found in aquifers at depths of around 100 m, and is "fossil" groundwater with a high mineral content.[17] Most economic uses demand surface freshwater, and its scarcity has resulted in competing demands to fulfil the needs of the mining sector, water supply utilities, indigenous groups and wetlands.

The region is Chile's principal copper mining area, copper being the country's most important export. The region has a large number of mines, many of which are owned by foreign mining companies. Mining demands huge flows of water for mineral

Chilean Water Markets ≈ 259

production processes: for example, Chuquicamata requires 12 cu m of water per second. The mining industry requires surface or subsurface freshwater for two reasons. First, surface water can be extracted in situ, whereas extracting groundwater requires deep wells and mechanized pumps, which are expensive to instal and operate. Second, groundwater is too saline and purification is costly. Freshwater scarcity has induced some large mines to economize water by recycling and instaling desalination plants on the coast.[18]

The region's state-owned waterworks company, ESSAN, supplies drinking water to the region's urban centers, as well as industrial consumers. ESSAN draws its water from surface sources for the same reasons. The region's growing tourist industry is also increasing the demand for piped water.

Atacameños live in small rural communities and practice traditional Andean subsistence-level terraced agriculture (cultivation of alfalfa, maize and quinoa) and petty commerce (in vegetables), as well as raise livestock. Their sources of irrigation water are surface freshwater streams and springs. Given the scarcity of water, they only irrigate once every two weeks. The region's wetlands, which consist of patchy marsh areas, are fed by subsurface freshwater springs. The wetlands are an important resource for Atacameños, primarily for livestock grazing, and also as a cultural feature of their landscape.[19]

The growth of mining since the 1980s has brought about significant changes in the economy, society and landscape of the region. Control over water, shaped by the Water Code, has been central to these changes. A combination of mechanisms to access water–regularizing existing water rights, requesting for new rights and purchasing rights from other users–allowed mining companies to gain large supplies of water, essential for existing and future mining operations. However, this situation quickly became contentious, not only because of the mining companies' control over large volumes of water, but also because their swift applications for new water rights meant that they claimed water that appeared as "available" even though it was used by other parties who had historic rights to it. Once available surface water had been exhausted, mining companies in particular looked to purchasing water from other users, including indigenous groups. This was largely done indirectly, via intermediaries who regularized the rights in order to resell them for a large profit. Anecdotal evidence indicates that indigenous people were coerced into selling water rights at well below the market price.[20]

260 ～ *Jessica Budds*

A wider debate revolves around the issue of informed consent. Humberto Peña used the case of Quillagua to illustrate the "effective" functioning of the water market, by transferring water from low-value uses (subsistence agriculture) to high-value uses (mining). Peña legitimized such transactions by asserting that indigenous sellers fully understood their actions, and moreover he considered that they had acted rationally by deciding to sell their water for a substantial sum of money, rather than to continue practicing traditional agriculture. However, the National Indigenous Development Corporation (CONADI) disputes this claim. It counterclaims that some Atacameños sold their water by signing papers that they could not read and accepting a price without knowing the market value, while others neither fully comprehended the act of "selling" nor its implications. This is because Atacameños view water as a holistic and inseparable part of nature, one that cannot be owned, let alone bought and sold.[21] However, the evidence is conflicting. On the one hand, some Atacameños continued to use the water they had sold, apparently not having understood the meaning of selling. On the other hand, the Water Director of CONADI (herself an Atacameña) visited potential Atacameño sellers to discourage them, invoking powerful arguments of ancestry and culture. Ultimately, the high value of water is often hard to resist by people who practice largely subsistence-level agriculture and are increasingly attuned to a non-indigenous lifestyle.

The Indigenous Law lays down provisions for demarcating indigenous resources, including ancestral land and water, and for passing the control over them to indigenous communities. Although it states that indigenous water rights must be protected, it prescribes no specific procedures for this. The Water Code makes no explicit reference to indigenous water rights, but these qualify for regularization on the basis of historic use. Significantly, the Indigenous Law enables regularized rights to be registered *communally*, rather than *individually*.

Using the Indigenous Law in response to the denial of water rights to Atacameños, CONADI initiated an indigenous water rights regularization program, as had been done in peasant communities throughout Chile (CONADI 1999; Cuadra 2000). Most regularizations proceeded smoothly; however, some sought to reclaim indigenous rights that had since been registered by other users, and some were challenged.

CONADI also implemented a program to repurchase (expropriate) water rights sold by indigenous people at the current market value.[22] The repurchased rights were registered as communal rights and could not be sold for 25 years, and thereafter only with the agreement of the entire community. The situation with groundwater is very different. In order to obtain groundwater rights, the applicant must demonstrate that the flow of the quantum of water requested exists, and this in turn requires drilling a well to extract it. Groundwater exploration has been extensive in the region and has led to encroachments on both the land inhabited by Atacameño communities and the land proposed for demarcation, although any subsequent water rights applications have been rejected.[23] Groundwater extraction has caused much resentment among Atacameños, not only because they oppose the extraction of groundwater from under their land for cultural reasons, but also because of its adverse impacts on the wetlands. However, they are powerless to claim groundwater rights themselves precisely *not* to use them because well-drilling is prohibitively expensive. Groundwater prospecting has since declined because mining companies were unwilling to buy water rights of questionable quality, reliability and origin.[24]

Atacameños have received few benefits from the development generated by mining, although it has brought about significant changes in their culture, livelihoods and landscape. Some companies have sought to reposition mining as socially and environmentally responsible, such as Minera Escondida. This company established the Minera Escondida Foundation in San Pedro de Atacama to promote local development around themes such as education, health and cultural identity–but not water.[25] However, the volume of investment in the Foundation is only a tiny fraction of either the profits generated by mining, or the value of the freshwater rights owned by Escondida, which is equivalent to just 10 liters per second. Although it has engaged with local people, its vision of local development is predicated upon the integration of indigenous communities into the modern economy, rather than allowing them to pursue their traditional lifestyle.[26] These sentiments have been expressed by Sandra Berna, Mayor of San Pedro de Atacama, herself an *Atacameña*:

> Escondida took our water but created the Foundation to assist us. Other mining companies take water and don't give anything . . . so,

262 ≈ *Jessica Budds*

it is "generous" . . . but I would prefer to own the water and sell it to Escondida at its real value.

Conclusions

The two case studies presented in this chapter challenge claims that water rights markets have led to social benefits for low-income water users. Both cases are characterized by demand for water from commercial interests that reduced the availability and/or security of water among low-income water users. In both cases, low-income groups experienced violations of their water rights by other parties and were unable to properly approach the courts or the government for redress in the absence of appropriate state regulations. Indeed, in both cases, government intervention was necessary to secure their water rights. Both peasant smallholders and indigenous groups faced particular challenges in controlling groundwater.

Much of the focus of Chile's Water Code is on market mechanisms. Although the water market was more significant in producing social outcomes in the Atacama, social impact was also evident in La Ligua despite the lack of trade in water rights. In addition, both cases showed evidence of depletion of water resources in the absence of regulation. This has several implications. First, the La Ligua case challenges the claim that water markets are inactive due to the optimal initial distribution of rights, because groundwater rights were unevenly distributed between large commercial farmers and peasant smallholders, with no change in market activity. Second, it suggests that water is fundamentally seen as both a *strategic* and a *symbolic* resource, and not a regular commodity that can simply be traded, even if people are not using it. Third, it refutes the idea that water trading can increase water use efficiency, because once resources have been fully assigned, re-allocation will occur through the market. The La Ligua case in particular showed that farmers looked to fresh *supplies* when faced with the exhaustion of present resources, which contradicts the ability of markets to manage *demand*. Four, it implies that it is not just the *tradable* nature of private water rights that produces these effects, but the broader gamut of neoliberal reforms, especially administration by private law and lack of regulation, as well.

In turn, these analyses challenge some of the broader economic arguments made about water markets, including the simplistic

Chilean Water Markets ≈ 263

assessment that water transfers demonstrate efficiency if they re-allocate water from low–to high-value uses. These standard cost–benefit assessments fail to incorporate the impact of the loss of traditional lifestyles and community cohesion, or environmental degradation. Such a material reading of water use reflects a wholly *utilitarian* argument that rights should reflect both economic and efficient use, rather than cultural or ecological uses.

One of the principal social benefits claimed to be associated with private water rights is increased water security. This also can be contested on two grounds. First, legal water rights can only be defended in the civil courts. In practice, groups with a low socio-economic status neither have the social skills nor the resources to use the legal system. Second, private property rights are a double-edged sword. Paradoxically, the tradability of legal water rights brings them *into* the market, and thus subject to acquisition by others.

The social impact of the Water Code has often been dismissed by the assertions that water use has not changed since its implementation, or that the law "applies to all Chileans alike." Both cases show that water use has indeed changed since 1981. The cases also highlight inequality of access to water rights. The idea of the law as equitable rests on a conceptualization of legal mechanisms as *technical* and *neutral,* but in practice they depend on *socio-economic status* and *resources,* particularly access to information, knowledge, money and social institutions.

The Water Code enabled economic sectors to exert greater control over water resources, to the detriment of low-income users, traditional water rights and water resources. However, these social outcomes should not be understood as impacts of the water markets model per se. Rather, they are embedded within wider social relations that produce social inequality, including in terms of access to water. In this regard, it is very important not to detach the Water Code from the historical-political context within which it was produced. The Water Code formed a key part of the *political* project assembled by the "technocrats" under the military government; the Code was less about an effective way to manage water and more about benefiting Chile's key industries in line with their own vested interests and long-term goals. The outcomes of the Water Code cannot, therefore, be understood in isolation from this context.

Notes

1. See Bauer (1998) for a comprehensive account of the formulation of the 1981 Water Code and a description of its features.
2. This section draws on press records from Chile from 1990 to 2004, publications of think tanks and documents released by the Senate.
3. Interview with Humberto Peña, former Director, DGA, Santiago, August 4, 2003.
4. For a more in-depth account of the La Ligua case, see Budds (2004).
5. Interview with Carlos Carrera, formerly responsible for water rights regularizations at SAG, Santiago, July 28, 2003.
6. An INDAP survey of peasants' wells in La Ligua identified 1,049 wells, of which 817 were built after 1977.
7. Interview with Christian Neumann, formerly Regional Director, DGA Fifth Region, Quillota, September 10, 2003.
8. This problem is substantiated by two water lawyers interviewed in La Ligua on August 7, 2003, and in Santiago on September 17, 2003, and by an analysis of regularizations at La Ligua Civil Court (1995–2003).
9. Analysis of applications for regularization, La Ligua Civil Court (1995–2003).
10. Ibid.
11. US $ 1,500–3000 and up to US $ 5,000 per liter per second (Interview with a large farmer, La Ligua, June 13, 2003).
12. Interview with a leader of peasant smallholders, El Carmen village, La Ligua, July 29, 2003.
13. Claimed by NGOs and INDAP, and openly admitted by large farmers.
14. Pablo Jaeger, former legal representative, DGA, Santiago.
15. Interview with a leader of smallholder peasants from El Carmen village, Li Ligua.
16. For a more in-depth account of the Atacama case, see Budds (2010).
17. Interview with Hugo Alonso, Professor of Chemistry, Catholic University of Northern Chile, Antofagasta, December 1, 2003.
18. Interview with Jorge Zeballos, Director of Corporate Affairs, Minera Escondida, Antofagasta, December 3, 2003.
19. Interview with Milka Castro, Professor of Anthropology, University of Chile, Santiago, September 1, 2003.
20. Interview with Marco Soto, Regional Director, DGA Second Region, Antofagasta, December 2, 2003.
21. Interview with Liliana Cortéz, Regional Director, CONADI, Calama, November 27, 2003; interview with Sandra Berna, Mayor of San Pedro de Atacama, November 26, 2003.
22. CONADI paid approximately US$27,000 per liters per second (2003).
23. Analysis of records of water rights applications, San Pedro de Atacama, December 2003.
24. Interview with Jorge Zeballos.

Chilean Water Markets ≈ 265

25. Interview with Manuel Escalante, Director of Indigenous Affairs, Minera Escondida Foundation, San Pedro de Atacama, November 28, 2003.
26. Interview with Liliana Cortéz.

References

Bauer, C. 1997. "Bringing Water Markets Down to Earth: The Political Economy of Water rights in Chile, 1976–95," *World Development,* 25(5): 639–56.

———. 1998. *Against the Current? Privatization, Water Markets and the State in Chile.* Boston: Kluwer.

———. 2004. *Siren Song: Chilean Water Law as a Model for International Reform.* Washington: Resources for the Future Press.

Briscoe, J. 1996. *Water Resources Management in Chile: Lessons from a World Bank Study Tour.* Washington: The World Bank.

Briscoe, J., P. Anguita and H. Peña. 1997. "Managing Water as an Economic Resource: Reflection on the Chilean Experience." Working Paper 62, The World Bank, Washington.

Budds, J. 2004. "Power, Nature and Neoliberalism: The Political Ecology of Water in Chile," *Singapore Journal of Tropical Geography,* 25(3): 322–42.

———. 2009. "The 1981 Water Code: The Impacts of Private Tradable Water Rights on Peasant and Indigenous Communities in Northern Chile," in W. Alexander (ed.), *Lost in the Long Transition: Struggles for Social Justice in Neoliberal Chile,* pp. 35–56. Lanham, Maryland: Lexington Books.

———. 2010. "Water Rights, Poverty and Environmental Management in Chile: Water, Mining and Indigenous Groups in the Atacama," in R. Boelens, D. H. Getches and J. A. Guevara Gil (eds), *Out of the Mainstream: Water Rights, Politics and Identity,* pp. 197–211. London: Earthscan.

Chilean Indigenous Development Corporation (CONADI). 1999. *Proyecto regularización de derechos de agua Provincia El Loa: II Región* [Water Rights Regularization Project in El Loa Province: Second Region]. Calama: CONADI.

Cuadra, M. 2000. "Teoría y práctica de los derechos ancestrales de agua de las comunidades atacameñas [Theory and Practice of Ancestral Water Rights Pertaining to Communities in the Atacama]," *Estudios Atacameños,* 19: 93–112.

Donoso, G. 2006. "Water Markets: Case Study of Chile's 1981 Water Code," *Cien cia e Investigaction Agraria,* 33(2): 157–71.

El Diario. 2002. "Fuertes discrepancias entre gobierno y empresarios por Código de Aguas," January 22, www.eldiario.cl (accessed October 12, 2012).

Gazmuri, R. 1994. "Chile's Market-oriented Water Policy: Institutional Aspects and Achievements," in G. Le Moigne, K. Easter, W. Ochs and

266 ≋ *Jessica Budds*

S. Giltner (eds), *Water Policy and Water Markets*, pp. 65–78. Washington, DC: The World Bank.

Gazmuri, R. and M. Rosegrant 1996. "Chilean Water Policy: The Role of Water Rights, Institutions and Markets," *Water Resources Development*, 12(1): 33–48.

Gundermann, H. 2000. "Las organizaciones étnicas y el discurso de la identidad en el norte de Chile, 1980–2000 [Ethnic Organizations and the Discourse of Identity in Northern Chile, 1980–2000]," *Estudios Atacameños*, 19: 75–91.

Hearne, R. and K. Easter. 1995. "Water Allocation and Water Markets: An Analysis of Gains-from-Trade in Chile." Technical Paper 315, The World Bank, Washington DC.

———. 1997. "The Economic and Financial Gains from Water Markets in Chile," *Agricultural Economics*, 15(3): 187–99.

Huneeus, C. 2000. "Technocrats and Politicians in an Authoritarian Regime: The 'ODEPLAN Boys' and the 'Gremialists' in Pinochet's Chile," *Journal of Latin American Studies*, 32(2): 461–501.

Muchnik, E., M. Luraschi and F. Maldini. 1997. *Comercialización de los Derechos de Aguas en Chile [Water Rights Markets in Chile]*. Santiago: Economic Commission for the Latin America and the Caribbean (ECLAC).

Ríos, M. and J. Quiroz. 1995. "The Market for Water Rights in Chile: Major Issues." Technical Paper 285, The World Bank, Washington, DC.

Romano, D. and M. Leporati 2002. "The Distributive Impact of the Water Market in Chile: A Case Study in Limarí Province, 1981–1997," *Quarterly Journal of International Agriculture*, 41(1–2): 41–58.

Rosegrant, M. and R. Gazmuri 1994. "Reforming Water Allocation Policy through Markets in Tradable Water Rights: Lessons from Chile, Mexico and California." Environment and Production Technology Division (EPTD) Discussion Paper 6, International Food Policy Research Institute (IFPRI), Washington.

Silva, E. 1993. "Capitalist Coalitions, the State and Neoliberal Economic Restructuring: Chile, 1973–88," *World Politics*, 45(4): 526–59.

Silva, P. 1993. "Intellectuals, Technocrats and Social Change in Chile: Past, Present and Future Perspectives," in A. Angell and B. Pollack (eds), *The Legacy of Dictatorship: Political, Economic and Social Change in Pinochet's Chile*, pp. 198–223. Institute of Latin American Studies, Liverpool: University of Liverpool.

Simpson, L. and K. Ringskog. 1998. *Water Markets in the Americas*. Washington, DC: The World Bank.

The World Bank. 1992. *Water Resources Management*, Washington, DC: The World Bank.

Thobani, M. 1995. "Tradable Property Rights to Water: How to Improve Water Use and Resolve Water Conflicts." FPD Note 34, Public Policy for the Private Sector, Washington, DC: The World Bank.

12

South Africa's Reformed Water Law and Its Challenging Implementation

Eiman Karar

—

This essay is largely focussed on institutional reforms in the management of water resources in South Africa. It briefly describes how water reforms in South Africa were formalised and why they were initiated, and highlights some of the ground realities and challenges in the implementation of a water law hailed internationally as one of the best in recent times. Many progressive clauses are included in South Africa's new water policy. How they are being implemented probably merits some explanation. However, this chapter mainly dwells on the aspects of decentralization of water resources management rather than the implementation of water policy itself.

The local management of water resources, as it has evolved to date, is first mapped out to illustrate the sequence of events and motives resulting in the decentralization of water management. This is followed by a select account of some of the challenges faced in and lessons learnt from such decentralization. The targets realized are stated, as also those that could not be realized due to various reasons that, in turn, are analyzed on the basis of a review of the existing literature and author's expert knowledge. The slow pace of

268　≈≈　*Eiman Karar*

change in the management roles and in the devolution of power is discussed, along with the challenges attendant upon those changes, such as limited co-operation and co-ordination between the state and the local actors as well as the shortage of adequately skilled water resource managers to match the demand created by decentralization. In terms of access to water, only marginal improvement has been witnessed, largely because of the perception that the river catchments are over-allocated, resulting in the dearth of additional water which can be allocated to those who were marginalized or denied access to water in the past. Needless to say, priority is given to the projected demands for domestic use of water as well as to those for developmental uses, such as new platinum mining in the Limpopo basin since 2006.

Sources, Availability and Use of Water Resources

South Africa is located in a predominantly semi-arid part of the world. It has a total surface area of 1.2 million sq. km and receives an average rainfall of 450 mm per year, well below the world average of 860 mm (see Map 12.1). The climate varies from desert type and semi-desert type in the west to sub-humid type along the eastern coast. South Africa's water resources are, in global terms, scarce and extremely limited. The country has no truly large navigable rivers, and the combined flow of all the rivers in the country amounts to approximately 49,000 million cu m per year (m^3/a), less than half of that of Zambezi, a large river closest to South Africa. The poor spatial distribution of rainfall and runoff is compounded by strong seasonality as well as high intra-season variability of rainfall over virtually the entire country, causing water-related disasters such as floods and droughts. Moreover, urban and industrial development, as well as growth of some dense rural settlements, has occurred in areas remote from large watercourses, a phenomenon governed by either the occurrence of mineral wealth or the political dispensation in the past. As a result, the requirement for water in several river basins far exceeds its natural availability, and often large-scale transfers of water across catchments have, therefore, already been made in the past decades (DWAF 2004).

Because of the predominance of hard rocks in the South African geology, only about 20 percent of groundwater occurs in major aquifer systems that can be utilised on a large scale.

South Africa's Reformed Water Law and Its Challenging Implementation

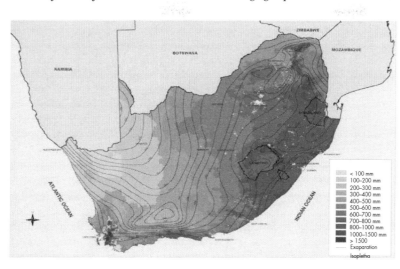

Map 12.1: Annual rainfall and evaporation

Source: Adapted from DWAF (2004).

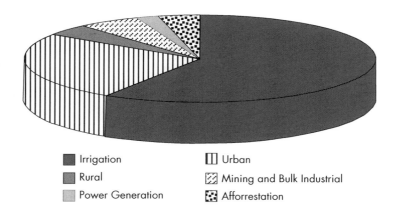

Figure 12.1: Sectoral break-up of water requirements

Source: DWAF (2004).

However, groundwater plays a pivotal role, especially in rural water supplies. Of the available water, 62 percent is used for agriculture, 23 percent for urban water supply, four percent for rural water supply, 6 percent for mining and heavy industry, 2 percent for power generation and 3 percent for afforestation (ibid.) (see Figure 12.1).

270 ≈ *Eiman Karar*

Pre-1994 Water Policy

Inequalities in land and water distribution in the country are closely linked to its history of European colonial rule and apartheid. Under the Native Land Act of 1913 (Act No. 27 of 1913), only 9 percent of the total land area was designated for Blacks who formed about three quarters of the total population.[1] The Act further prohibited transfer of land between Blacks and Whites. Not only land acquisition, access to water was made difficult by the prevalent laws at that time.[2]

In support of these laws and regulations, processes and institutions were developed which increasingly intervened in the development of water resources in favor of the White agricultural community. An important consequence of the recognition of riparian water rights under these laws was that not only did the White land owners have solid water rights attached to their land, but they also enjoyed preferential use of public water flowing alongside their properties (Hollingworth 2008). Under the apartheid regime, which began in 1948, entire communities were forcibly relocated to the "homeland areas/Bantustans" in order to make productive land available for commercial forestry, national parks, etc. These homelands[3], mostly located in arid areas, were characterized by poor soils and limited water resources (Francis 2005). In addition to the discriminatory water laws already discussed, access to water was available to a privileged few who controlled land and had economic power.

Why was the Water Reform Introduced?

The main triggers behind water reforms were not very different from those behind national political reforms, though with some specific implications. The water crisis and supply-driven approaches had exhausted the limited available resources through the building of numerous large dams meant to supply water to the White minority population (Muller 2001). Thus, by the time the apartheid ended, the demand for water had increased manifold.

The post-apartheid democratic government was confronted with a situation in which majority of South Africans had been ousted from their lands and hence denied access to water for productive uses. Therefore, the main aim of the water reform was to redress the imbalances in the access to water resources for the purposes of subsistence, sanitation or commercial use. To be able to do that,

South Africa's Reformed Water Law and Its Challenging Implementation ≈ 271

the policy had to allow for the deviation from one of the Dublin Principles[4] that water is an "economic good" only, for in South Africa, as elsewhere, water had to be seen as a "social good" as well.

The main reforms that fundamentally deviated from the water law of 1956 were:

a. The abolition of riparian water rights which led to water being treated as private property by White land owners. In the National Water Act (No. 36 of 1998; henceforth NWA) water is a public good which is entrusted to the state. As its custodian, the state guarantees the rights of its use for basic human needs and environmental flow requirements.[5] International obligations[6] are also protected by the state.
b. The need for redressing inequities in water resource allocation.
c. The ability of all water users to partake in decision-making through the decentralization of management of resources to basin-based water management institutions such as Catchment Management Agencies (CMAs) and Water User Associations (WUAs).

From 1994 onwards, various processes of water reform have been carried out. Several policy documents, acts and regulations (Figure 12.2) have been introduced and public institutions have been developed in support of those reform processes and to ensure that they have appropriate community, racial and gender representation.

Institutional Reform

As the custodian of the country's water resources, the state represented in the Department of Water Affairs and Forestry (DWAF) (now the Department of Water Affairs, and henceforth referred to in this chapter as "the Department") remains the ultimate body accountable for sustainable, equitable and efficient use of water resources. However, the Department is not required to perform all management functions itself, and is mandated under the NWA to delegate functions to CMAs and other water management institutions such as WUAs, as and when it deems appropriate. The delegation of functions to CMAs is based on the principle of subsidiarity which requires the management of resources at the lowest

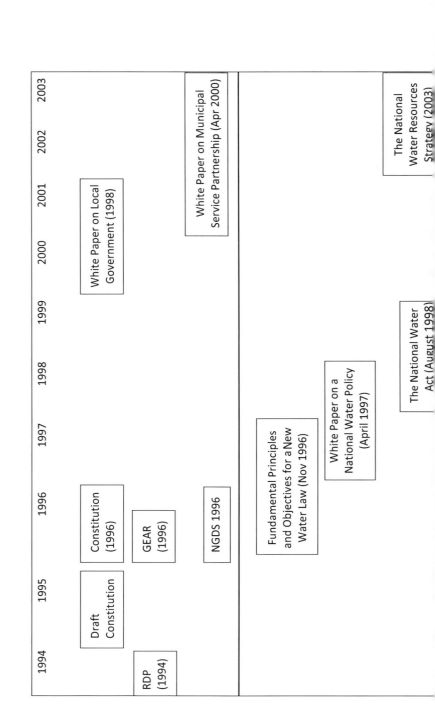

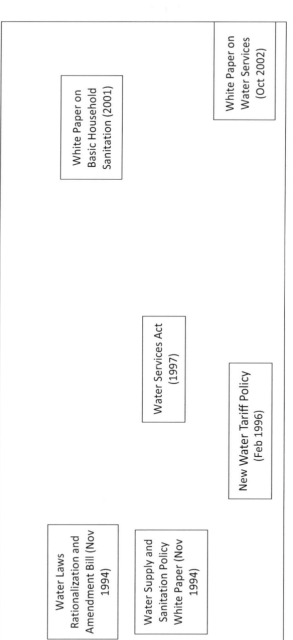

Figure 12.2: Macro-policy developments: water and related areas in South Africa (1994–2003)

Source: Adapted from De Coning and Sherwill (2004: 13).

274 〰 *Eiman Karar*

appropriate level, as described in Agenda 21 of the UN Conference on Sustainable Development at Rio de Janeiro in 1992. The Department, however, remains responsible for ensuring that these water management institutions deliver according to the stipulations of the NWA. The Department must, therefore, take up a stronger regulatory and oversight role vis-a-vis the water management institutions, so that it is prevented from undertaking the role of both a referee and a player.

The purpose of CMAs is described in the introductory notes to Chapter 7 of the NWA: "The purpose of establishing these agencies is to delegate water resource management to the regional or catchment level and to involve local communities, within the framework of the national water resource strategy established in terms of Chapter 2."

Shortly after the promulgation of the NWA, and after a process of public consultation, 19 WMAs were formed, and their boundaries defined using watercourse catchment boundaries, social and economic development patterns, efficiency considerations and communal interests within the area in question (NWA 1998: 22) (see Map 12.2).

During this early process various institutional challenges began to be recognized, including the difficult task of striking a balance between the size of a WMA and the need for having a local institutional presence therein; the disjuncture between hydrological and political boundaries; the mismatch between surface water boundaries and those of groundwater aquifers; and the relationship between WMAs and the larger basins of which they formed parts. This resulted in refining the boundaries which were described in the NWRS document (see Appendix E in DWAF 2004).

Each regional office of the Department put in place a process for the establishment of CMAs, although these processes varied considerably in accordance with the needs of particular WMAs, resulting in different outcomes and timeframes of their establishment (Karar and Pietersen 2009). Some took a very direct route, i.e., "top-down" approach towards the establishment of CMAs of which public participation in briefing meetings was a part. Others placed more emphasis on the "bottom-up" approach of establishing forums and WUAs as a precursor to the establishment of CMAs.

Once a CMA is fully functional, it should ultimately be responsible for most water resource management functions within its area of jurisdiction, including the authorization of water use. Certain

Map 12.2: Water Management Areas (WMAs)

Source: DWAF (1999).

strategic functions such as the determination of trans-boundary water-sharing obligations/agreements, water allocations to strategic industries and determination of inter-basin transfers will continue to be performed by the Department. However, a CMA starts with a set of initial functions set out in the NWA. Further, functions will be delegated as and when the capacity of the institution grows.

A WUA is a co-operative association of individual water users who wish to undertake water-related activities for their mutual benefit. The specific nature of the service that a WUA provides differ from case to case: as the name suggests, a water *user* association is an institution that serves its members. Because their needs differ from one area to another, a WUA is normally established in response to the aspirations of its members, i.e., its design conforms to their specifications. In cases where the Minister of Water Affairs and Forestry establishes a WUA on his/her own initiative, it should be ensured that it meets the aspirations of the people.[7] Where national imperatives may override local prerogatives, i.e., prerogatives of WUA members, the issue needs to be debated or discussed to arrive at an agreement. A WUA may be established for a range of activities including stream flow reduction, treatment of effluents and waste and their disposal, and controlling the use of water for recreational and/or environmental purposes (DWAF 2001). Upon its establishment, a WUA will carry out its principal functions as laid down in its constitution.

Alongside its principal functions, a WUA may have a range of other functions that affect its structure and management. In terms of the NWA, such functions may be performed only if they do not limit the WUA's capacity to perform its principal functions or financially prejudice it and its members. A common example of such an ancillary function is the provision of management services and training to water services institutions and rural communities.[8] An additional example, which is explored in some detail in this document, is the use of a WUA as an institution through which the empowerment of the poor can be facilitated by boosting agricultural production.[9]

Progress with Implementation of Water Law Reforms

It might still be too early to assess the outcomes of reform and if they have yielded the desired deliverables in terms of poverty eradication, basic human rights, gender equity and environmental sustainability. However, after almost 10 years since the promulgation of the NWA in 1998, observations, reflections and lessons can be useful for continuing the quest for integrated water resource management (IWRM)–is a vision that can only be realized progressively over a long period of time. In this chapter, subsequently, I offer to share some reflections and critical but constructive observations on the institutional reform plans and their implementation. The chapter does not account for the specific content of the new policy, as this has been adequately covered in South African literature such as

South Africa's Reformed Water Law and Its Challenging Implementation ≈ 277

the NWA (1998), DWAF and Water Research Commission (WRC) publications in 2004, 2005 and 2006.

Major Achievements/Successes to Date

The implementation of reform plans, has yielded some tangible results as exemplified in the following areas:

a. *Wide commitment and buy in*: Since the promulgation of the NWA in 1998, South Africa has seen a "buzzing" water sector wherein government, academia, private sector and non-governmental agencies as well as international experts have striven to produce a state-of-the-art legislation based on the "best practices" of the time, embodied by the 1992 IWRM Dublin Founding Principles such as subsidiarity, gender equity, water as an economic as well as social good and water management along hydrological boundaries.

b. *Restructuring of the former DWAF*: The Department that was historically responsible for meeting demand for water mainly through building infrastructure has been restructured to include the vast personnel and expertise requirements to fulfil the mandates of the new Act which include: stakeholder empowerment, institutional oversight, source and resource protection, integrated planning, monitoring of water quality and quantity within hydrological units (WMA), etc. Moreover, all nine regional offices have been regrouped into proto-CMA functional units which reflect all 19 WMAs.

c. *Catchment Management Agencies*: By the end of 2008, eight CMAs had been formally established through the Government Gazette. Two governing boards and two CEOs of Breede Overberg and Inkomati CMAs had been appointed, and whilst the Breede Overberg CMA was appointing its first line managers, only one, viz., the Inkomati CMA, had a significant staff in place under the CEO.

d. *Water User Associations*: More than 200 WUAs have been established to date. Most of them are transformed Irrigation Boards (IBs) which had been established under the old 1956 Act and were either responsible for the management of government water infrastructure or based on collective private ownership of dams. The IBs were responsible for collecting fees

278 ∽ *Eiman Karar*

for operating and maintaining water infrastructure, scheduling of water releases, etc., from all the commercial farmers. Their transformation into WUAs entailed that they become more inclusive of all water users in a locality. They are thought to be, in essence, the second tier of water management institutions executing local management of water resources, a function delegated by CMAs, once the latter are up and running.

e. *The Water Tribunal:* It is an independent body which has jurisdiction over water-related disputes in all the provinces and consists of a chairperson, a deputy chairperson and additional members. Members of the Water Tribunal are appointed by the Minister on the recommendation of the Judicial Service Commission, the body which chooses judges. The Water Tribunal replaced the *Water Court* in 1998.

f. *Strategic Planning:* The first NWRS was gazetted in 2004, to be reviewed every five years. The revised strategy is under construction for 2009–10. The purpose of the NWRS is to strategically direct the management of water resources from a national perspective. With the WMAs as primary geographic elements, the NWRS also directs the management of interdependencies among WMAs in the national interest such as with respect to provisions for the Reserve[10], water quality management and inter-WMA transfers of water. The directives of the NWRS are prescriptive according to the NWA, and provide the overall framework within which Catchment Management Strategies (CMSs) are to be developed.

Challenges and Lessons Learnt from Implementation

Blanket Approach to Decentralization

During his 2003 State of the Nation address, President Govan Mbeki acknowledged, for the first time, that South Africa is a "dual economy." The "dual economy" comprises two separate economies that operate differently. One is comparable to industrialized nations and another to developing countries. Consequently, he advised that they required different sets of policies and programs to stimulate their development and growth.

South Africa's Reformed Water Law and Its Challenging Implementation ≈ 279

For example, if we consider one CMA in a highly developed WMA such as the Crocodile (West) Marico and another in a less developed WMA such as the Gouritz,[11] the funds that can be raised for the functioning of CMAs will be from the following sources:

Table 12.1: Relative water use distribution in two WMAs

Description	Crocodile West Marico	Gouritz
Total yield 2,000 (m³/a)	718	275
Total requirements 2,000 (m3/a)	1,184	337
Use per sector (in percent)		
Irrigation	38	75
Urban	46	15
Rural	3	4
Mining and bulk industrial	11	1
Power generation	3	0
Afforestation	0	5

Source: DWAF (2004).

Chapter 5 of the NWA and the *Pricing Strategy for Raw Water Charges* (DWAF 2007) provides the financial framework within which CMAs operate. Section 56(2) of the NWA provides for fixing of water use charges as part of the *Pricing Strategy* for:

a. funding water resource management,
b. funding water resource development and operation, and
c. achieving the equitable and efficient allocation of water

What can be expected in both examples is the following (DWAF 2005):

a. Financially, CMAs will fund their activities through the Water Resource Management Charge and the Waste Discharge Charge levied for the industrial uses of water. The Crocodile (West) Marico will potentially generate about 50 percent of its revenue from the Waste Discharge Charge levied on account of the highly industrialized nature of the catchment (DWAF 2005). The Water Resource Management Charge on irrigated agriculture will contribute a substantial 40 percent of the CMA revenue. Since decisions will be made by a governing

280 ～ *Eiman Karar*

body composed of these users, there is a threat of CMAs being captured by the strong vested interests whereby the purposes of redress might be compromised.

b. Each CMA in these WMAs will be very different in function and hence in form and shape to cope with the management requirements resulting from the different uses.

c. As clearly shown in Table 12.1, the CMA's core business will be very different and hence, it is proposed that urban and rural CMAs be differentiated in their approaches and that the criteria for their establishment reflect the vision for redressing the imbalance in this "dual economy."[12] Another observation that can be drawn is that it is likely that the NWA was predominantly based on the "first economy" as benchmarked against the developed and developing ones. In this model, informal user groups such as "subsistence productive users" and small black emerging farmers both making modest financial contributions to the CMA, will have little say in decisions on water resource allocation and management. This is probably the reason for the state's presence in CMAs.

The Role of the State as a Player and a Referee

Although the decentralization-based reforms in water management defines a critical role for communities and users at large, the state will continue to play the most fundamental and central role because of its responsibility for managing water as a public good and for ensuring equitable allocation of water and equitable representation in decision-making; safeguarding the sustainable provision of ecosystem goods and services; and protecting the interests and welfare of all water users especially the poor, women and the disabled (Merrey et al. 2007). CMAs may be established either on the Minister's initiative or as per a proposal submitted to and approved by the Minister. Thus, either, the Department can take the lead in establishing CMAs, providing the bulk of funds and making special efforts of involving stakeholders, or the stakeholders supported by the Department can take such initiative (DWAF 2004).

Public involvement in this process is considered essential, because it contributes to establishing the legitimacy of the institution. Once a CMA is established, an Advisory Committee is constituted. The latter nominates before the Minister, select representative stakeholder

South Africa's Reformed Water Law and Its Challenging Implementation ≈ 281

groups for the membership of the governing board, and thereby builds a foundation for the CMA to promote public involvement in water resource management. Accordingly, the extent to which stakeholders are involved in the drafting of a proposal to establish an agency is one of the most important criteria against which the Minister will judge the merit of the proposal.

It is observed that generally ordinary South Africans are apathetic towards involvement in water resources management. As a matter of fact such involvement is not an attractive prospect for the poor, since it does not offer immediate rewards such as clean water supply in the home or community, or better sanitation facility. Providing the latter is squarely a responsibility of the local administration. Water resources management remains an abstraction for the poor who have more immediate needs to attend to.

The promise for equitable allocation of water that can be put to commercial uses such as agricultural production is meaningful only when there is access to land, credit and extension support, etc. Hence, regardless of the political will to devolve management functions to all water users, there is no demand on the ground especially from those marginal users who do not perceive much immediate gain from being involved in such functions. The risk of "elitist capture" referred to above, pushes the state towards greater involvement in order to protect the interests of the majority, i.e., the poor who in most cases are not meaningfully involved.

By virtue of state assuming the custodianship of all water resources, there is some centralization of checks and balances that are ultimately aimed to decentralize management. For instance, CMAs have to be established by the Minister, their governing boards of CMA have to be appointed by the Minister, any function apart from the "initial functions"[13] of CMAs has to be approved for delegation by the Minister, and the establishment of WMAs has to be approved by the Minister. However, the authority to allocate water is not likely to be delegated to a CMA by the Minister in the foreseeable future until the latter is satisfied that the former is capable of fulfilling the target of redressing inequities in the water allocation. The threat is that CMA can continue to be shaped by the state right from the onset. This is evident in the fact that most CMA establishment processes are predominantly "top-down." Although there are good reasons for the role that the state found itself playing as a referee in the absence of "level playing field," efforts should be made to create

282 ≈ *Eiman Karar*

incentives for the poor in order for them to be involved, and enhance awareness specially among the youth, civil society and other local organized structures (e.g., local governments, local authorities, water committees, ward committees, etc.), in order for the processes to be truly "bottom-up."

The articulation of a "developmental state" required the introduction of policies that would not allow for further discrimination against the marginalized poor and disempowered majority. In this sense, the South African government views itself as the referee and also a voice for the poor who are not in a position to readily grab the opportunities created by the new-found democracy. Hence, one finds policies such as affirmative action, black economic empowerment, social grants, land restitution and redistribution, water allocation reform, etc.

CMA Establishment: Is It a Dream?

The central pre-requisite in the South African water law is people's participation in decision-making processes as well as developmental activities. In this context, the policy of devolution of power and authority to sub-national institutions, referred to as decentralization is considered a major pillar for "good governance." Whilst the merits of decentralization are many, there are a number of prerequisites for it to work. According to the UNDP's Human Development Report (2003), these prerequisites include effective state capacity; empowered, committed and competent local authorities; and engaged, informed and organized citizens and civil society.

By the end of 2008, eight CMAs had been formally established by notification in the Government Gazette, but only two governing boards and two CEOs of Breede Overberg and Inkomati CMAs had been appointed. The desire to establish CMAs waned when there was a change of political and administrative leadership in the Department from 2005. The new leadership lacks the motivation to establish CMAs. Serious questions were asked by the South African Parliament and the Line Department about the NWA and the purpose of establishing CMAs and their future viability. After many workshops—which were meant for raising awareness about the Dublin principles, international benchmarking and the rationale for decentralized water management, and wherein most stakeholders were involved—were held, there was an overall

South Africa's Reformed Water Law and Its Challenging Implementation   ≈   283

agreement that decentralized management of water resources by local structures such as CMAs and WUAs was the desired route and that all the founding principles of the NWA for the decentralization of management were adequate. The main question was to what extent should the decision-making process be localized? How this vision of decentralized management needs to be implemented was challenged. Further, questions about the feasibility of 19 functional CMAs and about the possible threats to their viability such as elitist capture, financial viability, regulatory capacity of the state and the inefficacy of weak civil society structures to counterbalance the elitist capture were raised. Kauzya (2002) explains that in practice, the slow progress in the decentralization process is due to the lack of readiness of the Government of South Africa to relinquish or share power, which can be a major impediment to effective decentralization. In fact, the inability to make a transition to people-centered governance with its commensurate implications for popular participation and empowerment is perhaps a bigger bottleneck in the process of decentralization than legislative changes which in their own right are also crucial. The reduced number of CMAs is intended to resolve capacity issues in staffing, oversight and regulation of the CMAs. Equally, and quite importantly, the reduced number of CMAs would provide for stronger governance within the new institutions, which is currently a matter of concern for the departments of Water Affairs and Forestry, Public Service Administration and National Treasury.

The lesson to be drawn from the discussion is that it is desirable to reflect and assess policy implementation process and bring policies in sync with the ground reality, but at the same time, it is wise to exercise caution about not falling back into a comfort zone of reverting to the old bureaucratic style of water management. The regional offices of the Department are located in all the nine provinces of South Africa, where the proposed nine CMAs that are to be located. They have been operating along WMA boundaries rather than their historically demarcated areas of provincial jurisdiction. They might start engaging more with stakeholders and user groups and themselves turn into CMAs. Although this might be a reasonable institutional arrangement for the present and for South Africa, some serious questions about boundary issues and subsidiarity can and should be asked to clarify the appropriate level of decentralizing the management of water resources.

284 ≈ *Eiman Karar*

In the Inkomati WMA, most of the transformations of IBs into WUAs were aborted due to non-compliance with the requirement that emerging farmers be made members of WUAs. Either due to the perceived absence of emerging farmers in the area or due to the fact that many claims to proprietary rights over land did not materialize, the transformation did not happen. Local government was described as a major water user and its representatives were to be members of WUAs. Local government showed general apathy toward the whole process of decentralization and was not keen to engage the new WUAs. Most of the other users, who could be classified as local users of water mainly for small-scale subsistence agriculture, were not organized in order to be represented in the management of WUAs. The fact that the NWA did not make it compulsory for all water users in a locality to be members of the local WUA was cited as the major factor behind the inability of IBs to "force" water users to take them seriously (Brown and Woodhouse 2004).

A study of WUAs in the Olifants-Doorn WMA compiled by Wellman (2008) found that historically disadvantaged individuals (HDIs)[14] are well represented in the WUAs in the Olifants-Doorn. However, although constantly improving, the level of inclusion and participation still remains low. Some reasons for the current low level of inclusion of such individuals is their lack of experience, limited knowledge of the issues and limited understanding of the functioning of WUAs. Further, an evident lack of commitment in some WUA board members from previously disadvantaged groups, and a notable lack of feedback (on decisions made at the WUA meetings) by board members to their constituents are matters of concern. It is not possible to ascertain the extent of influence that board members from previously disadvantaged have over actual decision-making, as all Olifants-Doorn WUA boards arrive at all decisions through consensus. However, old power relations have proven highly resilient, and commercial farmers still dominate most WUAs. Another aspect that requires attention is the male domination (irrespective of race) in the water sector in the Olifants-Doorn WMA. Public meetings are still male-dominated and there is a noticeably low level of participation by women in WUAs. Their male counterparts (irrespective of race) often describe these women as just a "warm body" on the board.

Lack of Co-operation and Co-ordination between Responsible Departments

The dryland and stock farming areas in South Africa constitute 82 mha (million hectares) of private and 16 mha of communal land. Irrigation farming involves 40,000 to 45,000 commercial farmers, the majority of whom are white men, and 200,000 to 250,000 traditional subsistence farmers the majority of whom are black women. Agricultural laborers comprise approximately 120,000 permanent workers and an unknown number of seasonal workers. Irrigation constitutes close to 60 percent of the total water requirement in the country, while contributing less than 1.5 percent of each of the GDP and of the total employment (DWAF 2004: 25). A quarter of agriculture's contribution to GDP comes from irrigation (NDA 2002). There are approximately 320 smallholder irrigation schemes in the former homeland areas (Denison and Manona 2007).

On April 12, 2005, the then Minister of Water Affairs and Forestry, Buyelwa Sonjica, launched the Water Allocation Reform (WAR) Strategy. In his keynote address, The Minister said: "We will continue to strive to help our people along the journey from being small subsistence water users to, if they so wish, large commercial, productive and competitive users not just in South Africa but internationally" (2005).

The Draft Strategy on WAR, being prepared by the Department in consultation with stakeholders, defines equity and redress in water use as equitable access to water, as well as the actions that promote redressal of racial and gender inequity in water use, underpinned by the equitable distribution of the benefits of water use. This does not refer to the equal distribution of water (DWAF 2006). Several other supporting documents, including the WAR Toolkit, have been developed by the DWAF. Although these documents have not been officially adopted, the principles spelt out therein are being applied in various areas in line with the objectives of the WAR program. The WAR Strategy also stipulates national targets, which are inclusive of black women and are to be progressively achieved by 2024. In terms of these targets, 60 percent of allocable water should be allocated to black people, of which half should be in the hands of black women. The rationale behind setting these targets is to ensure that resources are channeled towards meeting the objectives of the WAR program.

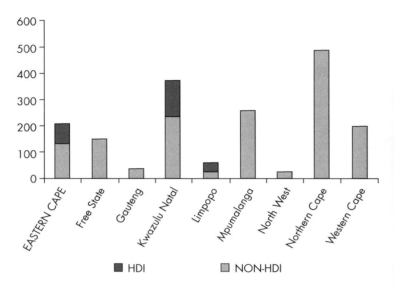

Figure 12.3: Number of licences issued to HDIs (Historically Disadvantaged Individuals) vs Non-HDIs by region (1998–2008)

Source: WRC (2011).

To date, implementation of the WAR program has not resulted in the kind of redressal that one would expect it to, given so much political will to effect change in the agricultural water use scenario of South Africa. The development of policy and strategy for reforms in water allocation has not yet led to any actual re-allocation of water on the ground (Schreiner et al. 2009). Dlamini (2009) has attributed the absence of effective implementation on the ground to the lack of co-ordination between government departments, especially that of Agriculture and Land Affairs and that of Water Affairs and Forestry.

Moreover, Hollingworth (2008) studied the reasons why during the term of the first Water Affairs Minister Kader Asmal (1994–2000) of the post-apartheid democratic regime, the quantum of water set aside for the emerging disadvantaged black farmers was not allocated to them satisfactorily. The select areas where water was meant for targeted allocation to the emerging black farmers were Mhlatuse (2,000 ha), Uhluhluwe (1,000ha), Blyde (800 ha), Lower Orange (4,000 ha) and Freestate (3,000 ha). He attributes this failure to a number of reasons. First, black irrigation farmers continue to

South Africa's Reformed Water Law and Its Challenging Implementation ～ 287

have mainly small plots within communal land in the absence of institutional development of a sound land distribution and water allocation system to address the problem of small uneconomic landholdings which are not conductive to commercial farming. This model is not sustainable without continuous and extensive financial and institutional support. Hence, the prospects of creating independent commercially orientated irrigation farmers, who would be able to not only pay for additional water allocations but also have more land at their disposal to increase cultivation and thereby change the water distribution landscape in South Africa, are negligible. Second, the mechanisms of inter-departmental co-operation at the national level and in several provinces are ineffective. It seems that the new government elected to office in 2009 has realized this lack of co-ordination between government departments and has hence established a new Ministry for Rural Development for addressing the water-related problems of the black emerging farmers, among other tasks. As a new ministry, it will require a few years before tangible results can be observed, but the move to establish the ministry itself is promising for redressal of a long-standing problem.

Decentralization Requires Adequate Human Resources

The new water sector reforms in South Africa have come up at a time when new challenges to the retention of quality human resource in the water sector are posed by such phenomena as ageing workforce, emigration of skilled professionals or brain drain, language barrier on entry to tertiary institutions and constraints on university training. To put it simply, the supply of skilled people is not able to cope with the demand.

One of the reasons for this crisis of human capital in water sector, as pointed by Karar and Pietersen (2009), could be South Africa's legacy of apartheid in education sector. Of the several challenges facing university science departments, the lack of adequate entry-level skills in maths and science, most agree, is one of the most serious ones. The white male dominance in South Africa's scientific research is mainly the result of this past racial discrimination in the access to the same quality of education at tertiary level as that in the white-dominated universities. The challenge then is to "square the circle," i.e., retain and even strengthen the existing human capital in

288   ≈   *Eiman Karar*

scientific research and development, whilst promoting innovation and widening racial representation.

Slow Change

As discussed before, South Africa is continuously reviewing its reform processes. There is a general criticism that implementation of certain aspects of this reform program takes a long time. Complex planning and over-regulation result in the lack of delivery in some instances. The reason for this might be a fear of "making mistakes." Examples like the articulation of environmental reserve for individual rivers will have implications on water availability for the poor when most of the water in many rivers is already allocated to commercial users (resource-rich commercial farmers and power and mining industries) and the trade-off between development and protection hangs in balance. Schriener and Heyden (2009) refers to this as weak and strong sustainability drives. There seems to be no clear direction from the government to endorse either weak or strong sustainability paths.

Implementation of compulsory licensing will have implications on the economic viability of commercial agriculture which is by far the largest user with very little contribution to GDP (unlike that to job creation). Even after more than 10 years of the promulgation of the NWA, no water has been re-allocated through compulsory licensing and few licenses have been issued to black users. Schreiner et al. (2009) have indicated that the policies and strategies developed under the WAR program have not led to any actual enhanced re-allocation of water at the ground level for redress purposes. In fact, in some areas land reform is likely to drive higher rates of re-allocation than WAR would. Instead, there is a move towards looking at an integrated approach towards water allocation and utilization for economic growth and development. A framework for "Water for Growth and Development" is being developed by the Department and has been referred to in the President's State of the Nation's address (DWAF 2009).

The reticence of some regional offices of the Department in continuing with the establishment of CMAs might be explained by the likely shift in power from regional offices of the Department to CMAs which would mean no clear mandate for regional offices. Again reverting to a "comfort zone" of reducing the number of

South Africa's Reformed Water Law and Its Challenging Implementation 〜 289

CMAs to nine might reinstate regional offices in the nine provinces. Whatever the case might be, this indecision is causing instability in the regional offices as reflected in the numerous unfilled vacancies. Moreover, measures aimed at poverty alleviation, gender equity, community empowerment and greater public participation are weakly implemented probably due to the lack of understanding of the provisions made in the NWA, or due to the untested efficacy of the Act itself, thereby leaving much to be desired. Transformation of the old IBs into more inclusive WUAs deprives the IBs of their power base gained by virtue of either the ownership of irrigation infrastructure or the size of land holdings, and thereby prevents them from being a majority user with a strong unified voice. Although more than 200 WUAs are established, their desired role as "agents of change" is still not evident.

Conclusions

Although major strides were made in the development of the NWRS in 2004, the establishment of the Inkomati CMA in the same year and the establishment of more than 200 WUAs, certain weaknesses have been observed recently, weaknesses that have led to a slowing down in the rollout of the policy for some legitimate reasons. Some of these reasons could be the complexity of administrative processes needed for redressal; the unique character of water management agencies based on management complexity on the ground; the dual role of the state as a player and a referee, the lack of sustained and documented institutional memory to allow for a follow-through, inadequate human resources and the lack of alignment between land and water reforms.

The lessons learnt from the slow implementation of the new water law in South Africa are a step towards identifying the way forward. What is most inspiring in the South African water sector is that robust debates and re-actualization of purpose continues to take center stage. The author considers this to be a healthy sign, a sign of the fact that the quest for improvement is not waning.

To conclude, decentralization can be successful when the state demonstrates its trust in people's resource management capacity and its commitment to their empowerment by parting with some of its authority and transferring it to the common water users, and when the latter in turn are capable to making fair and just

290 ≋ *Eiman Karar*

decisions on water resource management for the benefit of all South Africans. The social and historic imbalance in the access to water resources, the disempowerment of the poor and the perpetuation of marginalization are realities cited as reasons for the reluctance of the center to devolve authority. The increasing involvement of the state not only in the regulation of the decentralization process but also in its implementation, playing the dual role of a referee and a player can be the result of this reluctance. Another reason for the slow implementation is the keenness to perfect administrative procedures to address these imbalances making them too complex and cumbersome to implement. Some of these procedural complexities are the mandatory pre-requisites of public participation for establishing CMAs and WUAs, and reserving determinations (e.g., amount of water, state of monitoring water use, update of registered users, etc.) for issuing of licenses. That there are limitations to physical and hydrological availability of water such as in "closed basins" is also cited as a deterrent to effecting water access allocation reforms.

As a result, despite the existence of an enabling environment for the decentralization of water resources through a visionary and progressively revised water policy in the country, there persist factors that impede its implementation. In the wake of the advent of democracy in the post-apartheid period, the ambitious vision that through implementation of the new water policy, South Africa will become an egalitarian society in terms of access to opportunities and wealth is somewhat sobered by the reality that equitable access to water is but one factor of development and social justice, much wider reforms need to be effected for this vision to be realized.

Notes

1. Barbara van Koppen, IWMI, pers. comm.
2. For the progress in regulations on access to water, see Pienaar and van der Schyff (2007: 179).
3. The old "Homelands" in South African history, refer to those areas that were designated for the black population to live in, and that were managed by local administration of the central "apartheid rule."
4. The Dublin Principles announced at the International Conference on Water and the Environment (ICWE), Dublin, Ireland, 1992, are: *a*) fresh water is a finite and vulnerable resource, essential to sustain life, development and the environment; *b*)water development and

South Africa's Reformed Water Law and Its Challenging Implementation ≈ 291

management should be based on a participatory approach, involving users, planners and policy-makers at all levels; *c)* women play a central part in the provision, management and safeguarding of water; and *d)* water has an economic value in all its competing uses and should be recognized as an economic good.

5. Environmental flow requirements mean the quantity, timing and quality of water flows required to sustain freshwater and estuarine ecosystems, and the human livelihoods and well-being that depend on these ecosystems.

6. International obligations include river water sharing agreements, compliance with the South African Development Community (SADC) Water Protocol of which South Africa is a signatory as well as all international water laws such as those of the UN.

7. See Section 92 (1) (a) of the NWA, Act no. 36 of 1998.

8. See Schedule 5, Sections 5 (1) (a) & (b) and 5 (2) (a) & (b) of the NWA.

9. Using a WUA to facilitate empowerment does not mean abdicating responsibility for the management of a water service, which remains the primary objective of a WUA. It simply means that a water management institution is also being used for the purpose of uplifting the poor.

10. The Reserve is specific in the South African legislation which consists of two parts; the basic human needs reserve and the ecological reserve (Chapter 3, Part 3 of the NWA).

11. The Crocodile (West) and Marico WMA borders on Botswana to the northwest. Its main rivers, Crocodile and Marico, give rise to the Limpopo River at their confluence. The climate is generally semi-arid with mean annual rainfall ranging from 400 mm to 800 mm. Extensive irrigation occurs along the courses of the main rivers, viz., Crocodile, Marico and the Limpopo, while grain, livestock and game farming is carried out in other parts which are not irrigated. Economic activity in the WMA is dominated by the urban and industrial complexes of northern Johannesburg and Pretoria, and platinum mining to the northeast of Rustenburg. It is the second most populous WMA in the country and makes the largest contribution to the national GDP. A substantial portion of the water used in the WMA is transferred from the Vaal River and further afield. Small transfers out of the WMA are to Gabarone in Botswana and to Modimolle in the Limpopo WMA. Increasing volumes of effluent flow from urban and industrial areas offer considerable potential for re-use, but the effluent is at the same time a major cause of pollution in some rivers.

The Gouritz WMA is situated along the southern coast of South Africa and extends inland across the Little Karoo and into the Great Karoo. The area has two primary climatic regions that display distinctly different characteristics: the large arid inland Karoo area drained by

292 ≋ *Eiman Karar*

river Gouritz and the smaller humid strip of land along the coastal belt to the south of the Outeniqua Mountains which is drained by several small rivers. Rainfall ranges from less than 200 mm/a to over 1,000 mm/a. Economic activity is centered on sheep breeding and ostrich farming in the arid areas, with extensive irrigation farming of lucerne, grapes and deciduous fruits in the Little Karoo, and on forestry, tourism and petrochemical industries in the coastal region. Forests, wetlands and estuaries of high conservation status are found in the humid areas. The water in the arid areas has high salinity as a result of the geology and climate (NWRS 2004).

12. Explaining the concept of "dual economy," President Thabo Mbeki stated:

> [O]ur country is characterised by two parallel economies, the First and the Second. The First Economy is modern, produces the bulk of our country's wealth, and is integrated within the global economy.
>
> The Second Economy (or the Marginalised Economy) is characterised by underdevelopment, contributes little to the GDP, contains a big percentage of our population, incorporates the poorest of our rural and urban poor, is structurally disconnected from both the First and the global economy, and is incapable of self-generated growth and development (Address to the National Council of Provinces, 11 November 2003, http://www.dfa.gov.za/docs/speeches/2003/mbek1111.htm).

13. "Initial functions" of a "responsible" CMA includes allocations decisions (NWA, Chapter 7 Part 3).

14. Historically disadvantaged individual (HDI) means a South African citizen *a*) who, due to the apartheid policy that had been in place, had no franchise in national elections prior to the introduction of the Constitution of the Republic of South Africa,1983 (Act No 110 of 1983) or the Constitution of the Republic of South Africa,1993 (Act No 200 of 1993) ("the Interim Constitution"); and/or *b*) who is a female; and/or *c*) who has a disability.

References

Brown, J. and P. Woodhouse. 2004. "Pioneering Redistributive Regulatory Reform. A Study of Implementation of a Catchment Management Agency for the Inkomati Water Management Area, South Africa." Working Paper 89, Centre on Regulation and Competition (CRC), University of Manchester, UK. Also available online at http://www.competition-regulation.org.uk/publications/working_papers/.

South Africa's Reformed Water Law and Its Challenging Implementation ≈ 293

Denison J., and S. Manona. 2007. *Indigenous Water Harvesting and Conservation Practices: Historical Context, Cases and Implications.* WRC Report TT309/07. Pretoria: WRC. Also available online at http://www.wrc.org.za/Pages/DisplayItem.aspx?ItemID=8551&FromURL=%2fPages%2fKH_AdvancedSearch.aspx%3fk%3dtt309%26 (accessed September 11, 2012).

Department of Water Affairs and Forestry (DWAF). 1999. "Government Notice Gazette No. 1160," www.dwaf.gov.za/CM/Docs/WORD/Govt%20Gazette%201160.doc (accessed August 16, 2012).

———. 2001. *Establishing a Water User Association.* CMA and WUA Guide Series, Guide 3.

———. 2004. "National Water Resource Strategy (NWRS)," http://www.dwaf.gov.za/Documents/Policies/NWRS/Default.htm (accessed June 28, 2012).

———. 2005. "Note on the Financial Viability of Catchment Management Agencies and Possible Financial Support Requirements (Version 2.01)," http://www.dwaf.gov.za/IO/Docs/CMA/CMA%20Establishment%20Guide/NoteonCMAViability.pdf (accessed June 28, 2012).

———. 2006. "A Strategy for Water Allocation Reform," www.dwaf.gov.za/WAR/documents/WARStrategyNov06.pdf (accessed September 11, 2012).

———. 2007. "Pricing Strategy for Raw Water Charges," http://www.dwaf.gov.za/IO/Docs/CMA/Policy%20Documents/Pricing%20Strategy.pdf (accessed October 12, 2012).

———. 2009. "Water for Growth and Development Framework," http://www.dwaf.gov.za/WFGD/documents/WFGD_Frameworkv7.pdf (accessed June 28, 2012).

Dlamini, P. 2009. *An Analysis of Gaps in Policy and Legislation Relating to Water Use and Water Resources Management in South Africa.* Progress Report, WRC Project K5/1855. Pretoria: WRC.

Francis, R. 2005. "Water Justice in South Africa: Natural Resources Policy at the Intersection of Human Rights, Economics, and Political Power." BePress Legal Series Paper 518.

Hollingworth, B. 2008. *Water Allocation Studies: Why Are Black Farmers Not Taking Up Existing Allocations?.* WRC Report K8/761. Pretoria: WRC.

Karar, E and K. Pietersen. 2009. "Challenges Faced for Human Capital Development and Technological Innovations in the Water Sector in South Africa." Working Paper Series 13, Development Bank of South Africa (DBSA), Midrand, South Africa. Also available online at http://www.dbsa.org/Research/DPD%20Working%20papers%20documents/DPD%20No13.pdf (accessed June 28, 2012).

B. Schreiner, B. and R. M. Hassan (eds). 2011. *Transforming Water Management in South Asia: Designing and Implementing a New Policy Framework.* Global Issues in Water Policy Series, vol. 2. London: Springer.

294 ≈ *Eiman Karar*

Kauzya, J. M. 2002. "Local Governance Capacity Building for Full Range Participation: Concepts, Frameworks, and Experiences in African Countries." Background Paper presented at the 4th Global Forum on Re-inventing Government: Citizens, Businesses and Governments: Dialogue and Partnerships for Development and Democracy, December 13–14, Marrakech, Morocco, http://unpan1.un.org/intradoc/groups/public/documents/un/unpan007003.pdf (accessed October 12, 2012).

Merrey, D., R. Meizen, P. Milonga and E. Karar. 2007. "Policy and Institutional Reform: The Art of the Possible," in D. Molden (ed.), *Water for Food, Water for Life: Comprehensive Assessment of Water Management Agricultural Water*, pp. 193–231. London: Earthscan; Colombo: IWMI.

Muller, M. 2001. "How National Water Policy is Helping to Achieve South Africa's Development Vision," in C. Abernethy (ed.), *Intersectoral Management of River Basins: Proceedings of an International Workshop on Integrated Water Management in Water-Stressed River Basins in Developing Countries: Strategies for Poverty Alleviation and Agricultural Growth. Loskop Dam, South Africa, 16–21 October, 2000,* pp. 3–10. Colombo: IIWMI and German Foundation for International Development (DSE).

National Department of Agriculture (NDA). 2002. "Draft National Guidelines for Integrated Management of Agricultural Water Use," www.nda.agric.za/docs/Policy/SustainableDev.pdf (accessed September 4, 2012).

National Water Act (NWA). 1998. Republic of South Africa, Government Gazette No. 19182, www.info.gov.za/view/DownloadFileAction?id=70693 (accessed September 12, 2012).

Sonjica, Buyelwa. Opening speech, National Consultative Workshop on Water Allocation Reform in South Africa, CSIR Conference Centre, Pretoria, 12 April, http://www.google.co.za/#hl=en&site=&source=hp&q=speech+minister+csir+april+2005&oq=speech+minister+csir+april+2005&gs_l=hp.3...1437.18891.0.19515.31.31.0.0.0.0.269.3296.19j0j10.29.0...0.0.fU3xZaYQpo4&bav=on.2,or.r_gc.r_pw.,cf.osb&fp=bbcff42a77fd8d17&biw=1680&bih=828 (accessed June 28, 2012).

Pienaar, G. J. and E. van der Schyff. 2007. "The Reform of Water Rights in South Africa," *Law, Environment and Development Journal*, 3(2): 181–94. Also available online at http://www.lead-journal.org/content/07179.pdf (accessed June 28, 2012).

Schreiner, B., G. Pegram and C. von der Heyden. 2009. "Reality Check: Are We Doing the Right Things the Best Way Possible to Achieve the Desired Objectives in the Water Sector." Working Paper Series 11, Development Planning Division, DBSA, Midrand, South Africa. Also available online at http://www.dbsa.org/Research/DPD%20Working%20papers%20documents/DPD%20No11.pdf (accessed June 28, 2012).

South Africa's Reformed Water Law and Its Challenging Implementation ≋ 295

United Nations Development Programme (UNDP). 2003. *Human Development Report 2003, Millennium Development Goals: A Compact among Nations to End Human Poverty.* New York: UN.

WRC. 2011. *Water Allocation Reform in South Africa: History, Processes and Prospects for Future Implementation.* Report K5/1855.

Wellman, Gwendolyn. 2008. "Water User Associations in the Olifants-Doorn Water Management Area," Surplus People Project, Cape Town, http://www.spp.org.za/reports/water_user.pdf (accessed June 28, 2012).

13

Innovation in European Water Policy and the Need for Exchange on Water Policy Reform at a Global Scale

Claudia Pahl-Wostl

Over the past decade, a major change in the rhetoric surrounding water resources management has been evident. The debate is now dominated by an increased awareness of integrated management approaches taking into account environmental, economic and social considerations, and by a search for strategies which go beyond technical end-of-pipe solutions. In particular, the importance of improving water governance is now widely recognized. Challenges for water governance are manifold. Normative principles of "good" water governance such as accountability, transparency and equitability should be respected (Rogers and Hall 2003). Governance regimes should be adaptive and flexible in order to be able to deal with the complexity and uncertainty which are expected to even increase with the growing pace and impact of global climate change. Stakeholder participation in water management and governance too has assumed increasing importance.

The debate is now dominated by an increased awareness of inte-grated management approaches, taking into account environmental,

Innovation in European Water Policy ≋ 297

economic and social considerations, and by the search for strategies that go beyond technical end-of-pipe solutions.

Water crises have often been caused by problems of governance and inefficient and ineffective management, not by resource or technology problems. Correspondingly, more and more voices have advocated the need for a radical change, for a paradigm shift in water management (Gleick 2000; Pahl-Wostl 2002; 2007a and b). The arguments put forward differ in detail and emphasis but not in the essential elements of the nature of the needed paradigm shift which are (Pahl-Wostl et al. 2011):

a. move towards participatory management and collaborative decision-making,
b. increased integration of issues and sectors,
c. management of problem sources not effects,
d. decentralized and more flexible management approaches,
e. more attention to management of human behavior by "soft" measures,
f. explicit inclusion of environmental considerations in management goals,
g. open and shared information sources (including linking science and decision-making), and
i. integration of iterative learning cycles.

The emphasis on the hitherto rather neglected human dimension is evident. The importance of improving water governance is now widely recognized. Normative principles of "good" water governance such as accountability, transparency, equitability should be respected (Rogers and Hall 2003). Governance regimes should be adaptive and flexible to be able to deal with complexity and uncertainty which are expected to even increase with the growing impact of global change. Stakeholder participation has also gained increasing importance.

All in all, the perceived need to change water management concepts and practices, to involve a wide range of stakeholders and to foster social learning can be explained by several insights that are not entirely new but have only recently been seriously taken into account. They include increasing interdependence between government bodies for a more interactive way of working; identifying the complexities of natural resources management to be able to engage with a wider group of stakeholders and to be able to

298 ≋ *Claudia Pahl-Wostl*

handle uncertainties of climate change coupled with social dynamics through more flexible management approaches.

The rising demand to better account for the full complexity of the systems being managed is driven in part by a better appreciation of increasing uncertainties due to climate change and globalization. In developing, and threshold countries in particular, socio-economic changes are occurring at an unparalleled fast pace. Established planning approaches in water management, developed in industrialized countries that rely strongly on their technological competence to predict the effect of management measures, and design systems that can be controlled are less appropriate in highly uncertain and complex situations.

However, barriers to innovation are often more conceptual than technical. Progress in developing, and in particular implementing, innovative policy frameworks and management approaches has not kept pace with the express need for change in management paradigms and practices. Integrated and adaptive management approaches are required that perform well under complex and unpredictable conditions and that can be tailored to the institutional, cultural, environmental and technological settings of river basins. This chapter gives an overview how these challenges have been addressed in European water policy.

Recent Developments in European Water Policy

Latest developments in European water policy have taken such considerations into account. The European Water Framework Directive (WFD) which came into force in 2000 signaled a new area in the European Water Policy which had become increasingly compartmentalized by numerous specific directives such as the Nitrate Directive, Bathing Water Directive, etc. The WFD adopts an integrated approach and emphasizes the involvement of all interested parties in the development and implementation of river basin management plans.

The major objectives of the WFD[1] are:

    a. expanding the scope of water protection to all waters, surface waters and groundwater

    b. achieving "good status" for all waters by a set deadline

Innovation in European Water Policy ～ 299

c. water management based on river basins
d. "combined approach" of emission limit values and quality standards
e. getting the prices right
f. getting the citizen involved more closely
g. streamlining legislation

The WFD is also the first major European directive to prescribe formally the involvement of stakeholders and the public at large. The official website of the European Commission states the clear need for strong participation of all the involved parties for the successful implementation of the WFD:

> The first for strong participation is that the decisions on the most appropriate measures to achieve the objectives in the river basin management plan will involve balancing the interests of various groups. The second reason concerns enforceability. The greater the transparency in the establishment of objectives, the imposition of measures, and the reporting of standards, the greater the care Member States will take to implement the legislation in good faith, and the greater the power of the citizens to influence the direction of environmental protection, whether through consultation or, if disagreement persists, through the complaints procedures and the courts. Caring for Europe's waters will require more involvement of citizens, interested parties, non-governmental organisations (NGOs). To that end the Water Framework Directive will require information and consultation when river basin management plans are established and implemented (ibid.).

The WFD prescribes an ambitious schedule with the first implementation cycle ending in 2015. In order to support efficient and effective implementation, a number of guidance documents have been developed and tested in pilot river basins as part the Common Implementation Strategy (CIS) process.[2] Management plans have to be revised every 15 years, a provision which supports an adaptive approach to developing and implementing measures.

The European Flood Directive (FD) on the assessment and management of flood risks entered into force in November 2007. The Directive was a response to a number of severe floods between 1998 and 2004 including the catastrophic floods in the Danube and Elbe basins in summer of 2002. The FD now requires EU member states

300 ≈ *Claudia Pahl-Wostl*

to assess if all water courses and coastlines are at a risk of flooding, to map the extent of floods and of the risk to assets and human lives in these areas, and to take adequate and co-ordinated measures to reduce this flood risk. The FD also reinforces the rights of the public to access this information and participate in the planning process. The implementation process requires harmonization with the WFD.

To sum up, one can state that the European water policy has undergone profound changes. The WFD and the FD offer opportunities and provide support for a shift from the conventional command-and-control approach to an integrated and adaptive water management and governance. However, the practice of policy implementation lags behind in innovation compared to the guiding policy frameworks (e.g., Olsson and Galaz 2009; Isendahl et al. 2010; Pahl-Wostl et al. 2011). This may change given the prospects of climate change and the need for pro-active adaptation in the water sector. European and EU member states' water policies currently developed for adaptation to climate change argue for even more profound changes than already advocated by the latest European directives. One might even talk of a paradigm shift in water management. This is very pronounced in the Netherlands where the government promotes a radical rethinking of flood management—more "room for rivers" and an emphasis on "living with water" rather than on "controlling water." However, despite this shift in public and political discourse, change in management practices is very slow. Such inertia can be explained by the want of radical changes in the management regime that are needed to realize the postulated paradigm shift.

A Paradigm Shift in Water Policy and Management

The paradigm shift in water management may be interpreted as a sign of an increased awareness of the complexity of the issue and a fundamental change in understanding what management implies, not only in the field of natural resources and water (Pahl-Wostl 2007b).

More recently, the debate on improvement of water management has been increasingly dominated by the need for adaptation to climate change. This debate has shifted the importance of addressing

Innovation in European Water Policy ≈ 301

increasing uncertainties to the centre stage. Experience from the past is no reliable guide for the future, and water management is confronted from all fronts with unprecedented situations.

All in all, the perceived need to change water management concepts and practices, to involve a wide range of stakeholders and to foster social learning can be explained by several insights that are not entirely new but have only recently been seriously taken into account. They are:

a. Increasing interdependence between government bodies and other stakeholders (e.g., in collective decision-making, harnessing specific competence from government departments and their combined contribution) reduces the efficacy of a traditional command-and-control management style and demands a shift towards a more interactive and participatory style.
b. Increasing complexity of natural resources management (manifest in a shift towards integrated approaches in management objectives and heightened awareness of the complex nature of socio-ecological systems) requires an enhanced capacity for learning and innovation that functionally engages a wider group of stakeholders.
c. Increasing uncertainties (e.g., climate change, dynamic socio-economic conditions) require a more adaptive and flexible management approach to realize a faster coping cycle that allows the rapid assessment and implementation of the changes derived from new insights. This requires new skills and capabilities, informal management structures and the inclusion of expert knowledge as well as local lay knowledge.

Therefore, the need to account for the complexity in the natural system has driven managers of water to appreciate the uncertainties arising out of climate change in a globalizing world and plan accordingly. The present situation, however, is quite different in the developing world, where development is happening in a rather haphazard manner and the nations moving on the path of industrialization are more dependent on and believe in the use of technologies to manage water in the event of climate change, or to predict extreme climatic events rather than approach it from an

302 ∼ *Claudia Pahl-Wostl*

integrated perspective, especially because systems are more complex in nature.

However, barriers to innovation are often more conceptual than technical. Progress in developing, and in particular implementing, innovative management approaches has not kept pace with the express need for change in management paradigms and practices. Integrated and adaptive management approaches are required that perform well under complex and unpredictable conditions and that can be tailored to the institutional, cultural, environmental and technological settings of river basins.

Gap between Policy Decision and Implementation

Policy implementation lags behind the guiding policy frameworks in innovation (e.g., Olsson and Galaz 2009; Isendahl et al. 2010; Pahl-Wostl et al. 2011). Experience up to now suggests that despite innovative legislative frameworks, the paradigm shift is yet to happen in management practice.

Olsson and Galaz (2009) and Galaz (2005), cited in Pahl-Wostl et al. (2011: 850) have analyzed if there are signs for a "transition to adaptive water management in Sweden." They conclude that despite the opportunities offered by the WFD, current state of implementation does not take into account resilience and complexity, and that more efforts are required to change the dominant water management practices and behavior and support social learning and active stakeholder involvement.

The European project RISKBASE, a workshop with river basin managers to facilitate the exchange of insights drawn from their experiences on developing river basin management plans, was organized in the spring of 2009. The major conclusions drawn from the workshop were:

> It seems that the 1st generation of WFD RBMPs will reflect a rather "low" level of ambition and will include only measures of which the river managers have the long-time practical experience that they are effective. At the same time in many cases more innovative non-legally binding management plans have been developed in parallel which are more innovative and reflect space for "learning-by-doing" (Riskbase 2009: 5).

Innovation in European Water Policy ≋ 303

The observation that informal learning processes seem to start taking place is at least a positive first sign for change. One may argue that the prospects of climate change may trigger additional learning processes. More recently, the debate on improvements in water management has been increasingly dominated by the need for adaptation to climate change. This debate has shifted the importance of addressing increasing uncertainties to the centre stage. Past experience is no reliable guide for the future, and water management is confronted from all fronts by unprecedented situations. The adoption of more innovative approaches may be promoted by the prospects of climate change and the need for pro-active adaptation in the water sector. European and EU member states' policies currently developed for the adaptation to climate change argue for even more profound changes than already advocated by the latest European directives.

The European Commission has begun to develop a climate change adaptation strategy summarized in the Commission's White Paper on climate change adaptation (COM 2009a). One of the annexes deals explicitly with challenges for water policy (COM 2009b), wherein the Commission expresses an optimistic view regarding the possibilities of including climate change adaptation strategies in the current implementation of the major water-related directives:

WFD: The Water Framework Directive requires a river basin management plan to be established for each river basin district (including those with cross national frontiers). The first river basin management plans are required by 22 December 2009 and must be updated every six years. This flexible management framework is well-suited to managing adaptation to the impacts of climate change as it will enable new information on the impacts of climate change and the measures necessary to adjust to be incorporated into the revised river basin management plans. The requirement under the Water Framework Directive for Member States to take a cross-sectoral approach to water management will also facilitate the necessary cross-sectoral action on adaptation and provide a framework for consideration of the relationship between the use and management of the natural environment (e.g., land) and the quality and availability of water resources. Further, the achievement of "good ecological status" for all waters as provided in the Water Framework Directive will contribute strongly to improving and maintaining biodiversity in

304 ≈ *Claudia Pahl-Wostl*

the aquatic environment, as well as those ecosystems which rely on the aquatic environment.

FD: In line with the integrated river basin approach taken under the Water Framework Directive, the Flood Directive also requires Member States to co-ordinate their flood risk management practices in shared river basins, including with third countries, and to avoid taking measures that would increase the flood risk in neighbouring countries. Co-ordination with the implementation of the WFD is required under Article 9 of the Floods Directive from the second River Basin Management Plan. The Floods Directive therefore provides a comprehensive mechanism for assessing and monitoring increased risks of flooding due to climate change and for developing appropriate adaptation approaches. The co-ordinated approach with the river basin management plans will ensure an overall effective approach and help avoid maladaptation measures.

The document highlights that the regulatory frameworks pose no constraints and offer sufficient freedom for innovative management approaches in the operational implementation. The directives even encourage a radical rethinking of water policy and management, and provide a good base to address the challenges posed by climate change. However, the experience with the current state of the implementation of European water policies casts some doubt about whether the operational implementation will really make use of these opportunities and move towards a new water management paradigm embracing complexity and the human dimension. Some of the barriers that are often ignored are illustrated for the example of flood management.

Moving towards Adaptive and Integrated Flood Management

Flood management is currently undergoing a major paradigm shift towards an integrated management paradigm. This implies taking into account different kinds of regulatory services in landscapes more prone to floods, services that have been ignored for a long time.

The implementation of integrated and adaptive flood management strategies and the reduction of trade-offs between flood protection and floodplain restoration can be achieved by taking into account ecosystem services of flood plains and by moving towards multifunctional dynamic landscapes. As highlighted by Pahl-Wostl (2006), efficient integration requires processes of social learning since fundamental changes are needed in the governance structure (Table 13.1).

Table 13.1: Comparison of characteristics of the current management regime in regulated and controlled rivers with those of a future state that has multifunctional and dynamic landscapes.

	Current State with Regulated and Controlled Rivers	Potential Future State with a Multifunctional Dynamic Landscape
Dominating stakeholder groups and their roles	Authorities as regulators in a highly regulated environment. Engineers who construct and operate dams, reservoirs and levees. Environmental protection groups fighting for flood plain restoration. Insurance companies selling insurances against flood damage. House-owners ignorant about the risks of living in flood plains. Agriculture on lands in the vicinity of rivers. Shipping industry interested in well-functioning waterways.	Authorities act as contributors to an adaptive management process with shared responsibilities. Neutral third parties act as facilitators of the decision-making process. Landscape architects and engineers who have skills in systems, design and co-operate with ecologists in integrated landscape management. Environmental protection groups. House-owners in retention areas at a higher risk of floods. Tourism industry and tourists using the flood plains for recreation.
Stakeholder participation	Small stakeholder participation—occasional consultation with different stakeholder groups and the public at large who are asked to give their opinion on a management plan or scenario that	Stakeholders and the public are actively involved in river basin management. This can be described as co-production of knowledge and co-decision-making. Involvement can range from

(Contd.)

306 ≋ *Claudia Pahl-Wostl*

Table 13.1 (Contd.)

	Current State with Regulated and Controlled Rivers	Potential Future State with a Multifunctional Dynamic Landscape
	has already been prepared by experts.	discussions with the authorities and experts, to actively contributing to policy development (co-designing), influencing decisions (co-decision-making), or even full responsibility for (parts of) river basin management.
Paradigm water management	Management as control. Technology-driven. Risk can be quantified and optimal strategies can be chosen. Zero-sum-games in closed decision space. Implementation of controllable and predictable technical infrastructure (reservoirs, dams) based on fixed regulations for acceptable risk-thresholds.	Adaptive and integrated of water management. "Living with water." Acceptable decisions are negotiated. Implementation of a multi-functional landscape and increased adaptive capacity of the system. Designed risk dialogue and cascade of adaptation measures to live with extremes. Increased importance of real-time forecasting systems.
Institutional setting and governance	Centralized and top-down approaches. Institutional fragmentation: responsibilities for protection from floods, nature conservation, regional planning and water management are often vested in different authorities.	Polycentric governance and better institutional interplay. Better horizontal and vertical integration of formal insti--tutional settings to ovecome fragmentation which might imply new institutions such as river basin management panels with defined responsibilities and decision-making capabilities. Stronger role of informal institutions and participatory approaches.

(Contd.)

Table 13.1 (Contd.)

	Current State with Regulated and Controlled Rivers	Potential Future State with a Multifunctional Dynamic Landscape
Adaptive capacity	"Hard" approach to systems design aimed at implementing long-lasting optimal solutions. Generally very low adaptive capacity due to heavy investment in infrastructure and often inflexible legal regulations.	"Soft" approach to systems design allows new insights to be taken into account, including responses to changing environmental and socio-economic boundary conditions. This is more in line with the new paradigm of adaptive water management.

Source: Prepared by the author.

A transition to a new management regime which is perceived as a precondition for the restoration of multifunctional dynamic landscapes will require substantial changes in the role and power of different stakeholder groups. Engineers have to upgrade their skills and share the responsibility for the work with ecologists and landscape architects. However, water engineering is a profession with well-established rules of good practices that engineers have to follow in order to be recognized in their community. Such rules are not easy to change even when convincing alternatives are available. Some house owners will suffer a loss in the value of their property if certain areas now protected from flooding are assigned to temporally flooded zones. Some segments of industry (e.g., agriculture) will incur losses, while others (e.g., tourism)will benefit. The influence of governmental authorities will partly decline if the whole management scheme becomes more participatory.

Furthermore, current water management regimes have evolved over a long period of time. One reason for the lack of innovation is the strong interdependence of the factors that stabilize current management regimes. One cannot, for instance, move easily from top-down to bottom-up or participatory management practices without changing the whole approach to information and risk management.

In addition, one cannot expect that simplistic panaceas will provide guidance and that universal blueprints exist. Science and

308 ≈ *Claudia Pahl-Wostl*

policy will always be faced with the challenge of designing processes of change without completely understanding the system and the problems to be managed. This is also the key challenge for dealing with the impact of climate change.

Adaptive management is defined in the chapter as a structured process of improving management policies and practices by systemic learning from the outcomes of implemented management strategies and from taking into account new knowledge that becomes available during the implementation process. However, the implementation of adaptive management is only possible if certain structural conditions are fulfilled (Pahl-Wostl 2007a; Pahl-Wostl et al. 2007a). A polycentric governance regime with strong stakeholder participation and a balance between bottom-up and top-down processes is assumed to be more adaptive than a centralized regime with hierarchical top-down control. Sectoral integration is required to identify emergent problems and integrate policy implementation. A comprehensive understanding is achieved by open, shared information sources that facilitate bridging gaps and take into account different kinds of knowledge. Infrastructure does not rely on long-lived centralized infrastructure but emphasizes diverse sources of design and more decentralized technologies. Financial resources are diversified using a broad set of private and public financial instruments. These characteristics of integrated adaptive regimes are yet to be seen as working hypotheses since the change towards more adaptive regimes is still slow, and empirical data and practical experience are thus limited. One possible reason for this lack of innovation is the strong interdependence of the factors that stabilize current management regimes. One cannot, for instance, move easily from top-down to participatory management practices without changing the whole approach to information and risk management. Further, despite these general patterns, one cannot expect that simplistic panaceas will provide guidance. Science and policy will always be faced with the challenge of designing processes of change without completely understanding the system and problems to be managed. This is also the key challenge for dealing with climate change.

The Global Dimension

The global dimension of this unprecedented water governance challenge is manifold and one can observe an increasing awareness that water management is a global issue. Water problems have traditionally been considered local or regional problems. However, there are strong arguments to take the global dimension into account (Pahl-Wostl et al. 2008; Alcamo et al. 2008). First, the hydrological system is a global system and exchange processes (e.g., impact of climate change, other teleconnections, for instance, between deforestation and precipitation) occur at global level over relevant time periods. Second, global environmental change (GEC) and socio-economic phenomena at the global level increasingly create situations in which the driving forces behind water-related problems and conflicts lie outside the reach of local, national or basin-oriented governance regimes (e.g., impact of global trade on water quantity and quality). Third, many local phenomena occur globally such as erosion, eutrophication, urbanization, biodiversity loss, or the introduction of invasive species. The same is valid for many issues impacting human health like the poor quality of drinking water supply and of sanitation in poor countries. Such local phenomena may imply alarming global trends. For example, the construction of dams have led to a fragmentation and flow alteration of the world's river basins with major and sometimes irreversible impacts on associated freshwater ecosystems (Nilsson et al. 2005). Furthermore, lessons learnt in one part of the world, can be useful and relevant for other parts of the world, and comparative learning justifies a global approach.

Unfortunately, dealing with water issues has often been linked to technological or institutional panaceas. Global processes are needed to share and evaluate in a systematic fashion lessons learned to develop a "diagnostic approach" that allows linking specific characteristics of a climate change adaptation problem with appropriate governance approaches towards its solution. Too generic and simplistic approaches will hardly be able to address the complexity of real governance regimes which differ in history, political, cultural and socio-economic characteristics. Panaceas have proven to be weak in their explanatory power and not very useful or even detrimental for policy advice (Ostrom et al. 2007). On the other hand, too detailed analyses will hardly lead to insights that can be generalized across individual cases. Thus, what is required is a concerted research by the scientific community for sharing concepts and data to build the knowledge base needed to address pressing research questions.

310 ~~ *Claudia Pahl-Wostl*

Conclusions

Water governance is currently undergoing a major paradigm shift. In a number of countries innovative policy frameworks have been introduced over the past decade. However, despite innovation in regulatory frameworks, change in the policy discourse at the operational level remains slow. This is also the case with European water policy and the implementation of the two major directives, viz., WFD and FD. Change at the operational level is still hindered by quite a few structural constraints. Overcoming these constraints requires processes of social and societal learning.

Climate change has exposed vulnerability of current water management regimes and is another driver for water policy reform. Hence, we can expect to witness a whole range of policy experiments in the years to come to improve water governance. What is needed is a globally co-ordinated learning process to be able to share the lessons learned and to jointly build a global knowledge base. This would also support the development of the "diagnostic" approach which develops tools to analyze problems embedded in context and supports the development of context-specific integrated solutions instead of advocating simplistic technical and institutional panaceas.

Notes

1. European Commission. n.d. "Introduction to the New EU Water Framework Directive," http://ec.europa.eu/environment/water/water-framework/info/intro_en.htm (accessed August 24, 2012).
2. European Commission. n.d. "Implementing the EU Water Framework Directive & the Floods Directive," http://ec.europa.eu/environment/water/water-framework/objectives /implementation_en.htm (accessed August 24, 2012).

References

Alcamo, J., C. Vörösmarty, R. J. Naiman, D. P. Lettenmaier and C. Pahl-Wostl. 2008. "A Grand Challenge for Freshwater Research: Understanding the Global Water System," *Environmental Research Letters.* 3 (1): 1–6.

Commission of the European Communities (COM), 2009a. "Adapting to Climate Change: Towards a European Framework for Action." EU Commission White Paper, Brussels, 1.4.2009. SEC(2009) 386, 397, 388.

Also available online at http://eur-lex.europa.eu/LexUriServ/Lex UriServ. do?uri=COM:2009:0147:FIN:EN:PDF (accessed August 27, 2012).

———. 2009b. "Climate Change and Water, Coasts and Marine Issues." EU Commission Working Document accompanying the White Paper titled "Adapting to Climate Change: Towards a European Framework for Action," Brussels, 1.4.2009 SEC(2009) 386. Also available online at http://eur-lex.europa.eu/LexUriServ/Lex UriServ. do?uri=COM:2009:0147:FIN:EN:PDF (accessed August 27, 2012).

Galaz, V. 2005. "Does the EC water framework directive build resilience? Harnessing socio-ecological complexity in European water management, Policy Paper no. 1. Swedish Water House, Stockholm.

Gleick, Peter, H. 2000. "The Changing Water Paradigm: A Look at 21st Century Water Resources Development," *Water International,* 25(1): 127–38.

Huntjens, P., C. Pahl-Wostl, B. Rihoux, Z. Flachner, S. Neto, R. Koskova, M. Schlueter, I. Nabide Kiti and C. Dickens. 2011. "Adaptive Water Management and Policy Learning in a Changing Climate," *Environmental Policy and Governance,* 21(3): 145–63.

Isendahl, N., A. Dewulf and C. Pahl-Wostl. 2010. "Using Framing Parameters to Improve Handling of Uncertainties in Water Management Practice," *Environmental Policy and Governance,* 20(2): 107–22.

Nilsson, C., C. A. Reidy, M. Dynesius and C.Revenga. 2005. "Fragmentation and Flow Regulation of the World's Large River Systems," *Science,* 308(5720): 405–08.

Olsson, P. and V. Galaz. 2009. "Transition to Adaptive Water Governance and Management in Sweden," in D. Huitema and S. Meijerink (eds), *Water Policy in International Perspective: A Research Companion to the Role of Policy Entrepreneurs in Water Transitions,* pp. 304–24. Cheltenham: Edward Elgar Publishing.

Ostrom, E. 2007. "A Diagnostic Approach for Going Beyond Panaceas," *Proceedings of the National Academy of Sciences of the United States of America,* 104 (39): 15181–187.

Ostrom, E., M. A. Janssen and J. M. Anderies. 2007. "Going Beyond Panaceas," *Proceedings of the National Academy of Sciences of the United States of America,* 104(39): 15176–178.

Pahl-Wostl, C. 2002. "Towards Sustainability in the Water Sector: The Importance of Human Actors and Processes of Social Learning," *Aquatic Sciences,* 64 (4): 394–411.

———. 2006. "The Importance of Social Learning in Restoring the Multi-Functionality of Rivers and Floodplains," *Ecology and Society,* 11(1): 11–24. Also available at http://www.ecologyandsociety.org/vol11/iss1/art10/ (accessed November 13, 2012).

———. 2007a. "Transition towards Adaptive Management of Water Facing Climate and Global Change," *Water Resources Management,* 21(1): 49–62.

312　≋　*Claudia Pahl-Wostl*

———. 2007b. "The Implications of Complexity for Integrated Resources Management," *Environmental Modelling and Software*, 22(5): 561–69.

———. 2009. "A Conceptual Framework for Analysing Adaptive Capacity and Multi-Level Learning Processes in Resource Governance Regimes," *Global Environmental Change*, 19(3): 354–65. Also available online at http://dx.doi.org/ 10.1016/j.gloenvcha.2009.06.001.

Pahl-Wostl, C., J. Gupta and D. Petry. 2008. "Governance and the Global Water System: Towards a Theoretical Exploration," *Global Governance*, 14(4): 419–35.

Pahl-Wostl, C., P. Jeffrey, I. Isendahl and M. Brugnach. 2011. "Maturing the New Water Management Paradigm: Progressing from Aspiration to Practice," *Water Resources Management*, 25: 837–56.

Pahl-Wostl, C., J. Sendzimir, P. Jeffrey, J. Aerts, G. Berkamp and K. Cross. 2007a. "Managing Change toward Adaptive Water Management through Social Learning," *Ecology and Society*, 12(2), Art. 30. http://www.ecologyandsociety.org/vol12/iss2/art30/ (accessed November 13, 2012).

Pahl-Wostl, C., M. Craps, A. Dewulf, E. Mostert, D. Tabara and T. Taillieu. 2007b. "Social Learning and Water Resources Management," *Ecology and Society*, 12(2), Art. 5. http://www.ecologyandsociety.org/vol12/iss2/art5/ accessed November 13, 2012).

Rogers, P. and A. W. Hall, 2003. "Effective Water Governance." Technical Advisory Committee (TAC) Background Paper 7, Global Water Partnership (GWP), Stockholm, Sweden.

Young, O. 2007. "Designing Environmental Governance Systems: The Diagnostic Method." Keynote address at "10 Years Institutional Dimensions of Global Environmental Change: A Synthesis," Institutional Dimensions of Global Environmental Change (IDGEC) Synthesis Conference, 2006, Bali. Summary published in International Human Dimensions Programme (IHDP) Newsletter, 1.2007, pp. 9–11.

About the Editors

Anjal Prakash is Executive Director of the South Asia Consortium for Interdisciplinary Water Resources Studies (SaciWATERs), Hyderabad, India. He has worked extensively on the issues of groundwater management, gender, natural resource management, and water supply and sanitation in India. He has also worked with the New Delhi-based policy team of Water Aid India, handling research and implementation projects related to integrated water resources management (IWRM). He has to his credit several papers in leading journals, chapters in edited books and a book titled *The Dark Zone: Groundwater Irrigation, Politics and Social Power in North Gujarat* (2005). He is presently working on forthcoming edited volumes on water and health, and on water resources policies in South Asia.

Sreoshi Singh is Research Fellow in the Peri-urban Water Security project at SaciWATERS and a doctoral candidate at the Center for Economic and Social Studies, Hyderabad, India. She has worked on subjects concerning poverty, livelihood, health and gender. She specializes in urban development and planning and has special interest in various socio-economic and environmental aspects of urban areas for policy planning. She has also been working on the Crossing Boundaries project of SaciWATERs since 2008 and presently leads the Hyderabad research team of the Peri-urban Water Security Project.

Chanda Gurung Goodrich is Principal Scientist–Empower Women at the International Crop Research Institute for the Semi-Arid Tropics (ICRISAT), Hyderabad, India. She specializes in participatory research and development, and gender, particularly in the area of natural resources management. She has worked extensively on issues concerning social and gender equity rights, particularly in the spheres of agriculture, natural resources management and sustainable livelihoods in India and Nepal since 1996. She has published several papers and chapters in edited volumes on gender and agriculture/natural resource management.

314 　 *About the Editors*

S. Janakarajan is Professor of Economics at the Madras Institute of Development Studies (MIDS), Chennai, India. His areas of interest are development studies; rural development and agrarian institutions; climate change; costs and limits of adaptation to climate change and disaster risk reduction; water management and irrigation institutions; urban water resources, water conflicts and conflict-resolution; environment; and urban and peri-urban issues and markets. He has published several books and many papers in national and international journals. He is also the founder and convener of "Cauvery Family," an initiative in conflict-resolution that has established a sustained dialogue between farmers of Karnataka and Tamilnadu to resolve the most vexed inter-state water dispute in the history of contemporary India.

Notes on Contributors

Sultan Ahmed is Deputy Secretary of the Government of Bangladesh and a member of the Bangladesh Civil Service Administration cadre. He works at the Center for Environmental and Geographic Information Services (CEGIS) as Chief Specialist and Director. Dr Ahmed provides professional inputs on policies and institutions to the studies conducted at CEGIS ranging from master planning water, environment and climate to institutional strengthening of water sector planning and institutions in charge of water policy implementation. He has also authored chapters in edited books.

Jayanath Ananda is Senior Lecturer at the School of Economics, Albury-Wodonga Campus, La Trobe University, Australia. His research interests are in water policy and decision-making; efficiency and productivity analysis and sustainability of water resource management. He has authored many articles for internationally reputed journals and chapters for edited volumes. Currently, he is involved in several projects on enhancing the performance of water management institutions and climate change adaptation strategies.

Jessica Budds is Lecturer in Environment and Development at the Department of Geography and Environmental Science, University of Reading, UK. With an interdisciplinary background in Latin American studies, development studies, environmental studies and geography, she works on water, politics and social exclusion, with particular emphasis on the introduction and effects of neoliberal mechanisms in water policy, and a regional focus on South America. Her current research examines the relationship between water, mining and social change in the Andean region.

Thinley Gyamtsho is Assistant Water Management Officer at the Renewable Natural Resource Research Centre, Bajo, Bhutan, under the Ministry of Agriculture. His interest lies in working with local farming communities in the management of water resources for food production and in general rural development activities.

316 ≈ *Notes on Contributors*

Muhammad Mehmood Ul Hasan is Senior Scientist at the International Center for Agroforestry (ICRAF) Nairobi, Kenya. Previously, he worked as Senior Researcher in Innovation Systems at the Centre for Development Research (ZEF), University of Bonn, where he was responsible for facilitating and researching transdisciplinary approaches in validating scientific innovations. He has had a prolific professional career spanning over 21 years, during which he worked with the Faisalabad Agricultural University and the provincial government of Punjab in Pakistan; and with International Water Management Institute (IWMI). He also has 23 peer reviewed, and over 50 country/research reports, conference and workshop publications to his credit.

David Ip is currently Associate Head and Associate Professor at the Department of Applied Social Sciences in the Hong Kong Polytechnic University. He has published widely on transnationalism and Chinese transmigrants in Australia in the last decade and was an active consultant on social planning and development with various international development organizations including UNDP and AusAID.

Eiman Karar is the Director for Water Resources Management at the South African Water Research Commission, Johannesburg since 2005. She has almost 20 years experience in natural resources management, mainly water. She has an MSc in Environmental Sciences and a project management Diploma. She was the Director in the national Department of Water Affairs of South Africa responsible for developing policies related to all Water Management Institutions. She was a commissioner on the Limpopo Joint Transboundary Commission. She was a co-author in the global agricultural water Comprehensive Assessment of the CGIA as well as having authored numerous chapters and papers mainly dealing with governance related work. She was the co-Chair of the recent River Basin International Waters GEF initiative in defining Science in all its projects. She is a registered professional natural scientist with the South African Association of Natural Scientists and is registered for an LLM degree.

Seema Kulkarni is a founding member and Senior Research Fellow of the Society for Promoting Participative Eco-system Management (SOPPECOM), Pune, India. She has been working in

Notes on Contributors ≈ 317

the area of natural resource management and rural livelihoods since 1991, and is actively engaged in policy advocacy and gender training in the area of gender and rural livelihoods. She has been consistently associated with the women's movement in Maharashtra, particularly in south Maharashtra on the question of deserted women as part of the Stree Mukti Sangharsh Chalwal or the Women's Liberation. She has published several articles on the issues of gender, water and rural livelihoods and contributed chapters on the same themes in edited volumes.

Daanish Mustafa is Reader in Politics and Environment at the Department of Geography, King's College, London. He was Visiting Assistant Professor of Geography at George Mason University, and an assistant professor of Geography at the University of South Florida, St. Petersburg. His academic interest lies in critical water resources geography, social networks and environmental management and approaches to terrorism.

Priya Sangameswaran is Fellow in Development Studies at the Centre for Studies in Social Sciences, Calcutta, India. She works broadly at the intersection of developmental studies and environmental studies, drawing on heterodox economic theory, post-development theory and political ecology to understand how community-based efforts and questions of equity (particularly in the realm of water) have been conceptualized and practiced. Her most recent research has been on water sector reforms in Maharashtra, particularly on how they are shaped by the interaction between hegemonic discourses of water and development and the motivations of diverse actors, and how these changes are linked to larger debates on neoliberal development, rights, equity and commodification of resources.

Amita Shah is an economist and Director of Gujarat Institute of Development Research, Ahmedabad, India. She has a wide-ranging research experience in various aspects of rural economy. Her major areas of research interest include natural resource development with a special focus on dryland agriculture and forestry; environmental impact assessment; gender and environment; agriculture–industry interface; small-scale and rural industries; diffusion of technologies; and employment and livelihood issues. More recently, she has been involved in a number of studies pertaining to participatory watershed

318 〜 *Notes on Contributors*

development, protected area management, economic valuation of biodiversity, chronic poverty in remote rural areas, migration and status of women in agriculture. Over the past 22 years she has worked closely with a number of government and non-government organizations and participated in an informed process of policy formulation. She has also been a consultant to various donor agencies and has undertaken collaborative research both within and outside India. She has published around 100 research papers in professional journals and books, and been a visiting fellow to academic institutions in the UK, China, France and the Netherlands.

Tushaar Shah is Senior Fellow at International Water Management Institute (IWMI), where he has built and led the IWMI–Tata Water Policy Program in India, the first ever collaboration between an international center and an Indian foundation. He is the recipient of the 2002 Consultative Group (CG) award for "Outstanding Scientist of the Year". He was the Director of the Institute of Rural Management, Anand, and has consulted with scores of NGOs, government and lending institutions as well as private Indian foundations. He has also served on the boards of 25 Indian NGOs and research centers including as the Chairman of International Development Enterprises (IDE), India and PRADAN. He also serves on the Academic Council of the Chinese Center for Agricultural Policy (CCAP). Most recently, Prof. Shah has served on several committees of the Government of India for developing the irrigation component of India's 11th Five Year Plan as well as a committee of the Indian Planning Commission on sustainable groundwater management.

Saravanan V. Subramanian is a senior researcher at the Center for Development Research (ZEF), Department of Political and Cultural Change, Bonn University, Germany. He specializes in exploring the linkages between urbanization/globalization, agriculture and human health in the water resources management sector of the developing countries. His areas of research interest include analysis of power dynamics, policy processes, and spatial scales in water management.

Claudia Pahl-Wostl is Professor of Resources Management, and Director of the Institute for Environmental Systems Research in Osnabrück, Germany. She is an internationally reputed expert

Notes on Contributors ≈ 319

in adaptive management, water governance and participatory integrated assessment and agent-based modeling. Prof. Pahl-Wostl has worked for more than 10 years in the field of mathematical modeling, integrated assessment and human ecology at the Swiss Federal Institute for Science and Technology, Zürich, and the Swiss Federal Institute for Aquatic Science and Technology (EAWAG), one of the leading water research institutes in Europe. She is co-chair of the Global Water System Project, which is tasked with developing a global change research program on the water issue from a social science perspective. She is also President of The International Society for Integrated Assessment (TIAS). Prof. Pahl-Wostl participates in and has co-ordinated several European projects, particularly the European Union (EU) project HarmoniCOP and the Integrated Project NEWATER.

Margreet Zwarteveen is a researcher and Lecturer at the Irrigation and Water Management Group of Wageningen University, the Netherlands. In her work, Dr Zwarteveen combines critical feminist thinking with the analysis of water management. Her publications range from documentation and analysis of gendered rights and responsibilities in water management (among others in Nepal, Burkina Faso and the Andean countries) and critical feminist analyses of water policies and professional water cultures to the questioning of established ways of "knowing" in water and unravelling the power and politics of water knowledge. She is also involved in various capacity-building and research projects on gender and IWRM in South Asia and the Andes.

Index

adaptive irrigation 214

adaptive management 14, 298, 302, 308

agricultural bio-technology 22

agro-ecological system, Balochistan 199

ahar-pyne system, of water harvesting 222, 240n5

Andhi Khola Irrigation Scheme, Nepal 161

Andhra Pradesh Farmers Management of Irrigation Systems Act (1996) 102

aquifers 13, 21, 170, 214, 220–21, 223, 226, 230, 234–35, 237–38, 255, 258, 268, 274

Atacameños 258–61

atomistic irrigation 215–16

Balochistan 194–195, 196, 197, 198, 199, 202, 207

Bangladesh: BUET–DUT Linkage Project-III (2001–06) in 125–26; Flood Action Plan (FAP) in 120; flood control and management 119–20; flood control drainage and irrigation (FCDI) projects in 119; Guidelines for Participatory Water Management (GPWM) in 117, 123–27, 129; IWRM policy in 118, 123; Local Government Engineering Department (LGED) in 123–24, 128–29; Master Plan Organization (MPO) in 119; Narayanganj–Narsingdi Irrigation Project (NNIP) in 125–29; National Water Management Plan (NWMP) in 117, 122–23; National Water Plan (NWP) in 119; National Water Policy (NWPo, 1999) in 117, 120–21; national water resources in 117; National Water Resources Council (NWRC) in 119–21; participatory water management (PWM) in 123–29; policy development in water sector of 130–32; Water Development Board in 119; water institutions in 121–22; Water Management Groups (WMGs) in 124; Water Management Organizations (WMOs) in 125; Water Master Plan in 118; water sector planning and development in 118–20

Bangladesh Water and Flood Management Strategy (BWFMS) 120

Bauer, Carl 248–51, 254

Bayesian network (BN) 80, 88; as an analytical tool 68–69; benefits of 68; elements of 68; for flood management 68; for integration of water policies 67; probability model of 73; significance of 68–69

Bhutan: availability of water resources to farmers 137–38; Basic Health Units (BHUs) in 135; Field Crops Research Program (FCRP) in 142; First Five-Year-Plan (FYP) of 134; Gamri Watershed Management Plan of 144; Gross National Happiness (GNH) of 135, 136, 141; Gross National Product (GNP) of 141; hydropower development in 139–41; inter- and intra-community conflicts due to water scarcity in 138; Lingmuteychu Watershed Management Project (LWMP) in 137–38, 142, 144–45; National Environment Commission (NEC) of 142; National Watershed Management Unit (NWMU) in 143; other institutional programs in 144; Radhi Watershed Management Project (RWMP) in 145; renewable water resources 140; Rural Water Supply Scheme in 144; Vision 2020 of 141; Wang Watershed Management Project (WWMP) of 145–46; water management research program of 141–42; Water Resources Coordination Division of 142–43; water resources management in 137–44; water resources policies and programs of 136; water scarcity, situation of 138–39; Watershed Management Division of 143; watershed management research in 143–44; watershed policies and programs of 141–44; watershed projects in 144–46

Bhutan Water Partnership (BWP) 142

boro cultivation 126

Bourdieu, Pierre 52, 59n2

British East India Company 214

BUET–DUT Linkage Project-III (2001–06), Bangladesh 125–26

Business As Usual (BAU) 221

Buttala irrigation system, Sri Lanka 52

canal irrigation systems 10, 99, 109, 217, 234, 238

Carbon Capture and Storage (CCS) 240n4

carbon footprint, of India's groundwater economy 224–29

cash crops: access to market for selling 80, 82; area under 77, 80, 82–83; cultivation of 82; income from 80, 84, 85

Catchment Management Agencies (CMAs) 271, 277

Catchment Management Strategies (CMSs) 278

Chicago Boys (neoliberal technocrats) 13, 250

Chile: Agricultural and Livestock Service (SAG) in 256; Chicago Boys in 13, 250; ESSAN (waterworks company) in 259; Indigenous Law (1993) of 258, 260; Institute for Peasant Agricultural Development (INDAP) in 256; La Ligua river basin in 249, 255–62; mining and water in Atacama 258–62; National Indigenous Development Corporation (CONADI) of 260–61; National Water Directorate (DGA) of 251, 252; neoliberal model of water rights in 249–52; political debate over the water code in 252–54; tradable water rights in 247–48, 251, 258; Water Code (1951) of 249; Water Code (1967) of 255; Water Code (1981) of 13, 248, 249–52; water markets in 249, 254–55

Chi-square testing 73, 77

climate change 191, 198, 207; effects of 7, 12; General Circulation Modelling (GCMs) of 194; impact on groundwater resources 219–21; policy for 192; risks of flooding due to 304; sea level rise due to 220; and water storage alternatives 222

322 ~ *Index*

coal-based electricity 230
Common Guidelines for Watershed Development Projects 86
community-based management in Uppala Rajana 86
Community-Based Watershed Management (CBWM) 76, 85
crop markets in India 83

dam building activities 5
Decision Support System (DSS) 68
demand-oriented drinking water projects 165
Department for International Development (DFID) 76, 86, 87, 91n13, 91n14
Disaster Risk Reduction (DRR) 206–7
Distributary Canal Organizations 101
Distributary Committee (DC) 102
distribution of water 4, 174, 285 *see also* water distribution systems
District Rural Development Agencies (DRDAs) 76
diverse economies, concept of 11, 153, 159–65
drip irrigation 233–34, 237
droughts, impact of 21
dugwell recharge 235

East Pakistan Water and Power Development Authority (EPWAPDA) 118–19
ecofeminism 24, 47
electric tube well technology 194–95
Environment (Protection) Act (1986), India 108
ESSAN (waterworks company) 259
European Commission 299, 303
European Flood Directive (FD) 299, 304
European Water Framework Direc-

tive (WFD) 298, 302–4; Common Implementation Strategy (CIS) of 299; implementation of 299; objectives of 298–99
European Water Policy 13; for flood management 304–8; paradigm shift in 300–302; policy decision and implementation 302–4; recent developments in 298–300; River Basin Management Plan 303n04
evapotranspiration (ET) 7, 218

Falkenmark indicator 138
Farmer Organizations (FOs) 105, 172, 177
feminist project in irrigation 47
Field Canal Organizations (FCOs) 101
Field Crops Research Program (FCRP), Bhutan 142
flood hazard, in Lai 202–5, 207
flood management 68, 119, 300; adaptive and integrated 304–8
floodplain restoration 304
Flood Plan Co-ordination Organization (FPCO) 120
flood protection 304
flood warning system 206
food security 30, 117, 119, 123, 129
freshwater ecosystems 309
freshwater management 3
"Fruit Bowl of India" 76, 77, 82

Gal Oya Project, Sri Lanka 111, 112n4
Gamri Watershed Management Plan, Bhutan 144
Ganga–Bramhaputra–Meghna (GBM) basin 14n1
gender discrimination 30, 33
gender empowerment 28, 33–34, 36
gender relations, in irrigation systems 47, 58
geological sequestration 240n4

Index ≈ 323

GHG emissions 229–30, 234
Gibson-Graham, J. K. 157, 159–62
global environmental change (GEC) 309
Global Environmental Change (journal) 194
global–local dualism, notion of 157
global warming 7, 99
Gram Pradhans 110
Gram Sabhas 106
Gramsci's concept of hegemony 163
gravity flow irrigation 215, 221, 224, 237
groundwater contamination 235
groundwater irrigation 7, 216, 217, 223, 224, 229, 238; carbon emission from 226, 228
groundwater management 106, 108; electric tube well technology for 194–95; *karez* system for 194–98; productivity maximization *versus* resilience in 194–99
groundwater recharge 22, 31, 219, 221; for adaptation and mitigation 229–35
groundwater resources 3, 6, 99, 199; depletion of 21; exploitation with electric tube wells 197; impact of climate change on 219–21; overexploitation of 229–30; sustainability of 21–22
groundwater wells 216, 221

hazard mitigation, policies of 193, 207
hazardscapes: concept of 192–94; of Lai basin 204, 206–7; urban 202–7
hazards management 192
Himachal Pradesh Forest Sector Reform Project 76, 87
Hindu Kush Himalayas 7
historically disadvantaged individuals (HDIs) 284, 286, 292n14

Horticulture Mission *see* Technology Mission for Integrated Development of Horticulture
HP Mid-Himalayan Watershed Development Project 76
hydro-climatic change 218, 239
hydroelectricity, generation of 11; in Bhutan 139–41; in Chile 254
hydro-hazards 191, 200, 207; definition of 192–94

India: adaptive irrigation in 214; agricultural groundwater use in 215; atomistic irrigation in 215–18; Business As Usual (BAU) scenario in 221; canal construction in 214–15; canal irrigation technology in 217; carbon footprint of groundwater economy in 224–29; Central Ground Water Board of 235; crop markets in 83; electricity consumption by pumpsets in 227; Environment (Protection) Act (1986) of 108; groundwater demand management in 236; groundwater irrigation in 217; groundwater management in 217; groundwater-stressed areas of 231; groundwater wells in 216; hydro-climatic future of 218–19; irrigation economy in 221; irrigation, evolution of 214; *Jalswarajya* (drinking water project) in 159, 167n11; *Jyotirgram* scheme, Gujarat 233; Land Reforms Act of 75, 80, 85, 91n7; land-to-man ratio in 215; Managed Aquifer Recharge program of 223; Master Plan for Groundwater Recharge in 235; micro-watershed projects in 21; Minor Irrigation Census in 230; power generation in 224; riverine agriculture in 214; Sreeramsagar project in 53; surface irriga-

324 ≈ *Index*

tion systems in 216, 218; surface water storages in 221–24; water availability in 3; water budgets in 164; water harvesting structures in 222; water policy-making in 216; water sector reforms in 34, 153–55, 159, 164

Indira Gandhi Canal 238

Indo-Gangetic aquifer system 220

Indo-Gangetic basin 213, 218

Indo-Pakistan Indus Basin Treaty (1960) 199, 201

Indus basin: and its major infrastructure 200; management of 193–94, 199

Indus Basin Replacement Project, Pakistan 171

Indus Basin Water Development Project, Pakistan 199

Institute for Peasant Agricultural Development (INDAP), Chile 256

Institutional Analysis Development (IAD) 69

Institutional Organizers (IOs) 111

integrated area development program (IADP) 76

Integrated Management of Irrigation Schemes (INMAS) 101

integrated wasteland development program 76

integrated water resources management (IWRM) 66–68, 296; in Bangladesh 118, 123; in South Africa 276; in Uppala Rajana hamlet 85–87

International Development Research Centre, Canada (IDRC) 27

International Financial Institutions (IFIs) 13, 171, 180

International Food Policy Research Institute (IFPRI) 224, 229

International Water Management Institute (IWMI) 139, 233

irrigated farming 46–47

irrigation: decision-making 54; development programs in 86; evolution in India 214; feminist project in 47; gender relations in 47; and irrigated farming 46–47; *karez* system of 194–98; key performance indicators of 55; management of 26; people's decisions on 49–50; river water, sharing of 108; social positioning of 53; sources of 21; surface irrigation system 40; by tube well 196, 198; women in *see* women in irrigation

irrigation engineering 38, 49, 181

irrigation institutions: assessment of 104; classification of 100; definition of 99–100; design principles, to manage common pool resources 100; farmer-managed 103, 111

irrigation management institutions 51, 174 *see also* irrigation institutions

Irrigation Management Transfer (IMT), in Pakistan 10, 11, 23, 26, 101; conception of 172–73; design and implementation of policies 173–80; implementation of 178–80; lack of political will and resistance from stakeholders 175–76; legal pluralism and the resultant controversies 176–78; objectives of 173–75

irrigation performance, conceptualization of 48

Jackson, Cecile 27

Jalswarajya (drinking water project), India 159, 167n11

Jawaharlal Nehru National Urban Renewal Mission 158

johad system, of water harvesting 222, 240n6

Jyotirgram scheme, Gujarat 233

Index 〰 325

Kalabagh Dam project, Pakistan 201
karez irrigation system 194–98
katchi abadis 205
Kharif crops 218
Kohli community 74–75, 80, 83, 86–87
Krug Mission 118, 130

Lai basin 203–6
La Ligua river basin 249; agriculture and irrigation in 255–62
Land Reforms Act, India 75, 80, 85, 91n7
lift irrigation system 77, 84, 224, 226, 229
Lingmuteychu Lum Zhinchong Tshogpa (LLZT) 145
Lingmuteychu Watershed Management Project (LWMP), Bhutan 137–38, 142, 144–45

MacKinnon, Catharine 44
Mahaweli Development Project, Sri Lanka 101
"Managed Aquifer Recharge" program 223, 230, 231
Management of Irrigation Systems (MANIS) program, Sri Lanka 101
Mendhapurkar, Subhash 82
micro-watershed projects in India 21
Minera Escondida Foundation 261
Minor Irrigation Census, India 216, 224–26, 230
minor irrigation schemes, Sri Lanka 105
Mir-e-aab (water leader) 196

Narayanganj–Narsingdi Irrigation Project (NNIP), Bangladesh 125–29
National Indigenous Development Corporation (CONADI), Chile 260–61

National Integrated Water Resources Management Plan (NIWRMP), Bhutan 143
National Water Act (1998), South Africa 13, 271
National Water Policy (1999), Bangladesh 10, 117, 120–21, 129
Netherlands Development Organization (SNV) 141–42
Norsys Software Corporation Canada (NETICA) software 73

on-farm water management 82, 141
ontological choreography, notion of 54

Pakistan: Area Water Boards (AWBs) in 172; domestic water supply and sanitation in 200; Farmer Organizations (FOs) in 172; farmer's water rights in 172; federal water authority in 170; flood hazards in 202–5; groundwater management in 194–99; *harim* rule in 196; Indus Basin Replacement Project in 171; Irrigation Management Transfer (IMT) *see* Irrigation Management Transfer (IMT), in Pakistan; Islamabad Master Plan of 204; *karez* irrigation system in 194–98; National Drainage Program (NDP) of 172; PIDA Act (1997) of 174, 177; Provincial Irrigation and Drainage Authorities (PIDAs) in 172; provincial irrigation departments (PIDs) in 172, 181; public utilities (PUs) in 172, 174; Punjab's reform legislation 174, 177; surface irrigation in 173, 192, 199–202; water policy (2004) of 171; water resource development in 170; water supply services in 173; water user associations in 179

326 ~ *Index*

Panchayat 106, 109–10, 112
Panchayati Raj 106
Parthasarathy Committee 86
Participatory Irrigation Management (PIM) 10, 50, 99, 111; assessment of institutions 104; basic structure in Andhra Pradesh 102–3; projects in Sri Lanka 105; in South Asia 101–3; World Bank evaluation of 109
participatory water resources management 32, 308; in Bangladesh 123–29
policies of agricultural development 86
poverty alleviation programs 33, 86, 117, 123, 289
Proshika (non-governmental organisation) 161

Rabi crops 218
Radhi Watershed Management Project (RWMP), Bhutan 145
Rais 196
Rajana watershed 73–76
Rajana Watershed Committee 84
Rajput community 74–75, 80, 83–84, 86
Renewable Natural Resources Research Centre (RNR RC), Bajo 141
renewable water resources 3, 138–40
RISKBASE (European project) 302
risk management 14, 304, 307, 308
river basin management 141, 149, 298–99, 302–4, 306
river valley projects 108
river water disputes 108
rural-to-urban migration 198, 206
rural unemployment 86

Sardar Sarovar Project, Gujarat 239
scientific water knowledge 39, 41, 43–44

Self Help Groups (SHGs) 34
Sindh–Punjab Agreement (1945), for sharing of Indus basin waters 201
snowmelt-based runoff 220
social learning 297, 301–2, 305
Social Upliftment for Rural Action (SUTRA) 82
Society for Promoting Participative Ecosystem Management (SOPPECOM) 26
South Africa: agricultural water use scenario of 286; annual rainfall and evaporation of 269; aquifer systems in 268; Catchment Management Agencies (CMAs) in 271, 282–84; co-operation and co-ordination between responsible departments in 285–87; decentralization of water management in 267, 282–83; Department of Water Affairs and Forestry (DWAF) of 271, 285; dryland and stock farming areas in 285; human capital in water sector of 287–89; institutional reforms in 271–76; macro-policy developments in 273; major achievements and successes in water reforms of 277–78; Native Land Act (1913) of 270; pre-1994 water policy of 270; riparian water rights, abolition of 271; role of the state as a player and a referee in water management 280–82; sectoral break-up of water requirements in 269; spatial distribution of rainfall and runoff in 268; Water Allocation Reform (WAR) Strategy in 285–86, 288; water law reforms, implementation of 276–77; water management areas (WMAs) in 275; water reforms in 267, 270–71; water resources,

Index ∾ 327

sources, availability and use of 268–69; water tribunal in 278; water use distribution in 279; water user associations (WUAs) in 271, 277–78, 284

South Asia: distribution of electric and diesel pumpsets in 225, 227; water governance system in 6

Spivak, G. C. 44

Sreeramsagar project, India 53

Sri Lanka: Buttala irrigation system in 52; Gal Oya Project in 111, 112n4; Mahaweli Development Project in 101; Management of Irrigation Systems (MANIS) program in 101; Participatory Irrigation Management (PIM) in 105

State of Environment South Asia 2001 (UNEP) 5

subsistence agriculture 26, 134, 260, 284

subsistence poverty 135, 150n1

surface irrigation system 21, 40, 109, 207, 216, 218, 238; in India 216, 218; in Pakistan 173, 192, 199–202

surface reservoirs 216, 223, 234, 237–38

surface storages 13, 219, 221–23, 234, 237–38

surface water management 106, 202

Swajaldhara 159

tank irrigation systems 10, 99

Tata Institute of Social Sciences (TISS) 26

Technical Committee on Watershed Programmes *see* Parthasarathy Committee

Technology Mission for Integrated Development of Horticulture 76, 82, 86

tube wells 196–99, 226, 229, 238, 240n12; irrigation 196–98

UN Conference on Sustainable Development (1992), Rio de Janeiro 274

United Nations Environment Programme (UNEP) 5

United States Agency for International Development (USAID) 112n4, 118

Uppala Rajana hamlet: area under cash crops in 80, 82–83; demand of water in 77–85; implication for IWRM in 85–87; lack of irrigation facilities in 84; variables influencing framing of problems in 78–79, 88–90; watershed management in 74–76

upstream–downstream conflict resolution 200

village irrigation schemes 105, 158

Village Water and Sanitation Committees (VWSC) 34

Wang River Basin Management Framework (WRBMF), Bhutan 143

Wang Watershed Management Project (WWMP), Bhutan 145–46

warabandi 108

water allocation: decisions using BN on farmers 68; scenarios of 23

water budgets 164

water crisis 4–5, 270, 297

water distribution systems 239

water engineering 197, 307

water governance 87, 310; challenges for 296; global dimension of 308–9; importance of 296; principles of 296–97; in South Africa 250; South Asian 6; strategies for 236; and water supply 109–10

water harvesting 21, 222

328 ≈ *Index*

water-induced poverty 20, 30, 33
water policies: Bayesian network for
formulation of *see* Bayesian network (BN); concepts for theorizing 155–59; conceptual approach
for formulation of 69–72; development of 1; and ethnographies
of the state 162–65; European *see*
European Water Policy; framework for analyzing processes for
70; global–local dualism 157;
significance of 1; for sustainable
development 67
water pollution 3
water–poverty discourse 19–20;
alternative perspective 22–23;
evidence and issues 20–21; sustainability of groundwater 21–22;
water-use, efficiency and economic viability 22
water–poverty–gender interface: analytical framework for examining
28–32; feminist methodologies
35; key areas of exploration 32–
35; pro-poor agricultural growth
33; scenarios of, in production
sphere 29
water quality 3, 6, 143, 198, 241n13,
277, 278
water reforms 11, 99, 289; analyses
of 154–55; and neoliberalism
165–66; in South Africa 13–14,
267, 270–71; in South Asian
countries 10
water-related conflicts 207
Water Resource Planning Organization (WARPO), Bangladesh
120–21
water resources: distribution of 70;
National Water Policy (1999) for
management of 10; structure and
development of 2; urban stress
on 5

water resources management 1, 3–4,
12, 26, 31, 296; actors and stakeholders in 70–71; in Bangladesh
10, 117–23, 125; Bayesian network (BN) for integration of 69;
in Bhutan 137–44; effectiveness
of programs for 33; gender inequities related to 56–57; gender
role in *see* women in irrigation;
institutional mechanisms for 99;
inter-familial relationships in 51;
methodology for 72–73; National
Water Policy (1999), Bangladesh
10, 117, 120–21; Rajana watershed, case study 73–76; rules for
70–71; socio-political process of
70; women's exclusion 33
water rights: to the landless 161;
leasing of 254; monopolization
of 255; as private property 251;
regularization program for 260;
tradable 247
water scarcity, problem of 2, 23, 77,
138, 149–50, 201, 208, 257–59
water sector reforms in India 34, 153;
analyses of 154–55; *Swajaldhara*
159; water budgets 164
water security 5–6, 263
watershed management (WsM) 11,
31, 68; in Bhutan 141–44; Radhi
Watershed Management Project
(RWMP) 145; Rajana Watershed
Project 73–76; Wang Watershed
Management Project (WWMP)
145–46
watershed management group
(WsMG) 145
water storage: climate change and
alternatives for 222; mechanism
for 138; reservoir 258; seepage
losses from 214; surface 219, 223
water stress index 138
water table 6, 195–96, 198–99, 257

Index ≋ 329

water tanks 214, 216, 222, 238
water use: authorization of 274;
efficiency and economic viability
of 22; gender issues in 41, 56–57
Water Users' Associations (WUAs)
50–52, 60n13, 101–2; adaptiveness of 106–7; appropriateness
of scale of 107–9; capacity constraints of 110–11; compliance
capacity of 109–10; inter-connect-
edness with other institutions 106;
objectives of 104–11; in Pakistan
179; performance of 107; in South
Africa 271, 277–78, 284; sustainability of 107; upscaling problems
of 105
water users groups (WUGs) 67, 144,
146

West Gandak irrigation system,
Nepal 58
White, Gilbert 192
Wittfogel, K. 214
women in irrigation 39–41; gendered metaphors and dichotomies 45–48; power, perspective
and knowledge 41–45; technical
and management systems and
boundaries 48–55
women's rights collectives 34
World Bank 76, 86, 107, 109, 159,
172–73, 175, 178, 180, 182, 248
World Water Council (2000) 23
World Water Development Report-3
3–4
World Water Vision 23